Study Guide

for

Rathus, Nevid, and Fichner-Rathus

Human Sexuality in a World of Diversity

Eighth Edition

prepared by

Steve Weinert
Cuyamaca College

Allyn & Bacon

Boston   Columbus   Indianapolis   New York   San Francisco   Upper Saddle River
Amsterdam   Cape Town   Dubai   London   Madrid   Milan   Munich   Paris   Montreal   Toronto
Delhi   Mexico City   Sao Paulo   Sydney   Hong Kong   Seoul   Singapore   Taipei   Tokyo

10 9 8 7 6 5 4 3 2 1   14 13 12 11 10

Allyn & Bacon
is an imprint of

www.pearsonhighered.com

ISBN-10: 0-205-78609-X
ISBN-13: 978-0-205-78609-1

Table of Contents

INTRODUCTION

This study guide is designed to offer you a variety of ways to reinforce your knowledge of the subject of human sexuality, as presented in your textbook; *Human Sexuality in a World of Diversity,* 8/e, by Rathus, Nevid and Rathus-Fichner. The authors of your text have done a wonderful job of giving you an overview of some of the complex and interdisciplinary information related to human sexuality. They have made the information academically rigorous while remaining attached to the application of the information—along with using their collective wit and humor.

Human sexuality is far more complicated than most of us realize before we study it academically. It is one of the few classes your friends will be interested that you are taking! With that in mind, we have designed this study guide in a way to allow you to connect to the material through active learning experiences, critical thinking and synthesis, and from having experienced the material in multiple ways. We believe this combination will help you do well in your course while having some fun.

You will notice as you read your text, that each chapter is structured in a similar way. This structure better enables you to organize your thoughts and prioritize the wealth of information in each chapter. Each chapter in this study guide corresponds with an identically-number chapter of your textbook. Each chapter here though is always sub-divided into four major sections, "Before You Read," "As You Read," "After You Read," and "When You Have Finished."

The *"Before You Read"* section provides you with an overview of the content of the text chapter. It consists of a brief chapter summary, a list of major learning objectives, and a list of key terms in the chapter. You can use this section to make sure you have absorbed the most important points made by your textbook in any given chapter. It will also help you organize notes you will find useful in preparing for your exams. For example, when you can confidently address all of the issues listed in the chapter objectives, you should then be well-prepared both for the practice tests and the "real" tests in your classes. You will notice that your chapters include tips for learning the key terms in each case. Please also note that the chapter summaries here are not "Cliff's Notes" and are therefore not meant to be substituted for reading the entire textbook chapters—there is a great deal more detail in the text. The summaries are simply a narrative overview of the material covered in the chapter and you will find that we refer you at times to specific areas of the textbook for additional details.

The *"As You Read"* section provides you with learning opportunities corresponding to each of the main sections in each chapter outline. You will notice that these activities cover a wide range of study skills. At one moment, you might be asked to recall information in a traditional way, such as a matching exercise…. At the next moment you might be asked to synthesize information in a critical way that allows you to make sense of it in terms of your own life experiences, or in a way that lets you make connections with information in the other chapters.

As critical thinking is important, we have gone out of our way to make activities engaging and as fun as possible. We hope you find yourself doing them without counting the seconds until study time is over, and, at best, we hope you have an occasional "lightbulb moment" as you work your way through these sections.

The next section, *"After You Read,"* provides you with a few different ways to test yourself on the material. Each chapter has three detailed Practice Tests (ten items per test), in which the corresponding Learning Objectives and page numbers are referenced. Once you have utilized these, you will find a Comprehensive Practice Test. This test consists of fifteen multiple-choice questions (taken from the various detailed practice tests), eight True/False questions, and two essay questions.

Our goal with the multiple-choice questions is for them to help you know the material confidently without hesitation. We have tempted you whenever possible with correct *sounding* alternatives, in hopes that you will leave these sections feeling confident that you *know* the right answers, rather than feeling that you might recognize the right answers when you see them isolated "properly." With the correct-sounding alternatives, we have not tried to trap you with "second best" answers. If you get a question wrong and feel it was "tricky," we recommend that you revisit the text on that topic to further clarify it. You will find the answers to all of the multiple-choice questions in the appendix at the end of this study guide.

For the True/False questions (which are within a chapter's comprehensive examination), much of what applies to the multiple-choice questions also applies here as well. Please read each statement slowly and carefully as one (important) detail can make an otherwise correct statement false. They are designed to keep you from falling into a testing rhythm where you react to what you think the question says instead of what it *really* means. If you know the statement is false, make a note about what could be changed to make it true. If you can do this, it is a sign of mastery of the concept and it can help you immensely.

On the essay questions that compose the final part of the comprehensive examination, wherever possible, we have included details that give you opportunities to interpret the material critically rather than simply parroting what is in your text. Critical and integrative understanding is particularly important in that this is an upper-level textbook and you must be equally prepared for any "upper-level" tests in your course of study. Also, being able to answer an essay question clearly, accurately, and concisely can be the ultimate demonstration of your mastery of the concepts.

The *"When You Have Finished"* section allows you to browse the internet for information related to the chapter contents. Here we have selected links that bolster lessons in your text and also provide some light-hearted fun. A politeness warning on use of the web: We encourage you to use search engines at times for some of the terms, though you might intentionally or *unintentionally* bring up images and information that could be uncomfortable if using a public computer so please use care here.

Our hope is that you will find this study guide useful and enjoyable in addition to your textbook and your class. May your new knowledge of human sexuality keep on giving throughout your life—*and* to those whom you love both now and in the future. The interdisciplinary study of Human Sexuality is fascinating and always evolving. May you leave this text and study guide even more fascinated than when you began your journey.

Stephen Weinert
Cuyamaca College

Chapter 1
What Is Human Sexuality?

Before You Begin…

Chapter Summary

Human sexuality—a topic where some, or perhaps most, people think they have either the right or best answers even without any kind of formal education. If you doubt this, as you learn the material here, start asking some sex questions at your next party and see what happens. (Hint: This can be a popular and even divisive topic.) Your adventure in studying human sexuality will expose you to a breadth of knowledge across many disciplines. You will also have exposure to some of the methods used in scientifically determining answers—or at least removing some of the mystery. Also, we provide emphasis on development and use of your critical thinking skills, which are essential to successfully navigating your sexuality and, more broadly, both your future career(s) and relationships. Now let's get started on this exciting and rewarding adventure!

Chapter 1 provides an overview of a variety of issues related to human sexuality, beginning with an exploration of the definition and the scope of the field of human sexuality. Anthropologists, biologists, medical researchers, sociologists, and psychologists all contribute to the research in this field. The authors recognize the great diversity within and across cultures, subcultures, races, social classes, and value systems, and include such information throughout the text. Knowledge about human sexuality, along with the development of critical thinking skills, helps students make informed sexual decisions and take an active role in enhancing their sexual health.

Seven perspectives on human sexuality are presented along with two recent theories. The perspectives include:

- Historical
- Biological
- Evolutionary
- Cross-species
- Cross-cultural
- Psychological
- Sociocultural

The theories recently added include both Feminist Theory and Queer Theory.

The history of sexuality is described beginning with the human groups who lived approximately 20,000–30,000 years ago, during the pre-historic age, and continuing through the ancient Hebrews, Greeks, Romans, and early Christians. Eastern approaches to sexuality are compared and contrasted with those in Western tradition. This section also includes European sexual history from the Middle Ages to the present, and U.S. sexual history from colonial times on. Within each time period, topics such as the roles of men and women, attitudes toward sex, marriage customs, and sexual prohibitions are examined.

The biological perspective focuses on the genetic, hormonal, vascular and neural influences on human sexual behavior. The cross-species perspective searches within animal behavior for analogs of human sexual behavior. Anthropologists provide information for the cross-cultural perspective, which confirms that societies differ widely in their social attitudes, customs, and practices.

An evolutionary perspective attempts to explain variability in human mating and sexual behavior as a function of Darwinian natural selection principles. The genetic predisposition to adapt well to one's environment enhances reproductive success and ensures continuation of one's genes in the next generation. Because reproductive success is dependent upon sexual behavior, evolutionary psychologists identify broad cultural mores to postulate that social behavior can be transmitted genetically.

Within the psychological perspective, the authors examine the psychoanalytic and behavioral theories. The sociocultural perspective focuses on the behavioral and attitudinal differences in sexuality among subgroups within societies.

Research informing the seven perspectives attempts to explain the complexity of human sexual behavior. The chapter concludes with a valuable reminder that not only is human sexual behavior complex and ever-changing—it is highly dependent on sociocultural context. We must take care not to use our own value systems as a way to judge the sexual behavior of others as normal, natural, or moral.

Feminist theory includes identifying its origins and its evolution to today. This theory challenges the conventional ideas (or, more precisely, the gender roles) of men as breadwinners and sexual aggressors, for example. From the female perspective, it challenges the stereotypes of women as emotional and irrational, with a primary duty of being a homemaker. Cross-cultural comparisons between developed nations and those less so are explored.

Despite the use of the word "queer"—which has long been viewed derogatorily by lesbian and gay people—queer theory challenges commonly held assumptions that heterosexuality is not only the only "normal" sexual behavior but that it is also superior. Besides the concept of heteronormativity just alluded to, queer theory also examines heterosexism and homophobia.

1. State the authors' definition of human sexuality.

2. Describe the contributions made by the many involved disciplines to the study of human sexuality.

3. Discuss the role of various value systems in making "rational" sexual choices.

4. List the characteristics of critical thinking and explain how critical thinking skills can be applied to the study of human sexuality.

5. Identify the value and limitations of using the Internet for reliable information on sexuality.

6. Identify the characteristic sexual attitudes and practices of the historical eras described in this chapter.

7. Relate how the origins of contemporary sexual attitudes and behaviors can be traced to earlier eras.

8. Explain the foundations and recent history of sexuality as a "legitimate" area of scientific study.

9. Identify the major focuses of biological sexual research and its contributions to the field.

10. List the conclusions evolutionary psychologists draw from the evolutionary perspective, and identify the assumptions underlying each one.

11. Explain what we can and cannot learn from cross-species comparisons of sexual behavior.

12. Describe some of the cross-cultural variations in sexual behaviors and attitudes, and discuss possible conclusions about the universality of human sexual behavior from the material presented.

13. Explain the psychoanalytic theory and several learning theories of human sexual behavior.

14. Describe the contributions that the sociocultural perspectives make to the study of human sexual behavior.

15. Explain the importance of including multiple perspectives to understand sexuality.

16. Describe the essence of "feminist theory"

17. Outline and explain elements of "queer theory."

Term Identification: The following terms are identified in this chapter as important to understanding the material.

Helpful Hints:

1. To help in your recollections, consider creating flashcards using the terms. (Make the cards first, then fill in the details as you go, to save time and increase their effectiveness) On one side of the flashcard, write the term and page number. On the other side, write the glossary definition (from the back of the book or the text) and then the example from the book explaining the term.
2. When you write the definitions in your own words, you will remember them better!

Chapter 1 Key Terms

Behaviors	Gender
Bestiality	Homophobia
Bisexual	Monogamy
Chromosomes	Mutations
Coitus	Natural Selection
Concubine	Oedipus complex
Copulation	Pederasty
Courtesan	Phallic Symbols
Cunnilingus	Phallic worship
Defense Mechanisms	Polygamy
DNA	Psychoanalysis
Erogenous zones	Psycho sexual development
Evolution	Queer Theory
Evolutionary Psychologist	Repression
Fellatio	Sadism
Feminist Theory	Social Cognitive theory
Fornication	Values
Gay Activism	

As You Read...

❖ ***What Is Human Sexuality?***

➢ *The Study of Human Sexuality*

This part of your book gives a brief overview of the main disciplines that make contributions to the scholarly knowledge on human sexuality. Before you read any further into the chapter, stop for a moment to consider how much effort must go into combining the information contributed by each of these disciplines to arrive at a thorough consideration of human sexuality. Use the space below to make notes about the first things that pop into your mind:

_____

_____

_____

_____

_____

_____

Think back on the inevitable awkward moments that come when you learn about sex as a young person. Did your parents avoid the subject? The confusion about how to teach you about your sexuality makes a lot more sense as you get older.

On a discussion board or in class, take the time to find out where your classmates learned about sex. If this is too uncomfortable for you, try to produce a stereotypical scenario of someone learning about sex. Use the spaces below to jot down notes.

❑ How did you find out about your sexuality?

_____

_____

_____

_____

❑ How old were you when you found out about sex?

_____

_____

_____

_____

❑ What did you think/feel when you found out?

_____

_____

_____

_____

❑ What kind of definition would you have given about the things that make up human sexuality based on the information you got as a young person?

_____

_____

_____

_____

❑ How did your childhood definition compare with the kind of information the contributing disciplines in your text represent? (i.e., How many are included? Be sure to note which disciplines your definition leaves out as well.)

_____

_____

_____

_____

❑ Looking back on the experience through your "adult eyes," why do you think the things that were included got included? Why were the things unmentioned left out?

_____

_____

_____

_____

❑ What does all of this say about the social context of your childhood? (Don't worry if you don't have much to say about this yet—but definitely keep it in mind as your learn the information in this chapter. It should help it stick better by making it personal.)

_____

_____

_____

➢ *Sexuality & Values*

The authors of the text have chosen to share with you the values about sexuality that have guided their development of their book. To remind you of them, please see them below:

1. *Sexual knowledge and critical thinking skills are of value because they allow us to make informed sexual decisions.*

2. *Students should take an active role in enhancing their health.*

The study of sexuality opens us up to many topics that people might find offensive, rude, and morally wrong. These differences bring up the types of values that we all hold and that guide the development of this book. Each perspective offers us the ability to critically think about different perspectives outside of ourselves.

I agreed with the values guiding the development of this book listed below:

Because…

I disagreed with the values guiding the development of this book listed below:

Because…

➤ *Value Systems for Making Responsible Sexual Decisions*

For each of the following situations, use the various value systems in your text to arrive at a decision about how a person using each value system might handle it. Include the reasoning behind your choices.

1. Your 14-year-old younger brother comes to you for advice. He's having these constant sexual feelings he never had before, and he can't concentrate on school. A close friend told him that he's been feeling that way lately too, and that masturbating helps relieve the tension so that he's able to think more clearly during the day. He asks you what you think he should do. What do you tell him?

   Asceticism: Rationalism:

2. You and your significant other have been together for over a year, and you are both in love and committed to one another. You are both ready to have sex, but you are worried because it is against your religion to have premarital sex and, up until now, you've never wanted to do something that your religious tenets say is wrong. You are not sure whether you and your partner will eventually marry. What do you choose to do?

   Legalism: Relativism:

3. You recently met a new group of friends, and have been having a lot of fun hanging out with them, even though you have never been much of a party person. The first time you hang out with them overnight, they leave you alone towards the end of the night and disappear somewhere into the house of the person having the party. They tell you to wait for them and you do. The next morning, you ask where they were. They tell you they like group sex but didn't want to put you on the spot. They ask you whether you'd like to join them next time, and that you don't have to do anything you don't want to do—you can even watch instead of participating, if you like. What do you choose to do?

   Hedonism: Legalism:

4. You are away at college, and you have been in a serious relationship with your significant other who is thousands of miles away. You've been sexually active with each other for most of the relationship, so it's hard being so far apart. Usually you handle it pretty well, but, for some reason, lately you've found yourself thinking about someone in your psych class and getting aroused. Now you're at a party and your classmate approaches you—it's clear the attraction is mutual. Your classmate catches you off guard with a passionate kiss and asks if you want to go upstairs to be alone. What do you choose to do?

   Situationalism: Utilitarianism:

❖ *Thinking Critically About Human Sexuality*

➢ *Principles of Critical Thinking*

Critical thinking will help you both in this class and in life—the more practice you get questioning the status quo in a thoughtful way, the better you will get at it. Using the eight principles of critical thinking detailed in your text, develop an opinion on the validity of at least two of the following contemporary clichés about sexuality, and argue your point in the space following the list.

❑ It's not a choice, it's a child.

❑ If you teach children about sex, they'll have sex sooner.

❑ A woman without a man is like a fish without a bicycle.

❑ Most male athletes would rape someone on a date.

❑ In the 1950s, no one had premarital sex like they do now.

_____

Cliché #1:

Argument to support my opinion:

_____

Cliché #2:

Argument to support my opinion:

TRY PRACTICE TEST #1 NOW!
GOOD LUCK!

Perspectives on Human Sexuality

Read each statement below and fill in the name of the perspective(s) to which it refers.

1. We look to the _____ perspective(s) to explain variability of physical characteristics and mating behavior among and across species. The same perspective(s) also argue(s) that both physical and behavioral traits may be genetically transmitted.

2. Scientists who do research using the _____ perspective(s) have found that most qualities we see as masculine or feminine may have become so because particular cultural norms encourage men and women to behave in certain ways. Without the groundwork laid by this/these perspective(s), the recent research that challenges gender-role stereotypes might not be possible.

3. The _____ perspective(s) give(s) us a way to place sexual attitudes and behaviors in context, so that we can see whether our current practices and values reflect a particular culture or era, or whether they have been the same over a long period of time. This/these perspective(s) often includes consideration of the impacts that religions often have on human sexuality.

4. It is hard to imagine where therapists would be without the work done in keeping with the _____ perspective(s). It/they make(s) it possible to treat sexual addiction effectively, thus increasing the chances for successful procreation within the relationship of the recovering addict. _____ perspective(s) also help us understand recent trends towards lewd public behavior and increased incidences of couples' videotaping themselves during sexual encounters.

5. _____ perspective(s) on sexuality has/have taught us that there are animal analogues of human sexual behavior of many kinds. For example, foreplay is widely practiced in the animal world, as are things like same-sex sexual behavior and oral-genital contact.

6. Some research explores the influence of things like perception, emotion, personality, and motivation on human sexuality. One such scholar argues that behavioral reinforcements must be considered; they will increase or decrease the likelihood of certain sexual behaviors over time. These mental processes receive the most consideration from the _____ perspective(s).

7. If it weren't for the _____ perspective(s), we would not know the mechanisms of sexual arousal and response, nor would we be able to help infertile couples conceive. One of the interesting topics included in this/these perspective(s) is the orgasm; it was found by scholars to be both a spinal reflex and a psychological event.

TRY PRACTICE TEST #2 NOW!
GOOD LUCK!

➢ *The Sociocultural Perspective: The World of Diversity*

For each factor given consideration under the sociocultural perspective, use the information in your text to give a brief summary of the influence(s) of that factor on human sexuality (even though we know that in reality there is great variability on each topic and that these are simply trends). Also, be sure to consider whether this information rings true with your own anecdotal evidence about the influence of these factors, so you can keep building those critical thinking skills. If possible, form groups to discuss the degree to which the sociocultural research findings agree with your personal experiences on the subject and whether using the new information in the chapter and your critical thinking skills has had an influence on your personal opinions.

❑ Age

❑ Sociocultural research indicates: _____

_____

My life experience indicates: _____

_____

❑ Level of Education

Sociocultural research indicates: _____

_____

My life experience indicates: _____

_____

❑ Religious Experience

Sociocultural research indicates: _____

_____

My life experience indicates:

❑ Ethnicity

Sociocultural research indicates: _____

_____

My life experience indicates: _____

> *Multiple Perspectives on Human Sexuality*

Review the statements below about the multiple perspectives on human sexuality discussed in your text, and check off the category into which the authors of your text would probably sort them. In the box provided, include the page number where you found the information that guided your answers.

Statement	Page	Category		
		I think not.	*A little yes, a little no.*	*Most definitely.*
Most patterns of sexual behavior hold true universally.				
Studying other humans is useful, but there is not much we can learn about sex from other species.				
When we choose which personal cultural values we want to use to decide what kind of sexual behavior is right, they tend to be values we believe have deep meaning.				
Overall, human sexuality seems to reflect a combination of factors that interact in ways that are complex.				
When it comes to sexuality, right is right, wrong is wrong, and most folks agree which is which.				
Although all of the perspectives are useful in some way, most of human sexuality can be explained using a consideration of psychological factors.				
The nature of human sexuality makes it easy to conduct valid research.				
If we use our own cultural values to decide what is normal sexual behavior, we can usually agree across our own cultural groups. It's when we try to consider other countries' cultures that we have to be careful about applying our own values.				
Largely, women and men fit best into specific roles that are well-defined historically.				
While gay, lesbian, bisexual, or transgendered people should not be treated disrespectfully, heterosexuality remains the best, most normal orientation for people.				

TRY PRACTICE TEST #3 NOW!
GOOD LUCK!

After You Read...

(LO = Learning Objective)

1. Which of the following statements, if any, are true in respect to the definition of human sexuality given by your text?
    a. Sexual intercourse is part of human sexuality; gender is not.
    b. Human sexuality includes the way we express ourselves as sexual beings.
    c. Sexuality is important to some people, but it is not an essential part of ourselves.
    d. Both B and C are true.
    e. None of the above are true.
             p. 4   LO 1

2. Medical science teaches us about human sexuality with respect to:
    a. The influence of motivation on sexual attitudes.
    b. The biological bases of sexual dysfunctions.
    c. The information one needs to decide when it's time to begin engaging in sex.
    d. The ways in which we can balance our sexual arousal with our spiritual beliefs.
             p. 4   LO 2

3. Sociocultural theorists contribute to the interdisciplinary nature of the study of human sexuality by providing information relating to:
    a. The relationship between the learning processes and sexual behavior.
    b. Our physiological responses during arousal.
    c. The relationship between sexual behavior and religion, race, or social class.
    d. The cross-cultural similarities and differences in sexual behavior.
             p. 4   LO 2

4. Studying human sexuality can offer us all of the following benefits, EXCEPT:
    a. A better understanding of how sexuality is influenced by family, culture, and societal traditions and beliefs.
    b. Assistance in recognizing and choosing appropriate intervention for sexual problems.
    c. An increase in ability to communicate effectively with sexual partners.
    d. Specifying which sexual behaviors are moral and which are not.
             p. 4-5   LO 2

5. Sexual knowledge and _____ are of value because they allow us to make informed sexual decisions.
    a. emotional commitment
    b. physiological arousal
    c. critical thinking skills
    d. an up-to-date copy of *The Joy of Sex*
             p. 5   LO 3

6. If our society was hedonistic, we would be driven to seek:
    a. Moral validation.
    b. Pleasure.
    c. Religious Piety.
    d. Rule-driven behavior.
        p. 7   LO 3

7. According to your text, the following all provide frameworks that guide our value systems EXCEPT:
    a. Asceticism.
    b. Hedonism.
    c. Sado-masochism.
    d. Rationalism.
        p. 7-8, 19   LO 3

8. Critical thinking requires:
    a. Rejection of any claims and arguments of others.
    b. Reliance upon our intuitive "gut impressions."
    c. Examination of the logic of arguments.
    d. Acceptance of conventional wisdom.
        p. 8   LO 4

9. Christopher reads a newspaper article about new research findings that say eating fresh peaches may increase male longevity during sexual intercourse. This leads him to think critically about whether or not this might be possible. Which of the following thoughts that go through his mind seem to be following the steps used in thorough critical thinking?
    a. That doesn't sound right to me. I've always heard that pomegranates are the only fruit that has an impact on sexual performance.
    b. It's hard to believe but I guess it's possible. Eating peaches could be part of a healthy lifestyle that allows for more sexual longevity.
    c. I think this research might be biased. Last week I saw an article that said the same thing about fresh cherries. I wonder if this one was sponsored by the Confederation of Fresh Produce Growers too.
    d. Both A and B are reflective of critical thinking.
    e. Both B and C are reflective of critical thinking.
        p. 9-10   LO 4

10. The convenience of the Internet is a great benefit in finding information. When a critical thinker is using it to find reliable information on sexuality, he/she can:
    a. Consider the overall professionalism in website appearance as one contributing indicator of reliability.
    b. Allow the website author to only make *one* (or possibly two) extravagant claims before becoming suspect of the website's reliability.
    c. Just as with conventional written sources, like books and journals, examine the professional credentials behind the author(s).
    d. All of the above are reasonable in assessing the reliability of a given sexuality website.
    e. Only A and C are true.
        p. 9-10   LO 5

(LO = Learning Objective)

1. The Ancient Greeks viewed men and women as:
    a. Heterosexual.
    b. Homosexual.
    c. Bisexual.
    d. Asexual.
                    p. 14   LO 6

2. Which of the following taboos do historians and anthropologists believe to be present in all human societies?
    a. Pederasty
    b. Incest
    c. Masturbation
    d. Adultery
                    p. 12   LO 6

3. A widely known conflict exists between two concepts of women: woman as temptress and woman as virtuous and pure. This is often referred to as a "Madonna-whore complex." During what period of history did this duality of thought first become dominant?
    a. The Pre-historic Era
    b. The Middle Ages
    c. The Era of Early Christianity
    d. The Golden Age of Ancient Greece
                    p. 17   LO 7

4. The sexual revolution was characterized by the following attribute(s)?
    a. Heightened use of illicit drugs
    b. Occurred during the mid-1960s to the mid-1970s.
    c. Heightened pregnancy rates as it started before "the pill" became available.
    d. All of the above are true
    e. Only A and B are correct attributes
                    p. 19   LO 7

5. Alfred Kinsey's major goal was to:
    a. Study the physiology of sexual functioning.
    b. Offer psychological advice about healthy types of sexual expression.
    c. Describe patterns of sexual behavior in the United States.
    d. Provide a guidebook for improving one's sexual relationships.
                    p. 19   LO 8

6. Which of the following statements is most descriptive of the main influence of Sigmund Freud on the science of human sexuality?
   a. He led the research team that completed the first large-scale surveys of sexual behaviors in the US.
   b. He developed a theory of personality that emphasized sexual drives and the unconscious mind.
   c. He found that one's sexual appetite could be controlled by eating food made with whole grain flours.
   d. He developed a theory of behaviorism that emphasized rewards and punishments in the learning process.

              p. 28   LO 8

7. Choose the major focuses of biological sexual research from among the following options:
   a. The mechanisms of reproduction
   b. The roles of genes in human sexuality
   c. The function of dating rituals in human mating strategies
   d. Both A and B.
   e. Both B and C.

              p. 21   LO 9

8. Some evolutionary psychologists think there may be a genetic basis to social and sexual behavior among both animal and human species. Which of the following have been raised as criticisms of this belief with respect to human sexuality?
   a. Culture and life experiences play such vital roles that genetics cannot be relied upon to be the single explaining factor.
   b. It is primarily hormones that influence human sexuality; genetics do not have much influence on sexual behavior.
   c. Genetics are often determined by sociocultural factors during pregnancy; thus they cannot drive social behavior.
   d. If we emphasize the influence of genetics, people will lose their motivation to learn appropriate ways to initiate sexual contact.

              p. 22   LO 10

9. Which of the following, if any, are examples of animal analogues of human sexual behavior?
   a. Some animals practice male-male sexual behavior.
   b. Some animals kiss as part of sexual foreplay.
   c. Some animals bring their sexual partners offerings of certain plants pulled off at the stems.
   d. Both A and B are true.
   e. Both A and C are true.

              p. 23   LO 11

10. Why is it so important for us to study cross-cultural variations in sexual behaviors and attitudes?
    a. Its diversity lets us know that sexuality is determined by a lot more than just biology.
    b. It gives us information with which we can eventually help other cultures improve their sexual value systems, making them more like our own.
    c. It strengthens the argument that human sexuality is complex, dynamic, and expressed in many ways.
    d. Both A and C are true.
    e. All of the above are true.
                 p. 4   LO 12

(LO = Learning Objective)

1. Watson is to Freud as:
   a. Behaviorism is to social-learning theory.
   b. Sociobiology is to psychoanalysis.
   c. Behaviorism is to psychoanalysis.
   d. Social learning is to the cross-cultural perspective.
      p. 28-29   LO 13

2. Although both behaviorism and social-learning theory discuss rewards and punishments, social-learning theorists also emphasize:
   a. The importance of learning by observation.
   b. The importance of cognitive activity.
   c. The importance of constant reinforcement.
   d. Both A and B are emphasized.
   e. Both B and C are emphasized.
      p. 29, 30   LO 13

3. According to social-learning theorists, your sexual preferences, values and patterns of behaving are developed through:
   a. The stages of psychosexual development.
   b. Receiving direct rewards and punishments.
   c. Observation and imitation of significant models.
   d. The unfolding of your genetic program.
      p. 29   LO 13

4. The MAIN role of sociocultural theorists is to:
   a. Explain why people within a particular subgroup all hold the same sexual attitudes.
   b. Determine the influence of past experiences on the current sexual behavior of individuals.
   c. Examine differences in sexuality among the subgroups of a society, along issues such as ethnicity, religion, and social class.
   d. Contribute to our understanding of cross-cultural variance in sexuality.
      p. 4   LO 14

5. According to socioculturalists, people who have more education tend to be more sexually:
   a. Restrained.
   b. Promiscuous.
   c. Fickle.
   d. Liberalized.
      p. 24   LO 14

6. Teresita is a Latina American participant in the NHSLS study referred to by your text. When comparing her own number of sexual partners to the trends reported in a report on this survey, she notices that she has had more partners than average for her age. When she reads the sociocultural discussion of the results and sees that, on average, persons of her ethnicity tend to have fewer sexual partners than members of most other ethnic groups, she is worried that something might be wrong with her sex drive. What would a socioculturist be most likely to remind her in order to reduce her distress about this?
    a. Since you are Latina American, you must be Catholic; you can receive absolution at confession.
    b. Not all members of any group act alike; it is normal for there to be a range of attitudes and behaviors within any given group.
    c. Don't worry; there are counselors who can help you with your promiscuity.
    d. Both A and B might be offered to comfort her.
    e. All of the above might be offered to comfort her.
              p. 24   LO 14

7. It is important to include multiple perspectives in order to understand sexuality because:
    a. There are many different viewpoints about what is right or wrong.
    b. Multiple perspectives reflect the complex nature of sexuality.
    c. It is important to keep in mind that our beliefs about sexuality may not be fitting for others.
    d. All of the above.
    e. Only A and B are true.
              p. 31   LO 15

8. Feminist theory challenges the following element(s):
    a. Women should now be considered sexual aggressors—even overtaking the male role as aggressor over time.
    b. The idea that men must be breadwinners and women are to be homemakers
    c. That women, despite becoming far more rational, remain the emotional sex and men remain the unemotional sex.
    d. Only B and C are true.
    e. All of the above are true.
              p. 30   LO 16

9. Queer theory contains the following element(s):
    a. Argues that sexuality has naturally contained more variation than those in power, who are usually heterosexual, are willing to admit.
    b. Suggests that homosexuality is—in several cases—superior to heterosexuality.
    c. It is a theory of both gender roles and sexuality with its origins from psychology and sociology.
    d. Only A and C are true.
    e. Only B and C are true.
              p.30   LO 17

Multiple Choice

1. Our society is _____. If it were not, we might not be able to express such a wide range of sexual attitudes and values.
    a. pro-choice
    b. pluralistic
    c. in favor of sex outside of marriage
    d. Both B and C are true.

2. Which of the following statements is most descriptive of the main influence of Sigmund Freud on the science of human sexuality?
    a. He led the research team that completed the first large-scale surveys of sexual behaviors in the U.S.
    b. He developed a theory of personality that emphasized sexual drives and the unconscious mind.
    c. He found that one's sexual appetite could be controlled by eating food made with whole grain flours.
    d. He developed a theory of behaviorism that emphasized rewards and punishments in the learning process.

3. Medical science teaches us about human sexuality with respect to:
    a. The influence of motivation on sexual attitudes.
    b. The biological bases of sexual dysfunctions.
    c. The information one needs to decide when it's time to begin engaging in sex.
    d. The ways in which we can balance our sexual arousal with our spiritual beliefs.

4. The MAIN role of sociocultural theorists is to:
    a. Explain why people within a particular subgroup all hold the same sexual attitudes.
    b. Determine the influence of past experiences on the current sexual behavior of individuals.
    c. Examine differences in sexuality among the subgroups of a society, along issues such as ethnicity, religion, and social class.
    d. Contribute to our understanding of cross-cultural variance in sexuality.

5. Critical thinking requires:
    a. Rejection of any claims and arguments of others.
    b. Reliance upon our intuitive "gut impressions."
    c. Examination of the logic of arguments.
    d. Acceptance of conventional wisdom.

6. A widely known conflict exists between two concepts of women: woman as temptress, and woman as virtuous and pure. This is often referred to as a "Madonna-whore complex." During what period of history did this duality of thought first become dominant?
    a. The Pre-historic Era
    b. The Middle Ages
    c. The Era of Early Christianity
    d. The Golden Age of Ancient Greece

7. Which of the following statements, if any, are true in respect to the definition of human sexuality given by your text?
    a. Sexual intercourse is part of human sexuality; gender is not.
    b. Human sexuality includes the way we express ourselves as sexual beings.
    c. Sexuality is important to some people, but it is not an essential part of ourselves.
    d. Both B and C are true.
    e. None of the above are true.

8. Although both behaviorism and social-learning theory discuss rewards and punishments, social-learning theorists also emphasize:
    a. The importance of learning by observation.
    b. The importance of cognitive activity.
    c. The importance of constant reinforcement.
    d. Both A and B are emphasized.
    e. Both B and C are emphasized.

9. It is important to include multiple perspectives in order to understand sexuality because:
    a. There are many different viewpoints about what is right or wrong.
    b. Multiple perspectives reflect the complex nature of sexuality.
    c. It is important to keep in mind that our beliefs about sexuality may not be fitting for others.
    d. All of the above.
    e. Only A and B are true.

10. Which of the following, if any, are examples of animal analogues of human sexual behavior?
    a. Some animals practice male-male sexual behavior.
    b. Some animals kiss as part of sexual foreplay.
    c. Some animals bring their sexual partners offerings of certain plants pulled off at the stems.
    d. Both A and B are true.
    e. Both A and C are true.

11. Alfred Kinsey's major goal was to
    a. Study the physiology of sexual functioning.
    b. Offer psychological advice about healthy types of sexual expression.
    c. Describe patterns of sexual behavior in the United States.
    d. Provide a guidebook for improving one's sexual relationships.

12. The Ancient Greeks viewed men and women as:
    a. Heterosexual.
    b. Homosexual.
    c. Bisexual.
    d. Asexual.

13. Why is it so important for us to study cross-cultural variations in sexual behaviors and attitudes?
    a. Its diversity lets us know that sexuality is determined by a lot more than just biology.
    b. It gives us information with which we can eventually help other cultures improve their sexual value systems, making them more like our own.
    c. It strengthens the argument that human sexuality is complex, dynamic, and expressed in many ways.
    d. Both A and C are true.
    e. All of the above are true.

14. Choose the major focuses of biological sexual research from among the following options:
    a. The mechanisms of reproduction.
    b. The roles of genes in human sexuality.
    c. The function of dating rituals in human mating strategies.
    d. Both A and B.
    e. Both B and C.

15. The convenience of the Internet is a great benefit in finding information. When a critical thinker is using it to find reliable information on sexuality, he/she can:
    a. Consider the overall professionalism in website appearance as an indicator of reliability.
    b. Allow the website author to only make *one* (or possibly two) extravagant claims before becoming suspect of the website's reliability.
    c. Just as with conventional written sources, like books and journals, examine the professional credentials behind the author(s).
    d. All of the above are true in assessing the reliability of a given sexuality website.
    e. Only A and C are true.

True/False

_____ 1. Margaret Mead was the Queen of England from 1837 to 1901; her name has become virtually synonymous with sexual repression.

_____ 2. According to recent research from the evolutionary perspective, men show greater erotic plasticity than women do.

_____ 3. History shows little evidence of universal sexual trends.

_____ 4. Vaginal lubrication is the result of a "sweating" action of the vaginal walls.

_____ 5. The Roman Empire viewed men and women as bisexual.

_____ 6. Increased access to birth control was the one momentous event that marked the mid-1960s onset of the sexual revolution in the U.S.

_____ 7. Ancient Hebrews viewed sex within marriage as a fulfilling experience.

8. The higher you go up the evolutionary ladder, the more important the influence of experience and learning on sexuality.

Essay Questions

1. Explain the value systems that are said to provide guiding frameworks for making informed sexual choices. Please include one example of a sexual decision and the probable choice one would make based on each value system.

_____

_____

_____

_____

_____

_____

_____

_____

2. In its discussion of the foundations of scientific study on sexuality, your text mentions how tedious the original Kinsey books on male and female sexual behavior were to read. Knowing what a revolution in the study of human sexual behavior these books began, it is difficult to imagine them being boring. Use what you have learned in this chapter about critical thinking to discuss some possible reasons that Kinsey might or might not have made the text into a "dry" read on purpose.

_____

_____

_____

_____

_____

_____

_____

_____

When You Have Finished...

There are some thought provoking questions raised by the authors in the introduction to this chapter. We have listed a few of them below, for reference. Choose at least one of them (or find another one more to your liking if you prefer), and see what you get when you try to find the answers on the Web. Practice your critical thinking skills and consider how useful and accurate you believe the information to be.

- ❑ Can people who are paralyzed from the neck down become erect or lubricated?
- ❑ What factors determine a person's sexual orientation?
- ❑ Can you infect others with a sexually transmitted infection without having any symptoms yourself?

1. Go to Google and find a website that has information about human sexuality (you can put "-.com" after human sexuality to filter out commercial sites if you are nervous about what might show up on your browser. For a benign site, try: http://www.expertdatingadvice.com. Choose one of the many links that promise to address all of your relationship concerns, and read the advice using your critical thinking lenses. What do you think of it? Do you feel you can trust the content? What might you need to consider before you take this advice to heart?

2. Visit the Breakup Girl website, which offers advice with a little spice. This link will take you to a particular letter, within which the Madonna-whore complex is referenced: http://www.breakupgirl.net/advice/980216/980216j.html. Although this letter is approximately ten years old, the idea is still current. It shows that the complex is alive and well—and still influencing some of our relationship choices. How do you feel about that? The letter also mentions the way this complex was applied to the Clinton/Lewinsky affair during President Clinton's tenure in the White House a number of years back. Do you think her comments make sense in light of what you're learning about this schism between "good" and "bad" girls?

3. Have you seen the movie "The Ice Storm?" It provides a look at some of the less carefree aspects of the sexual revolution. One of the things it explores is the idea of "key parties," where couples would come to a party, put all of their keys in a big bowl, and have a member of each couple pick a key. The person to whom the key belonged became your sexual partner for the evening. Although the public dialog on "swinging" seems a bit quieter than it was during the sexual revolution, the phenomenon still exists. Try searching Craigslist.org for swinging couples in your area or Google "swingers" and see what you get. Proceed with caution unless you're comfortable viewing sexually explicit materials online. Are you surprised with the results of your search? Why/Why Not?

Chapter 2
Research Methods in Human Sexuality

Before You Begin...

Chapter Summary

Sometimes one may hear of a new study on television, radio, or on the Internet that seems to conflict with a prior one. We hope it causes you to wonder more about just how scientific research is done! While this chapter will not teach you how to do research for a doctoral dissertation, it will give you much greater insight into the empirical research process. Greater understanding, coupled with the previous chapter's lessons on critical thinking, will allow you to become a more informed user of research findings.

Chapter 2 begins with a description of the classic scientific method: research question formulation, hypothesis formation, hypothesis testing, and drawing conclusions. The goals of the scientific study of human sexuality are to describe, explain, predict, and control behavior. To achieve these goals, researchers must first specify an operational definition of variables they expect to study. Various sampling methods for choosing subjects within a population are discussed. Bias problems are explained—more specifically both volunteer bias and social desirability bias. Woven throughout this chapter, emphasis is placed on the overarching importance of critical thinking and its impact on careful research design. (A poorly designed study can be a waste of time and effort!)

Your text presents six models (or methods) for sex research, the:

1. Case study
2. Survey
3. Naturalistic observation (field study)
4. Ethnographic observation
5. Participant observation
6. Laboratory observation

For each method, the related terminology, variants, advantages and best uses, disadvantages, and limitations are examined. Examples of studies employing each method are described and selected results are presented.

The case-study method emphasizes individual or small group sexual practices. It presents the advantages of close attention to the dynamics of many factors, but also faces problems of generalizability. Looking at the survey method, it is less expensive to use and often it is the only realistic way to study a large sample to glean insight into its sexual attitudes and practices. You will notice that six distinct limitations of the survey method are identified.

The naturalistic-observational method, or field study approach, uses direct observation of humans and animals in the context of a natural environment. Similar to the naturalistic observational method, the ethnographic observational method facilitates study of differing cultures/ethnic groups in their settings. Participant observation involves direct interaction, and historically some of its scientific value has been questioned—but current users of this method have made changes. The laboratory observation method is similar to participant observation, but it moves the subjects to the laboratory instead. Collectively, the advantages of these types of methods are similar to the case-study method and, in keeping with that similarity, they present significant problems with sampling bias along with heightened ethical concerns.

Masters and Johnson, users of the laboratory method, invented an artificial penis (containing photographic equipment) and employed yet other medical instruments in their studies. These instruments allowed them to quantify vasocongestion, myotonia, and other physiological responses as noted in your text. The study of such responses (or dependent variables) allowed quantifying and understanding the physical aspects of sexual response to a degree not previously done.

There are two approaches to data analysis, which are predictably explained well by your text authors. The approaches divide along the lines of correlational and experimental. The chief distinction between correlational and "true" experimental (i.e., empirical in the traditional sense of the word) is that correlational merely associates two or more variables, while the classic experimental approach attempts to demonstrate a cause-effect relationship between them. In the social sciences, with its emphasis on the ethical study of human behavior, it can often be very difficult to establish a definite, experimentally-verified relationship between two variables and instead the correlational method must be used.

Correlation is a statistical technique that is used to establish the both the strength and directionality of relationship between two variables. For example, the use of a heavy coat (that, when wearing it effectively thickens one's amount of clothing) has an opposite relationship to outside temperature for most people. Clearly, this would help explain why one does not wear a heavy parka on a Florida beach during Spring Break. Stated scientifically now, the thickness of one's clothing negatively correlates to outside temperature—so as one goes up, the other goes down. Directionality between the variable pairs can be positive or negative and the strength of relationship, as measured by the correlation coefficient, ranges from 0 to 1 (or 0% to 100%) and for negative correlates, 0 to -1. Note that there are significant caveats in relying on correlation even though sometimes it is the only tool available—do read the text section carefully; the caveats make for good class examination questions.

In contrast to the correlation method, the experimental (or true empirical) method does allow definite determination of cause and effect relationships between a pair of variables. Though, to make *some* research truly empirical, it could effectively require the researchers to compromise ethics. As noted by the Tuskegee Syphilis Study, history does reveal some terrible lapses in ethics. Fortunately, such outcomes have led to greater oversight on the use of deception and in providing participants with informed consent.

Your authors note that ethical considerations include items such as the potential for either physical or psychological harm. Aspects of possible psychological harm include protecting confidentiality, informed consent, and the use of deception. Before undertaking a study, sex researchers must submit for approval detailed explanations of experimental design and protocol to institutional ethics review committees nowadays. The goals are to ensure both the safety of the study's participants as well as protection of the researchers and their institution from litigious entanglements with participants who feel they have experienced harm.

1. Explain the four essential elements of the classic scientific method of research.

2. List the four broad goals of the science of human sexuality.

3. Describe the sampling methods used to choose research subjects. Identify the advantages and disadvantages associated with these methods.

4. Describe the case-study method and its advantages and limitations.

5. Critique the sampling techniques used in several large-scale surveys discussed in this chapter.

6. Identify and explain advantages and problems associated with using the survey method, providing examples for each.

7. Distinguish the four observational methods and suggest research questions each might be used to answer.

8. Identify the principle weaknesses of the various observational methods.

9. Compare and contrast the correlational and experimental methods of data analysis. Explain why correlations cannot indicate a cause-and-effect relationship.

10. Discuss the experimental method in terms of the variables involved and the assignment of subjects to groups.

11. Cite the limitations of the experimental method and give examples of situations in which it could not be used.

12. Discuss the major ethical issues researchers encounter when conducting sex research and how they are resolved.

13. Discuss at least one lapse in sound ethical judgment from earlier in the last century as applied to the study of one sexually transmitted disease. Outline some of the safeguards that would be used to prevent such an experiment today.

Term Identification

As in the prior chapter, the various terms that are introduced throughout the chapter are summarized below and organized alphabetically.

Helpful Hints:

1. To help in your recollections, consider creating flashcards using the terms. (It is usually best to do this as you go.)
2. Many terms are defined in the margins of the chapter. Also, the index in the back of the textbook can point you to the correct page.
3. When you write the definitions in your own words, you will remember them better!

Chapter 2 Key Terms

Anthropomorphism	Informed consent
Case study	Laboratory observation
Confidentiality	Myotonia
Control group	Naturalistic observation
Correlation	Participant observation
Correlation Coefficient	Penile strain gauge
Demographic	Population
Dependent variable	Random Sample
Ethnographic observation	Selection factor
Experiment	Social desirability
Experimental group	Survey
Frequency	Treatment
Generalize	Vaginal Photoplethysmograph
Hypothesis	Validity and Reliability
Incidence	Variables
Independent variable	Vasocongestion
Inference	Volunteer bias

As You Read...

❖ *A Scientific Approach to Human Sexuality*

➢ *The Scientific Method*

The scientific method applies broadly amongst all the science disciplines—and the study of human sexuality is no different. The scientific method is instrumental in helping sexuality researchers construct studies so that reliable findings emerge. Broadly, the process is called research methods, and before going further in our attempt to become scholars of human sexuality, it is important to learn enough about research methods. Understanding them allow us to be good consumers of existing research and, possibly, good designers of our own research projects in the future. Although the study of human behavior most often involves making some compromises on the traditional scientific method due to ethical and practical considerations (making them what is usually referred to as "quasi-experimental designs"), it is important to have a thorough knowledge of the "gold standard" of scientific methodology. With that in mind, rearrange the following elements of the scientific method in their order of occurrence and note the key features of each. Eventually, they will become easy to use as a basis for comparison to the other methods in the chapter.

❑ Testing the hypothesis

❑ Drawing conclusions

❑ Formulating a research question

❑ Framing the research question in the form of a hypothesis

	Correct Order of Elements:	Key Features:
1.		
2.		
3.		
4.		

Why is it important to perform the above steps in order? For example, would it be reasonable for a scientist to develop a hypothesis after examining their data and drawing conclusions? Why not?

➢ *Goals of the Science of Human Sexuality*

❖ The goals of the science of human sexuality are congruent with those of other sciences: to describe, explain, predict, and control the events (in this case, the sexual behaviors) that are of interest. Name the three major categories of variables your book cites as commonly used to explain sexual behavior, give examples of each one, and make up what seems to be a reasonable example of the kind of behavior each predicts. Use information from research you have read and the trends discussed in this chapter to rationalize your assessment of the statements as reasonable or unreasonable.

For example, if hair color were a major variable (which it is NOT, just for the record), we might predict, based on the conventional wisdom, that blondes have more fun, that women with blonde hair have a higher number of sexual partners than do their cohorts with other hair colors. We do not think the statement is reasonable because there is no research linking hair color with sexual performance, despite conventional wisdom about blondes' love lives.

1. Major Category: _____

   Variable: _____

   Behavior Predicted by Variable: _____

   _____

   How valid is the prediction? _____

2. Major Category: _____

   Variable: _____

   Behavior Predicted by Variable: _____

   _____

   How valid is the prediction? _____

3. Major Category: _____

   Variable: _____

   Behavior Predicted by Variable: _____

   _____

   How valid is the prediction? _____

❖ *Populations and Samples: Representing the World of Diversity*

➢ *Sampling Methods*

As your text points out, despite the diversity of human sexual behavior in the world, many research studies are performed using convenience samples of European American, middle-class college students who volunteer for studies conducted at the schools they attend.

Consider the following issues and discuss how these convenience samples tend to influence the results found in studies that utilize them for participants. As usual, please state your reasons for choosing your answers.

❑ Would your sample be representative of college students in general?

_____

_____

❑ How would you determine if your sample represented the students at your particular college?

_____

_____

❑ On what variables might they be biased?

_____

_____

❑ What steps could you take to reduce some of the biases inherent to convenience samples?

_____

_____

❑ In what ways do you think volunteers for studies on human sexuality might differ from other convenience sample volunteers?

_____

_____

TRY PRACTICE TEST #1 NOW!
GOOD LUCK!

❖ Methods of Observation

> ➢ *So many observational methods, so little time….*

Because there is no such thing as a perfectly designed research study of human behavior, it is important that you think critically about which biases you can afford to accept and which you need to work extra hard at minimizing. In sum, you need to consider your research question and decide what elements are most important to control in order to best answer it. One of the most crucial elements to consider is the fit between your method of observation and the question your research is trying to answer. With that in mind, examine the hypothetical research questions below, and choose the method you think would best fit. When making your choice, be sure to consider why you think it offers the best chance at helping to reach your research goals.

1. Is there a difference in how often couples who live in urban areas on the East and West Coasts have intercourse per week during the first year of their marriage?

   I would choose the _____ method of observation because:

   _____

   _____

2. Do homosexual female couples decrease the physical space between each other when an attractive female approaches and engages them in conversation using very "open" body language?

   I would choose the _____ method of observation because:

   _____

   _____

3. Do persons residing in rental apartments: a) make note of the comings and goings of their neighbors' overnight guests, b) make assumptions about the nature of these visits, c) have an awareness of which neighbors are regular participants in such dialogues, and d) express willingness to include someone who is both researcher and neighbor in such dialogues upon informed request?

   I would choose the _____ method of observation because:

   _____

   _____

4. Who displays some form of physical contact most often among unmarried heterosexual couples in public settings: males or females?

I would choose the _____ method of observation because:

_____

_____

5. When a couple has married, divorced, and then remarried, how does it affect things like their choice of living arrangements, financial decisions, and relationships with each other's immediate family members?

I would choose the _____ method of observation because:

_____

_____

6. Do same-sex adoptive parents of newborns living in San Francisco who are members of the Castro Street Community Center Adoptive Support Network experience any changes in the frequency and/or nature of their lovemaking as a result of the arrival of the newborns into their homes?

I would choose the _____ method of observation because:

_____

_____

TRY PRACTICE TEST #2 NOW!
GOOD LUCK!

❖ *The Experimental Method*

➤ *Limitations of the Experimental Method*

Despite the fact that it is the best (perhaps the only) method through which we can examine causal relationships between variables, the experimental method has its share of drawbacks when it is applied to the study of human behavior—and especially of human sexuality. As potential researchers of sexual behavior, it is important to maintain a sense of empathy for participants, despite the urge to control variables in ways that will allow for experiments that can address unanswered questions about human sexuality.

With that in mind, this is an opportune situation in which to practice using empathic critical thinking. In other words, the problems this method may produce are much easier to troubleshoot if you're able to imagine yourself as the participant instead of the researcher, and use the information to take care that due consideration has been given to the degree of discomfort that might arise during the experiment.

Take some time to journal about your personal and scholarly reactions to the following experimental scenario. If it helps to decrease your desire to respond to this scenario in a socially desirable, research-compliant way, despite your personal feelings about the issue, please keep in mind that this journal entry is for your eyes only—no one will judge your reply. Just because you might want to perform experiments about human sexuality, you need not feel it is wrong not to want to participate in one yourself.

"You Are There...."

Imagine yourself a participant in an experimentally designed research project about the effect of "party drugs" (such as GHB or Ecstasy) on one's ability to achieve sexual arousal. You have signed off on the informed consent form, but you skimmed it because it seemed to be written in legal mumbo-jumbo. The researcher asked you if you had any questions, but you are kind of embarrassed to stop everything to ask them what the form meant, especially because you're starting to wonder why you thought it would be fun to be in this research. Nevertheless you are committed to following through in the interest of science—and some much needed extra credit points in your Human Development Class. You've never taken party drugs, but you have talked to people you trust who have, and you feel ok about trying them, especially since the environment will be controlled and you know no one will let you be endangered. You enter the room where the experiment will take place. It is set up like a bedroom—sort of like a hotel room, but with cameras, and a table on the side with some complicated looking equipment with electrodes. After you get all wired up so that your sexual responses can be measured, you are made comfortable and told to watch a film so they can record your baseline sexual response to the content. They've put you in an easy chair and you're starting to relax a little, despite the fact that you have electrodes on your erogenous zones and cameras observing you. The sexually explicit film begins. It starts off with some harmless looking stuff—still nudes, some of them sleeping—and then things get a little more racy, including things like masturbation and love-making. After viewing it for a while, you become aroused. You remain so during the rest of the film. Now you are given one of the drugs. You are not told which party drug it is because it is more experimentally sound if you don't react in a way you expect a drug might make you react, rather than reacting naturally to its effects. Another movie is inserted into the DVD player and you are told that it will contain both the images you saw before, as well as some new ones. As you watch, you notice that you are more easily aroused than before. You start to see that the new additions to the film include some scenes in which the sleeping nude is "taken unaware" sexually, and others where the sex is fairly aggressive. You remain aroused throughout these scenes, despite the fact that these are not the kind of images that run through your head when you are trying to think arousing thoughts. How do you feel about your experience?

My Personal Reaction (i.e., How am I feeling about participating in the research now?):

_____

_____

_____

_____

_____

My Scholarly Reaction (i.e., What are the problems with this research design? If I were the researcher, what would I do differently in terms of design and informed consent?):

_____

_____

_____

_____

_____

_____

❖ *Ethics in Sex Research*

One of the most important rights that researchers must provide participants is the right to be protected from exposure to harm. That sounds straightforward, but it can become complicated in an instant. Let's go back to using our mental imagery for a moment….

"You Are There…. AGAIN!"

Imagine that you are conducting a series of case studies with persons who are HIV positive, examining how being HIV positive has affected their sexual activity in various ways, such as frequency, means of gratification, and social context of any sexual activity experienced with others. During one of the interviews, your interviewee, a heterosexual female, discloses that she has not yet told her significant other that she has tested HIV positive, and that she is particularly nervous about it now because she got caught up in the moment and allowed herself to engage in unprotected sex. She is afraid if she tells the truth now, she will lose her lover, and, to be fair, her physical symptoms are very favorable, and she believes this might mean she has not transmitted the disease. She tells you that she has decided she will not tell her partner unless he develops some symptoms of his own, even though she knows it's dishonest. You have worked hard to gain her trust, and you know that the fallout would be devastating to her if her lover broke off the relationship right now due to other complications, like her dependency on him for rent money and food for herself and her 2 kids. Her medical record shows more signs of good health than any other you've seen for a person who has HIV. No one but you will have access to her complete interview transcripts, and she is one of your key informants—you need her endorsement to get most of the other people in your target sample to consider participating in your research.

What do you do with the information? When you consider your answer, take note of the sort of issues upon which you base your decision, and remember to keep in mind the potential harm to the participant as well as to her significant other.

Issues Influencing My Decision: _____

_____

_____

Potential Harm to Participant:_____

_____

Potential Harm to Participant's Significant Other: _____

_____

The Action I Would Take Based on All of the Above: _____

TRY PRACTICE TEST #3 NOW!
GOOD LUCK!

After You Read...

PRACTICE TEST #1

(LO = Learning Objective)

1. The empirical research approach is based on:
   a. Intuition.
   b. Research evidence.
   c. Anecdotal evidence.
   d. Legal restrictions.

   p. 37   LO 1

2. According to your text, what is the main element shared by both critical thinking and the scientific approach?
   a. Skepticism
   b. Legalism
   c. Hedonism
   d. Political correctness

   p. 37   LO 1

3. The four essential elements of the classic scientific method of research include which of the following?
   a. Formulating a research question
   b. Testing the hypothesis
   c. Securing permission for the research
   d. Both A and B
   e. All of the above

   p. 37   LO 1

4. The goals of the science of human sexuality are _____ those of other sciences.
   a. less scientifically rigorous than
   b. not comparable to
   c. divergent from
   d. congruent with

   p. 37   LO 2

5. The often misused practice of applying human standards to explain animal behavior is called:
   a. Correlational description.
   b. Anthropomorphism.
   c. Transmogrification.
   d. Intuitive matching.

   p. 38   LO 2

6. All of the following are goals of the science of human sexuality EXCEPT:
    a. Providing information to help couples conceive.
    b. Providing rules that tell people how they should behave.
    c. Providing means through which people could enhance their sexual experiences.
    d. Providing cures for sexually transmitted infections.
                        p. 38   LO 2

7. Bob and Carol are seeing a couples therapist in hopes of resolving their difficulties in expressing themselves emotionally to one another. Despite the fact that they have both indicated their reluctance to do so, the therapist continues to insist that based on scientific knowledge, their best course is to spend some time dating others to make sure they want to be with each other. This therapist may need:
    a. Lessons on how to persuade clients to follow advice more eagerly.
    b. To remember that it is not her job to convince clients to follow the therapist's goals.
    c. To bring in an additional treatment provider to help make Bob and Carol understand.
    d. To help Bob and Carol by introducing each of them to a suitable date.
                        p. 38   LO 2

8. If you were surveying the students at your college about their sexual behavior, a _____ would be the best way to describe your use of randomly selected groups of Freshmen, Sophomores, Juniors and Seniors in proportion to their number in the student body.
    a. population
    b. control group
    c. stratified random sample
    d. target sample
                        p. 39   LO 3

9. Both scholarly research and conventional wisdom tell us that sex research causes many more people to refuse to participate than might a less personal research topic. This kind of self-selection is also known as a type of:
    a. Sexual discrimination.
    b. Researcher bias.
    c. Volunteer bias.
    d. Population enhancement.
                        p. 40   LO 3

10. What kind(s) of issues listed below tend to accurately describe a sample of convenience?
    a. They are truly representative of the target group being studied.
    b. They are often found within the university at which the researcher is employed.
    c. They tend to be of low socioeconomic status.
    d. Both A and B are true.
    e. All of the above are true.
                        p. 40   LO 3

(LO = Learning Objective)

1. Which of the following, if any, is considered an advantage of using the case-study method?
   a. It yields information that can be generalized to the rest of the population.
   b. It yields rich, in-depth information about the participants' personal experiences.
   c. It is easy to find participants that are representative of the larger target population.
   d. None of the above are advantages of this method.

   p. 40   LO 4

2. By definition, the focus of a case study is:
   a. To understand one or several individuals as fully as possible.
   b. Obtaining descriptive information applicable to a larger group.
   c. Confined to one prolonged interview session
   d. Finding causality of the dependent variable(s).

   p. 41   LO 4

3. Most of the scientific research on sexuality has been a result of using which of the following methods?
   a. Direct observation
   b. Surveys
   c. Case studies
   d. Randomized scientific experimentation

   p. 41   LO 5

4. Kinsey's famous surveys on human sexuality utilized samples that underrepresented which group or groups?
   a. People in urban areas
   b. People of color
   c. Younger people
   d. All of the above
   e. None of the above

   p. 42   LO 5

5. In a research project, the degree to which the questionnaire measures the construct it purports to measure is an indication of its:
   a. Validity.
   b. Reliability.
   c. Sample probability.
   d. Incidence.

   p. 43   LO 6

6. In his famous survey, Kinsey compared the response of each member of a number of married couples regarding the frequency of intercourse in an attempt to minimize one of the limitations of survey methodology. If both spouses agreed on the frequency of intercourse, then Kinsey would have more assurance that his results were:
    a. Valid.
    b. Reliable.
    c. Unbiased.
    d. Interpreted correctly.
        p. 43   LO 6

7. The National Survey of Family Growth was conducted by the _____ to assess concerns about _____.
    a. League of women voters; discrimination
    b. Scientific community; pregnancy
    c. Kinsey Group; morality
    d. Center For Disease Control; public health
    e. Both B and C are true.
        p. 43   LO 7

8. Dr. Brooks goes to a massage parlor as a potential customer and records how offers for sexual services are made. The research method used here is:
    a. Ethnographic observation.
    b. Participant observation.
    c. Obtrusive observation.
    d. Naturalistic observation.
        p. 49   LO 7

9. Unfortunately, participants in studies of human sexuality tend to supply distorted or biased information, even if it is obtained by observational methods. This limitation is often due to the pressure towards social desirability, in which participants responses may:
    a. Make them sound more adventurous than they are.
    b. Reflect what they think the researcher wants to hear.
    c. Keep them from feeling judged.
    d. All of the above.
    e. None of the above.
        p. 47   LO 8

10. One of the biggest limitations of direct observation of sexual behavior is that it is usually performed in private where others cannot see it. What does your text suggest as a way to minimize this effect?
    a. Use a hidden camera to record sexual activity of participants.
    b. Provide an incentive for someone who can secretly get access to act as an informant.
    c. Conduct personal interviews with those being observed and ask them about it.
    d. None of the above are done; they are all unethical practices.
        p. 47   LO 8

(LO = Learning Objective)

1. A/n _____ is a method of measuring the relationship between two variables, whereas a/n _____ is a method of studying cause-and-effect relationships between variables.
    a. experiment; correlation
    b. correlation; intervention
    c. experiment; ethnography
    d. correlation; experiment
            p. 51, 53   LO 9

2. The systematic manipulation of independent variables used in the experimental method is most useful in providing scientists a way to draw conclusions about:
    a. Their frequency.
    b. Their validity.
    c. Their causal relationship.
    d. Their tendency towards social desirability.
            p. 53   LO 9

3. Using the correlational method, it has been found that being married is correlated positively with a sense of well-being. In light of this finding and our knowledge of the advantages and disadvantages of correlational methods, we can conclude that:
    a. Being single may predict a sense of unhappiness.
    b. Being married causes happiness.
    c. Being single causes unhappiness.
    d. Both A and C are true.
    e. Both B and C are true.
            p. 51-52   LO 9

4. In an experiment to study the effects of a drug that is touted to have an aphrodisiac effect on the user, the _____ group receives the _____ of the drug, while the _____ group does not.
    a. control; treatment; experimental
    b. treatment; dependent variable; control
    c. experimental; treatment; control
    d. experimental; dependent variable; control
            p. 54   LO 10

5. If a researcher measures the degree of penile enlargement as related to the viewing of sexually explicit movie clips, the movie clips are the _____ variable and the degree of penile enlargement is the _____ variable.
    a. independent; dependent
    b. dependent; independent
    c. treatment; independent
    d. dependent; treatment
            p. 53   LO 10

6. In experimental research design, the _____ variables are systematically manipulated by the researchers.
    a. representative
    b. dependent
    c. randomized
    d. independent
            p. 53   LO 10

7. Which of the following statements about experimental research, if any, is/are false?
    a. It does not allow for the exploration of cause-and-effect relationships.
    b. It allows the researcher to control variables thought to influence the sexual behavior being studied.
    c. It is being used regularly in studying human sexual behavior.
    d. All of the above are false.
    e. None of the above are false.
            p. 53   LO 11

8. The experimental method cannot be used to determine the effects of exposure to pornography on children and adolescents because _____ concerns make it impossible to manipulate the variables.
    a. copyright
    b. privacy
    c. ethical
    d. correlational
            p. 54   LO 11

9. In experiments about the effect of violent pornography on violent behavior, men are led to believe they are anonymously shocking a woman by pressing a lever when, in fact, they are not harming anyone. This example presents an ethical dilemma related to which ethical practice?
    a. Ensuring confidentiality.
    b. Exposing participants to harm.
    c. Notification of informed consent laws.
    d. Avoiding the use of deception.
            p. 56-57   LO 12

10. The following are all examples of ways to ensure the confidentiality of participants EXCEPT:
    a. Using anonymous questionnaires.
    b. Obtaining only minimal information from face-to-face interviewees.
    c. Mixing up responses to individual questions within a data set.
    d. Destroying original data after analysis.
                    p. 55   LO 12

Multiple Choice

1. In a research project, the degree to which the questionnaire measures the construct it purports to measure is an indication of its:
    a. Validity.
    b. Reliability.
    c. Sample probability.
    d. Incidence.

2. All of the following are goals of the science of human sexuality EXCEPT:
    a. Providing information to help couples conceive.
    b. Providing rules that tell people how they should behave.
    c. Providing means through which people could enhance their sexual experiences.
    d. Providing cures for sexually transmitted infections.

3. The experimental method cannot be used to determine the effects of exposure to pornography on children and adolescents because _____ concerns make it impossible to manipulate the variables.
    a. copyright
    b. privacy
    c. ethical
    d. correlational

4. One of the biggest limitations of direct observation of sexual behavior is that it is usually performed in private where others cannot see it. What does your text suggest as a way to minimize this effect?
    a. Use a hidden camera to record sexual activity of participants.
    b. Provide an incentive for someone who can secretly get access to act as an informant.
    c. Conduct personal interviews with those being observed and ask them about it.
    d. None of the above are done; they are all unethical practices.

5. Choose the major focuses of biological sexual research from among the following options:
    a. The mechanisms of reproduction.
    b. The roles of genes in human sexuality.
    c. The function of dating rituals in human mating strategies.
    d. Both A and B are correct.
    e. Both B and C are correct.

6. In experiments about the effect of violent pornography on violent behavior, men are led to believe they are anonymously shocking a woman by pressing a lever, when, in fact, they are not harming anyone. This example presents an ethical dilemma related to which ethical practice?
    a. Ensuring confidentiality
    b. Exposing participants to harm
    c. Notification of informed consent laws
    d. Avoiding the use of deception

7. A/n _____ is a method of measuring the relationship between two variables, whereas a/n _____ is a method of studying cause-and-effect relationships between variables.
    a. experiment; correlation
    b. correlation; intervention
    c. experiment; ethnography
    d. correlation; experiment

8. In his famous survey, Kinsey compared the response of each member of married couples regarding the frequency of intercourse in an attempt to minimize one of the limitations of survey methodology. If both spouses agreed on the frequency of intercourse, then Kinsey would have more assurance that his results were:
    a. Valid.
    b. Reliable.
    c. Unbiased.
    d. Interpreted correctly.

9. If you were surveying the students at your college about their sexual behavior, a _____ would be the best way to describe your use of randomly selected groups of Freshmen, Sophomores, Juniors and Seniors in proportion to their number in the student body.
    a. population
    b. control group
    c. stratified random sample
    d. target sample

10. According to your text, what is the main element shared by both critical thinking and the scientific approach?
    a. Skepticism
    b. Legalism
    c. Hedonism
    d. Political correctness

11. Which of the following statements about experimental research, if any, is/are false?
    a. It does not allow for the exploration of cause-and-effect relationships.
    b. It allows the researcher to control variables thought to influence the sexual behavior being studied.
    c. It is being used regularly in studying human sexual behavior.
    d. All of the above are false.
    e. None of the above is false.

12. By definition, the focus of a case study is:
    a. To understand one or several individuals as fully as possible.
    b. Obtaining descriptive information applicable to a larger group.
    c. Confined to one prolonged interview session.
    d. Finding causality of the dependent variable(s).

13. Dr. Brooks goes to a massage parlor as a potential customer and records how offers for sexual services are made. The research method used here is:
    a. Ethnographic observation.
    b. Participant observation.
    c. Obtrusive observation.
    d. Naturalistic observation.

14. The systematic manipulation of independent variables used in the experimental method is most useful in providing scientists a way to draw conclusions about:
    a. Their frequency.
    b. Their validity.
    c. Their causal relationship.
    d. Their tendency towards social desirability.

15. Using the correlational method, it has been found that being married is correlated positively with a sense of well-being. In light of this finding and our knowledge of the advantages and disadvantages of correlational methods, we can conclude that:
    a. Being single may predict a sense of unhappiness.
    b. Being married causes happiness.
    c. Being single causes unhappiness.
    d. Both A and C are true.
    e. Both B and C are true.

True/False

_____ 1. The nature of the participant-observation method makes it well suited to explaining cause-and-effect relationships.

_____ 2. Participants in surveys of sexual behavior may feel pressured to answer questions in the direction of social desirability.

_____ 3. Alfred Kinsey's survey methodology includes a good example of a representative sample of people in the U.S.

_____ 4. One of the purposes of the NHSLS Study was to get information that might be used to predict and prevent the spread of AIDS.

_____ 5. Another name for the naturalistic-observation method is the "field study."

_____ 6. In Masters and Johnson's research, the unmarried people only participated in studies that did not require intercourse.

_____ 7. By definition, a case-study cannot be performed on someone who is deceased.

_____ 8. Convenience samples often include an oversampling of middle-class people.

Essay Questions

1. Discuss the major ethical considerations in conducting research on human sexuality. Using the principles outlined in your text, consider whether there are situations when the ethics should be overridden for the sake of scientific advancement. For each principle, provide an example that supports your argument that it is or is not an "optional" ethical consideration.

_____

_____

_____

_____

_____

_____

_____

_____

_____

2. Both Kinsey's and the NHSLS Study represent landmark survey research about sexuality. Compare and contrast these studies, giving attention to the methods they utilized, the composition of their samples, their findings, and their design limitations.

_____

_____

_____

_____

_____

_____

_____

_____

_____

_____

When You Have Finished...

Where will the Web take you as you explore the following activities about Research Methods in Human Sexuality.

1. One of the most (in)famous studies about sexuality presents some very interesting ethical dilemmas. This study, done by Laud Humphries as part of his dissertation, was detailed in a book called *Tearoom Trade.* In this study, he went in as a participant observer, without obtaining informed consent, and played the role of a "watcher" in a "tearoom," the expression used for certain bathrooms where anonymous public sex could take place among consensual homosexual males before the age of AIDS made such practices a virtual game of Russian Roulette. Search Amazon.com for the title "**Tearoom Trade**" as it includes the non-scholarly reviews of others who have read the book. Once you've gotten a feel for the study, consider the ethical violations it presents. Most people are ready to indict Humphries for clearly violating the trust of his subjects. But at the same time, he gave us access to a subculture that was completely unexamined by scholars prior to his study, and we have yet to meet anyone who was not fascinated by the findings in some way. Look at these sites and think about whether his ends justified his means in this research. http://www.ithaca.edu/beins/methods/demos/tearoom.htm

2. By the new millennium, the information age had provided us with a new source of research—the Internet. Many scholars, both school-aged and credentialed, think about and use Internet surveys as a means of accessing formerly unreachable people. Search the Web for information about how to do this, and think about what kind of sample it might yield you. Can you develop a probable "profile" of this sample based on the kind of reasoning that allowed the authors to describe the demographic characteristics of most convenience samples? Are there ways the anonymity of the Internet might provide a lessened sense of social desirability bias in a study on human sexuality? What kind of things might be appropriate to study using the Internet to recruit subjects?

3. While your text authors have done an excellent job summarizing the Tuskegee Syphilis Study, the US Centers for Disease Control (CDC) website remains a great place to visit to learn more. (The CDC has a wealth of information on many sexual health topics—of which we'll relate even more in successive chapters.) Regarding Tuskegee, you will find a link to a timeline, frequently asked questions, such as "Were the men purposely infected with the disease?" and a link that details the presidential apology to the study's victims. http://www.cdc.gov/nchstp/od/tuskegee/

4. Have you read any good blogs lately? Chances are, if you're a traditionally aged undergraduate, you have, and you already know that it's a buzzword for Internet journaling. Things like personal journals have never been so accessible to public viewing before. What kind of issues concerning human sexuality might be observable in the text of various blogs? How would you construct a study to examine the issue? Take some time to look for blogs and scan them for any interesting references to human sexuality. You can easily get started by using your favorite Internet search engine and the keywords "sexuality blog."

5. Check out Web resources related to some of the landmark studies in your text. For example, here is a link to a well-done summary on the NHSLS Study: http://cloud9.norc.uchicago.edu/faqs/sex.htm. See if you can find any non-scholarly commentary on these kinds of studies, and think about the implications of what you find.

6. Author Mary Roach has been on NPR and the national best seller list. Her book *Bonk* is about the history of sex research. Check out video on www.ted.com (search Mary Roach) and the podcast on NPR Google "NPR Mary Roach"

Chapter 3
Female Sexual Anatomy amd Physiology

Before You Begin…

Chapter Summary

For the females exploring this chapter, you will have a natural advantage over the males especially if you have taken some time to examine yourself over the years—but if you have not, it is not too late! For the males reading this chapter, knowledge of female anatomy and physiology—along with its diseases and disorders—can be instrumental to helping the females in your life live better lives. The health concept preceding is especially relevant given that comprehensive sexuality courses like what you are now in are not universally available. Also for the males, since a significant part of female genitalia system lies inside the body, you are perhaps less likely to know intuitively exactly the best spots to pleasure a female (unlike your own body). For both sexes, we endeavor to address all of this and more in this chapter.

Your text authors have begun the chapter with a Truth & Fiction section that has a good number of popular ideas that are either not right or not exactly right—of which the exact answers are grouped by the topical area that applies. You will notice those answers, just as with prior chapters, are interspersed as you progress through the entire chapter. It is wise to know the real answers and why.

The first section begins with a description of the external female sex organs (the pudendum) which includes the mons veneris, labia majora, labia minora, clitoris, vestibule, perineum, and both the vaginal and urethral openings. Next, the structures that underlie these external organs are detailed. This includes the crura, vestibular bulbs, and Bartholin's glands. Relative to the clitoris, its unique role in sexual pleasure is explained. You will learn what a clitoridectomy is, how common it is (or the incidence rate), procedures used, and reasons for the historic and current practice of it.

The myths and rituals concerning the hymen and virginity are presented. Throughout the chapter, the authors include useful self-help health information on such topics as avoiding cystitis, preventing vaginitis, getting regular pelvic exams and Pap smears. New cancer guidelines are discussed, including lessened emphasis on routine breast self-exams and the implications of lessened urgency to perform these exams. Also new, your text explores the relationship between cervical cancer and the Human Papilloma Virus (HPV) along with how HPV vaccinations interplay. Updates have been included on ovarian and endometrial cancers too. Finally, newer information on hormone replacement therapy (HRT) is highlighted.

The female internal sex organs (the vagina, cervix, uterus, fallopian tubes, and ovaries) and their functions are carefully described. Next, normal breast appearance and function and the incidence of breast cancer are presented. Surgical breast removal, one treatment for breast cancer, triggers varying reactions in women and are explained more fully. The increased likelihood of breast cancer among African American women relative to other American women is discussed.

Typical hormonal changes associated with the menstrual cycle, as well as numerous historical and cross-cultural negative ideas about menstruation, are presented. Menstruation is compared to estrus. The menstrual cycle is regulated by a complex endocrine system. The myths and facts about the changes associated with menopause are discussed. Variations among women's experience of menopause are attributed to differences of ethnicity, socioeconomic status, and lifestyle.

Women commonly experience some unpleasant symptoms during the premenstrual and menstrual phases of the menstrual cycle. Problems with menstruation and the symptoms associated with dysmenorrhea, amenorrhea, premenstrual syndrome (PMS), and premenstrual dysphoric disorder (PMDD) are identified. The controversy surrounding use of hormone replacement therapy (HRT) to eliminate the monthly period is explained. The chapter concludes with an examination of research on the causes of PMS and includes suggestions for reducing menstrual discomfort, as well as a number of recommendations designed to improve quality of life .

Learning Objectives

1. Recognize that the female sexual organs have been historically maligned, and explain the attitudes that underlie this persistent bias.

2. Identify, describe, and explain primary function of the female external sex organs, or vulva.

3. Name the structures that underlie the vulva.

4. Recognize that the clitoris is the only sexual organ whose sole known function is pleasure.

5. Describe ritual female genital mutilation, why it is practiced, name the types of mutilation, and the medical complications associated with the practice.

6. Explain why the condition of the hymen cannot be used to prove or disprove virginity.

7. Identify, describe, and explain the primary functions of the female internal sex organs, or reproductive system.

8. Describe the pelvic exam procedure and explain the importance of routine pelvic exams.

9. Describe normal breast appearance and function and explain the importance of breast self-examination, mammograms, and regular medical checkups.

10. Discuss the incidence of breast cancer in women, the major treatments available, survival rates and the support needed by women following breast removal.

11. Identify the four phases of the menstrual cycle and discuss the hormonal and physical changes associated with each.

12. Explain how menopause affects women.

13. Summarize the research regarding the cultural, social, psychological, and biological correlates of dysmenorrhea.

14. Identify the common symptoms of PMS, cite the prevalence of women who experience symptoms and list the possible causes of PMS and its proposed treatments. Compare these to the symptoms, and treatments for PMDD.

15. More cancers: Identify the relationships between cervical cancer and the human papilloma virus (HPV); and endometrial cancer and of hormone replacement therapy (HRT); ovarian cancer and hysterectomy.

Key Terms

Term Identification

Hold on to your hats—there are a lot of key terms to learn about anatomy! As usual, make flashcards using the following terms as you go. Use the definitions in the margins of this chapter for help. Focus on learning the function of any body parts on the list, and be sure to pay special attention to the exercises in this chapter related to labeling female anatomy; connecting the appearance and functions of the terms will make them easier to recall for tests.

Chapter 3 Key Terms	
Amenorrhea	Clitoridectomy
Amenorrhea, primary	Clitoris
Amenorrhea, secondary	Corpora cavernosa
Analogous	Corpus luteum
Anorexia nervosa	Crura
Areola	Cystitis
Bartholin's glands	Cysts
Benign	Douche
Cervix	Dysmenorrhea
Climacteric	Dysmenorrhea, primary
Dysmenorrhea, secondary	Ova
Ectopic pregnancy	Ovaries
Endocrine gland	Ovulation
Endometriosis	Oxytocin

Chapter 3 Key Terms (Continued)

Endometrium

Episiotomy

Estrogen

Fallopian tubes

Fibroadenoma

Follicle

Follicle-stimulating hormone (FSH)

Fundus

Gonadotropin releasing hormone (GNRH)

Gonadotropins

Gynecologist

Homologous

Hormone

Hymen

Hypothalamus

Hysterectomy

Hysterectomy, complete

Hysterectomy, partial

Introitus

Labia majora

Labia minora

Lumpectomy

Luteinizing hormone (LH)

Malignant

Mammary glands

Mammography

Mastalgia

Mastectomy

Menarche

Menopause

Osteoporosis

Pap test

Perimenopause

Perimetrium

Perineum

Pituitary gland

Premenstrual dysphoric disorder (PMDD)

Premenstrual syndrome (PMS)

Prepuce

Progesterone

Prolactin

Menstrual phase

Menstruation

Mittelschmerz

Mons veneris

Myometrium

Os

Prostaglandins

Pudendum

Radiotherapy

Secondary sex characteristics

Secretory phase

Sphincters

Testes

Testosterone

Urethral opening

Uterus

Vagina

Vaginitis

Vestibular bulbs

Vulva

As You Read...

❖ *External Sex Organs & The Structures That Underlie Them*

➤ *The Discovery Zone*

Compared to the ease with which a man can examine his own genital anatomy, a woman's attempts at the same can seem like some sort of mysterious expedition into the unknown. Pair this with the cultural baggage that often connects self-deprecating feelings to female sexuality and it's a wonder that any of us really know what's going on "down there."

So, before we settle into some unavoidably traditional activities to help you learn more about female sexual anatomy, take a few moments to look back on your life, and jot down all of the words you remember hearing associated with female genitalia, from the amusing to the offensive.

Nicknames for Female Genitalia		
Funny to me	Neutral to me	Offensive to me

Once you are finished, consider the meaning the nicknames seem to convey, and apply this information as you answer the following questions. Choose one nickname per question, where needed.

Nickname:_____

Where did I learn this nickname, and what does it seem to tell me about the attitudes endorsed by the person/group from whom I learned it?

_____

_____

_____

Nickname:_____

What does this name say about the subcultures I belong to based on my gender? Ethnicity? Social class? Sexual orientation?

_____

_____

_____

Nickname:_____

What does this nickname suggest about how messages from the larger "mainstream" culture are filtered down and practiced within my sphere of influence?

_____

_____

_____

****

How do you feel about your conclusions?

_____

_____

Would you choose to make any changes in your own experiences if you knew your own female child would have to experience them? Why? Why not?

_____

_____

Considering questions like these can go a long way towards fostering an informed, shame-free, proactive attitude toward your own sexuality.

❖ *Internal Sex Organs*

➢ *The Discovery Zone: The Sequel*

If you are a woman, look back on the first time you really examined your own genitals and answer the following questions.

OR

If you are a man, look back on the first time you got a good look at women's sexual anatomy, whether it was "live," or looking at a book or movie. Ask yourself the same questions. Are your answers any different than they would be if you were considering how you felt when you first examined your own genitalia?

If at all possible and comfortable for both of you, find an opposite sex study partner willing to compare answers with you.

How old were you? _____

What brought on your curiosity? _____

Where were you and with whom (if anyone)? _____

Did you feel that you were doing something wrong? _____

Again, what messages were you internalizing if you felt good or bad about what you were doing?

_____

_____

_____

➢ *The Cervix, Cancer of it, & HPV Vaccination*

Research noted in your text reveals that if a female, before she becomes sexually active, receives the vaccination against the Human Papilloma Virus (HPV), her chances of suffering from cervical cancer later in her life are sharply reduced. In the large U.S. state of Texas, recently there was a divisive political battle about whether the state should compel parents to have their young girls vaccinated—and it was exactly for this reason.

How do you feel about vaccinating your future (or even current) adolescent girl(s) to reduce chances of cervical cancer?

_____

_____

Some citizens and politicians have argued that the costs of these vaccinations are too much to mandate them, that the research is specious, and/or that there could be long-term side effects. In your opinion, is the benefit of such vaccination worth having your state (or provincial) government compel it so girls of less enlightened parents are protected too? Why or why not?

_____

_____

TRY PRACTICE TEST #1 NOW!
GOOD LUCK!

❖ *The Breasts*

Before you explore your feelings about how you would deal with breast cancer in yourself or a loved one, take some time to consider your feelings about breasts in general. For example, answer the questions below:

Do you associate breasts with femininity? _____

Do a women's breasts advertise her sexuality? _____

Do you enjoy including breasts in your sexually pleasurable activities? _____

Are there any negative associations with breasts for you? _____

Are breasts a source of pride (for women) or admiration (for men and women who prefer women)?

➢ *Breast Cancer*

How well-equipped are you to deal with breast cancer in yourself or a loved one? Consider how you would react and problem solve if faced with the following situations associated with breast cancer. They are written in the second person, so if you are choosing to think of how you would deal with someone else, please keep that in mind. And for the men, don't forget that, although it's rare, you can get breast cancer too; if you are able to do so, please imagine yourself in the following situations as well. Use what you have learned in this chapter to support your answers.

What would you do if:

❑ You are doing a monthly self-exam of your breasts and you notice a lump where it used to be smooth?

_____

_____

_____

❑ You have been diagnosed with cancer and are told that a mastectomy is the only way to maximize your chances of beating the disease.

_____

_____

_____

❑ You have a lump removed and are waiting for the biopsy results. You have never been good about self-care, but are making all sorts of promises to the universe about how much more you'll do if you can just avoid cancer this time. The lump is benign.

_____

_____

_____

❑ You come from a family where your mother and two of your three sisters have had aggressive breast cancer. Only one of them is currently alive, and she is still battling the disease actively. Your doctor reminds you that you have the choice to take strong drugs and/or have a double mastectomy as a protection against your family history.

_____

_____

_____

❑ You just found out last that your mammogram results were abnormal. You had an emergency biopsy at your doctor's request. Today you got the results, and because of the severity of the situation, your doctor pulls some strings to get you to the oncologist to discuss your treatment options TODAY. You are so overwhelmed you are not sure you are processing any of this, and you have no idea where to start in choosing a treatment method that would best suit your needs.

_____

_____

_____

❑ With your breast cancer in remission, you are finally feeling like getting your life closer to your pre-treatment routine. Your partner is excited about this because with all of the stress neither of you has had much chance to address your sexual needs. You realize you have never had intercourse without your breasts, remembering how big a part they were of your sexual interaction with your partner.

_____

_____

_____

TRY PRACTICE TEST #2 NOW!
GOOD LUCK!

❖ The Menstrual Cycle

➢ *Regulation & Phases of the Menstrual Cycle.* Women are complex. Just look at how many terms it takes to explain the monthly hormone cycle. Define the following components of menstruation, and explain their roles in the process.

Term	Definition	Role/Function
Estrogen		
Progesterone		
Proliferative phase		
Ovulation		
Secretory/Luteal phase		
Corpus luteum		
Endocrine gland		
Menstrual phase		
Anovulation		
Menarche		
Hypothalamus		
Pituitary gland		
Hormones		
Testosterone		
Prolactin		
Oxytocin		
Gonadotropins		
FSH		

Term	Definition	Role/Function
LH		
Gn-RH		
Graafian follicle		
Fallopian tube		
Clomiphene		
Basal body temperature		
Mittelschmerz		

➤ *Choosing when to have sex.*

Every person who is sexually active must know their own (or their partners) cycle. There is an app for that (there are even apps for the iPod that help you calculate monthly cycles).

Where do you stand on the issue of sex during menstruation, and why?

_____

_____

_____

When is the best time to have sex during the cycle? Can you determine which days of the month are better?

_____

_____

_____

> *Menopause, Perimenopause, & the Climacteric*

Explain the relationship between the terms above, placing emphasis on what makes each of them distinct from the others.

_____

_____

_____

_____

_____

_____

❖ **Menstrual Problems**

> *Dysmenorrhea, Amenorrhea, Premenstrual Syndrome (PMS) & Premenstrual Dysphoric Disorder (PMDD)*

Given what we know about each of the abovementioned difficulties that arise, consider a woman with the characteristics listed below, and predict which menstrual challenge she seems to have experienced. Explain your choices by providing information about the cause of each problem where possible.

1. Sophie had always experienced a lot of PMS symptoms before her period. Some months, she noticed difficulties from the day she felt herself ovulate, all the way through her period. However, the last 6 months or so were definitely the worst she ever remembers feeling—it was like she was an entirely different person when it was coming on.

   She seems to have experienced _____, which is usually brought on by _____.

2. Sally used to have painful cramping every time she menstruated. Strangely enough, after her last pregnancy two years ago, the problem seems to have gone away.

   She seems to have experienced _____, which is usually brought on by

   _____.

3. Despite the fact that her last several OB/GYN routine examinations had gone without a hitch, Tanita was often unable to sleep through the night during the week before her menstruation occurred; her breasts were so tender it woke her up when she turned onto her stomach in her sleep.

She seems to have experienced _____, which is usually brought on by

_____.

4. Lora trained hard for last season's track competitions; she wanted to compete at her best during her last year of NCAA eligibility. She had never run the 10-mile race at a better pace in her life; she did everything right to stay in optimum condition. During that season, she was looking at her calendar one day and noticed she had not had her period for about 3 months.

She seems to have experienced _____, which is usually brought on by

_____.

➢ *How to Handle Menstrual Discomfort*

Your text outlines several helpful suggestions for dealing with menstrual discomfort. How do you tend to cope with your own, or that of the significant women in your life? Do you act as if nothing is wrong, or admit that there is a problem deserving of your attention and try to apply your coping skills? How did you arrive at this way of coping? Do you feel it meets your needs? If not, are you willing to consider some of the book's suggestions? Below, please respond as to your willingness to try the suggestions and indicate your rationale.

Suggestion	*Would you try it?*	*Why/Why not?*
Keep a menstrual calendar to track patterns		
Develop pleasant distraction strategies for the days that you experience the most distress		
Examine your attitudes about menstruation		
See a gynecologist about your symptoms		
Alter the content and patterns of your eating habits to minimize menstrual distress		
Do vigorous exercise regularly		

Suggestion	Would you try it?	Why/Why not?
Take vitamin & mineral supplements		
Take over-the-counter medicines for pain		
Take prescription medicines for anxiety/depressive symptoms		

TRY PRACTICE TEST #3 NOW!
GOOD LUCK!

After You Read...

(LO = Learning Objective)

1. The cultural roots of the word pudendum, which refers to the outer part of female genitalia, are indicative of the negative messages women have had to endure about their sexuality. The derivation of the word literally means:
    a. Something to keep secret.
    b. Something demonic.
    c. Something to be ashamed of.
    d. Something that could break down society.
    p. 61   LO 1

2. All of the following statements about the mons veneris are accurate, EXCEPT:
    a. It becomes covered with hair at puberty.
    b. It serves as a protective cushion during coitus.
    c. It has few nerve endings, and is relatively insensitive to touch.
    d. Its hairy covering retains chemical secretions from the vagina.
    p. 61   LO 2

3. The clitoris serves as a(n):
    a. Essential structure during conception.
    b. Channel for urine.
    c. Organ of sexual pleasure.
    d. Vestigial organ.
    p. 63, 64   LO 3

4. All of the following structures are enclosed by the labia majora EXCEPT:
    a. The introitus.
    b. The uvula.
    c. The urethral opening.
    d. The clitoris.
    p. 62   LO 3

5. Female sexual arousal and orgasm during masturbation is usually due to stimulation of the:
    a. Vaginal walls.
    b. Perineum.
    c. Clitoris.
    d. Kegel muscles.
    p. 64   LO 4

6. The ritual practice of surgically altering the female genitals:
    a. Is currently against the law throughout the world.
    b. Continues today in some countries of Africa and the Middle East.
    c. Was a social custom that disappeared at the turn of the 20th century.
    d. Is a painless procedure performed under sterile conditions in some African countries.
        p. 68   LO 5

7. Why is the lack of an intact hymen not a reliable indicator of whether or not a woman has engaged in coitus?
    a. Many women are born with no hymen.
    b. Some women's hymens have been altered during a clitoridectomy.
    c. The hymen can be torn by engaging in physical activities other than coitus.
    d. Some women's hymens grow back, even after coitus.
        p. 66   LO 6

8. All of the following are internal female sexual organs EXCEPT:
    a. The perineum.
    b. The vagina.
    c. The cervix.
    d. The fallopian tubes.
        p. 68, 69   LO 7

9. Vaginal lubrication is produced by:
    a. The Bartholin's glands.
    b. The vestibular bulbs.
    c. A type of sweating of the vaginal walls.
    d. Fluid released through the urethral opening.
        p. 70   LO 7

10. The pelvic exam procedure for women:
    a. Includes a Pap smear to detect cervical cancer.
    b. Should only be performed after a woman is pregnant.
    c. Includes a bimanual vaginal and recto-vaginal exam.
    d. Both A and C are true.
    e. Both A and B are true.
        p. 76   LO 8

(LO = Learning Objective)

1. The instrument routinely used to hold open the walls of the vagina during pelvic exams is called a:
   a. Colposcope.
   b. Pelvic dilator.
   c. Speculum.
   d. Catheter.

           p. 74   LO 8

2. During the part of a routine pelvic exam where the doctor addresses any questions the patient may have about her sexual health, a woman expresses concern about how to maintain optimal vaginal health. A list of suggestions from the doctor might include which of the following?
   a. Regular douching
   b. Use of feminine hygiene sprays
   c. Wearing nylon underwear
   d. Taking care to wipe from front to back, vulva to anus

           p. 75   LO 8

3. Female breasts are considered to be _____ sex characteristics.
   a. primary
   b. secondary
   c. tertiary
   d. proprietary

           p. 75   LO 9

4. Despite the claims of the miracle cream manufacturers in the back of women's magazines, variation in breast size is largely a function of:
   a. The quality of her nutritional regimen.
   b. The size of her mammary glands.
   c. The amount of fatty tissue in her breasts.
   d. The size of her maternal grandmother's breasts.

           p. 76   LO 9

5. Which of the following types of lumps, if any, can occur in the breasts?
   a. Cysts
   b. Fibroadenomas
   c. Myometriosis
   d. Both A and B
   e. Both A and C

           p. 77   LO 9

6. Which of the following characteristics, if any, are associated with a lower risk of breast cancer among women?
   a. No childbirth
   b. Low-fat diet
   c. Hormone replacement therapy
   d. Late timing of menopause
   e. None of the above apply
   p. 78-79   LO 10

7. Once they are diagnosed with it, _____ American women are more likely to die from breast cancer than are their _____ American counterparts.
   a. African; Latina
   b. European/White; African
   c. Latina; African
   d. African; European/White
   p. 79   LO 10

8. Although the American Cancer Society (ACS) has recently relaxed its recommendation that women perform monthly self-exams on their breasts, your text suggests that it might be beneficial to continue the habit because:
   a. Many claims of the ACS have later been disproven.
   b. It might foster a sense of psychological empowerment.
   c. Stopping the exams after routinely performing them increases one's cancer risk.
   d. Mammograms are much less accurate at detecting changes in breast tissue texture.
   p. 80   LO 10

9. Genes for breast cancer not only appear to predict whether women will contract the disease, but also how:
   a. Long remission will last.
   b. Deadly it will be.
   c. It will affect their sense of sexual attractiveness.
   d. Long they should take anti-cancer drugs like Tamoxifen.
   p. 78   LO 10

10. Engaging in sexual intercourse during the menstrual phase:
   a. Is harmful to the female.
   b. Is dangerous for the male.
   c. Triggers the development of certain STIs.
   d. Is a matter of personal preference.
   p. 88   LO 11

(LO = Learning Objective)

1. An ova is released during which phase of the menstrual cycle?
    a. Proliferative (first phase)
    b. Ovulatory (second stage)
    c. Secretory or Luteal (third phase)
    d. Menstrual (fourth phase)
    e. Mittelschmerz
            p. 82   LO 11

2. Which of the following is/are NOT symptoms of menopause?
    a. Nausea
    b. Night sweats
    c. Dizziness
    d. Both A and C are not menopausal symptoms.
    e. None of the above is a menopausal symptom.
            p. 88,91   LO 12

3. Which of the following functions, if any, do the ovaries stop performing during menopause?
    a. Ripening egg cells
    b. Responding to FSH
    c. Producing estrogen
    d. Initiating mittelschmerz
            p. 88-89   LO 12

4. _____ is defined as a lack of menstruation.
    a. Menstrual synchrony
    b. Endometriosis
    c. Amenorrhea
    d. Dysmenorrhea
            p. 92   LO 13

5. Some research indicates that _____ can reduce the occurrence of dysmenorrhea.
    a. ovulation
    b. orgasm
    c. insertion of a diaphragm
    d. acetaminophen
            p. 92-93   LO 13

6. Which of the following, if any, is a proven cause of PMS?
   a. The use of birth control pills
   b. High production of FSH
   c. Childbirth
   d. Both B and C are proven causes.
   e. None of the above is a proven cause.
           p. 93,94   LO 14

7. The difference between PMS and PMDD is primarily one of:
   a. The severity of symptoms.
   b. The ability to obtain sick leave.
   c. The types of symptoms.
   d. The validity of symptoms.
           p. 94   LO 14

8. Besides relieving symptoms associated with gynecological disorders, a hysterectomy may be performed when there is:
   a. Cancer in the ovaries.
   b. Endometriosis.
   c. Breast cancer.
   d. Cystitis
   e. Vaginitis.
           p. 73   LO 15

9. Endometrial cancer is associated with all of the following risk factors EXCEPT:
   a. Early menarche with high estrogen levels accompanying it.
   b. Hormone replacement therapy (HRT).
   c. Estrogen replacement therapy.
   d. Early menopause.
           p. 72   LO 15

10. Cervical cancer has all of the following attributes associated with it EXCEPT:
    a. The primary cause of this cancer is the presence of HPV.
    b. An HPV vaccine has been developed that makes most women immune to this cancer.
    c. Is more common in women with more sexual partners.
    d. Is more common amongst women who have been sexually active at a relatively early age.
    e. Occurs more commonly amongst women who do not smoke.
            p. 71   LO 15

Multiple Choice

1. Some research indicates that _____ can reduce the occurrence of dysmenorrhea.
    a. ovulation
    b. orgasm
    c. insertion of a diaphragm
    d. acetominiphen

2. Engaging in sexual intercourse during the menstrual phase:
    a. Is harmful to the female.
    b. Is dangerous for the male.
    c. Triggers the development of certain STIs.
    d. Is a matter of personal preference.

3. Cervical cancer has all of the following attributes associated with it EXCEPT:
    a. The primary cause of this cancer is the presence of HPV.
    b. An HPV vaccine has been developed that makes most women immune to this cancer.
    c. Is more common in women with more sexual partners.
    d. Is more common amongst women who have been sexually active at a relatively early age.
    e. Occurs more commonly amongst women who do not smoke.

4. Female breasts are considered to be _____ sex characteristics.
    a. primary
    b. secondary
    c. tertiary
    d. proprietary

5. The difference between PMS and PMDD is primarily one of:
    a. The severity of symptoms.
    b. The ability to obtain sick leave.
    c. The types of symptoms.
    d. The validity of symptoms.

6. Why is the lack of an intact hymen not a reliable indicator of whether or not a woman has engaged in coitus?
    a. Many women are born with no hymen.
    b. Some women's hymens have been altered during a clitoridectomy.
    c. The hymen can be torn by engaging in physical activities other than coitus.
    d. Some women's hymens grow back, even after coitus.

7. Which of the following functions, if any, do the ovaries stop performing during menopause?
    a. Ripening egg cells
    b. Responding to FSH
    c. Producing estrogen
    d. Initiating mittelschmerz

8. All of the following structures are enclosed by the labia majora EXCEPT:
    a. The introitus.
    b. The uvula.
    c. The urethral opening.
    d. The clitoris.

9. Endometrial cancer is associated with all of the following risk factors EXCEPT:
    a. Early menarche with high estrogen levels accompanying it.
    b. Hormone replacement therapy (HRT).
    c. Estrogen replacement therapy.
    d. Early menopause.

10. Vaginal lubrication is produced by:
    a. The Bartholin's glands.
    b. The vestibular bulbs.
    c. A type of sweating of the vaginal walls.
    d. Fluid released through the urethral opening.

11. During the part of a routine pelvic exam where the doctor addresses any questions the patient may have about her sexual health, a woman expresses concern about how to maintain optimal vaginal health. A list of suggestions from the doctor might include which of the following?
    a. Regular douching
    b. Use of feminine hygiene sprays
    c. Wearing nylon underwear
    d. Taking care to wipe from front to back, vulva to anus

12. Female sexual arousal and orgasm during masturbation is usually due to stimulation of the:
    a. Vaginal walls.
    b. Perineum.
    c. Clitoris.
    d. Kegel muscles.

13. The cultural roots of the word pudendum, which refers to the outer part of female genitalia, are indicative of the negative messages women have had to endure about their sexuality. The derivation of the word literally means:
    a. Something to keep secret.
    b. Something demonic.
    c. Something to be ashamed of.
    d. Something that could break down society.

14. The ritual practice of surgically altering the female genitals:
    a. Is currently against the law throughout the world.
    b. Continues today in some countries of Africa and the Middle East.
    c. Was a social custom that disappeared at the turn of the 20th century.
    d. Is a painless procedure performed under sterile conditions in some African countries.

15. Once they are diagnosed with it, _____ American women are more likely to die from breast cancer than are their _____ American counterparts.
    a. African; Latina
    b. European/White; African
    c. Latina; African
    d. African; European/White

True/False

_____ 1. A newborn girl already has all the ova she will ever produce.

_____ 2. Experts agree that male circumcision is an accurate analogue to female clitoridectomy.

_____ 3. A punctured hymen does not prove a lack of virginity.

_____ 4. By the time a malignant breast lump is large enough to be felt by touch, it already contains millions of cells.

_____ 5. The clitoris is one of many sexual organs whose only known function is the experience of pleasure.

_____ 6. When at rest, the walls of the vagina touch like fingers of an empty glove.

_____ 7. The lubrication that accompanies female sexual arousal is secreted by the Bartholin's glands.

_____ 8. The opening in the middle of the cervix, the os, can expand from the width of a straw to an opening large enough for a baby to pass through during childbirth.

Essay Questions

1. Describe the four phases of the menstrual cycle, and explain what changes occur during each phase.

_____

_____

_____

_____

_____

_____

_____

_____

_____

2. Detail the major cultural and biological issues that surround the controversial practice of clitoridectomy. Include your opinion on the topic, and the rationale for your choice.

_____

_____

_____

_____

_____

_____

_____

_____

_____

When You Have Finished....

<u>What Does the World Think?</u>

Let us see where the Web takes you as you explore the following issues concerning Female Sexual Anatomy and Physiology.

1. Despite the tendency to think of things like anatomy and physiology as unbiased and unchanging due to their "factual" nature, there seem to be constant changes in explanations for physiological functioning and best practice for sexual health. Since the nature of the Internet often gives it the ability to disseminate new information more quickly than traditional methods such as this text, choose a topic from the chapter for which information is clearly still emerging (e.g., the practice of menstrual suppression therapy). Make note of whether the Web's current offerings indicate the availability of more or different knowledge than was available at the time this text went to press.

2. Where did you first learn about menstruation? How accurate were your sources? Lucky for today's young people, a great many of them have Internet access so they can research their questions instead of waiting for the kid in their class that always seems to "know things" to serve as their fountain of information. Think like a 10-year-old; where would you look? What does using this approach yield? Compare the accuracy of the information you gather with what your learned in your text.

3. After what you have just read about sexual anatomy, functioning, and health, what do you think about piercings of external female genitalia, including the clitoris and labia? What kind of statement do you think it makes? Would you consider getting one or dating a woman who had one? What would you do if your young child found out you did? Read this story about a woman whose 6-year-old found out about hers, and then check out the site it's attached to so you can find out more about the process: http://tattoo.about.com/library/bltest13.htm

4. All that talk about hymens and proving virginity… Does anyone worry about that anymore? Then we remembered hearing about a movement towards "secondary virginity"—women who had once engaged in coitus, but made a pledge to be celibate until marriage, thus reclaiming their status as virgins. They often refer to themselves as "born again virgins." What do you think about that? Here's a link to get you started: http://pamf.org/teen/sex/virginity/second-gen.html
If you supplement this with the use of a search engine, you should then be able to find some random commentary by others on this issue as well.

5. Where can you go for help when you need help with some of the concerns about female sexual health raised in the text? Take some time and search for information and online support networks for some of the wide range of illnesses mentioned. Because the illnesses are related to sexual health, what are the potential benefits and liabilities of having your own access to information online, as well as access to what amounts to anonymous social support? Here are some links to get you started:

PMDD—http://www.pmdd.factsforhealth.org

Menopause—http://www.womentowomen.com

Breast Cancer—http://www.nationalbreastcancer.org

HPV—http://www.plannedparenthood.org/sexual-health/std/hpv.htm

Chapter 4
Male Sexual Anatomy and Physiology

Before You Begin...

Chapter Summary

A common stereotype is that male sexual anatomy is simpler than that of female sexual anatomy. Too, some men refuse to be examined for the presence of prostate cancer because of fear that the digital rectal exam is connected with homosexuality. Often younger people think of cancer as something that largely only affects older people—and yet prostate cancer and testicular cancer have very different age profiles in men. This chapter clarifies the errors in popular ideas and it provides males, and the females that love or will love them, with useful and perhaps life-saving information. So let's get started!

Your text authors note that the male sex organs, like those of the female, have both internal and external parts. Historians have found that early Western civilizations worshiped the male genitalia and showed this in many ways, from phallic jewelry to penile symbols in art, as well as celebratory tributes to the penis. This sense of pride about men's genitals can still be found in some forms today; for example, it is why some people are occupied with the thought that "size matters," both in terms of sexual performance and manliness.

External male anatomical structures include the penis, its complex underlying parts, and the scrotum. The scrotum, which develops from the same embryonic tissue as the female labia majora, contains the testes, which are held in place by a spermatic cord containing the vas deferens and cremaster muscle. The scrotum enables the maintenance of optimal temperature for sperm production. Temperature is regulated, as well, by the brain structures of the hypothalamus and pituitary gland in a negative feedback loop. Figure 4.1 in your text clearly shows the structure of the penis while Figure 4.2 depicts the entire system. Just as with the prior chapter on female genital anatomy, we urge you to make your own diagrams of relative relationship of the various parts—and no, it does not need to be artistic.

Male circumcision, the surgical removal of the prepuce (also known as the foreskin), is widely practiced in some countries and cultures for religious and/or hygienic reasons. Research evidence regarding the public health debate over circumcision is detailed. Issues include sexual pleasure functions, urethritis, sexually-transmitted infection (STI) transmission—especially HIV—and other rare penile anatomical problems. Although the authors acknowledge the role of circumcision in preventing the transmission of STIs, they cite recent research that asserts the risks of STIs are not enough to recommend universally that men be circumcised. Contrary to common misconception, there is no correlation between penis size and masculinity or sexual performance.

The internal sex organs are the testes, the tubes and ducts that conduct sperm, and the organs that nourish and activate sperm. Sperm are produced by seminiferous tubules; they are stored and mature in the epididymis. The sperm exit the scrotum through the vas deferens and combine with fluids from the seminal vesicles, prostate gland, and Cowper's glands to produce semen. The testes are in some respects functionally analogous to the female ovaries because they secrete sex hormones and produce germ cells. Testes secrete androgens and produce sperm.

Just as with females, hormones play an important role in proper function of the male reproductive system—along with related effects on a man's energy level and such things as propensity for depression. Along this line, your text authors introduce the relatively new concept of andropause—a male equivalent to the female's menopause that you have already studied. Figure 4.7 shows the feedback loop that keeps testosterone levels stable in a healthy man. You will recognize from last chapter the presences of LH (luteinizing hormone) and FSH (follicle-stimulating hormone). Predictably, these hormones operate differently in the male. Further, your authors explain LH-RH—which is the LH releasing hormone. Again, the figure and related text clarify the regulation process.

Male sexual function, erection and ejaculation, involves both the brain and the autonomic nervous system. The physiology of typical male sexual functions is described in detail, and abnormalities in both erection and ejaculation are described briefly. The significance of spinal cord injury and its relationship to orgasm, ejaculation, and successful reproduction is explained thoroughly.

There are several diseases that affect sexual anatomy of the male. The incidence, types, detection strategies, and treatments for these diseases are described. These diseases include:

- Urethritis (which both men and women can contract)
- Testicular cancer (which is the most common cancer to strike men aged 20–34), and
- Prostate cancer (of which its incidence increases with age).

As with all forms of cancer, emphasis is put on early detection to assure, or at least improve the odds of, living a healthy and reasonably unencumbered life post-recovery. Hint: The cancers occur often enough that many course instructors are likely to ask questions to confirm your knowledge about them and how to detect them early on your next test—so please study up!

Learning Objectives

1. Describe the penis and the internal structures and bodily systems that make the male sexual arousal cycle possible.

2. Cite the reasons people give for having males circumcised and the research evidence on both sides of this topic.

3. Distinguish between myths and facts derived from research on the effects of penis size on sexual performance and a partner's sexual satisfaction.

4. Describe the scrotum and its role in maintaining optimum temperature for sperm production.

5. Describe the structure of the testes and explain their functions in sperm and testosterone production.

6. Trace the route of the sperm as they leave the testes and combine with the several glandular fluids that form semen.

7. Discuss the incidence, symptoms, treatments, and survival rates associated with testicular cancer.

8. Describe the testicular self-examination procedure, as well as the importance of self-exams and regular medical checkups for early detection of testicular and prostate cancer.

9. Identify the disorders of the prostate and their symptoms and treatments.

10. Describe the conditions under which erections can occur and explain why the process of erection is a spinal reflex.

11. Explain the effect of spinal cord injuries on erection and ejaculation.

12. Discuss the role of the brain and the autonomic nervous system in erection.

13. Describe several erectile and ejaculatory abnormalities.

14. Describe the process of ejaculation, including the roles of the spinal cord and the autonomic nervous system.

15. Define andropause, when it typically arrives, and the physical changes that often accompany it. Discuss the risks and rewards of hormone replacement therapy (e.g., testosterone) in the treatment of andropause.

Term Identification: Focus on learning the function of any body parts on the list, and, just like when you learned about female anatomy, be sure to pay special attention to the exercises in this chapter related to labeling male anatomy; connecting the appearance and functions of the terms will make them easier to recall for tests.

Chapter 4 Key Terms	
Ampulla	Penis
Androgens	Performance anxiety
Andropause	Peyronie's disease
Autonomic nervous system	Phallic symbols
Benign prostatic hyperplasia	Phimosis
Bulbourethral glands	Premature ejaculation
Cilia	Prostate cancer
Circumcision	Prostate gland
Corona	Prostatitis
Corpora cavernosa	Reflex
Corpus spongiosum	Retrograde ejaculation
Cowper's glands	Root
Cremaster muscle	Sacrum
Cryptorchidism	Scrotum
Dartos muscle	Secondary sex characteristics
Ejaculatory duct	Semen
Emission phase	Seminal vesicles
Epididymis	Seminiferous tubules
Erection	Shaft
Expulsion stage	Sperm
Foreskin	Spermatic cord
Frenulum	Spermatids
Germ cell	Spermatocyte
Interstitial cells	Spermatogenesis
Koro	Spermatozoa
Leydig's cells	Sympathetic
Orgasm	Testes
Paraplegic	Testicles
Parasympathetic	Testicular cancer
Testosterone	Urologist
Urethral bulb	Vas deferens
Urethritis	Vasectomy

As You Read...

❖ *External Sex Organs & The Structures That Underlie Them*

➢ *Think it over*

You may recall from the last chapter review on female anatomy that it is important to think about the meaning of the words we use to refer to our sexual organs and what they say about our social world. Just as we did in Chapter 3, take a few moments to look back on your life and jot down all of the words you remember hearing associated with male genitalia, from the amusing to the offensive.

Nicknames for Male Genitalia		
Funny to me	Neutral to me	Offensive to me

Once you are finished, consider the meaning the nicknames seem to convey, and apply this information as you answer the following questions. Choose one nickname per question, where needed.

Nickname: _____

Where did I learn this nickname, and what does it seem to tell me about the attitudes endorsed by the person/group from whom I learned it?

_____

_____

_____

Nickname: _____

What does this name say about the subcultures I belong to based on my gender? Ethnicity? Social class? Sexual orientation?

_____

_____

_____

Nickname: _____

What does this nickname suggest about how the messages from the larger "mainstream" culture are getting filtered down and practiced within my sphere of influence?

_____

_____

_____

****

How do you feel about your conclusions?

_____

_____

Would you choose to make any changes in your own experiences if you knew your own male child would have to experience them? Why? Why not?

_____

_____

What are some of the ways that historic Western cultures indicated their belief in the glory of the male genitalia? Do any of those practices have modern counterparts? If so, what are they?

_____

_____

_____

❖ *Internal Sex Organs*

➢ *Think it Over: The Sequel*

If you are a man, look back on the first time you really examined your own genitals.

OR

If you are a woman, look back on the first time you got a good look at a man's sexual anatomy, whether it was "live," or in a book or movie. Ask yourself the same questions. Are your answers any different than they would be if you were considering how you felt when you first examined your own genitalia?

If at all possible (and comfortable), find an opposite sex study partner willing to compare answers with you.

How old were you? _____

What brought on your curiosity? _____

Where and with whom were you (if anyone)? _____

Did you feel that you were doing something wrong? _____

Again, what messages were you internalizing if you felt good or bad about what you were doing?

_____

_____

Considering your reflections from the questions above, along with the information in your text, apply them by supplying a short answer to the question below:

Your 13-year-old son tells you he thinks he might need to see a doctor because one of his testicles seems to hang a little lower than the other. He looks very distressed, and adds that he's afraid he's somehow permanently hurt them. How will you answer him, and why? How can you use this question as a way to talk to him about his anatomy in a healthy way?

_____

_____

_____

_____

TRY PRACTICE TEST #1 NOW!
GOOD LUCK!

❖ Health Problems of the Urogenital System

What kind of doctor does a man need to see when he has a problem with his urinary system?

Answer: _____

What about his reproductive system?

Answer: _____

Are the answers to the above two questions related to one another? How? Why?

Answer: _____

➢ Urethritis

Please answer the questions below:

a. What is urethritis?

   _____

b. What are the symptoms associated with it?

   _____

c. What can be done to prevent it?

   _____

   _____

❖ Cancer of the Testes

A close male family member just came home from a regular checkup. He says that his doctor is going to test him for testicular cancer and that he was so upset, he really doesn't remember much else. Knowing what you learned in your text, write what you know about the following issues, so he can ease his mind by being better informed.

❑ How common is it?

_____

_____

_____

❑ What are his chances of survival?

_____

_____

_____

❑ What might increase his odds of having it?

_____

_____

_____

❑ What kinds of treatments are available if he does have it?

_____

_____

_____

❑ If he finds out that he is cancer-free for now, what can he do to avoid a scare like this in the future?

_____

_____

_____

❖ *Disorders of the Prostate*

Given the high rate at which it occurs, everyone should be aware of prostate cancer. Once a man is diagnosed, there are many available treatment options. It is important to choose the treatment with the best fit for each man's lifestyle and the degree to which the cancer has invaded his body. Use the chart below to review the pros and cons of the treatments available.

Evaluating different prostate treatment options

Treatment	Advantages	Limitations	Disadvantages
Surgical removal of the prostate			
External-beam radiation			
Highly targeted proton radiation			
Radioactive seed implants			
Testosterone-blocking hormone treatments			
Combination therapies			
Watchful waiting			

TRY PRACTICE TEST #2 NOW!
GOOD LUCK!

❖ *Male Sexual Functions*

Your text provides information about the following male sexual functions: erection, spinal reflexes and sexual response, and ejaculation. Consider what you have read and provide short answers to the questions below:

1. Describe the complex process of erection. What accounts for the firmness of an erection?

_____

_____

_____

_____

2. What are nocturnal erections? When do they occur?

_____

_____

_____

_____

3. Describe the role of the spinal cord in the reflex that produces erection in response to tactile stimulation.

_____

_____

_____

_____

_____

4. What is a "no-hands" erection and how does it occur?

_____

_____

_____

_____

5. Describe the roles of the sympathetic and parasympathetic branches of the autonomic nervous system in erection and ejaculation.

_____

_____

_____

_____

_____

TRY PRACTICE TEST #3 NOW!
GOOD LUCK!

After You Read...

(LO = Learning Objective)

1. The flaccid penis stiffens when:
   a. The internal penile bones lock into place during sexual arousal.
   b. The penile muscles become rigid due to sexual excitement.
   c. The corpus cavernosa and corpus spongiosum sustain vasocongestion.
   d. The meatus becomes engorged with blood.
      p. 104   LO 1

2. The most sensitive part of the penis is the:
   a. Glans.
   b. Corona.
   c. Frenulum.
   d. Meatus.
      p. 104-105   LO 1

3. Circumcision is the surgical removal of the:
   a. Urethral flap.
   b. Seminal vesicle.
   c. Prepuce.
   d. Epididymis.
      p. 105   LO 2

4. People in favor of male circumcision say that it _____. However, people against it argue that _____.
   a. reduces chances of infection; cleaning the area is enough
   b. is a ritual signifying the covenant between God & the people of Abraham; there is no way to know how much pain it causes a baby
   c. increases sexual sensations; it decreases them
   d. Both A and C are true.
   e. Both A and B are true.
      p. 105   LO 2

5. Which of the following statements is/are true about penis size?
   a. The average erect penis ranges from 5 to 7 inches in length.
   b. The size of a flaccid penis is a good predictor of its size when erect.
   c. Size differences are mostly cancelled out by erection.
   d. A and B, but not C
   e. A and C, but not B
      p. 107   LO 3

6. If a man is engaged in sexual intercourse in a cold room, you would expect the:
   a. Vas deferens to lengthen and expand to allow for vasocongestion.
   b. Cremaster muscle to bring the testicles closer to the body.
   c. Dartos muscle would relax to allow the testicles to dangle farther from the body.
   d. Interstitial cells to increase production of testosterone.
   p. 107   LO 4

7. Testosterone carries out all of the following functions, EXCEPT stimulating:
   a. Development of secondary sex characteristics.
   b. Prenatal differentiation of primary sex characteristics.
   c. Sperm production.
   d. The Bartholin's gland.
   p. 109   LO 5

8. Spermatogenesis refers to the process in which:
   a. Sperm are transported through the seminiferous tubules.
   b. Sperm cells are produced and stored.
   c. Hormone levels in the male reproductive system are regulated.
   d. Spermatocytes split.
   p. 110   LO 5

9. The spermatozoan pathway from testes to ejaculation from the penis as semen is:
   a. Vas deferens, epididymis, urethra.
   b. Urethra, vas deferens, epididymis.
   c. Epididymis, vas deferens, urethra.
   d. Vas deferens, urethra, epididymis.
   p. 110   LO6

10. What role does the prostate gland have in the formation of semen?
    a. It produces all of the ingredients of semen.
    b. It provides fluid that is milky and alkaline.
    c. It makes semen acidic, as is the vaginal tract.
    d. It produces a small drop of clear, slippery fluid at the tip of the penis during arousal.
    p. 112-13   LO 6

(LO = Learning Objective)

1. Which of the following has been implicated as a sign or cause of testicular cancer?
   a. Childhood cryptochidism
   b. One enlarged testicle
   c. Mother taking DES while pregnant
   d. Sexual overactivity

           p. 115   LO 7

2. Cancer of the testes is the most common form of solid-tumor cancer to strike men between the ages of:
   a. 13–27.
   b. 20–34.
   c. 30–44.
   d. 34–48.

           p. 115   LO 7

3. Which of the following is NOT a warning signal of testicular cancer?
   a. A change in the consistency of a testicle
   b. A sensation of dragging and heaviness in a testicle
   c. A dull ache in the lower abdomen or groin
   d. An increased difficulty in urinating

           p. 116   LO 7

4. When is the best time to perform self-examination of the testes?
   a. Shortly after waking in the morning
   b. Shortly after sexual activity
   c. Shortly after a warm shower or bath
   d. Shortly before bedtime

           p. 116   LO 8

5. The best technique for self-examination of the scrotum for evidence of pea-sized lumps is:
   a. Palpating each testicle with both hands in imitation of female breast examination.
   b. Pulling each testicle away from the body to check for lumps behind it.
   c. Rolling each testicle gently between the thumb and fingers.
   d. Using a mirror to look carefully for visible lumps.

           p. 116   LO 8

6. Early symptoms of prostate cancer may mimic those of:
   a. Testicular cancer.
   b. Benign prostate enlargement.
   c. Colon cancer.
   d. Benign penile dysfunction.

           p. 117   LO 8

7. PSA, a substance measured to detect the presence of prostate cancer, consists of:
    a. A protein that helps the prostate form a liquid that transports sperm.
    b. A particle that leaks from cancer-affected cells in the prostate.
    c. A protein that provides nutrition to sperm cells.
    d. A particle that is removed from the body in urine.
        p. 117   LO 8

8. Why is enlargement of the prostate problematic?
    a. It prevents the free passage of sperm during ejaculation.
    b. It constricts the urethra causing urinary disturbances.
    c. It increases vulnerability to testicular cancer.
    d. It interferes with sexual arousal.
        p. 117   LO 9

9. Prostate cancer is usually first detected by:
    a. Testicular self-examination.
    b. The penile strain gauge.
    c. Rectal examination or a blood test.
    d. A magnetic resonance imaging examination.
        p. 117-118   LO 9

10. Prostatitis, also known as inflammation of the prostate, can be very painful. Which of the following is NOT an effective way to lessen or eliminate its symptoms?
    a. Antibiotics
    b. Ejaculation through masturbation or coitus
    c. Aspirin or ibuprofen
    d. Drinking cranberry juice
        p. 117   LO 9

(LO = Learning Objective)

1. Males begin to have penile erections:
    a. Only after the first year of life.
    b. After they have reached puberty.
    c. As soon as they are able to ejaculate.
    d. Even while in the fetal environment.
        p. 119   LO 10

2. The reflexes that govern erection and ejaculation are controlled in the:
    a. Cerebral cortex.
    b. Spinal cord.
    c. Nerve endings on the penile surface.
    d. Brainstem.
        p. 121-122   LO 10

3. The sacral erection center controls erections occurring in response to:
    a. Visual stimuli.
    b. Dream content.
    c. Emotional reactivity.
    d. Tactile stimulation.
        p. 122   LO 11

4. Which of the following, if any, are true statements about the sexual function of men with spinal cord injuries?
    a. Erections can occur if the injury is above the sacral center.
    b. Erections can occur in response to tactile stimulation.
    c. Sex can continue to be psychologically pleasurable.
    d. All of the above are true.
        p. 122   LO 11

5. Sally and Steve are in their late 30's. She is concerned that Steve is losing interest in her because he requires more direct penile stimulation to become erect. What advice is a sex therapist likely to give?
    a. Steve is probably having an extramarital affair.
    b. You should probably seek another lover.
    c. Males take longer to achieve an erection as they age.
    d. Males in their climacteric are less sexually focused.
        p. 122   LO 12

6. The _____ system largely governs erection, and the _____ system largely governs ejaculation.
   a. autonomic nervous; somatic nervous
   b. parasympathetic; sympathetic
   c. somatic nervous; autonomic nervous
   d. sympathetic; parasympathetic

   p. 123   LO 12

7. A man with Peyronie's disease has a penis that:
   a. Will not become erect.
   b. Is excessively straight.
   c. Burns during ejaculation.
   d. Is excessively curved.

   p. 123   LO 13

8. Priapism, a condition in which an erection persists for hours or days, can become a medical emergency because:
   a. The erection is extremely painful.
   b. It can cause testicular cancer.
   c. It can lead to the deterioration of penile tissue.
   d. It can damage the prostate.

   p. 124   LO 13

9. The force of the expulsion stage of ejaculation can vary, based on:
   a. The man's age and general health.
   b. The condition of the man's prostate.
   c. The intensity of the orgasm.
   d. All of the above
   e. None of the above

   p. 124   LO 14

10. Sean is prepubescent.
    a. He experiences orgasm and ejaculation with sufficient sexual stimulation.
    b. He cannot achieve an erection until puberty.
    c. He experiences "dry orgasms."
    d. He experiences ejaculation without orgasm.

    p. 124   LO 14

Multiple Choice

1. Which of the following statements is/are true about penis size?
   a. The average erect penis ranges from 5 to 7 inches in length.
   b. The size of a flaccid penis is a good predictor of its size when erect.
   c. Size differences are mostly cancelled out by erection.
   d. A and B, but not C
   e. A and C, but not B

2. The spermatozoan pathway from testes to ejaculation from the penis as semen is:
   a. Vas deferens, epididymis, urethra.
   b. Urethra, vas deferens, epididymis.
   c. Epididymis, vas deferens, urethra.
   d. Vas deferens, urethra, epididymis.

3. When is the best time to perform self-examination of the testes?
   a. Shortly after waking in the morning
   b. Shortly after sexual activity
   c. Shortly after a warm shower or bath
   d. Shortly before bedtime

4. The flaccid penis stiffens when:
   a. The internal penile bones lock into place during sexual arousal.
   b. The penile muscles become rigid due to sexual excitement.
   c. The corpus cavernosa and corpus spongiosum sustain vasocongestion.
   d. The meatus becomes engorged with blood.

5. Prostate cancer is usually first detected by:
   a. Testicular self-examination.
   b. The penile strain gauge.
   c. Rectal examination or a blood test.
   d. A magnetic resonance imaging examination.

6. The _____ system largely governs erection, and the _____ system largely governs ejaculation.
   a. autonomic nervous; somatic nervous
   b. parasympathetic; sympathetic
   c. somatic nervous; autonomic nervous
   d. sympathetic; parasympathetic

7. Priapism, a condition in which an erection persists for hours or days, can become a medical emergency because:
    a. The erection is extremely painful.
    b. It can cause testicular cancer.
    c. It can lead to the deterioration of penile tissue.
    d. It can damage the prostate.

8. Spermatogenesis refers to the process in which:
    a. Sperm are transported through the seminiferous tubules.
    b. Sperm cells are produced and stored.
    c. Hormone levels in the male reproductive system are regulated.
    d. Spermatocytes split.

9. Sean is prepubescent.
    a. He experiences orgasm and ejaculation with sufficient sexual stimulation.
    b. He cannot achieve an erection until puberty.
    c. He experiences "dry orgasms."
    d. He experiences ejaculation without orgasm.

10. Early symptoms of cancer of the prostate may mimic those of:
    a. Testicular cancer.
    b. Benign prostate enlargement.
    c. Colon cancer.
    d. Benign penile dysfunction.

11. The sacral erection center controls erections occurring in response to:
    a. Visual stimuli.
    b. Dream content.
    c. Emotional reactivity.
    d. Tactile stimulation.

12. Circumcision is the surgical removal of the:
    a. Urethral flap.
    b. Seminal vesicle.
    c. Prepuce.
    d. Epididymis.

13. Which of the following has been implicated as a sign or cause of testicular cancer?
    a. Childhood cryptochidism
    b. One enlarged testicle
    c. Mother taking DES while pregnant
    d. Sexual overactivity

14. Males begin to have penile erections:
    a. Only after the first year of life.
    b. After they have reached puberty.
    c. As soon as they are able to ejaculate.
    d. Even while in the fetal environment.

15. If a man is engaged in sexual intercourse in a cold room, you would expect the:
    a. Vas deferens to lengthen and expand to allow for vasocongestion.
    b. Cremaster muscle to bring the testicles closer to the body.
    c. Dartos muscle would relax to allow the testicles to dangle farther from the body.
    d. Interstitial cells to increase production of testosterone.

True/False

_____ 1. The penis serves as a passageway for both urine and semen.

_____ 2. Ancient Greeks carried oversized phallic symbols in celebration of human sexuality.

_____ 3. The penis is composed primarily of muscle tissue.

_____ 4. Koro, or genital retraction syndrome, occurs primarily among men from Australia.

_____ 5. Men's decline in the production of sex hormones and fertility is more gradual than the decline experienced by women.

_____ 6. Many male babies are circumcised as a treatment for phimosis, a condition in which it is difficult to retract the foreskin from the glans.

_____ 7. Men's sexual responses, erection, and ejaculation are reflexes.

_____ 8. Benign prostatic hyperplasia is a life-threatening problem.

Essay Questions

1. Compare and contrast benign prostate hyperplasia (BPH) with cancer of the prostate. Include attention to: which men are likely to experience the conditions, and when; what symptoms and prognoses are associated with each condition; and the treatments most commonly offered for each, including pros and cons (where possible) for the treatment options.

_____

_____

_____

_____

_____

_____

_____

_____

2. Detail the major cultural and biological issues that surround the practice of routine circumcision among young males. Include your stance on the topic and the rationale for your choice.

_____

_____

_____

_____

_____

_____

_____

_____

When You Have Finished...

What Does the World Think?

See where the Web takes you as you explore the following issues concerning Male Sexual Anatomy and Physiology.

1. It's only fair that we pay the same attention to male anatomy as we did to female anatomy in the last chapter. So let's see what information the Web has to offer about male anatomy and sexual function. As was true of women, we tend to think of things like male anatomy and physiology as unbiased and unchanging due to their "factual" nature, but are things ever really that simple? Since the nature of the Internet often gives it the ability to disseminate new information more quickly than traditional methods such as this text, choose a topic from the chapter for which information is clearly still emerging (e.g., maintaining prostate health as men age). Make note of whether the Web's current offerings indicate the availability of more or different knowledge with respect to the topic(s) than was available at the time this text went to press.

2. Where did you first learn how erections and ejaculation function? How accurate were your sources? Lucky for today's young people, a great many of them have Internet access, so they can research their questions instead of waiting for the kid in their class that always seems to "know things" to serve as their fountain of information. Think like a 10-year-old; where would you look? What does using this approach yield? Compare the accuracy of the information you gather with what your learned in your text.

3. After what you have just read about sexual anatomy, functioning, and health, what do you think about penile piercings? What kind of statement do you think it makes? Most importantly, do you even know what's really involved in caring for a penile piercing? Check out these authoritative websites about aftercare and potential problems, and then think about whether you're ready to make that kind of a commitment—and whether you are prepared to jeopardize your urethral health and risk tissue damage to future sexual partners.
http://www.pubmedcentral.nih.gov/articlerender.fcgi?artid=1496593
http://sciencedaily.mediwire.com/main/Default.aspx?P=Content&ArticleID=156070

4. Where can you go for help when you need help with some of the concerns about male sexual health raised in the text? Take some time to search YouTube or some information about male health issues. Because the illnesses are related to sexual health, what are the potential benefits and liabilities about having your own access to information online, as well as access to what amounts to anonymous social support? Here are some links for you:
Testicular self-examination —http://www.soyouwanna.com/site/syws/testexam/testexam.html
Prostate health—http://www.prostatehealth.com/
Sperm motility—http://www.advancedfertility.com/sperm.htm
Penile dysfunctions*— http://www.urologyhealth.org/adult/index.cfm?cat=11

Chapter 5
Sexual Arousal and Response

Before You Begin...

Chapter Summary

There are many popular ideas about sexual arousal—some true, some not, and some in between. Some of the questions that we will answer include:

- Exactly how much do hormones explain sexual interest and eagerness?
- Can you increase the arousal of your partner in subtle ways?
- Are there subconsciously-perceived scents that influence one's selection of a mate and his or her actual degree of excitement with that person?
- Does sexual orientation affect to which gender's scents one is attracted?
- What kinds of drugs improve or impede sexual functioning and the quality of decisions you are likely to make?
- Do females really have more than one type of orgasm?

This chapter explores all of this and more—so curl up in your chair and we'll get into the details.

We will start the chapter by examining the factors that contribute to sexual arousal and the processes that relate to sexual response. Your senses have an important role in sexual experiences and include vision, smell, the skin (or tactile sense), taste, and hearing—along with how they interplay. We'll look at the effects of pheromones (the unconscious scents) both on humans and on other animals. We'll also see where they fit in synchronizing the menstrual cycles of females who live together.

Your authors cover current research on aphrodisiacs (which are those substances thought to increase sexual arousal). Concurrent with the study of aphrodisiacs will be the effects on sexual functioning by psychoactive drugs. Psychoactive drugs include a wide variety of both legal and illicit substances like alcohol, Rohypnol, marijuana, amphetamines, and cocaine. Also, the role of anaphrodisiacs is explained.

The brain and two of its components plays a central role in sexual functioning. We'll look at the role of the cerebral cortex and limbic system. Too, we'll study the conceptual model of electrically stimulating the brain. Such stimulation makes the brain think it is getting pleasure sensations just like that of orgasm! Related animal research along this same line will be outlined too for you.

We'll also see both the organizing influence as well as the activating influence in sexual behavior of the sex hormones. Your text further highlights the role of testosterone in sexual behavior—and especially why it is very important to females as well. In your text, you will find the details divided into two sections on the basis of sex.

In terms of sexual response, the popular Masters and Johnson's sexual response cycle is explained. It identifies the physiological changes associated with sexual arousal and response. Also, the similarities between the physiological responses of men and women are emphasized. The four phases of the cycle are: excitement, plateau, orgasmic, and resolution. As an alternate, Kaplan has proposed another model of sexual response consisting of three stages: desire, excitement, and orgasm. The Kaplan model fits well into a clinical counseling setting designed to solve sexual dysfunctions. The focus on desire here is helpful since most reported problems occur in the desire phase.

Finally, the authors present research evidence on the orgasmic response: multiple orgasms in women as compared to men along with the idea of vaginal and clitoral sources of orgasms in women. Note, too, that at various points throughout this chapter, there is a focus on how aging modifies sexual arousal and response. Understanding this allows you to know what to expect about what is normal as you age and what is not—recognizing that the "not" can often be treated successfully nowadays.

Learning Objectives

1. Describe the role of vision in sexual arousal.

2. Describe the role of smell in sexual arousal and discuss the research on the influence of pheromones on human and other animal behavior.
   a. Relate pheromones with menstrual synchrony.
   b. Identify the interplay between sexual orientation and axillary odors.

3. The sense of touch: Define erogenous zones—both primary and secondary zones—and identify their locations. Understand where the brain fits (or does not fit) in this zone paradigm.

4. Compare and contrast the roles each of the five senses play in sexual arousal; which senses play minor roles and which play major roles.

5. Summarize the research on substances that have aphrodisiac or anaphrodisiac properties.

6. Identify the major categories of psychoactive drugs and explain their psychological and physical effects on sexual arousal. Identify several specific examples of these drugs, at least one per category.

7. Identify the parts of the cerebral cortex and the limbic system that play roles in sexual arousal and sexual behavior. Know diagrammatically the approximate location of these parts relative to one another. Relate how electrical stimulation may emulate sexual pleasure.

8. Summarize the research on the role of sex hormones as both organizing influences and activating influences—both for females and for males. Understand how human females differ from most other mammals (i.e., estrus cycles). Explain just how much of the "picture" hormones are in explaining sexual behavior in both sexes.

9. Name the four phases of the sexual response cycle proposed by Masters and Johnson, and describe the changes associated with each phase for the female and then for the male.

10. Compare Kaplan's three-stage model of sexual arousal with Masters and Johnson's four-phase model. Know in what instances one model is possibly superior to the other.

11. Summarize the research on the female and male capacity for multiple orgasms.

12. Evaluate the research concerning the types of orgasms women and men experience.

Key Terms

Term Identification

Make flashcards using the following terms about sexual arousal and response as you go. Use the definitions in the margins of this chapter, or from Figure 5.1 and its caption, for help. Focus on learning the function of any brain systems and/or hormones; connecting the terms with their purposes helps to make them seem less "foreign," and thus easier to recall later.

Chapter 5 Key Terms	
Anaphrodisiacs	Myotonia
Antiandrogen	Orgasmic platform
Aphrodisiac	Ovariectomy
Cerebral cortex*	Pheromones
Cerebrum*	Plateau phase
Erogenous zones	Refractory period
Erogenous zones, primary	Resolution phase
Erogenous zones, secondary	Sex characteristics, secondary
Excitement phase	Sex flush
Hypogonadism	Sex skin
Hypothalamus*	Sexual response cycle
Limbic system*	Transsexual
Multiple orgasms	Vasocongestion
*See Figure 5.3 and its caption, p. 148	

As You Read...

❖ *Making Sense of Sex: The Role of the Senses in Sexual Arousal*

As your text points out, all of our senses are involved to some degree in sexual arousal. Using the information you learned in this chapter—and your opinion on the matter—rank the five senses in terms of their importance in arousal and use information in the text to strengthen your argument. Be sure to include a mention of gender differences where you feel it is applicable.

Vision: The Better to See You With

Rank:_____

Rationale: _____

_____

Smell: Does the Nose Know Best?

Rank:_____

Rationale: _____

_____

The Skin Senses: Sex as a Touching Experience

Rank:_____

Rationale: _____

_____

Taste: On Savory Sex

Rank:_____

Rationale: _____

_____

Rank: _____

Rationale: _____

_____

TRY PRACTICE TEST #1 NOW!
GOOD LUCK!

❖ *Aphrodisiacs: Of Spanish Flies and Rhino Horns*

Ok, I'll admit it. I fell for the whole "somebody put Spanish Fly in the punch, be careful" thing at a middle school dance once. How about you? Think back on your life so far, and for each substance below, tell whether you believe(d) in them, what you thought they did, and what you really know now from your text. Be careful—there might be some anaphrodisiacs and psychoactive drugs mixed in there too….

Spanish Fly	*Opinion:* *Does it work?*	*Why/why not?*
	Text: *Does it work?*	*Why/why not?*

Saltpeter *(Potassium Nitrate)*	*Opinion:* *Does it work?*	*Why/why not?*
	Text: *Does it work?*	*Why/why not?*

Phallic Foods (e.g., Oysters, Bananas)	*Opinion: Does it work?*	*Why/why not?*
	Text: Does it work?	*Why/why not?*

Alcohol	*Opinion: Does it work?*	*Why/why not?*
	Text: Does it work?	*Why/why not?*

Arginine	*Opinion: Does it work?*	*Why/why not?*
	Text: Does it work?	*Why/why not?*

Amyl Nitrate ("Poppers")	*Opinion: Does it work?*	*Why/why not?*
	Text: Does it work?	*Why/why not?*

Testosterone	*Opinion: Does it work?*	*Why/why not?*
	Text: Does it work?	*Why/why not?*

| Hallucinogenics (e.g., Marijuana, LSD) | Opinion: Does it work? | Why/why not? |
| | Text: Does it work? | Why/why not? |

| Exercise | Opinion: Does it work? | Why/why not? |
| | Text: Does it work? | Why/why not? |

| Stimulants (e.g., Methamphetamine, Cocaine) | Opinion: Does it work? | Why/why not? |
| | Text: Does it work? | Why/why not? |

| Rohypnol ("Roofies," "La Rocha") | Opinion: Does it work? | Why/why not? |
| | Text: Does it work? | Why/why not? |

❖ *Sexual Response and the Brain: Cerebral Sex?*

Have you ever asked yourself what the role of your brain is in sexual response? Many of us joke about men "thinking with the little head instead of the big one," or about women thinking too much instead of "going with the flow" when they become aroused, but how does it really all work? This chapter answers the question as well as it can be answered at the present: human behavior is complex beyond belief! The text explores both the physical and emotional responses that involve the brain and nervous system. Using the information you read, give realistic examples, along with an explanation of the way each of the following might function in sexual arousal:

Spinal Reflexes: _____

_____

_____

_____

Cerebral Cortex: _____

_____

_____

_____

Limbic System: _____

_____

_____

_____

❖ Sex Hormones: Do They "Goad" Us Into Sex?

> ➤ Sex Hormones and Sexual Behavior: Organizing and Activating Influences

Just to make sure it makes sense, take a moment to reflect on how your text tells you to define the difference between the organizing and the activating effects of sex hormones in the space provided below.

_____

_____

_____

_____

_____

_____

Now let's try a little application. For each of the following scenarios, fill in the blank with the type of hormonal influence being described—organizing or activating. Please note that the scenarios involving human behavior have been designed to elicit a particular type of influence clearly; it is my hope that no one actually believes in nor has experienced them!

Scenario 1:
The field researcher noted that when in estrus, the alpha males in the herd of animals competed with one another in front of the females, with the winner taking his choice of female mates aside to perform coitus after the competition ended.

Type of Influence: _____

Scenario 2:
Although he was usually lukewarm, at best, to her advances, she could not help but notice that tonight, as the party air grew warmer and thicker, her crush was definitely giving her strong signals that he was aroused by the nearness of her as they danced. On top of that, he kept nosing up against her like he was sniffing her neck. She gasped slightly as she remembered that before the party, she had humored her roommate and dabbed a little of that new "attraction" perfume called "Testosteroni" on her pulse points. "I guess for once the advertising was true," she laughed to herself.

Type of Influence: _____

Scenario 3:
Whenever the scientist injected the lab rats in her experiment with testosterone, their mounting attempts over the next 6 hours tripled in frequency.

Type of Influence: _____

Scenario 4:
Amused with the predictability of their behavior patterns, the undergraduate woman noticed that every year, as soon as the weather rose above about 75° in the spring, several members of the most prestigious (and typically very attractive) sorority seemed to be outside relaxing in bikinis at any given moment, giggling in response to the interested looks they elicited from the most handsome men who passed by the house on their way to and from classes.

Type of Influence: _____

➤ *Sex Hormones and Male & Female Sexual Behavior*

Congratulations: if you are using this study guide, you must have survived the hormone rollercoaster also known as adolescence! By young adulthood most of us have had at least a little experience with the overwhelming feelings that accompany sexual arousal. As with the brain, the relationship between hormones and sexual arousal is complicated and has influence both in terms of physical and emotional arousal.

Take a moment to fill out the chart below. For each hormone-related condition, briefly describe its function in terms of sexual arousal, and indicate whether it tends to be more of a factor in the arousal and behavior of males, females, or both. Although your text clearly indicates that behavior can influence and often reverse the effects of many of the conditions noted below, for the purposes of this exercise, focus on the hormonal issues rather than behavioral influences.

Name	*Function(s)*	*Mainly Male, Female or Both?*
Estrogen		
Antiandrogens		
Testosterone		

Name	Function(s)	Mainly Male, Female or Both?
Progesterone		
Hypogonadism		
Ovariectomies		
Estradiol		
Chemical castration		

TRY PRACTICE TEST #2 NOW!
GOOD LUCK!

❖ *Sexual Response*

> *The Four-Phase Masters and Johnson Sexual Response Cycle*

In the following chart, list the physical changes in men and in women associated with each of the four stages of Masters and Johnson's Sexual Response Cycle.

PHASES	PHYSICAL CHANGES IN MALES	PHYSICAL CHANGES IN FEMALES
Excitement		
Plateau		
Orgasm		
Resolution		

➤ *Kaplan's Three Stages of Sexual Response: An Alternative Model*

By contrast, in this chart, list the physical changes in men and in women associated with each of the three stages of Kaplan's Sexual Response Cycle.

PHASES	PHYSICAL CHANGES IN MALES	PHYSICAL CHANGES IN FEMALES
Desire		
Excitement		
Orgasm		

➢ *Controversies About Orgasm*

Your text details some of the arguments and controversies about orgasms. For each of the questions it addressed, give your personal answer, using information from the text to support your responses.

1. How many kinds of orgasm do women experience?

_____

_____

_____

_____

_____

_____

2. What is the G-spot?

_____

_____

_____

_____

_____

_____

3. Is there such a thing as female ejaculation?

_____

_____

_____

_____

_____

4. Are men and/or women capable of experiencing multiple orgasms?

_____

_____

_____

_____

_____

_____

TRY PRACTICE TEST #3 NOW!
GOOD LUCK!

After You Read...

PRACTICE TEST #1

(LO = Learning Objective)

1. Visually mediated erotica (also known as "porn flicks") appeals to:
    a. Both sexes about equally.
    b. Females more than males usually.
    c. Males more than females usually.
    d. Neither males nor females in a significant amount.
        p. 131   LO 1

2. If Ellen and Susan are roommates, what is likely to happen?
    a. Their PMS symptoms will become almost identical.
    b. Pheromones will help them to bond emotionally.
    c. They will become sexually attracted to one another because of the effects of pheromones.
    d. Their menstrual cycles will become synchronized.
        p. 132   LO 2

3. Any substance that increases sexual arousal or desire is called a/an:
    a. Pheromone.
    b. Antiandrogen.
    c. Hypogonadal agent.
    d. Aphrodisiac.
        p. 137   LO 2

4. Recent research suggests that male _____ has positive effects on women, ranging from elevating their moods to facilitating the emergence of sexual feelings.
    a. cologne
    b. saliva
    c. perspiration
    d. urine
        p. 134-5   LO 2

5. Which of the following could be examples of secondary erogenous zones?
    a. Ears, mouth, and brain
    b. Brain, shoulders, and kneecaps
    c. Kneecaps, wrists, and shoulders
    d. Mouth, clitoris, and nipples
        p. 133-135   LO 3

6. Primary erogenous zones are erotically sensitive due to _____, but secondary erogenous zones are erotically sensitive due to _____.
    a. the presence of many nerve endings; experiences that eroticize them
    b. experiences that eroticize them; the presence of many nerve endings
    c. their emissions of testosterone; their emissions of perspiration
    d. their emissions of perspiration; their emissions of testosterone
        p. 133-135   LO 3

7. Preferences as to erogenous zones can vary from person to person, depending on their differing:
    a. Biological characteristics.
    b. Attitudes.
    c. Past experiences.
    d. None of the above.
    e. All of the above are true.
        p. 136-137   LO 3

8. Which of the following senses tends to take the most influential role in during sexual activity?
    a. Sight
    b. Taste
    c. Touch
    d. Smell
        p. 136-137   LO 4

9. Under which of the following circumstances can certain sounds become arousing?
    a. When they are social taboos
    b. When they are soft and low
    c. When they are melodious
    d. None of the above
    e. Any of the above, under certain circumstances
        p. 137   LO 4

10. Although there is some scholarly debate on the issue, _____ tend to be more interested in erotic visual images.
    a. women
    b. men
    c. men and women under 25 years of age
    d. men and women over 25 years of age
        p. 138   LO 4

(LO = Learning Objective)

1. Anaphrodisiacs:
   a. Can inhibit sexual drive.
   b. Enhance erectile response.
   c. Elevate mood which increases our capacity for orgasm.
   d. Complement the function of aphrodisiacs.
       p. 139-40   LO 5

2. Why have foods such as bananas, celery stalks, and clams been believed to be aphrodisiacs, even though there is not evidence to support that they are?
   a. Because Freud said they all were.
   b. Because of their phallic/erogenous shapes.
   c. Because of their use in ancient Greek celebrations of sexuality.
   d. Because of their ability to increase blood flow to one's genitals.
       p. 138   LO 5

3. All of the following help explain why alcohol is so strongly associated with sexual enjoyment, EXCEPT:
   a. Alcohol induces some feelings of euphoria.
   b. It impairs information processing and therefore judgment.
   c. Its vasodilating effects increase sexual arousal and prolong orgasm.
   d. Intoxication serves as a convenient reason for socially deviant behavior.
       p. 140   LO 6

4. The following are true about the use of central nervous system (CNS) depressants such as barbiturates EXCEPT:
   a. Depressants can interfere with reproduction because there can be a dramatic reduction in sperm count/spermatogenesis in most males.
   b. Depressants can enhance sexual arousal in some people by lessening fear or inhibitions.
   c. Some depressants actually dampen sex drive.
   d. Depressants impair erectile response and delay ejaculation.
   e. All of the above are true.
       p. 139-140   LO 6

5. Which of the following have been claimed to heighten arousal and sensations of orgasm, and in high doses can bring on irritability, insomnia, and loss of appetite?
   a. Viagra
   b. Wellbutrin
   c. Methamphetamines
   d. LSD
       p. 141-2   LO 6

6. Your memories of your first romantic kiss, your ability to recreate your favorite sexual fantasy, and your learned association between silk and sexual arousal are all contained in your:
   a. Limbic system.
   b. Cerebral cortex.
   c. Cerebellum.
   d. Thalamus.

   p. 142   LO 7

7. Mating behaviors and sexual physiological responses in laboratory animals can be induced by applying electrical stimulation to:
   a. Specific areas of the brain.
   b. Along the spinal cord.
   c. The genitals directly.
   d. Any of the above.

   p. 142   LO 7

8. Regarding the scientific understanding of the organizing effects and the activating effects of sex hormones, which statement is most accurate:
   a. More is understood about the activating effects than the organizing effect.
   b. More is understood about the organizing effect than the activating effects.
   c. Finally, both of these effects are now equally well understood.
   d. Only the organizing effect is well understood.

   p. 144   LO 7

9. Ultimately, the secretion of sex hormones by the ovaries and testes is regulated by the:
   a. Hypothalamus and pituitary gland.
   b. Pituitary and adrenal glands.
   c. Limbic system and Bartholin's gland.
   d. Pons and medulla.

   p. 144   LO 8

10. It is generally accepted that testosterone affects the frequency and intensity of sexual interest in both men and women. In other words, this hormone has a/an _____ effect.
    a. organizing
    b. activating
    c. developmental
    d. cyclical

    p. 145   LO 8

(LO = Learning Objective)

1. Identify the true statement(s) about transsexuals relative to sexual differentiation:
   a. The brains of transsexual individuals may have been prenatally sexually differentiated in one direction, while their genitals were being differentiated in the other.
   b. Prenatally, both the brains and the genitals of transsexuals are sexually differentiated in the same direction, but sometime between birth and approximately the age of five, the brain finishes its differentiation in a direction that is opposite to that of the existing genitalia.
   c. Transsexuals will often think his (or her) anatomical sex does not match what he (she) feels inside.
   d. Both A and C are true
   e. Both B and C are true

   p. 145   LO 8

2. Following orgasm, Tom is incapable of experiencing another orgasm or ejaculation. He is worried that he is suffering from a sexual dysfunction. What would you tell him?
   a. He should visit a urologist to determine if he has testicular cancer.
   b. This is normal and is called the refractory period.
   c. He should relax more and the problem will disappear.
   d. This is normal and is called the retraction period.

   p. 148   LO 9

3. Both men and women experience _____ early in the sexual response cycle proposed by Masters and Johnson.
   a. vasocongestion
   b. myotonia
   c. sex skin
   d. Both A and B
   e. Both B and C

   p. 148   LO 9

4. Most muscle tension, or myotonia, tends to fade away within _____ after an orgasm in both men and women.
   a. 2 minutes
   b. 5 minutes
   c. 7 minutes
   d. 10 minutes

   p. 148   LO 9

5. The stages of Kaplan's model of sexual response include all of the following EXCEPT:
   a. Orgasm.
   b. Excitement.
   c. Resolution.
   d. Desire.
      p. 153-154   LO 10

6. Whitney and Jerome are having difficulties in their marriage because she is a "night person" and he is a "morning person" when it comes to sex and neither of them seems to be able to compromise about the timing of their love-making. Which model(s) of sexual arousal is/are most likely to be useful to the counselor who helps them resolve this particular issue?
   a. Masters and Johnson's
   b. Kaplan's
   c. Both of the above
   d. Neither of the above
      p. 148-154   LO 10

7. What is the gender difference that occurs during the resolution phase of sexual arousal?
   a. Only women experience it.
   b. Only men experience it.
   c. Men's resolution phase takes longer than women's.
   d. Women's resolution phase takes longer than men's.
      p. 148   LO 10

8. A major gender difference in sexual response is:
   a. Men's greater levels of physical arousal and subsequent pleasure.
   b. Men's higher level of myotonia and vasocongestion.
   c. Women's greater capacity for multiple orgasms.
   d. Women's extended plateau period.
      p. 154-5   LO 11

9. According to Masters and Johnson:
   a. Women may experience either a clitoral or vaginal orgasm.
   b. Three types of orgasm occur in women.
   c. Stimulation of the G-spot produces an intense orgasm.
   d. There is only one kind of orgasm.
      p. 155   LO 12

10. A dry orgasm occurs:
    a. In both men and women.
    b. When a woman has not had sufficient foreplay to reach lubrication.
    c. When a man is dehydrated to the point of reducing his seminal fluid.
    d. When a man has an orgasm without ejaculating.
       p. 155   LO 12

Multiple Choice

1. Visually mediated erotica (also known as "porn flicks") appeals to:
   a. Both sexes about equally.
   b. Females more than males usually.
   c. Males more than females usually.
   d. Neither males nor females in a significant amount.

2. If Ellen and Susan are roommates, what is likely to happen?
   a. Their PMS symptoms will become almost identical.
   b. Pheromones will help them to bond emotionally.
   c. They will become sexually attracted to one another because of the effects of pheromones.
   d. Their menstrual cycles will become synchronized.

3. Which of the following could be examples of secondary erogenous zones?
   a. Ears, mouth, and brain
   b. Brain, shoulders, and kneecaps
   c. Kneecaps, wrists, and shoulders
   d. Mouth, clitoris, and nipples

4. Which of the following senses tends to take the most influential role in during sexual activity?
   a. Sight
   b. Taste
   c. Touch
   d. Smell

5. Anaphrodisiacs:
   a. Can inhibit sexual drive.
   b. Enhance erectile response.
   c. Elevate mood which increases our capacity for orgasm.
   d. Complement the function of aphrodisiacs.

6. The following are true about the use of central nervous system (CNS) depressants such as barbiturates EXCEPT:
   a. Depressants can interfere with reproduction because there can be a dramatic reduction in sperm count/spermatogenesis in most males.
   b. Depressants can enhance sexual arousal in some people by lessening fear or inhibitions.
   c. Some depressants actually dampen sex drive.
   d. Depressants impair erectile response and delay ejaculation.

7. Your memories of your first romantic kiss, your ability to recreate your favorite sexual fantasy, and your learned association between silk and sexual arousal are all contained in your:
   a. Limbic system.
   b. Cerebral cortex.
   c. Cerebellum.
   d. Thalamus.

8. It is generally accepted that testosterone affects the frequency and intensity of sexual interest in both men and women. In other words, this hormone has a/an _____ effect.
   a. organizing
   b. activating
   c. developmental
   d. cyclical

9. Following orgasm, Tom is incapable of experiencing another orgasm or ejaculation. He is worried that he is suffering from a sexual dysfunction. What would you tell him?
   a. He should visit a urologist to determine if he has testicular cancer.
   b. This is normal and is called the refractory period.
   c. He should relax more and the problem will disappear.
   d. This is normal and is called the retraction period.

10. The stages of Kaplan's model of sexual response include all of the following EXCEPT:
    a. Orgasm.
    b. Excitement.
    c. Resolution.
    d. Desire.

11. Whitney and Jerome are having difficulties in their marriage because she is a "night person" and he is a "morning person" when it comes to sex and neither of them seems to be able to compromise about the timing of their love-making. Which model(s) of sexual arousal is/are most likely to be useful to the counselor who helps them resolve this particular issue?
    a. Masters and Johnson's
    b. Kaplan's
    c. Both of the above
    d. Neither of the above

12. A major gender difference in sexual response is:
    a. Men's greater levels of physical arousal and subsequent pleasure.
    b. Men's higher level of myotonia and vasocongestion.
    c. Women's greater capacity for multiple orgasms.
    d. Women's extended plateau period.

13. According to Masters and Johnson:
    a. Women may experience either a clitoral or vaginal orgasm.
    b. Three types of orgasm occur in women.
    c. Stimulation of the G-spot produces an intense orgasm.
    d. There is only one kind of orgasm.

14. A dry orgasm occurs:
    a. In both men and women.
    b. When a woman has not had sufficient foreplay to reach lubrication.
    c. When a man is dehydrated to the point of reducing his seminal fluid.
    e. When a man has an orgasm without ejaculating.

15. Identify the true statement(s) about transsexuals relative to sexual differentiation:
    a. The brains of transsexual individuals may have been prenatally sexually differentiated in one direction, while their genitals were being differentiated in the other.
    b. Prenatally, both the brains and the genitals of transsexuals are sexually differentiated in the same direction, but sometime between birth and approximately the age of five, the brain finishes its differentiation in a direction that is opposite to that of the existing genitalia.
    c. Transsexuals will often think his (or her) anatomical sex does not match what he (she) feels inside.
    d. Both A and C are true
    e. Both B and C are true

True/False

_____ 1. Studies have found that women stop ovulating in the presence of male perspiration.

_____ 2. Primary erogenous zones have more nerve endings than most other body parts.

_____ 3. Music itself can contribute to sexual arousal.

_____ 4. Viagra was originally developed as a treatment for vertigo.

_____ 5. Coca-Cola® included cocaine in its original formula.

_____ 6. Studies have proven that "pleasure centers" in the brain exist in humans.

_____ 7. Some men who have been chemically castrated go on functioning sexually for years.

_____ 8. "Sex flush" is more prominent among women than among men.

Essay Questions

1. Your little sister goes to college this fall for the first time. Using the information from this chapter, what would you tell her to help her avoid being dosed with the "date rape" drug against her will? Include both information about the drug and strategies to prevent its abuse as a facilitator of blackouts.

_____

_____

_____

_____

_____

_____

_____

_____

_____

2. Discuss the major arguments made as to how many kinds of female orgasms exist. Include your opinion, supported by research cited in your text.

_____

_____

_____

_____

_____

_____

_____

_____

When You Have Finished...

Rev up your search engines and see where the Web takes you as you explore the following issues concerning Sexual Arousal and Response.

1. With all the myths surrounding aphrodisiacs and anaphrodisiacs, this seems like a good time for you to see what kind of urban legends there are out there about sexual arousal. For example, have you ever heard about how saltpeter keeps men from getting aroused? And how the Army used to sneak it into soldiers' food because of that? Well, guess what? Urban legend! See for yourself and go from there: http://www.snopes.com/military/saltpetr.htm .

2. Do you remember any of the things you learned about sexual arousal as a teenager? Were there any things that were crazy? Have you ever questioned them? Take some time to look them up and see what you get when you start to Google these myths.

3. Knowing what you know now about how important subjective emotions are in sexual arousal and response, maybe this is a good time to think about what you would want in a mutually satisfying relationship. Here's a link to a test to "Discover Your Sexual Personality": http://discoveryhealth.queendom.com/sex_personality_abridged_access.html

4. By now, hopefully, the idea that testosterone plays a huge role in sexuality for both men and women is old news to you. However, it is still most closely associated with men. Why not find out more about its impact on women's health? Be sure to pay attention to the details—do they match up with the information in your textbook or do they contradict it? If they go against it, think about why that might be and how valid the source is. Here's a good place to start: http://www.aphroditewomenshealth.com/news/20020311214759_health_news.shtml

Chapter 6
Gender Identity, Gender Roles, and Sex Differences

Before You Begin…

Chapter Summary

Gender and sex are often used interchangeably by those with less education than you will have quite soon! Have you wondered if cross-dressers are perhaps confused about what gender they are—or is it just the transsexuals? Is there even confusion there with transsexuals at all? Is there a third gender/third sex? What is the difference between an intersexual and a hermaphrodite and how common are these variations? Are all fetuses female for a time? All this and more… and you will see that many of the popular stereotypes range either from being a little off to just flat out wrong. If you'll get comfortable, we can now dig into the details!

This chapter discusses gender and its implications for men and women, using the lenses of biology, psychology, and sociology to examine its many aspects. At the opening, this chapter includes correspondence between a transsexual and her parents; it clearly showcases the individual and family difficulty associated with gender dysphoria and transsexualism. Do recognize that transsexualism is a gender-identity disorder in which people have the anatomic sex of one gender but have a persistent sense of themselves as members of the other gender. Also note that before one identifies as a transsexual, gender dysphoria surfaces—and it is a sense of incongruity between one's anatomic sex and his/her gender identity.

As explained in the text, sexual differentiation begins prenatally, at about the seventh week after conception. It occurs due to a combination of genetics, hormones, and brain development, with the hormone testosterone playing a particularly crucial role in the process. Development of reproductive organs begins high in the abdominal cavity, followed by the descent of the testes into the scrotal sac or of the ovaries into the pelvic area. The effects of sex chromosomal anomalies on sexual characteristics, physical health, and psychological development are presented.

The interwoven influences of nature and nurture on gender identity are explored. Gender identity is psychological, rather than physiological, but is almost always consistent with anatomic gender. In rare cases, non-normative prenatal hormonal development results in mixed indicators of gender. Gender assignment and rearing of people who have hermaphroditism and intersexualism are discussed. Your authors eagerly examine both transsexualism and transgenderism for you. Also, where homosexual transsexuals fit is outlined. The efficacy of hormone treatment and gender-reassignment surgery is examined. And, in the "closer look" box, you will discover information on real-life cases.

Gender roles are broad cultural expectations about men and women that can result in stereotyping. Examples of sexism and its effects are presented. Examples of research that examines male-female differences in cognitive abilities, personality, and social behaviors are discussed. The influence of gender roles on dating and sexual behavior are also examined.

Gender role stereotypes are considered from biological, cross-cultural, and psychological perspectives, as are the implications of each explanation. Within the psychological perspective, the psychodynamic, social-learning, cognitive-developmental and gender-schema (information processing) theories of gender typing are presented.

Your authors examine differences in cognition, personality, and behavior relative to the male and female sexes. Cognitive abilities affect areas like math and logical reason. Personality aspects include how the following variables differ between the sexes on these variables:

Extraversion	**Trust**	**Anxiety**	**Nurturance**
Tough-mindedness	**Assertiveness**	**Self-esteem**	

Behavior attributes, like personality above, also include a variety of attributes such as:
- Who discloses feelings and personal experiences
- Which sex does most of the talking
- Who is more willing to seek healthcare
- Who has the most interest in casual sex
- Who desires multiple sex partners
- Who is most aggressive, including who marches off to war or seeks fame/glory

Relative to gender typing, we explore several perspectives based both in biology and psychology. Biology examines both evolution and prenatal organization. Psychological perspectives look at the following theories:
- Psychoanalytic
- Social-cognitive
- Cognitive-developmental
- Gender schema

Lastly, the authors discuss psychological androgyny and build an argument for the reconstruction of traditional definitions of masculinity and femininity as opposite ends of one continuum. Considering the possibility that men and women can have both male and female traits at the same time, they discuss how psychological androgyny might allow one to deal with a wider range of social situations more effectively. Arguments against this reconstructed model of masculinity and femininity are also considered.

1. Trace the influences of sex chromosomes (genetic factors) and hormones on prenatal sexual differentiation of the brain and body anatomy.

2. Define gender identity and gender dysphoria and discuss the research relevant to the debate on genetic vs. socialized determination of gender identity.

3. Define hermaphroditism, intersexualism, transsexualism, and transgenderism. Discuss the theoretical perspectives on transsexualism and describe the techniques and limitations of gender-reassignment surgery.

4. Define sexism, give examples, and discuss the effects on women and men of gender role stereotypes.

5. Summarize the research on male-female differences in cognitive abilities, personality traits, and social behavior.

6. Summarize the biological and evolutionary perspectives on gender typing.

7. Summarize the cross-cultural evidence on gender typing.

8. Explain the psychological perspectives and the role of socialization in gender typing.

9. Examine the arguments for and against reconstructing the concepts of masculinity and femininity, and examine the influence of psychological androgyny on psychological well-being and personal development.

Term Identification

As usual, make flashcards using the following terms as you go. Use the definitions in the margins of this chapter for help.

Chapter 6 Table of Key Terms	
Androgen-insensitivity syndrome	Identification
Androgens	Inguinal canal
Autogynephilic	Intersexual
Chromosome	Klinefelter syndrome
Congenital adrenal hyperplasia	Oedipus complex
Cryptochidism	Phalloplasty
Dominican Republic syndrome	Psychological androgyny
Embryo	Schema
Gender	Sex assignment
Gender constancy	Sexism
Gender dysphoria	Sexual differentiation
Gender identity	Socialization
Gender roles	Stereotype
Gender schema	Testosterone
Gender stability	Transsexualism
Gender typing	Transgenderism
Hermaphrodite	Transsexuals
Homosexual transsexuals	Zygote

As You Read...

Vocabulary Matching

Directions: Match each key vocabulary term listed in the left-hand column with the correct definition in the right-hand column.

a. hermaphrodites

b. congenital adrenal hyperplasia

c. androgen-insensitivity syndrome

d. Dominican Republic syndrome

e. transsexuals

f. gender dysphoria

g. homosexual transsexuals

h. autogynephilic

i. identification

j. phalloplasty

k. stereotype

_____ A form of intersexualism in which a genetic female has internal female sexual structures but masculinized external genitalia.

_____ Extremely feminine gay males who seek sex reassignment.

_____ The surgical procedure of creating and artificial penis.

_____ In psychoanalytic theory, the process of incorporating within ourselves our perceptions of the behaviors, thoughts, and feelings of others.

_____ A form of intersexualism in which a genetic enzyme disorder prevents testosterone from masculinizing the external genitalia.

_____ Descriptive of transsexuals who are sexually stimulated by fantasies that their own bodies are female.

_____ A fixed, conventional idea about a group of people.

_____ People who strongly desire to be of the other sex and live as a person of the other sex.

_____ A sense of incongruity between one's anatomic sex and one's gender identity.

_____ People who possess both ovarian and testicular tissue.

_____ A form of intersexualism in which a genetic male is prenatally insensitive to androgens such that his genitals are not normally masculinized.

➢ *Tracking the Differentiation Process: Analogous Male and Female Sex Organs*

Fill in the blanks in this statement:

Basically, embryos start off with _____ structures, and later develop in ways that produce male or female sex characteristics. Without the group of hormones commonly referred to as _____, all embryos would end up staying in their original anatomical structure, and thus all eventually develop _____ sexual structures.

Now, complete the chart below. Included are the undifferentiated external sexual organs visible on a typical fetus at about 5–6 weeks after conception; add the names of any corresponding male and female organs that each undifferentiated external organ will become when the fetus is fully developed.

UNDIFFERENTIATED	DEVELOPED MALE	DEVELOPED FEMALE
Glans area		
Urethral fold & groove		
Lateral buttress		
Anal pit & tubercle		

❖ *Gender Identity*

> ➢ *Reflection Assignment: Exercise Your Empathy*

You gender is fluid, somewhere between masculinity and femininity. It is such a huge part of our self-awareness, that most people do not have the opportunity to stop and think about what is means to be a man or a woman. Here is a hypothetical situation in which to consider your virtual self...

> You were raised as a young girl in a remote village in Africa. You have always been good at sports but you like to act like a girl, and play feminine games of your culture. A track coach noticed you in high school and you progressed very quickly into a world class athlete. At the world championships in Berlin, you will win the 800M run by 10 meters. You are at the top of the world.

> All of a sudden you gender is called into question by other women in the race. Your sexuality becomes the topic of discussion for the entire world. A review board orders a gender test. You are subjected to physical examinations, as well as more intrusive medical exams. The tests show (and are leaked to the public), that you have testicles that have never descended and an underdeveloped penis and scrotum. You are biologically male.

What is the condition that this 800M runner is experiencing? (You can search the Web for the answer).

_____

_____

How might this affect your relationships?

_____

_____

How might this affect your self-esteem?

_____

_____

Might there be advantages to having this condition?

_____

_____

Should you lose you medal? Even though you did not know you were male and you still feel like a woman?

_____

_____

Might there be disadvantages to having this condition?

_____

_____

Do you think there would be people with whom you could be open about your situation? If so, who and why? If not, why not?

_____

_____

How would you describe your level of (dis)comfort with this line of questions? Why do you think you are at this level of (dis)comfort?

_____

_____

❖ *Compare and contrast the following:*

Terms	Similarities	Differences
True hermaphroditism vs. pseudohermaphroditism		
Androgenital syndrome vs. androgen-insensitivity syndrome		
Pre-surgical vs. post-surgical transsexualism		

TRY PRACTICE TEST #1 NOW!
GOOD LUCK!

❖ *Gender Roles & Stereotypes*

➤ *Group Field Observation: Social Norming & Gender Roles*

Although it appears the scope of "acceptable" gender role behavior for both men and women has expanded over the past few decades, there are still some things about gender roles that we accept as "the way things are." When we behave in ways that we mainly choose "because that's the way things are done," we tend to be choosing things that are socially acceptable—we are either consciously or unconsciously choosing to follow our gender role scripts. The boundaries of social roles can be subtle; the easiest way to tell where a role begins and ends tends to be breaking it. Once the role script is violated or broken, there tend to be social consequences for the person who "colors outside the lines." This process of social sanctioning and rejection is often referred to as "social norming."

In this exercise, you will take some time to see what happens when you follow the rules, and when you break them. Form a group with enough members so that there is at least one person for each assignment below. If the class constraints do not permit the formation of groups for this activity, take a few moments to play out at least 2 of the scenarios yourself. You can choose the setting in which to play out the scenarios, but some suggested settings include: a store carrying items used by children; a discussion with same gender, opposite gender, or mixed gender friends; or a discussion with an older family member. In fact, if you have the opportunity to try it in more than one setting, please do; often the most interesting part is to consider why the expectations and outcomes tend to change as the social contexts do.

The scenarios:

In each case below, start off by saying that you need to find an appropriate gift for a baby shower, and you'd like to hear their suggestions. Use the details below to vary your requests for advice and note the implications about gender roles and stereotypes the resulting gift suggestions produce.

❑ It's going to be a boy/girl (choose one at a time), and the parents are very traditional.

Gift(s) suggested:

Implications:

❑ It's going to be a boy/girl (choose one at a time), and the parents are very progressive.

Gift(s) suggested:

Implications:

❑ The parents aren't sure whether it's going to be a girl or a boy, but they are very traditional/progressive (choose one at a time) people so I need to make sure they'll like the gift.

Gift(s) suggested:

Implications:

❑ It's going to be a boy/girl (choose one at a time), but I hate to give stereotypical gifts to little kids, and I'd love to get something the parents would never think of since they're so conservative about things like that.

Gift(s) suggested:

Implications:

❑ It's going to be a boy/girl (choose one at a time), and I hate to give non-traditional gifts to little kids, even though I know for a fact that the parents are really liberal, and they believe in doing things like making sure boys have dolls and girls get dump trucks to play with.

Gift(s) suggested:

Implications:

❖ **Sexism**

➤ *Sexism & Context: Behavioral Expectations*

The prejudice of sexism is nothing most people would want to claim as a practice. However, not all incidences of sexism are obvious. In each situation below, answer the associated question and explain why you chose your answer. Try hard not to think before you react—giving yourself time to consider the situation may change your reaction, and this is about automatic assumptions. After you have finished the exercise, note that most of the personal descriptors for the people were chosen from the lists in Table 6.1. Once you check the lists from which each person's characteristics came, are you tempted to change any of your answers? Why or why not?

1. Your female co-worker is ambitious and confident, yet she has made few friends at the office. She tends to show a lack of kindness in interpersonal situations, though it does not appear to be on purpose. She applies for a promotion, and goes up against a man with a very similar work record, but more friends at work. She gets the promotion. Who did you think would get it?

Immediate Response:

Reason for Response:

Are you tempted to change your answer after referring to Table 6.1?

Why or why not?

2. You are an elementary school teacher with a third grade class. You have noticed lately that, although his behavior does not stand out in the classroom in any way, there is one little boy who really stands out during recess. He always goes out of his way to play "house" with the little girls, and is eager to play no matter what role he is assigned—mother, father, child, etc. When there is not a game of "house" going, he is often seen playing alone with his stuffed animals in an almost dreamy reverie. No matter what he is playing, he is usually timid and often cries if another child acts aggressively toward him. Do you see any reason to notify his parents about this behavior when you send home his next progress report?

Immediate Response:

Reason for Response:

Are you tempted to change your answer after referring to Table 6.1?

Why or why not?

3. Your 18-year-old male friend's mother has always gone out of her way to make sure that both her male and female children know how to do all the work it takes to keep a household going. They all know how to cook, clean, do laundry, and baby-sit, and do so in ways that reflect their steady, capable, and yet somehow modest personalities. In fact, your friend is so imaginative, not to mention downright gentle, when it comes to taking care of the younger kids in the family, he's decided that instead of following his original career plan to become a plastic surgeon, he wants to become a pediatric nurse. He asks you what you think about his decision; will you encourage or discourage him to pursue this change of heart?

Immediate Response:

Reason for Response:

Are you tempted to change your answer after referring to Table 6.1?

Why or why not?

❖ ***Gender Differences: Vive la Différence or Vive la Similarité?***

➤ *A Closer Look: What Could the Differences Mean?*

The text is wise to point out that most male-female differences are found when examining GROUPS of men and women, and that there is tremendous individual difference to be found within each group. It is not difficult to find exceptions to even the most "established" gender differences. Nonetheless, there are trends that do appear to have some validity. Take a moment to form your own explanation of what could explain the following trends listed in your book. Be sure to consider what social advantages it might bring a man or woman to hold true to these trends; many times, social patterns endure because something about them is "working" for those involved. Be sure to support your answers with information from the chapter about gender roles.

❑ "Parents, on the average, prefer to have boys."

Possible explanation for stereotype:

❑ "Society has created an uneven playing field in which females have to perform better than males to be seen as doing equally well."

Possible explanation for stereotype:

❑ "As girls mature, it appears that they learn to 'take a back seat' to boys and let the boys do most of the talking when they are in mixed-gender groups."

Possible explanation for stereotype:

❑ "It is true that men act more aggressively, on the whole, than women do."

Possible explanation for stereotype:

❑ "Many men have a 'bullet-proof mentality' [when it comes to health care]."

Possible explanation for stereotype:

❖ On Becoming a Man or a Woman: Gender Typing

> ➤ *Rationale Roulette: The Diverse Explanations for Gendered Behavior*

For each of the following situations, supply a reasonable explanation that might be supplied by a scholar of the specified perspective.

1. A married American man has an affair with another woman.

   Evolutionary Perspective: _____

   _____

   Cultural Adaptation Perspective: _____

   _____

2. A female toddler announces that when she grows up, she's going to be a daddy.

   Psychodynamic Theory: _____

   _____

   Cognitive-Developmental Theory: _____

   _____

3. A male teen out with his friends chooses to buy a magazine about cars even though he is more interested in the one about home decorating.

   Social-Learning Theory: _____

   _____

   Gender-Schema Theory: _____

   _____

4. A mother is called in to meet with the principal concerning her son's unwillingness to stop using sticks as guns when playing with a certain group of boys during recess, despite several disciplinary warnings to all of the boys involved.

   Prenatal Brain Organization Perspective: _____

   _____

   Cultural Adaptation Perspective: _____

   _____

TRY PRACTICE TEST #2 NOW!
GOOD LUCK!

❖ Gender Roles & Sexual Behavior

➤ Social Assumptions & Sexuality

Your text makes it clear that there is still a double standard when it comes to men and women and sexual behavior. Complete the following sentences with the first answers that come to mind and consider the implications for men and women as they express their sexuality. Also assess your answers in terms of whether they fit the stereotypical responses for your gender, and why that might or might not be.

1. A 21-year-old man who has had 20 sexual partners is _____; a 21-year-old woman who has had 20 sexual partners is _____.

Do your answers fit the stereotypical responses for your gender?

Why might that be?

2. The _____ should pretty much always make the first move when it comes to sex.

Do your answers fit the stereotypical responses for your gender?

Why might that be?

3. If a woman tells a guy "no" the first time he asks for sex, but keeps making out with him afterwards, she really meant _____ when she said "no."

Do your answers fit the stereotypical responses for your gender?

Why might that be?

4. When it comes to an offer for group sex, any real man would _____, and any real woman would _____.

Do your answers fit the stereotypical responses for your gender?

Why might that be?

❖ ***Psychological Androgyny: The More Traits, the Merrier?***

➢ *Intergenerational Change: "When I Was Your Age..."*

Social trends seem to indicate that there is more self-acceptance to be found when one adopts psychological androgyny. Knowing that social trends tend to change a lot from generation to generation, it would be interesting to hear some opinions about androgyny among your parents' generation. Find one of your parents, or someone at least 20 years older than you are right now. Talk to them about at least one of the following two issues and record both your responses and theirs below:

1.   What does s/he think it took to be a well-adjusted man or woman when they were your age?

How does it compare to what you think it takes to be psychologically sound now?

Which description was more psychologically androgynous?

Why might that be so?

2.   When s/he looks back on the time that has passed since s/he was your age, do they think there are any differences now in terms of their psychological androgyny?

Most scholars see trends that as people age, they become more psychologically androgynous. Does the person you spoke with seem to fit that trend or not?

Why might that be so?

TRY PRACTICE TEST #3 NOW!
GOOD LUCK!

After You Read...

(LO = Learning Objective)

1. The same undifferentiated structure that develops into the scrotum in male sexual anatomy differentiates to become the _____ in females.
    a. clitoral shaft
    b. vagina
    c. labia majora
    d. clitoral glans
            p. 165   LO 1

2. For unknown reasons, an XY embryo fails to produce any androgens. What will happen to the embryo?
    a. It will be attracted to people of the same sex as an adult.
    b. It will become an anatomical male.
    c. It will become an anatomical female.
    d. It will become a transsexual.
            p. 166-167   LO 1

3. Male sex hormones are the primary influence of sexual differentiation during fetal development. However, female sex hormones also play an important role in the development of:
    a. Sexual differentiation of female embryos only.
    b. Secondary sex characteristics in puberty.
    c. Pseudohermaphroditism.
    d. Gender dysphoria.
            p. 173   LO 1

4. What relationship, if any, exists between gender dysphoria and patterns of sexual attraction?
    a. Most transsexuals are same-sex oriented.
    b. Gender dysphoria inhibits sexual attraction.
    c. Most transsexuals are heterosexual.
    d. There is no known relationship.
            p. 171   LO 2

5. The most common form of female intersexualism is:
    a. Androgen insensitivity syndrome.
    b. Hermaphroditism.
    c. Congenital adrenal hyperplasia (CAH).
    d. Dominican Republic syndrome.
            p. 169   LO 2

6. The following statement(s) is/are true about gender identity:
   a. Most children have acquired a firm sense of gender identity by the age of 24 months.
   b. Gender identity is often inconsistent with chromosomal sex.
   c. Gender identity is our psychological sense of being male or female.
   d. All of the above are true.
   e. Both A and C are true.

   p. 168   LO 2

7. The primary difference between intersexuals and hermaphrodites is that:
   a. Intersexuals have gonads that do not match their chromosomal sex.
   b. Hermaphrodites have an XXY chromosomal pattern.
   c. Intersexuals have undescended testes.
   d. Hermaphrodites have both ovarian and testicular tissue.

   p. 168   LO 3

8. In comparison to men who are considered homosexual transsexuals, autogynephilic transsexuals are more likely to _____ when they are in the pre-operative phase.
   a. appear very feminine in appearance and social behavior
   b. prefer traditional male masturbation more so than sexual activity with others
   c. seek both men and women as sexual partners for intercourse
   d. be sexually stimulated by fantasies of their own bodies as being female

   p. 171   LO 3

9. After gender-reassignment surgery, a transsexual can do all of the following EXCEPT:
   a. Engage in sexual activity.
   b. Experience orgasm.
   c. Impregnate or become pregnant.
   d. Live socially as a member of the other gender.

   p. 173-4   LO 3

10. Which of the following surgical procedures do most female-to-male transsexuals choose to undergo?
   a. Phonosurgery
   b. Partial hysterectomy
   c. Phalloplasty
   d. Double mastectomy

   p. 174   LO 3

(LO = Learning Objective)

1. Most current literature on the subject implies that gender role stereotypes are:
    a. Strictly an American phenomenon.
    b. Present primarily in Western European cultures.
    c. Widespread across many cultural settings.
    d. Mythical behavioral guidelines that do not currently exist.
                    p. 175   LO 4

2. Julie is considered to be "pushy" because she does not hesitate to make her point of view clear.
   Jerry is considered to be "assertive" because everyone always knows where he stands on issues.
   This is an example of:
    a. Gender differentiation.
    b. Sexism.
    c. Androgyny.
    d. Acculturation.
                    p. 178   LO 4

3. All of the following statements about gender differences are accurate, EXCEPT:
    a. Boys are slower to develop language skills.
    b. Boys have a slight advantage in visual-spatial skills.
    c. Girls have greater computational skills in elementary school.
    d. In adolescence, girls have greater problem-solving abilities.
                    p. 179-180   LO 5

4. Which of the following lists of personality traits would be most fitting of a *stereotypical* female?
    a. Capable, emotional, inventive, warm
    b. Appreciative, complicated, imaginative, talkative
    c. Resourceful, adventurous, pleasure-seeking, loud
    d. Charming, individualistic, modest, rational
                    p. 179-180   LO 5

5. A survey on relationships includes open-ended questions about what kind of sexual relationships
   men and women would choose if they had their way. If you had to leave your common sense at
   home and use ONLY the Sexual Strategies Theory to predict the differences between the responses
   of heterosexual male and female participants, which of the following would you predict to hold true?
    a. Men would be more likely to seek out women with high social status.
    b. Women would be more likely to seek out a youthful, attractive man.
    c. Men would express interest in having sex with as many women as possible.
    d. Both B and C would hold true according to this theory.
    e. Both A and C would hold true according to this theory.
                    p. 184-5   LO 6

6. Which perspective would assert that females are genetically predisposed to domesticity in order to perpetuate the survival of the species?
   a. Biological perspective
   b. Evolutionary perspective
   c. Psychoanalytic perspective
   d. Behavioral perspective
      p. 190   LO 6

7. The 2003 Schmitt survey on sexual relationship strategies around the world concluded that North American gender differences in the desire for sexual variety were:
   a. Echoed only by South Americans and Western Europeans.
   b. Found to be universal across the cultures surveyed.
   c. The opposite of those found among Southern Europeans and Africans.
   d. Unique compared with each of the other cultures surveyed.
      p. 185   LO 7

8. Anthropologists propose that cultural differences in gender roles reflect:
   a. Patriarchal attitudes toward masculine and feminine behaviors.
   b. Cultural adaptations to social and natural environments.
   c. Biological imprinting in the chromosomes of females and males.
   d. Survival strategies inherited through the process of natural selection.
      p. 191   LO 7

9. Freud believed children have an incestuous wish for their parent of the opposite gender. This:
   a. Is called the Oedipus complex for males.
   b. Is called the Electra complex for females.
   c. Occurs during the phallic period of psychosexual development.
   d. All of the above
   e. None of the above
      p. 187   LO 8

10. According to _____ theory, children form schemas about gender and then conform their behavior to their gender concepts.
   a. evolutionary
   b. psychoanalytic
   c. cognitive-developmental
   d. social-learning
      p. 189   LO 8

(LO = Learning Objective)

1. The term third gender or third sex is (or has been) used to describe:
    a. An intermediate state between man and women in some cultures.
    b. In Western societies, to label gay and lesbian people.
    c. The state of being neither male nor female or the ability to swap.
    d. In Western societies, to label transgendered and intersex people.
    e. All of the above
                    p. 176   LO 4

2. In terms of differences in social behavior, which statement(s) is (are) true?
    a. Males finally show a greater willingness to seek health care now and are about equal on this behavioral dimension with females.
    b. While not true historically, men are equal (or very close to equal now) in disclosing feelings and personal experiences.
    c. Women, in many cases, now seek glory and fame at rates equal to or greater than males.
    d. Women are now less likely to want to combine sex and a romantic relationship.
    e. All of the above are false.
                    p. 182   LO 5

3. What is true about the evolutionary view (or the "it's only natural perspective")?
    a. It allows scientists to definitively attribute complex behaviors (such as gender roles and aggression) to biological determinants.
    b. It is unnatural for society to promote monogamous relationships for males.
    c. Men, in contrast to women, have an inherited tendency to be interested in multiple sex partners.
    d. Both A and C.
    e. All of the above are true.
                    p. 183, 184   LO 6

4. By gender across cultures, which statement(s) are false about desire for multiple sex partners:
    a. In *none* of the ten studied regions did women, on a percentage basis, *ever* exceed men in any other region.
    b. Men in both Eastern and Southern Europe regions, along with the Oceania region, generally desire more sex partners than men in the North America region.
    c. In all regions, men's desire for multiple partners *always* exceeded that of the women in *their* corresponding region.
    d. Both A and B are false.
    e. A, B, and C are all false.
                    p. 186   LO 7

5. Gender identity itself is sufficient to inspire gender-appropriate behavior. After children develop a concept of gender identity, they begin to seek information concerning gender-type traits and try to live up to them. The latter describes what theory best:
   a. The gender-schema theory.
   b. The cognitive-developmental theory.
   c. The social-cognitive theory.
   d. The psychoanalytic theory.

           p. 189   LO 8

6. You take a psychological test and score high on androgyny. According to the research discussed in your text, most likely you:
   a. Have a stronger sex drive than others of your gender.
   b. Are better adjusted psychologically than people who score high on femininity or masculinity.
   c. Are a rare type among college students.
   d. Will have more difficulty than others in finding a satisfying partner.

           p. 190   LO 9

7. Some feminist scholars dislike the notion of psychological androgyny because:
   a. Men should not be allowed the privilege of taking on feminine traits; they have enough privileges already.
   b. The way it is defined perpetuates belief in masculine and feminine gender roles.
   c. Feminine traits are the best traits for women to have already.
   d. Both A and C are true.
   e. None of the above is true.

           p. 190   LO 9

8. Jamal is cooperative, science-oriented, assertive, moderately interested in sex, and emotionally expressive. He is:
   a. Experiencing low levels of testosterone.
   b. Stereotypically male.
   c. Considered androgynous.
   d. Likely to be transsexual.

           p. 190   LO 10

9. Richard Lippa's research is discussed at length in your text. Which of the following statements do his research findings support?
   a. Psychological androgyny is too complicated a construct to be useful.
   b. Measures of masculinity are oversimplified on measures of psychological androgyny.
   c. Psychological androgyny can only be accurately measured in women.
   d. Both A and C are supported in the research.
   e. None of the above is supported in the research.

           p. 191   LO 9

10. Which of the following behavioral tendencies did Lippa find to be associated with measures of masculinity used in the model of psychological androgyny?
    a. Working with people
    b. Bisexual orientation
    c. Prejudice
    d. Expressiveness
                p. 191   LO 9

Multiple Choice

1. Male sex hormones are the primary influence of sexual differentiation during fetal development. However, female sex hormones also play an important role in the development of:
    a. Sexual differentiation of female embryos only.
    b. Secondary sex characteristics in puberty.
    c. Pseudohermaphroditism.
    d. Gender dysphoria.

2. The same undifferentiated structure that develops into the scrotum in male sexual anatomy, differentiates to become the _____ in females.
    a. clitoral shaft
    b. vagina
    c. labia majora
    d. clitoral glans

3. The following statement(s) is/are true about gender identity:
    a. Most children have acquired a firm sense of gender identity by the age of 24 months.
    b. Gender identity is often inconsistent with chromosomal sex.
    c. Gender identity is our psychological sense of being male or female.
    d. All of the above are true.
    e. Both A and C are true.

4. Gender dysphoria is defined as:
    a. The sense of dissatisfaction with members of the opposite gender.
    b. The presence of an extra X chromosome.
    c. The sense that one's genital anatomy and gender identity or role do not match.
    d. The feeling of being sexually attracted to members of the same gender.

5. Which of the following surgical procedures do most female-to-male transsexuals choose to undergo?
    a. Phonosurgery
    b. Partial hysterectomy
    c. Phalloplasty
    d. Double mastectomy

6. According to stereotypical gender role scripts, which phrase would LEAST likely be used to describe a very "feminine" woman?
    a. She is confident, but modest, warm, and always offering a kind word.
    b. She is seldom patient, but somehow manages to be resourceful.
    c. She likes to show-off her sharp wit and strong opinions at social gatherings.
    d. She might be emotional and complicated, but she is always forgiving.

7. Women tend, on average, to outlive men by about 7 years. Scholars say this seems to be due to:
   a. Women's less stressful lives in the workplace.
   b. Men's tendency to ignore symptoms of health problems until they become serious.
   c. Women's use of home remedies to treat many illnesses.
   d. Men's tendency to act aggressively throughout their lives.

8. Which of the following lists of personality traits would be most fitting of a *stereotypical* female?
   a. Capable, emotional, inventive, warm
   b. Appreciative, complicated, imaginative, talkative
   c. Resourceful, adventurous, pleasure-seeking, loud
   d. Charming, individualistic, modest, rational

9. Which of the following statements describes a child who has developed gender constancy?
   a. A girl chooses a Spiderman costume for Halloween, ignoring her mother's continued objections to her portrayal of the male character.
   b. A boy tells his dad that he's not sure yet whether he wants to be a daddy or a mommy when he grows up.
   c. A girl recognizes her best male friend on the first day of Kindergarten, and notices that he has let his hair grow so long over the summer that he is wearing it in a ponytail.
   d. A boy calls his daddy "mommy" whenever the father puts on his apron and cooks dinner for the family, but never calls his mommy by another name, no matter what kind of household labor she is doing.

10. Anthropologists propose that cultural differences in gender roles reflect:
    a. Patriarchal attitudes toward masculine and feminine behaviors.
    b. Cultural adaptations to social and natural environments.
    c. Biological imprinting in the chromosomes of females and males.
    d. Survival strategies inherited through the process of natural selection.

11. Because they are considered the "gatekeepers" for sexual activities, which of the following are women expected to do?
    a. Allow men to make the first and all subsequent sexual moves
    b. Be as sexually "ready" as men at all times
    c. Guide men through sexual encounters with helpful instructions
    d. Insist on the female-superior sexual position the majority of the time

12. People who have personality traits with a lot of assertiveness, instrumental skills, cooperation, and nurturance, could be best described as:
    a. Sexually macho.
    b. Emotionally femme.
    c. Psychologically androgynous.
    d. Anatomically dissonant.

13. Which of the following is NOT seen as an important influence on gender socialization?
    a. Schools
    b. Popular culture
    c. Parental behavior
    d. I.Q.

14. At approximately what age are children most likely to begin acting rigid about their gender roles and discourage others who do not stay within the boundaries of their "scripts"?
    a. 6 months old
    b. 13 years old
    c. 3 years old
    d. 18 years old

15. Some feminist scholars dislike the notion of psychological androgyny because:
    a. Men should not be allowed the privilege of taking on feminine traits; they have enough privileges already.
    b. The way it is defined perpetuates belief in masculine and feminine gender roles.
    c. Feminine traits are the best traits for women to have already.
    d. Both A and C are true.
    e. None of the above is true.

True/False

Gender typing is the process by which males and females develop distinct reproductive anatomy.

_____ 1. Gender typing is the process by which males and females develop distinct reproductive anatomy.

_____ 2. During the first six weeks or so of prenatal development, the sexual structures of both male and female fetuses resemble primitive female structures.

_____ 3. Small amounts of androgens are produced in female fetuses.

_____ 4. Boys with Dominican Republic syndrome have an XY genetic code but lower-than-normal prenatal sensitivity to androgens.

_____ 5. Current statistics say that more than 50,000 transsexuals in the US are known to have undergone sex-reassignment surgery.

_____ 6. Sexism is the preference for associating socially only with people of one's own gender.

_____ 7. Females adhering to masculine gender role stereotypes are less likely to engage in unprotected sex than are men adhering to masculine gender role stereotypes.

_____ 8. Freudian theory argues that gender typing is connected with one's experiences during potty training

Essay Questions

1. Compare the definitions of intersexualism and hermaphroditism and discuss their implications for gender identity.

_____

_____

_____

_____

_____

_____

_____

_____

2. Discuss how, if at all, each of the following psychological perspectives on gender typing seems to take into account the influence of human agency (the ability of a person to play an active role in his or her development):
   a. Psychodynamic theory
   b. Social learning theory
   c. Cognitive developmental theory
   d. Gender schema theory

_____

_____

_____

_____

_____

_____

_____

_____

_____

_____

When You Have Finished...

What Does the World Think?

Rev up your search engines and see where the Web takes you as you explore the following activities related to Gender Identity, Gender Roles, and Sex Differences!

1. Google "transsexual" and, as access and personal comfort permits, check out some of the links and consider the issues below:
   a. What kind of links came up? Which kind was predominant? For example, were they support sites, porn sites, etc.?
   b. Be sure to look over at least one site offering support and information. How did the information compare with your text in terms of being up-to-date and accurate?
   c. If you hadn't read your text, how prevalent would you think transsexualism was based on the number of "hits" your search produced?
   d. How do you think the Internet may be influencing the lives of transsexual people and their loved ones?

2. By now, most of us have heard of the book, *Men are from Mars, Women are from Venus,* by John Gray. Visit his official website, http://www.marsvenus.com, and check out the offerings. How do you feel about it in light of what you've learned in this chapter? Be sure to notice the advertisement and links. What kind of messages do they send about the intent of the author and the kind of audience they think they're serving?

3. Visit the website for SIECUS, the Sexuality Information and Education Council of the United States, at http://www.siecus.org. Browse what they have to offer, and be sure to visit the links "for parents and other adults" and "for teens." What do you think of their offerings? Would you have found them useful as a teen? Can you imagine how you would have felt if your parents had used the resources there? Can you imagine whether you would find the information useful if you had children of your own? Think through the "why's" of your answers.

4. Google "Berlin 800M World Track and Field Championships" and read about the results from the race. How is it being talked about in popular media and within the track community? Should we genetically test our female athletes to make sure they have two X chromosomes?

5. Check out the local chapter of the Gay, Lesbian, Transgender and Bisexual Center in your town. For a list of sites in your area go to: "http://resources.lgbtcenters.org/Directory/Find-A-Center.aspx" and click on your area. You can search for help with gender issues and see what resources there are for people in your area. Check around the United States to see where there are centers and were resources are either scarce or plentiful.

Chapter 7
Attraction and Love—Binding Forces

Before You Begin...

Chapter Summary

Attraction and love—these are very popular topics when one listens to music, watches television, or sees a movie! Undoubtedly by this point in your life, we are sure you have heard much advice on relationships—including how to find Mr./Ms. Right and how to keep the love alive. We've got news for you: some of the popular notions are not quite right or are even flat out wrong. This chapter explores interpersonal attraction and the various types of love along with how they combine. Standards of beauty, both by Western standards and cross-culturally, are discussed including how sexual orientation relates to such standards. Now let's get going!

Interpersonal attraction is determined by a number of subjective factors. Physical attractiveness plays a filtering role in mate selection, and most cultures are fairly consistent in how they measure attractiveness in facial features. In mainstream American culture, women place relatively greater emphasis on traits like status and earning potential, whereas men give relatively more consideration to physical attractiveness. Numerous research studies on the determinants of interpersonal attraction are presented, with particular attention to several aspects of physical appearance. Some evolutionary psychologists believe that evolutionary forces favor the continuation of such gender differences in preferred traits because these traits provide reproductive advantages. The theory that attractiveness preferences may be inherited is examined and weighed against arguments that cultural context, instead, may explain most of the consistency in preferences.

According to the matching hypothesis, people tend to develop romantic relationships with people who are similar to themselves in physical appeal, including race and ethnicity, level of education, and age. Compatibility in attitudes and views is a strong contributor to attraction, friendships, and love relationships. Reciprocity, the exchange of positive words and actions, strongly enhances mutual attractiveness.

Romantic love is idealized in contemporary Western culture, and although romantic love is found across many cultures, the concept of love must be placed in cultural context to be understood properly. With the aid of computerized brain imaging, romantic love is really starting to be explained. During the classical age, Greeks distinguished four concepts related to the modern meanings of love: storge, agape, philia and eros. A vast majority of people in the United States see romantic love, instead of loving attachment or physical arousal, as prerequisite for marriage. Western society continues to maintain double standards with regard to sexuality and gender. Early in a relationship, infatuation and more enduring forms of romantic love may be indistinguishable. However, infatuation is not a mandatory first step towards developing long-term, deep feelings of love. All four of these types of love are further explained by your text authors.

Berscheid and Hatfield define romantic love in terms of intense physiological arousal and cognitive appraisal of that arousal as love, based on the perception of several simultaneous events. Hendrick and Hendrick suggest that there are six styles of love, as indicated among the college students in their research: romantic love, game-playing love, friendship, logical love, possessive love, and selfless love. In contrast, Sternberg suggests that there are three distinct components of love: intimacy, passion, and decision/commitment. Differing levels of these components and their presence or absence determine the kind of love that exists between people. These dimensions can be conceptualized in terms of a triangular representation indicating the strength of each component in the shape the triangle. In this framework, balanced, consummate love is represented by an equilateral triangle, and several other types of love are represented by varying triangular models.

Learning Objectives

1. Summarize the research on the role of physical appearance in attraction—including what aspects are universal cross-culturally. Recognize the typical waist-to-hip ratio preferred by both heterosexual males and females as well as lesbians. Identify the role of more masculine male voices in attractiveness. Understand how different female names influence attractiveness.

2. Identify the characteristics men and women look for in a potential partner for a long-term relationship. Know how such factors as vocational status, earning potential, kindness, dependability, cooking ability, and expressiveness fit.

3. Discuss evolutionary and social psychology's views of the different characteristics men and women desire in their mates.

4. Analyze how the attraction-similarity hypothesis accounts for partner choice. Said differently, do opposites really attract or do more similar people attract one another and why.

5. Describe the influence of compatible attitudes on attraction and on relationships.

6. Define reciprocity and describe its effect on attraction and on maintaining relationships.

7. Discuss the four Greek concepts of love: storge, agape, philia, and eros.

8. Identify the characteristics of and male-female differences in romantic love.

9. Understand infatuation and its role in romantic relationships. Describe physical manifestations of it and how necessary it is in sustaining fulfilling relationships.

10. Discuss contemporary models of love and the associated explanations of the origins of love. This includes the biological model, love as an appraisal of arousal (including its styles), and Sternberg's triangular theory.

Term Identification

You know the drill; these are the terms you need to learn to do well on your professor's examination. And again, making flashcards as you go will help you associate the terms with their meanings. Be sure to note the pronunciation of the Greek terms since three of those terms do not follow a usual pronunciation.

Chapter 7 Key Terms	
Agape	Intimacy
Anorexia nervosa	Passion
Attraction–similarity hypothesis	Philia
Commitment	Propinquity
Eros	Reciprocity
Infatuation	Storge

As You Read...

Activities

Vocabulary Matching

Directions: Match each key vocabulary term listed in the left-hand column with the correct definition in the right-hand column.

a.   anorexia nervosa

_____ The kind of love that is closest in meaning to the modern-day concept of passion.

b.   matching hypothesis

_____ A state of intense absorption in or focus on another person, which is usually accompanied by sexual desire, elation, and general physiological arousal or excitement; passion.

c.   reciprocity

_____ The concept that people tend to develop romantic relationships with people who are similar to themselves in attractiveness.

d.   *storge*

_____ A kind of love characterized by feelings of passion and intimacy.

e.   *agape*

_____ Loving attachment and nonsexual affection; the type of emotion that binds parents to children.

f.   *philia*

_____ A potentially life-threatening eating disorder characterized by refusal to maintain a healthful body weight, intense fear of being overweight, a distorted body image, and, in females, lack of menstruation (amenorrhea).

g.   *eros*

_____ Selfless love; a kind of loving that is similar to generosity and charity.

h.   infatuation

_____ Mutual exchange.

i.   romantic love

_____ Friendship love, which is based on liking and respect rather than sexual desire.

❖

❖ Attraction: The Force That Binds?

For each of the following factors that enter into personal attraction, list between 1 and 3 of the ways the text says they influence interpersonal attraction.

Factor	Influence(s)
Overall physical appeal	
Height	
Body shape	
Facial features	
Mood	
Name	
Psychological characteristics	
Social qualities	
Race and/or Ethnicity	
Income potential	

Factor	Influence(s)
Age and health	

TRY PRACTICE TEST #1 NOW!
GOOD LUCK!

❖ *The Matching Hypothesis: Who Is "Right" for You?*

The matching hypothesis says that people tend to enter romantic relationships with people similar to themselves in terms of physical attractiveness. Your book's authors also explained some of the different qualities that "matching" applies to. Please list five of these qualities and give a brief example of how each might work. *Note that these qualities should include examples related to attitudes and reciprocity as well.*

Extremely Unreal Example:

Quality: Shoes

How it might work: Women prefer men who compulsively buy shoes at roughly the same rate as they do.

Quality: _____

How it might work: _____

_____

Quality: _____

How it might work: _____

_____

Quality: _____

How it might work: _____

_____

Quality: _____

How it might work: _____

_____

Quality: _____

How it might work: _____

_____

TRY PRACTICE TEST #2 NOW!
GOOD LUCK!

❖ *Love: "The Morning and the Evening Star?"*

➢ *The Greek Heritage*

For each of the following examples of loving relationships, please note the type(s) of love it describes according to the Greek model of love stages. Be sure to include your rationale. Take care to think through the scenarios carefully—like in real life, some of these situations can represent more than one kind of relationship at once.

1. *Although she had secretly had a crush on him for over a year—since they entered high school together—Alyson would never have let Eric know it because they had been inseparable friends since the first day of kindergarten.*

_____
_____
_____
_____
_____

2. *The first thing Mr. & Mrs. Jackson did after they won the lottery was to establish a foundation dedicated to supporting programs working to prevent domestic violence. They had always felt strongly that it was important to "give back" to the community whenever possible, and now they could put their money where their hearts were.*

_____
_____
_____
_____
_____

3. *As soon as George saw her across the dance floor, he knew he had to overcome his shyness and ask her to dance. By the time the party was over, he and Jennifer had both begun to wonder whether they were wrong about "love at first sight" being a myth.*

_____
_____
_____
_____
_____

4. *On the first Saturday of every month, the whole family made the two-hour drive to their grandparents' house to make sure they had everything they needed and visit with them for the day. Sometimes it was hard to make the time, but they felt it was the right thing to do for someone so important in their lives.*

_____
_____
_____
_____
_____

5. *"Please???" she begged on the phone, "I know you're tired but I'm SOOO bored and I've got to get out of the house. You know we always have fun once we get going, just come on and rescue me, NOW!" Stephanie giggled on the other side of the conversation. "Oh all right, stop begging, it's undignified. I'll be there in 10 minutes. Check the movie listings so we won't lose any time—it's almost time for the first show and I'm too tired to wait for the second one." As she hung up the phone, Mae thought how lucky she was to have a friend who didn't mind being spontaneous when she really felt lonely and needed a change of scenery.*

_____
_____
_____
_____
_____

> *Romantic Love in Contemporary Western Culture*

As this chapter reminds us, there are many sources that influence our expectations about romantic love in relationships, from family patterns to fairy tales. Look back on your childhood and adolescence. Do you remember stories or events that fueled your thoughts about the nature of romantic love? Use the space below to recount at least one example and be sure to explain whether the resulting belief fit into societal norms using information from the book to support your rationale.

Example Most older Disney Princess Movies.:

Let's go back to almost any classic Disney movie where there is a princess involved. It is the same old story: girl is tormented by (fill in evil force here) until a knight in shining armor rides in and saves the girl showing her what true love is with a kiss. The princesses are all beautiful and the princes are all handsome. This is the perfect example of romantic love, where passion rules (Snow White, Cinderella and Sleeping Beauty), but at the same time, there is a compassionate love where the prince develops strong feelings for the protection of the princess (Beauty and the Beast).

_____

_____

_____

_____

_____

_____

_____

_____

_____

_____

_____

_____

_____

_____

_____

➢ *Contemporary Models of Love: Dare Science Intrude?*

Your text details three modern theorized models of love. Complete the chart below by summarizing each model in the left-hand column and listing the components of each model in the right-hand column.

Theorists	Components
Berscheid and Hatfield	Three simultaneous events 1. 2. 3.
C. and S. Hendrick	Six styles of love 1. 2. 3. 4. 5. 6.

Theorists	Components
Sternberg (Triangular theory of love)	Three components of love 1. 2. 3. Eight types of love 1. 2. 3. 4. 5. 6. 7. 8.

TRY PRACTICE TEST #3 NOW!
GOOD LUCK!

After You Read...

(LO = Learning Objective)

1. Roger examines his physique in the mirror. If he is typical of college men, he will conclude that:
    a. He is flabbier than the ideal man.
    b. He could stand to lose a little weight to be more appealing to women.
    c. His height is related to his feelings of attractiveness.
    d. He is more muscular than what most females find appealing.
        p. 198   LO 1

2. Which of the following (if any) are NOT mentioned in your book as physical attributes considered beautiful among women in certain cultures?
    a. Shortness
    b. Elongated labia majora
    c. Slenderness
    d. Hourglass figures
        p. 200   LO 1

3. In one of the studies your text discusses, women who identified their sexual orientation as lesbian or bisexual rated attractiveness of various female body shapes. Which of the following, if any, were among the findings of this research?
    a. They found women with hourglass figures (0.7 waist-to-hip body ratio) to be most sexually attractive.
    b. Their first preference was for heavy women with hourglass figures and small breasts.
    c. They rated women with long hair as somewhat sexually attractive, regardless of body shape.
    d. A and C, but not B
    e. A and B, but not C
        p. 200, 202   LO 1

4. According to a study that showed men and women a continuum of female figures that differed only in bust size, men preferred:
    a. Larger breasted women than those the women preferred.
    b. Smaller breasted women than those the women preferred.
    c. Women with small breasts, but larger than those the women *believed* they would prefer.
    d. Women with large breasts, but not as large as those the women *believed* they would prefer.
        p. 202   LO 1

5. In a meaningful relationship, _____ was rated as the most valued characteristic by college students.
    a. caring
    b. honesty
    c. tenderness
    d. personality
            p. 202   LO 2

6. Across cultures, the two features more highly valued by men in prospective mates are
    a. Physical attractiveness and fidelity.
    b. Domestic skills and reputation.
    c. Sexual interest and relative youthfulness.
    d. Physical attractiveness and relative youthfulness.
            p. 203   LO 2

7. The researcher who found that women prefer relatively older male mates interpreted this finding to mean that:
    a. Most women have unresolved Electra complexes that draw them to "father figures."
    b. Older men's psychological androgyny tends to make them better long-term partners.
    c. Women are looking for good providers, and age and income are linked in men.
    d. Younger men are less interested in starting a family or procreation.
            p. 203   LO 2

8. If you believe that clear eyes, a good complexion, firm muscle tone, and a younger age in your choice of a sexual partner are inherited preferences, then you are in agreement with:
    a. The love theorists.
    b. The evolutionary view.
    c. Cognitive-developmental theorists.
    d. Cross-cultural researchers.
            p. 204   LO 3

9. Couples in romantic relationships tend to be similar in physical attractiveness. This supports:
    a. The coupling hypothesis.
    b. The concept of gender matching.
    c. The attraction-similarity hypothesis.
    d. The sociocultural hypothesis.
            p. 204   LO 4

10. Of the following factors, which is best used to determine partner selection?
    a. Physical sameness
    b. Propinquity
    c. Genetic selection
    d. Chemical attraction
            p. 206   LO 4

(LO = Learning Objective)

1. Which of the following descriptors, if any, tend to apply to the matching theory?
    a. Ethnicity and age
    b. Level of education and religion
    c. Athleticism and adventurousness
    d. A and B, but not C
    e. A and C, but not B
                    p. 205   LO 4

2. People tend to choose as mates those whose backgrounds are similar to their own because:
    a. They resemble each other physically.
    b. Few people venture beyond their locales of origin.
    c. Similar backgrounds lead to similar attitudes.
    d. It is easier to be honest with someone of a similar background.
                    p. 206   LO 5

3. We tend to assume that people we find attractive share our:
    a. Attraction.
    b. Attitudes.
    c. Socioeconomic status.
    d. Educational level.
                    p. 207   LO 5

4. Though similarity can be important in determining initial attraction, _____ seems to be a stronger predictor of maintaining an intimate relationship.
    a. differences in interests
    b. social network strength
    c. compatibility
    d. ability to express anger
                    p. 206   LO 5

5. Reciprocity is:
    a. Mutual exchange of positive feelings between two people.
    b. Defined as our tendency to be attracted to people who are similar to us in physical attractiveness.
    c. A potent determinant of attraction.
    d. Both A and C
    e. Both B and C
                    p. 206   LO 6

6. Who places a greater emphasis on attitude similarity as a determinant of attraction to a stranger?
    a. Women
    b. Men
    c. Homosexuals
    d. Both A and C
    e. Both A and B
          p. 206   LO 6

7. Some research says that when we believe strangers like us, we are much more likely to:
    a. Think they are intelligent.
    b. Be vulnerable to stranger assault.
    c. Be warm and helpful.
    d. Give them false compliments.
          p. 208   LO 6

8. Although she makes only a moderate salary as an elementary school teacher, Carol donates 10% of her salary to the "Save the Children Foundation." Her love for children is best described as:
    a. Storge.
    b. Agape.
    c. Philia.
    d. Eros.
          p. 207   LO 7

9. Kay and Sharon talk on the phone almost every day. They often attend functions together and can depend on one another during times of crisis. They like and respect one another. This relationship reflects the Greek concept of:
    a. Eros.
    b. Storge.
    c. Philia.
    d. Agape.
          p. 207   LO 7

10. Which of the four Greek concepts of love seem to be the most difficult to differentiate from one another, and why?
    a. Storge and Agape, because they are both selfless in nature
    b. Eros and Philia, because they both indicate passionate love of some type
    c. Philia and Storge, because they are both bonds that can be experienced in loving friendships
    d. Both B and C
    e. Both A and C
          p. 207   LO 7

(LO = Learning Objective)

1. Labeling our attraction to another as "love" rather than "lust" allows us to:
   a. Discuss our romantic relationships even at the family dinner table.
   b. Ennoble attraction and sexual arousal to both ourselves and society.
   c. Be viewed as less primitive or animalistic.
   d. All of the above.
   e. None of the above.
   p. 209   LO 8

2. Western society is still maintaining many aspects of the double standard toward sexuality. Based on this, which of the following, if any, are assumptions about gender and sexuality discussed in your book?
   a. Women are more sexually assertive than men.
   b. Men are more likely to believe in love at first sight than women.
   c. Women are less likely to think that love is a "mushy" concept.
   d. Men are less likely to feel the need to attribute sexual urges to love.
   p. 209   LO 8

3. According to the text, for the first month or two of a romantic relationship, _____ and the more enduring forms of romantic love are difficult to tell apart from one another.
   a. philia
   b. infatuation
   c. love illusions
   d. pragmatism
   p. 210   LO 8

4. All of the following attributes about infatuation are true EXCEPT:
   a. Infatuation is a necessary first step towards a mutual lasting love.
   b. Even as time passes, a "positive illusion" effect still remains visible.
   c. At first, one may find it difficult to determine the difference between infatuation and romantic love.
   d. During the first month or two of a relationship, signs that distinguish it from romantic love appear.
   e. All of the above are true.
   p. 210   LO 9

5. Infatuation manifests in the following way(s) EXCEPT:
   a. Strong sexual desire
   b. Intense focus or absorption
   c. Idealization of one's partner
   d. Ensuring an enduring romantic love once it fades
   e. All of the above are true
   p. 210   LO 9

6. Kim can hardly wait to see Jason, whom she met while riding in a helicopter over a live volcano. It is possible that the degree of attraction she feels is due to:
    a. Her physiological arousal from the exciting helicopter ride.
    b. The emotional state induced by her hormonal levels.
    c. Her cognitive appraisal of her physiological arousal.
    d. Both A and C
    e. Both B and C
                    p. 211   LO 10

7. According to the Berscheid and Walster model, the definition of romantic love is being in a state of intense _____ and the appraisal of that state of being as love.
    a. emotional reactivity
    b. physiological arousal
    c. cognitive ideation
    d. mental confusion
                    p. 211-212   LO 10

8. The Hendricks' Love Attitude Scale suggests that there are six styles of love. Which of the following are NOT among them?
    a. Romantic love (eros)
    b. Game playing love (ludus)
    c. Logical love (pragma)
    d. Co-dependent love (enablus)
    e. Possessive love (mania)
                    p. 212   LO 10

9. Considering the Hendricks' styles of love, which statement is true?
    a. After a relationship has become established, one dominant love style tends to appear, and it remains stable over time.
    b. The game-playing style eventually leads to the selfless love style.
    c. Relationships exhibiting both romantic and selfless love styles tend endure.
    d. Relationships exhibiting both romantic and logical love styles tend endure.
    e. None of the above are true.
                    p. 212   LO 10

10. According to the Sternberg Triangular Theory of Love, which of the following kinds of love is best conceptualized by an equilateral triangle?
    a. Romantic love
    b. Passionate love
    c. Companionate love
    d. Consummate love
                    p. 213   LO 10

Multiple Choice

1. The Hendricks' Love Attitude Scale suggests that there are 6 styles of love. Which of the following are NOT among them?
    a. Romantic love (eros)
    b. Game playing love (ludus)
    c. Logical love (pragma)
    d. Co-dependent love (enablus)
    e. Possessive love (mania)

2. Roger examines his physique in the mirror. If he is typical of college men, he will conclude that:
    a. He is flabbier than the ideal man.
    b. He could stand to lose a little weight to be more appealing to women.
    c. His height is related to his feelings of attractiveness.
    d. He is more muscular than what most females find appealing.

3. Across cultures, the two features more highly valued by men in prospective mates are:
    a. Physical attractiveness and fidelity.
    b. Domestic skills and reputation.
    c. Sexual interest and relative youthfulness.
    d. Physical attractiveness and relative youthfulness.

4. If you believe that clear eyes, a good complexion, firm muscle tone and a younger age in our choice of a sexual partner are inherited preferences, then you are in agreement with:
    a. The love theorists.
    b. The evolutionary view.
    c. Cognitive-developmental theorists.
    d. Cross-cultural researchers.

5. Kay and Sharon talk on the phone almost every day. They often attend functions together and can depend on one another during times of crises. They like and respect one another. This relationship reflects the Greek concept of:
    a. Eros.
    b. Storge.
    c. Philia.
    d. Agape.

6. Couples in romantic relationships tend to be similar in physical attractiveness. This supports:
    a. The coupling hypothesis.
    b. The concept of gender matching.
    c. The attraction-similarity hypothesis.
    d. The sociocultural hypothesis.

7. The central motive for seeking "matching" partners in romantic relationships appears to be:
    a. Fear of exploitation by less appealing people.
    b. Fear of rejection by more appealing people.
    c. Fear of exploitation by more appealing people.
    d. Fear of rejection by less appealing people.

8. Reciprocity is:
    a. Mutual exchange of positive feelings between two people.
    b. Defined as our tendency to be attracted to people who are similar to us in physical attractiveness.
    c. A potent determinant of attraction.
    d. Both A and C
    e. Both B and C

9. Although she makes only a moderate salary as an elementary school teacher, Carol donates 10% of her salary to the "Save the Children Foundation." Her love for children is best described as:
    a. Storge.
    b. Agape.
    c. Philia.
    d. Eros.

10. Though similarity can be important in determining initial attraction, _____ seems to be a stronger predictor of *maintaining* an intimate relationship.
    a. differences in interests
    b. social network strength
    c. compatibility
    d. ability to express anger

11. According to the text, for the first month or two of a romantic relationship, _____ and the more enduring forms of romantic love are difficult to tell apart from one another.
    a. philia
    b. infatuation
    c. love illusions
    d. pragmatism

12. Kim can hardly wait to see Jason, whom she met while riding in a helicopter over a live volcano. It is possible that the degree of attraction she feels is due to:
    a. Her physiological arousal from the exciting helicopter ride.
    b. The emotional state induced by her hormonal levels.
    c. Her cognitive appraisal of her physiological arousal.
    d. Both A and C
    e. Both B and C

13. In one of the studies your text discusses, women who identified their sexual orientation as lesbian or bisexual rated attractiveness of various female body shapes. Which of the following, if any, were among the findings of this research?
    a. They found women with hourglass figures (0.7 waist-to-hip body ratio) to be most sexually attractive.
    b. Their first preference was for heavy women with hourglass figures and small breasts.
    c. They rated women with long hair as somewhat sexually attractive, regardless of body shape.
    d. A and C, but not B
    e. A and B, but not C

14. According to the Berscheid and Walster model, the definition of romantic love is being in a state of intense _____ and the appraisal of that state of being as love.
    a. emotional reactivity
    b. physiological arousal
    c. cognitive ideation
    d. mental confusion

15. Western society is still maintaining many aspects of the double standard toward sexuality. Based on this, which of the following, if any, are assumptions about gender and sexuality discussed in your book?
    a. Women are more sexually assertive than men.
    b. Men are more likely to believe in love at first sight than women.
    c. Women are less likely to think that love is a "mushy" concept.
    d. Men are less likely to feel the need to attribute sexual urges to love.

True/False

1. _____Research on physical attractiveness indicates that it is a minor determinant of interpersonal and sexual attraction.

2. _____In studies where people were shown several women who differed only in bust size, men consistently preferred the women with the largest possible busts.

3. _____Both men and women tend to be wrong about the physical preferences of the other sex.

4. _____According to research in your text, the single most desired quality that college students reported wanting in long-term relationships was honesty.

5. _____The attraction-similarity hypothesis applies only to physical appeal.

6. _____Romantic love is unique to Western European cultures.

7. _____The "Love Attitudes" Scale measures the degree to which people hold a romantic or realistic view of love.

8. _____College women are more likely than college men to develop "game-playing" and "romantic" love styles.

Essay Questions

1. Describe how research says college men and women feel about body shape, size, and attractiveness for themselves and their partners. Use this information to draw your own conclusions about potential pitfalls these feelings may give rise to for both self-esteem and interpersonal relationships. Support your answers with information from the text.

_____

_____

_____

_____

_____

_____

_____

_____

2. Compare and contrast the three contemporary models of love in your text. Include in your answer your opinion on which, if any, seems to capture the "reality" of love relationships best, including the rationale for your choice.

_____

_____

_____

_____

_____

_____

_____

_____

When You Have Finished...

What does the world think?

Rev up your search engines and see where the Web takes you as you explore the following activities related to Attraction & Love....

1. Clearly there is still a lot of information to be discovered before definitive statements can be made about the nature of attraction and love. See what else people are saying on the Web. For example, here's a PowerPoint lecture posted at the University of Utah and from a lecture on stress, arousal, attractiveness, and limerence (similar to infatuation as it is explained in this text): http://www.psych.utah.edu/classes/2006_fall/2800_001/lectures/9-19.pdf

2. Go to ted.com and search for Dr. Fisher and love. Watch and listen to what she has to say about romantic love and intimacy. It might surprise you what is going on in the brain when you fall in love!

3. Has this chapter got you thinking about what kind of people you find to be attractive? Search Google for "virtual attractiveness." You will find the "beauty check" site where they build attractive models using computers.

4. All this talk about attraction sets the stage nicely for a consideration of body image issues. You may have heard some of what is said about female body image issues, but see what the Web has to offer in terms of both information and support. While you're surfing, see what you can find about male body image too—it's a relatively new area of research, and long overdue. The links below will help you get started:

   Body image research summary—http://www.sirc.org/publik/mirror.html

   Self-acceptance that extends beyond physical appearance, and encourages empowerment for women and men who support healthy self-image in women (AND it's really fun & witty)— http://www.about-face.org/

   A collection of articles about various aspects of male and female body image, including more than just body size (e.g., image, ethnicity, weight, "good and bad hair," etc.) And again, it's actually fun, as you might notice from the name of the website—http://www.adiosbarbie.com/features/

5. Do you ever shop for clothes online? If so, you might be familiar with this next site, My Virtual Model, but let's use it in a new way. It's the virtual mannequin website (http://www.mvm.com) and it does exactly what it sounds like it would—after you select "women" or "men" on the home page. It asks a series of questions about your physical attributes and creates a virtual you, so that you can see what the clothes would look like on YOU, not the catalog models. Try out a few different sets of measurements and physical traits, and see how you feel about it. Is it hard to see yourself? Do you like what you see? What if you wanted to build your perfect mate? What would s/he have? Be sure

to take some time to search for discussion about this technology too, using "virtual mannequin" as a search term in dogpile.com or the search engine of your choice.

6. This chapter briefly mentions one kind of eating disorder, but it doesn't begin to cover the scope of the forms it can take or the diverse people whose lives are affected by this group of disorders. Below are some sites to get you started gaining a deeper understanding of eating disordered behavior its impact on body image, self-esteem, mental and physical well-being, and relationships:

The Renfrew Center Foundation (a nonprofit organization dedicated to advancing the education, prevention, research, and treatment of eating disorders)—http://www.renfrew.org/

Clinical aspects and treatment strategies related to body dysmorphic disorder, an illness characterized by distorted imagery of one's bodily appearance— http://www.biopsychiatry.com/bdd.html

Information specific to males and eating disorders— http://www.caringonline.com/eatdis/topics/males.htm

Chapter 8
Relationships and Communication

Before You Begin...

Chapter Summary

Romantic relationships—the source of excitement, challenges, growth, and even some grief in the life of an average person! In this chapter, we examine aspects of how romantic relationships start, continue, and end. We outline the principle of mutuality and a model that divides a relationship into a series of stages more than just start, end, or continue as just mentioned. How attraction and social-exchange theory fits into relationship-seeking behavior is keenly detailed. Additionally what intimacy is, and what it is not, is carefully explored in this chapter. How boredom and jealousy affect relationships is covered—along with what can and cannot be done to manage these two often unhelpful relationship "modifiers." Commonality among opposite-gender and same-gender couples is also explored in detail. Stalking behavior and behaviors strongly associated with it are explained. Too, relationship satisfaction information is shared across couple types (opposite-sex and same-sex).

Relationships undergo five stages of development, each with potential for positive or negative exchanges. These exchanges will predispose it to continue to the next stage or to end as a romance. The stages are given an easy-to-remember mnemonic (ABCDE) as proposed by Levinger:

- A for attraction
- B for building
- C for continuation

- D for deterioration
- E for ending

Your text authors explore the essence of each these five areas in greater detail—so please do not be fooled by thinking that the simple word association explains all that one needs to know! Let's jump to a simple summary though of some of those stages...

The attraction phase starts when two people become aware of one another and find one another enticing or appealing. Though, if details like good opening lines and effective small-talk are not mastered, a potential relationship will not get to the next stage. Also, if a proper progression of self-disclosure is not followed, this problem will thwart building a relationship too. Your authors do an excellent job in addressing all of these topics—so please eagerly read more about it!

Building a relationship is strongly contingent upon one recognizing similarities. Of course, the focus on similarities turns the popular adage of "opposites attract" into an old fable. Predictors motivating people to build relationships include:

- Similar levels of physical attractiveness
- Similarity in attitudes
- Mutual liking

While modern technology allows people to meet, "date," and establish an intimate relationship online, continuation rests upon several factors. These factors include items such as:

- Variety
- Caring
- Positive evaluations

- Lack of jealousy
- Perceived fairness in the relationship
- Mutual feelings of satisfaction

Deterioration of relationships and the factors that are associated with it—along with responses to it—are discussed. Factors include the failure to invest time and energy in the relationship, deciding to put an end to it, or simply permitting deterioration to proceed unchecked. Relationships tend to end when the partners find little satisfaction in the affiliation, alternative partners are available, couples are not committed to preserving the relationship, or they expect the relationship to falter.

Intimacy involves feelings of emotional closeness and connectedness with another person. It also includes the desire to share each other's innermost thoughts and feelings. In contrast to intimacy, loneliness is a state of painful isolation, of feeling cut off from others, and is most often noted in adolescence. The causes of loneliness are a function of attitudes and demeanors such as passivity, fear, cynicism, and pessimism. Suggestions for coping with loneliness are presented.

Factors leading to satisfaction in relationships are examined. Particular attention is given to communication skills, and Gottman's research with couples and communication patterns. Among his findings: deterioration in relationships is often preceded by defensiveness and avoidance in couples' communications, whereas satisfaction was often experienced by those who could remain open and calm while communicating during conflicts.

Conflict behaviors include male "stonewalling," a trait where there is little non-verbal acknowledgement of listening, and few verbal acknowledgments given to one's partner during a conflictual discussion. Stonewalling is noted as being particularly bad for relationships. Gottman's conclusions centered on the idea that it's not conflict that is bad for relationships, but *poor handling* of conflict that is difficult to overcome in relationships.

Along the line of communication, additional researchers have echoed the importance of developing effective communication skills and the ability to use them during conflict with a partner. This includes open and honest communication about sexual relations. Important skills related to this include both verbal and nonverbal forms, as well as mixtures thereof. Each can be misunderstood, which explains the need to work actively on improving communication in a relationship. When good communication skills are not enough to resolve an impasse, partners may need to take a break, agree to tolerate difference or agree to disagree on some issues.

Suggestions for enhancing communication, including empathy, patience, handling impasses, and active-listening skills—and these are eloquently discussed by your text authors in greater detail. Note though, particular attention is given to the importance of not expecting one's partner to be a mind-reader; to this end, there are ideas for communicating sexual desires and dislikes in a way that is least threatening to one's partner's ego.

Your authors also explore the differences and similarities between relationships where partners are gay, lesbian, bisexual, and heterosexual. In terms of satisfaction, it seems that whether the relationship is same-sex or opposite-sex there is scant difference. There are additional factors though weighing upon same-sex couples as noted in the textbook.

The text illuminates contrasting perspectives on jealousy, thus, nuances of it are carefully discussed. This includes its existence across cultures, the different types, gender differences, and some theories about the social function of jealousy. How it can be helpful or destructive is also clearly explained. How it applies amongst same-gender couples and among opposite-gender couples when the infidelity is with a person of the same gender.

Finally, the significance of stalking behavior (or unwanted pursuit) is outlined—along with some of the other behaviors that "cluster" with it as potential advance indicators. Minor jealousy is not associated with unwanted pursuit, but major jealousy is—along with physical violence and verbal abuse as noted by the authors.

Learning Objectives

1. Cite the five stages of development characteristic of romantic relationships.

2. Describe the process of building a relationship from initial conversation through mutual and increasing self-disclosure. Also, relate how social exchange theory fits along the continuum. Know the popular and most effective ways one meets a potential mate and how opening lines fit.

3. Identify the factors that generally lead to continuation of a relationship. Know about gender differences and commitment, and how commitment and trust contribute to mutual cyclical growth.

4. Explain the effects of jealousy in a relationship and identify characteristics of a jealous person. Identify what "unwanted pursuit" includes and some of the other behaviors during a relationship that are strongly associated with it.

5. Examine passive and active responses that will determine whether a deteriorating relationship ends or is renewed.

6. Summarize the causes of loneliness and suggest ways of coping with loneliness.

7. Identify the characteristics of intimate relationships and the skills necessary for building and maintaining an intimate relationship. Understand the differences in relationship satisfaction among heterosexuals, gay males, lesbians, bisexuals, and transgendered people.

8. Explain the importance of good communication, both verbal and nonverbal, in an intimate relationship.

9. Examine the irrational beliefs and fears about sexual communication that can cause difficulties in intimate relationships.

10. Give examples of ways to begin a conversation about your sexual relationship and examples of specific listening skills that will encourage the continuation of communication.

11. Identify the skills associated with giving and receiving information and requests in an intimate sexual relationship.

12. Explain the skills involved in giving and receiving criticism.

13. Give examples of how partners can handle disagreements that may not be resolved even with good communication skills.

Term Identification

You know the drill; these are the terms you need to learn, and making flashcards will help. Don't let this short list fool you; be sure you know enough about the function of the skills to which these words apply; this chapter is much more about application than it is about memorization.

Chapter 8 Table of Key Terms

ABCDE model	Small talk
Intimacy	Social-exchange theory
Mutual cyclical growth	Stalking
Mutuality	Surface contact
Self-disclosure	

As You Read...

❖ *The ABC(DE)'s of Romantic Relationships*

Directions: Supply the missing information to the following chart that refers to Levinger's ABCDE model of relationships. Use the filled-in areas as examples to help you complete the table.

STAGE	DESCRIPTION OF THE STAGE	BEHAVIORS OF THE PARTNERS
ATTRACTION		
BUILDING		Surface contact Small talk Gradually increasing Self-disclosure Attaining mutuality
CONTINUATION		
DETERIORATION	When one or more partners see the relationship as less rewarding than it has been.	
ENDING		

➢ *From (Not-So) Small Talk to Breaking Up Is (Often) Hard To Do: An Overview*

Directions: Each of the following short answer questions refer to the various parts of the "relationship lifespan" discussed in your text. Using your text to support your rationale, answer the questions. In addition, take time to reflect on your own experiences and those of others close to you in relationships. Form an opinion as to the importance of the issues and rank them accordingly from 1 to 5, with 1 being the "most important" and 5 being the "least important" relationship skill. Use the text to support your choices (or to acknowledge that they are in disagreement with the text, as needed).

❏ Describe the role of small talk in building a relationship.

ANSWER:

IMPORTANCE OF SKILL—RANKING:

REASON FOR RANKING:

❏ What factors lead to the building of a relationship?

ANSWER:

IMPORTANCE OF SKILL—RANKING:

REASON FOR RANKING:

❏ How are "early self-disclosers" viewed?

ANSWER:

IMPORTANCE OF SKILL—RANKING:

REASON FOR RANKING:

❏ How does jealousy affect a relationship?

ANSWER:

IMPORTANCE OF SKILL—RANKING: ☐

REASON FOR RANKING:

❏ What factors contribute to the deterioration of a relationship?

ANSWER:

IMPORTANCE OF SKILL—RANKING: ☐

REASON FOR RANKING:

TRY PRACTICE TEST #1 NOW!
GOOD LUCK!

❖ *Loneliness: "All the Lonely People, Where Do They All Come From?"*

Before we work on learning the causes of loneliness and ways to cope with it, it's worth taking a moment to reflect on what loneliness means to you. Loneliness can be very subjective. To paraphrase a famous quotation, one person's loneliness is another person's welcome solitude. As we cope with our busy lives in this first decade of the new millennium, there appear to be just as many people having trouble overcoming loneliness as there are people trying to find some time alone. Using the information in your text about loneliness and solitude to support your answers, fill in some items below to compare and contrast "being lonely" with "being alone."

Being Lonely	Being Alone

➤ *Causes of Loneliness & Coping With Them*

Your text does a wonderful job of detailing some of the causes of loneliness and some tools people can use to cope with and manage them. It is important to practice your critical thinking skills about this issue, because being lonely can have so many negative consequences, and, as we know, there is book knowledge and then there is the real world. Using the space below, list six of the nine causes of loneliness discussed in your book; use your "book knowledge" to describe a way to cope with each one, and your "real world" sense to give an example of how this might work.

Extremely Unreal Example:

Cause of Loneliness: Playing too many computer games.

Coping Strategy: Finding a way to make this a social activity instead of a solitary one.

Real World Example: Throw away that "Casino Poker" CD and get thee to Las Vegas!

1. *Cause of Loneliness:*

    Coping Strategy:

    Real World Example:

2. *Cause of Loneliness:*

    Coping Strategy:

    Real World Example:

3. *Cause of Loneliness:*

   Coping Strategy:

   Real World Example:
4. *Cause of Loneliness:*

   Coping Strategy:

   Real World Example:

5. *Cause of Loneliness:*

   Coping Strategy:

   Real World Example:

6. *Cause of Loneliness:*

   Coping Strategy:

   Real World Example:

❖ *Satisfaction in Relationships: Communication as a Key*

➤ *Gottman's Research on Satisfaction in Relationships*

It is clear that there is a lot of *un*clear communication going on between couples! Your book gives you a lot of tools to use to understand and improve communication within relationships, and it also makes the important point that there is no one right or wrong way to handle things—relationships are all about FIT. Pretend that you are a therapist who specializes in relationship counseling. Below are three hypothetical descriptions of partners' communication styles/traits during conflicts with each other. For each hypothetical couple, use the information about communication styles and strategies in your text to describe at least one possible difficulty that may arise for them and at least one strategy they might use to deal with it. Finally, based on the communication issues, give your opinion as to whether the imaginary couple has a poor, fair, good, or excellent chance of having a healthy and sustained relationship. Support your opinion with information from the text.

HYPOTHETICAL COUPLE #1

Partner 1-A has a tendency to shut down during arguments; the more hostile things get, the quieter this partner becomes.	
Partner 1-B is more confrontational and does not back down, often saying increasingly mean things in an attempt to get a response from Partner 1-A.	
Possible Difficulty:	Possible Strategy:
Chances of continued relationship with mutual satisfaction (circle one): POOR FAIR GOOD EXCELLENT	
Rationale for opinion:	

HYPOTHETICAL COUPLE #2

Partner 2-A just wants everything to be agreeable; this includes saying anything to comply with Partner 2-B's needs, even if they are not the same as his/her own.	
Partner 2-B also dislikes conflict, and has a tendency to get quieter the worse the fight gets. When Partner 2-A offers options, s/he is almost unable to respond for fear of saying the "wrong" thing, because past experience says 2-A doesn't always mean what s/he says during an argument.	
Possible Difficulty:	Possible Strategy:

Chances of continued relationship with mutual satisfaction (circle one):

POOR   FAIR   GOOD   EXCELLENT

Rationale for opinion:

HYPOTHETICAL COUPLE #3

Partner 3-A is able to express needs during an argument, but only if things stay quiet enough; yelling unnerves this Partner.	
Partner 3-B has a hot temper but has worked at learning how to cool off, and tries hard to listen during arguments. This Partner is likely to escalate to yelling during about 2 out of 5 arguments.	
Possible Difficulty:	Possible Strategy:

Chances of continued relationship with mutual satisfaction (circle one):

POOR   FAIR   GOOD   EXCELLENT

Rationale for opinion:

TRY PRACTICE TEST #2 NOW!
GOOD LUCK!

➤ *Communication Skills for Enhancing Relationships and Sexual Relations: How To Do It*

For each of the situations below, describe an effective way that you might communicate to your sexual partner about the situation.

1. The pressure of your partner's touch on your erogenous zones is too soft to stimulate you the way you need to be stimulated to enjoy yourself and possibly achieve an orgasm with him/her. You haven't mentioned it so far for fear of making him/her feel inadequate.

2. You would like to be a bit more reciprocal about oral sex (so far, you do far more giving than you do receiving).

3. You and your partner are doing everything right together…. But just not often enough. How do you let him/her know that you are interested in more sexual intimacy with him/her?

4. You are *really* curious about trying something you read in an erotic novel but are not sure if your partner would be interested.

TRY PRACTICE TEST #3 NOW!
GOOD LUCK!

After You Read...

(LO = Learning Objective)

1. The ABCDE model describes the stages of romantic relationships. This acronym represents:
   a. Attraction, building, commitment, deterioration, and ending.
   b. Affiliation, building, continuation, determination, and ending.
   c. Attraction, building, continuation, deterioration, and ending.
   d. Affiliation, budding, continuation, deterioration, and ending.

   p. 223   LO 1

2. According to social-exchange theory, romantic relationships develop as a series of _____ that convince each partner to maintain or dissolve the romance.
   a. dates and outings
   b. financial disclosures
   c. rewards and costs
   d. attractions and sexual encounters

   p. 222-223   LO 1

3. What kind of mood heightens feelings of attraction, according to Levinger's research?
   a. Pensive
   b. Frightened
   c. Happy
   d. Sad

   p. 223   LO 1

4. According to studies of how couples meet and become attracted to each other, which of the following ways of meeting are most common for *unmarried* couples to meet, if any?
   a. Mutual friends
   b. Self-introductions
   c. Co-workers and friends' introductions
   d. Both A and C
   e. Both A and B

   p. 223   LO 1

5. The purpose of "small talk" in a relationship is to:
   a. Uncover personality flaws and weaknesses.
   b. Reveal the more intimate aspects of each other's lives.
   c. Allow each person to try the other out for the possibility of friendship.
   d. Begin the process of reciprocal self-disclosure of deep feelings.

   p. 224   LO 2

6. What usually comes *before* "small talk" when a person is interested in getting to know someone?
    a. Instant messaging for more than 5 minutes
    b. Establishing eye-contact
    c. Getting the person's phone number
    d. Looking to see if the person is wearing a wedding ring
        p. 224-225   LO 2

7. What does research suggest about self-disclosure during the building of a traditional (i.e., offline) romantic relationship?
    a. The more things you self-disclose, the faster you can build trust.
    b. The fewer things you self-disclose, the more secure your partner perceives you to be.
    c. The earlier the self-disclosure, the bigger the increase in emotional closeness.
    d. The later the self-disclosure, the bigger the increase in emotional closeness.
        p. 226   LO 2

8. As couples age _____ becomes more valued component of their relationship.
    a. intimacy
    b. commitment to each other
    c. sexual expression
    d. Both A and B are true.
    e. Both A and C are true.
        p. 228   LO 3

9. Michael has managed to arrange a truly creative way to celebrate Valentine's Day with his partner for each of the five years they have been together. According to your text, Michael is encouraging continuation of his relationship by:
    a. Spending money on important dates.
    b. Taking initiative when it comes to planning events.
    c. Seeking ways to maintain interest.
    d. Distracting his partner from his shortcomings by being strong in this area.
        p. 229   LO 3

10. According to Wortman and her colleagues, a person who shares intimate information early in a conversation is:
    a. Perceived as genuine and honest.
    b. Perceived as less mature, less secure, and less well adjusted.
    c. More likely to get dates.
    d. Perceived as bold, assertive, and independent.
        p. 226   LO 3

(LO = Learning Objective)

1. Extreme cases of jealousy are associated with:
    a. Commitment and devotion.
    b. Depression and violence.
    c. Companionate and consummate love.
    d. Sexual passion and romance.
        p. 230-231   LO 4

2. Negotiating differences in a relationship that is deteriorating is an example of a(n) _____ response while just waiting for something to happen is an example of a(n) ____ response:
    a. Active, passive.
    b. Passive, active.
    c. Effective, ineffective.
    d. Ineffective, effective.
        p. 233   LO 5

3. When a relationship is perceived to be "falling apart,":
    a. Go with the flow and see what happens.
    b. Practicing improved communication skills is an active response.
    c. Doing nothing is a passive response.
    d. Abandon the relationship because if you are perfectly matched no effort needs to be invested.
    e. Both B and C
        p. 234   LO 5

4. According to recent research discussed in your text, _____ seems to be somewhat the new norm when people meet in cyberspace.
    a. rapid sexual intimacy
    b. delayed sexual intimacy
    c. rapid self-disclosure
    d. delayed self-disclosure
        p. 226   LO 5

5. Loneliness is characterized by all the following EXCEPT:
    a. Cynicism about human nature.
    b. An internal locus of control.
    c. Little or no interest in the lives of other people.
    d. Lack of interpersonal social skills.
        p. 235-236   LO 6

6. _____ is when we feel emotional closeness and connectedness with another person, sharing our innermost thoughts and feelings.
    a. Mutuality
    b. Intimacy
    c. Companionship
    d. Commitment
              p. 227   LO 7

7. Although _____ is a core feature of intimacy, intimate relationships involve a balance in which some things are revealed and others are not.
    a. strength
    b. silence
    c. mutual diagnosis
    d. honesty
              p. 228   LO 7

8. In healthy relationships, couples who have a strong sense of togetherness:
    a. Have given up their individuality.
    b. Attempt to dominate each other's lives.
    c. Maintain individual interests, likes, and dislikes.
    d. Have mutually decided to do everything together.
              p. 230   LO 7

9. Which of the following did Gottman's research find to be predicted by "stonewalling" behavior?
    a. Reduced conflict after the relationship ends
    b. Increased conflict after the relationship ends
    c. Reduced loneliness after the relationship ends
    d. Increased loneliness after the relationship ends
              p. 239   LO 8

10. To communicate effectively about sexual matters, couples:
    a. Need to agree on their choices of language when talking about sex.
    b. Should share their experiences about previous sexual encounters.
    c. Need to agree that they can be verbally abusive if angry.
    d. Must decide who will dominate the conversation.
              p. 242-243   LO 9

(LO = Learning Objective)

1. If you tell your partner, "It was really hard to talk about, but I'm glad that you told me how you feel about oral sex," this statement:
    a. Reinforces your partner for communicating about sex.
    b. Illustrates how to deliver criticism in a timely manner.
    c. Shows your partner that you are upset.
    d. Is an example of active listening.
        p. 242-243   LO 10

2. Kayla is frustrated with Steven because even after a year of dating each other exclusively, he does not seem to realize that she doesn't like to be rushed into making love, despite her never having expressed this to him verbally. Kayla's emotional situation is an example of which common misconception discussed in your text?
    a. Men don't like foreplay.
    b. Women shouldn't talk about sex to their partners.
    c. People should know what their partners need without being told.
    d. Talking about sex is vulgar.
        p. 240   LO 10

3. Starting a discussion with your partner about sexual issues by saying, "I have something on my mind. Is now a good time for us to talk?" is an example of:
    a. A poor way to discuss a sensitive issue.
    b. Passive aggressive communication.
    c. A good way to approach a difficult topic.
    d. Both B and C
    e. Both A and C
        p. 241   LO 11

4. Which of the following would your text say is a reasonable way to suggest to your partner that some improvements to your sexual "routine" are in order?
    a. Buy a book about sex and leave it on the nightstand.
    b. Have a close friend bring it up with him/her.
    c. Write a love letter and give it to him/her during a special evening together.
    d. Suggest to him/her that it's ok to tell you ways that you can become a more effective lover.
        p. 241   LO 11

5. When delivering criticism to your partner:
   a. Use "you" statements to make your point clear.
   b. Speak your mind as soon as you can.
   c. Frame your displeasure in terms of your own feelings.
   d. It is not necessary to be too specific.
           p. 244   LO 12

6. Listening actively involves which of the following skills?
   a. Asking helpful questions
   b. Taking notes
   c. Focusing attention on the verbal and non-verbal messages
   d. Both A and B
   e. Both A and C
           p. 241-242   LO 12

7. Which of the following does your text suggest as an exercise for couples to express their sexual likes and dislikes?
   a. Watching an erotic movie and discussing it together.
   b. Body painting each other's erogenous zones.
   c. Making up a signal to use when they feel sexual pleasure.
   d. Both A & C
   e. Both B & C
           p. 243   LO 13

8. Gottman's recent research suggests that you are more likely to achieve desired results by:
   a. Reminding your partner to act lovingly.
   b. Framing requests in I-talk.
   c. Offering something in exchange.
   d. Asking for what you want in a public place to avoid conflict.
           p. 239   LO 13

9. When people have a more solid sense of who they are as individuals, they are more apt to _____ their partners.
   a. break up with
   b. want to marry
   c. expect and receive fidelity from
   d. tolerate differentness in
           p. 229   LO 13

10. Sometimes, when you and your partner reach a stalemate, it helps to:
    a. Put aside the issue to let it "incubate."
    b. Stay up until you agree about the issue.
    c. Keep your own point of view in mind when looking at the problem.
    d. Have partners take turns "winning" the point to keep power balanced.
            p. 246   LO 13

Multiple Choice

1. Michael has managed to arrange a truly creative way to celebrate Valentine's Day with his partner for each of the five years they have been together. According to your text, Michael is encouraging continuation of his relationship by:
   a. Spending money on important dates.
   b. Taking initiative when it comes to planning events.
   c. Seeking ways to maintain interest.
   d. Distracting his partner from his shortcomings by being strong in this area.

2. Levinger's ABCDE model describes the stages of romantic relationships. This acronym represents:
   a. Attraction, building, commitment, deterioration, and ending.
   b. Affiliation, building, continuation, determination, and ending.
   c. Attraction, building, continuation, deterioration, and ending.
   d. Affiliation, budding, continuation, deterioration, and ending.

3. When people have a more solid sense of who they are as individuals, they are more apt to _____ their partners.
   a. break up with
   b. want to marry
   c. expect and receive fidelity from
   d. tolerate differentness in

4. In healthy relationships, couples who have a strong sense of togetherness:
   a. Have given up their individuality.
   b. Attempt to dominate each other's lives.
   c. Maintain individual interests, likes, and dislikes.
   d. Have mutually decided to do everything together.

5. What does research suggest about self-disclosure during the building of a traditional (i.e., offline) romantic relationship?
   a. The more things you self-disclose, the faster you can build trust.
   b. The fewer things you self-disclose, the more secure your partner perceives you to be.
   c. The earlier the self-disclosure, the bigger the increase in emotional closeness.
   d. The later the self-disclosure, the bigger the increase in emotional closeness.

6. According to recent research discussed in your text, _____ seems to be somewhat the new norm when people meet in cyberspace.
   a. rapid sexual intimacy
   b. delayed sexual intimacy
   c. rapid self-disclosure
   d. delayed self-disclosure

7. Extreme cases of jealousy are associated with:
    a. Commitment and devotion.
    b. Depression and violence.
    c. Companionate and consummate love.
    d. Sexual passion and romance.

8. To communicate effectively about sexual matters, couples:
    a. Need to agree on their choices of language when talking about sex.
    b. Should share their experiences about previous sexual encounters.
    c. Need to agree that they can be verbally abusive if angry.
    d. Must decide who will dominate the conversation.

9. Loneliness is characterized by all the following EXCEPT:
    a. Cynicism about human nature.
    b. An internal locus of control.
    c. Demanding too much too soon in a relationship.
    d. Lack of interpersonal social skills.

10. A key predictor(s) of unwanted pursuit (stalking) from a breakup is/are:
    a. Physical violence during the relationship.
    b. Display of even minor jealousy during the relationship.
    c. Verbal abuse during the relationship.
    d. A and B are correct
    e. A and C are correct

11. Which of the following did Gottman's research find to be predicted by "stonewalling" behavior?
    a. Reduced conflict after the relationship ends
    b. Increased conflict after the relationship ends
    c. Reduced loneliness after the relationship ends
    d. Increased loneliness after the relationship ends

12. If you tell your partner, "It was really hard to talk about, but I'm glad that you told me how you feel about oral sex," this statement:
    a. Reinforces your partner for communicating about sex.
    b. Illustrates how to deliver criticism in a timely manner.
    c. Shows your partner that you are upset.
    d. Is an example of active listening.

13. Starting a discussion with your partner about sexual issues by saying, "I have something on my mind. Is now a good time for us to talk?" is an example of:
    a. A poor way to discuss a sensitive issue.
    b. Passive aggressive communication.
    c. A good way to approach a difficult topic.
    d. Both B and C
    e. Both A and C

14. When delivering criticism to your partner:
    a. Use "you" statements to make your point clear.
    b. Speak your mind as soon as you can.
    c. Frame your displeasure in terms of your own feelings.
    d. It is not necessary to be too specific.

15. When a relationship ends:
    a. Emotionally-secure individuals, unfortunately, are most likely to turn to alcohol or drugs for "support."
    b. Emotionally-insecure individuals are most likely to turn to friends for social support.
    c. Many individuals will engage in stalking and other unwanted pursuit activities.
    d. All of the above are correct responses to breaking up.
    e. None of the above is the correct response to breaking up.

True/False

_____ 1. A mutual "agreement to disagree" can be healthy for a couple.

_____ 2. A feminine-typed male is more likely to be empathic and listen to other people's trouble than is a masculine-typed female.

_____ 3. Liking and knowing yourself is an important step towards becoming intimate with others.

_____ 4. Gottman found that deterioration of satisfaction in married relationships could be predicted by physiological measures while resolving verbal conflicts.

_____ 5. Engaging in "small talk" is a legitimate way to determine whether there is common ground between people who are attracted to one another.

6. Loneliness tends to peak during old age.

_____ 7. People who are emotionally intimate with each other must be in love with each other.

_____ 8. Jealousy from sexual infidelity is less when it can be attributed externally (to alcohol or social pressure) versus when it is because of one's own internal choice.

Essay Questions

1. Using issues raised in your text, compare and contrast some of the things that can lead to the continuation of a relationship with some things that can lead to the deterioration of a relationship. Please discuss at least three situations/traits each for continuation and for deterioration.

   _____
   _____
   _____
   _____
   _____
   _____
   _____
   _____
   _____

2. Discuss some of the causes and coping strategies for loneliness described in your text. Argue which coping method you find most promising and explain your choice using information in the text to support it.

   _____
   _____
   _____
   _____
   _____
   _____
   _____
   _____
   _____

When You Have Finished…

What Does the World Think?

Rev up your search engines and see where the Web takes you as you explore the following activities related to Relationships & Communication.

1. If "small talk" is the bridge to new relationships, then social anxiety is definitely one of the gremlins underneath that bridge pulling it apart before you can cross it. We all get a little anxious from time to time, but some people's lives are deeply affected by their discomfort in social situations. There seem to be commercials for drugs to deal with it on the television every two minutes, but have you ever stopped to think about what social anxiety really means? Do a little searching (and screen yourself if you have any concerns!). Here is a good, definitive site to get you started: http://www.social-anxiety.org/

2. We're sure at one time or another that we've all joked about stalking or being stalked, but we all know it can have devastating consequences. Arm yourself emotionally so that you can troubleshoot this type of behavior before it happens in your own relationship! Peruse these websites and learn some of the basics:
Overview—http://www.antistalking.com/aboutstalkers.htm
What to do if a victim—http://www.antistalking.com/victim.htm
Stalking behavior—http://www.stalkingbehavior.com/
Cyberstalking—http://www.wired.com/politics/law/news/2000/05/35728

3. Google "help with unhealthy relationships -.com" and you will find what to do with a situation that has progressed beyond a bump in the dating scheme.

4. All this talk about preventing emotional crises, as important as it is, shouldn't keep you from having a little fun with these Web activities. We've mentioned before how much trouble you can get yourself into by taking *Cosmopolitan*-type quizzes with a partner. We'll leave it up to you whether you let them look at this with you! Here is variety of links to questionnaires about love and sex:

Relationship quizzes— http://www.rateyourself.com/subject.cfm/Subject_ID/1

Slightly more official-looking quizzes about jealousy and communication skills; different versions are available for men/women, straight/gay, etc.—
http://discoveryhealth.queendom.com/jealousy_men_abridged_access.html
http://discoveryhealth.queendom.com/communication_short_access.html

5. According to your text, it's pretty important to know how to self-disclose "properly" as you build a romantic relationship. With that in mind, here is some information that might help you work through your assumptions and issues without having to ask someone a question you'd be too embarrassed to ask (since it's assumed we all know this stuff "naturally"—as if that were possible!): http://mentalhelp.net/psyhelp/chap13/chap13i.htm

6. <u>So</u> it is time to go to YouTube and search "how to be a better lover." What kind of material are you finding? Is there anything about communication and romance, or is it just all about sex?

Chapter 9
Sexual Behavior and Fantasies

Before You Begin...

Chapter Summary

Cultural expectations, personal values, and individual experience, in addition to the physical capacity for stimulation and arousal, determine our sexual behavior and the arousal techniques we participate in. This chapter explores sexual techniques and behaviors people engage in alone and with others. Despite the many methodological controversies associated with them, the Kinsey and University of Chicago group's sex surveys have been the primary sources of information we have about prevalence of sexual techniques—and are still widely used today. Adding to that have been findings from the National Health and Social Life Survey (also called the "Sex Survey")—you will notice the common abbreviation for this survey is NHSLS. Findings from these studies are mentioned throughout the chapter as solitary and non-solitary sexual behaviors are discussed.

Masturbation may be practiced by means of manual stimulation of the genitals, or with the aid of a device that provides tactile stimulation. Until recent years, masturbation was considered by some to be physically and/or mentally harmful, but no scientific evidence supports these views. Historical views of this misconception are explained. The authors present some benefits to masturbation. Surveys indicate that most people have masturbated at some point in their lives. Common techniques by which men and women masturbate are described.

Sexual fantasies often accompany masturbation or sex with another person. Although one of the most common fantasies is sex with one's partner, many people fantasize about sexual activities in which they would not engage.

Foreplay is non-coital sexual behavior. The pattern and duration of foreplay varies widely within and across cultures. Women usually desire longer periods of foreplay than men do. Couples kiss for enjoyment or as a prelude to intercourse. Kissing may also be affectionate and without erotic significance. Touching or caressing erogenous zones can be highly arousing. Men typically prefer direct stroking of their genitals by their partners early in lovemaking. Women, however, tend to prefer that their partners caress their genitals after a period of general body contact. Most women enjoy manual and/or oral breast stimulation. Use of breast stimulation among gay males and lesbians is discussed. The prevalence of oral-genital stimulation has increased dramatically since Kinsey's day; sociocultural factors that appear to influence the tendency to engage in oral sex are discussed, as are techniques associated with oral-genital stimulation.

The four most commonly used penile-vaginal intercourse positions are the male-superior position, the female-superior position, the lateral-entry position and the rear-entry position. Each position is discussed by your text authors, including the advantages and disadvantages for each

Copyright © 2011 Pearson Education, Inc. All rights reserved.
201

technique. The male-superior position is the most commonly used but the female-superior position allows the woman greater freedom of movement and may also help the male control ejaculation. The practice and prevalence of anal sex is discussed in some detail, including the increased risk for injury and STIs (sexually transmitted infections). Anilingus is also explained.

Learning Objectives

1. Summarize historical-medical and religious views on masturbation.

2. Cite the incidence of masturbation and describe the techniques used by males and females.

3. Explain the function and prevalence of sexual fantasy in males and females and the role fantasy plays in arousal and masturbation.

4. Describe common foreplay techniques, such as kissing, and breast or genital stimulation.

5. Describe fellatio and cunnilingus techniques and state how widely they are practiced among specific populations.

6. Summarize findings on the incidence of oral sex and sexual permissiveness by education and race/ethnicity.

7. Cite reasons people give for abstaining from oral sex.

8. List the four basic intercourse positions and the advantages and disadvantages of each.

9. Describe the incidence and frequency of fantasy during coitus and the effects of fantasy on relationships.

10. Discuss who engages in anal intercourse, as well as the necessary precautions to take.

Term Identification

You know the drill; these are the terms you need to learn, and making flashcards will help.

Chapter 9 Table of Key Terms

Anilingus	Foreplay
Coitus interruptus	Impotence
Cunnilingus	Masturbation
Dildo	Missionary position
Fellatio	

As You Read...

❖ ***Solitary Sexual Behavior***

➢ *Masturbation*

Directions: Masturbation is one of the most commonly used and least-likely-to-be-openly-discussed sexual behaviors there is. In some religions it is thought of as immoral, deviant behavior and a major sin. So how can we learn more about it?

Think back to your childhood. What kind of information did you hear from your peers and influential others (family, school, etc.) about masturbation? In retrospect, was any of it accurate? Take a few moments to reflect on this issue and jot down some of the myths you heard. If you were lucky enough to avoid being tricked like the rest of us, jot down things you have heard others say, or some of the "classics," like "you'll go blind if you do it too much." Record at least three such pieces of information. Then, using your text, make arguments concerning the accuracy of each myth and replace each with something more realistic about masturbation that you might have found more useful and realistic to know instead.

Extremely Unreal Example:

Masturbation Myth
If a girl masturbates before puberty, she might "break herself" and never be able to have an orgasm later in life.

How valid was it?
Not at all. Not only is it natural for children to want to explore themselves by touching their genitals to see how it feels, research does not show any association between early self-touching and later frequency of orgasms among females.

What could I have been told instead?
It is ok to want to touch yourself and explore your body. Just remember that this is something to be done in private, and that you are the only one who should be doing it—do not let anyone else tell you they have the right to touch you there for pleasure.

Masturbation Myth #1

How valid was it?

What could I have been told instead?

Masturbation Myth #2

How valid was it?

What could I have been told instead?

Masturbation Myth #3

How valid was it?

What could I have been told instead?

➢ *Use of Fantasy*

The power of sexual fantasy should not be minimized. The ability to fantasize must be one of the main reasons that the brain is often referred to as the most important sexual organ any of us have. Again, since this happens inside your head AND is often not something you'd ever want anyone else to know under any circumstances, it can often be an area of self-doubt. We must reiterate something the authors of the text touch upon briefly. It is very important to examine your own fantasies and know what role they play in your life (including whether or not you would actually want them to happen in real life). The work of author Nancy Friday on this subject is extensive and fascinating. Your text quotes her when discussing whether there is a connection between sadistic fantasies and wanting to victimize someone sexually, but her work includes a great deal more than just this issue. We would encourage you to seek out at least one of her books if you are at all curious about this. One "classic" text she has authored is *My Secret Garden*.

With this in mind, and using your text to support your answers, respond to the following short essay questions about fantasy.

1. What is the relationship between sexual fantasies and acting out those fantasies?

2. Summarize the gender differences in fantasy themes.

TRY PRACTICE TEST #1 NOW!
GOOD LUCK!

❖ Sexual Behavior with Others

➤ *Foreplay— Kissing, Touching & Stimulation of the Breasts*

In the course of discussing various forms of foreplay and the cultural- and gender-related patterns associated with them, your text raises two issues that have important implications for our sexually intimate relationships. First, it mentions in passing that many heterosexual women report that are "reluctant" to mention to their male partners that having their breasts suckled hurts because they don't want to keep their male partners from having pleasure. Second, it makes a connection between the gender differences in preferences about foreplay and the tendency for men to be "more genitally oriented" than women, who "are more likely to view sex within a broader framework of affection and love." So what does this mean?

At a basic level, it means that there are likely to be complications when sexual partners attempt to communicate their needs to one another. They aren't just focusing on what makes them feel good— they are also focusing on the ways they might be willing to sacrifice their needs to make their partners feel good. They may also be focusing on what it means emotionally to be allowing themselves to be vulnerable in a sexually intimate way. (At least let's hope the latter is a consideration most of the time!) Let's use the information in this chapter and combine it with what we have already learned in the text about communication between partners. How can we apply what we know about communication to foreplay? Below are three scenarios that might occur between couples at one time or another. Respond to the questions following each scenario using information from your text to support your replies.

1. *Shannon and Christopher have been having sex for two months. They have known each other for two months and two days, and have had a whirlwind romance, spending most of their free time together since their first hook-up at an NCAA basketball playoff party on the main campus quad. Despite the amount of "face time" they have, they don't know each other too well. They have a strong physical attraction to one another and find it difficult to keep their hands off each other most of the time that they are together. Their sex life appears to be the most satisfying part of their relationship so far, and Shannon thinks that he might be "the one." One day, Shannon's friends are talking amongst themselves and one of them mentions that he overheard some of Chris's friends saying that although Chris likes Shannon, he hasn't really thought too much one way or the other about whether he wants their time together to be something he thinks of as a relationship. Being good friends, Shannon's friends tell her what they heard so that she will have a better idea of how they stand. Shannon is floored by this and doesn't know what to do. She is torn between thinking that Chris really does have deep feelings for her based on their intense sex life and thinking that she has got to do something to make him realize that they belong together.*

    a. *If Shannon came to you with her dilemma, what would you tell her?*

    b. *Why would you tell her that?*

c. Do you think your own gender influenced your initial reaction to this scenario? Why/why not?

2. Oliver and Nola have been a couple for almost their entire college years. It is common knowledge that they are a couple and that they will, in all likelihood, marry after graduation. Their sex life is satisfying and they find ways to keep it interesting. However, Nola notices that Oliver is less and less likely to encourage or allow her to give him fellatio for any length of time. She knows he finds it an erotic activity, so she is puzzled. One night she gets brave and asks him what's up. After stalling for a while, he finally apologetically admits that he doesn't find her technique satisfying because she isn't careful enough with her teeth and sometimes it causes him discomfort. She asks him why he never told her before, and he says he didn't want to hurt her feelings. This makes Nola sad.

   a. If this couple came to you for help smoothing things out, what would you tell them?

   b. Why would you tell them that?

   c. Do you think your own gender influenced your initial reaction to this scenario? Why/why not?

3. *Ryan and Trista recently began dating. After a few dates, they decide they are ready to have sex together. They plan a romantic evening and everything goes just right; they are both flirtatious and receptive to one another, both aroused and anxious to get to the lovemaking, both happy with their decision.... However, once they are "getting down to business," things go a bit off course. It all started when, after a couple of passionate kisses and sweet nothings whispered, Ryan put his hand down inside Trista's panties. She is offended, and he is puzzled. The rest of the evening goes downhill from there. They are both frustrated because they are still very much attracted to each other, but just don't know how to fix it.*

    a. *You are a close friend of Ryan's and he just told you this story and asks you if you have any idea what went wrong. What would you say?*

    b. *Why would you tell him that?*

    c. *Do you think your own gender influenced your initial reaction to this scenario? Why/why not?*

4. *You are an especially-trusted adult and have the confidence of a teenage relative, neighbor, or even one of your own children. Both you and he (or she) are of a Judeo-Christian religious faith. This individual confides that he (or she) has been masturbating regularly and feels guilty about it.*

    a. *What do you think would be your initial thoughts upon this discovery or revelation?*

    b. *How would you then respond? (Would you or would you not use the scientific findings in the text, rely on your historical religious teachings, or somehow meld the two—and especially if the latter, how would you meld them?)*

➢ *Oral-Genital Stimulation*

Your text discusses a lot of issues relating to oral-genital stimulation, and they are all important to keep in mind. Use the cues below to write outline points you would want to include in a comprehensive essay about the subject.

❑ Definitions

❑ Risks

❑ Techniques (for each gender)

❑ Common Positions

❑ Prevalence (including sociocultural factors influencing it)

❑ Abstinence

TRY PRACTICE TEST #2 NOW!
GOOD LUCK!

➤ *Sexual Intercourse: Positions and Techniques*

Directions: Complete the following chart by describing each sexual intercourse position and then identifying the advantages and disadvantages of each position.

POSITIONS (Descriptions)	ADVANTAGES AND DISADVANTAGES
Male-superior	
Female-superior	
Lateral-entry	
Rear-entry	
Anal intercourse	

TRY PRACTICE TEST #3 NOW!
GOOD LUCK!

After You Read...

PRACTICE TEST #1

(LO = Learning Objective)

1. Why has masturbation been condemned by Judeo-Christian tradition?
   a. It is more pleasurable than intercourse.
   b. It spreads disease more easily.
   c. It is not a form of procreative sex.
   d. It debilitated those who engaged in it frequently.

   p. 253   LO 1

2. If you were a 19th century parent who was concerned that your teenager masturbated, you would be likely to do all of the following, EXCEPT:
   a. Prepare a daily bowl of corn flakes for him/her.
   b. Introduce the teenager to strong coffee and tea.
   c. Serve graham crackers and whole wheat bread frequently.
   d. Purchase a medically approved masturbation-prevention device.

   p. 254-255   LO 1

3. Which of the following did 18th century physician (and signer of the Declaration of Independence) Benjamin Rush believe to be caused by masturbation?
   a. Epilepsy
   b. Excessive body hair
   c. Tuberculosis
   d. Both A and B
   e. Both A and C

   p. 254   LO 1

4. How can masturbation help females improve the quality of orgasms (and their general reported levels of satisfaction) during partnered sex?
   a. It encourages physical self-exploration and increases self-knowledge.
   b. It increases a sense of control as they reject their usual sexual partners.
   c. It increases muscle tone in the pubococcygeus muscle.
   d. It allows partners freedom from responsibility for pleasing them.

   p. 258   LO 2

5. Among women, research has shown that there is an association between:
   a. Early masturbation and later sexual promiscuity later in life.
   b. Negative attitudes toward masturbation and difficulty reaching orgasm.
   c. Positive attitudes towards masturbation and multiple sex partners.
   d. Masturbation after marriage and marital dissatisfaction.

   p. 258   LO 2

6. Among men who report masturbating, most rely on _____, but do not _____.
    a. hand technique; fantasize while masturbating
    b. erotic visual stimulation; use sex toys
    c. fantasy; know the women in their fantasies
    d. lubricant; use erotic visual stimulation
           p. 259   LO 2

7. Which of the following is a common male myth about women's masturbation?
    a. They often fantasize about other women touching them and having a man watch.
    b. They never fantasize at all as a means of self-stimulation.
    c. They prefer direct stimulation of the clitoral glans.
    d. They usually insert fingers or phallic objects into their vaginas as the main stimulation.
           p. 259   LO 2

8. Who engages in sexual fantasies?
    a. Men and women without regular sexual partners
    b. Those who find tactile and visual stimulation insufficient
    c. Individuals who are reluctant to masturbate
    d. A vast majority of both men and women, especially during masturbation
           p. 273   LO 3

9. What would the authors of the text say about someone who fantasizes about other people during sex with his or her partner?
    a. They should seek couples counseling.
    b. They are perfectly normal.
    c. They should be sure to tell their partner so they can enjoy it together.
    d. They have unsatisfying sex lives.
           p. 274   LO 3

10. According to your text, sex drive and _____ are related to testosterone levels in both men and women.
    a. frequency of sexual fantasizing
    b. likelihood to use sex toys
    c. fantasies about members of the same gender
    d. ability to enjoy erotica or pornography
           p. 274   LO 3

(LO = Learning Objective)

1. Foreplay:
    a. May be a prelude to coitus.
    b. May be engaged in without coitus in mind.
    c. In some form, is engaged in by virtually all species of mammals.
    d. All of the above
    e. None of the above
    p. 261　　　　　　LO 4

2. All of the following are true regarding breast stimulation, EXCEPT:
    a. Some women report achieving orgasm from breast stimulation alone.
    b. The nipples are erotically sensitive in both genders.
    c. Female breast size is proportional to level of arousal when stimulated.
    d. The type of breast stimulation desired varies among individuals.
    p. 262　　　　　　LO 4

3. Which of the following, if any, are true of "genital apposition"?
    a. It is most often practiced by gay males.
    b. It is most often practiced by lesbians.
    c. It is most often practiced by adolescents to achieve orgasm without intercourse.
    d. All of the above
    e. None of the above
    p. 263　　　　　　LO 4

4. Fellatio refers to:
    a. Oral stimulation of the clitoris.
    b. Anal stimulation with the tongue.
    c. Anal intercourse.
    d. Oral stimulation of the male genitals.
    p. 265-266　　　　LO 5

5. Cunnilingus refers to:
    a. A type of venereal disease.
    b. Oral stimulation of the female genitals.
    c. Sexually deviant behavior with animals.
    d. Oral stimulation of the penis.
    p. 266-267　　　　LO 5

6. Partnered, mutual oral-genital stimulation is often called?
   a. Joint cunnilingus
   b. Anilingus
   c. Joint fellatio
   d. Sixty-nine

   p. 268   LO 5

7. Which statement most accurately describes the statistical relationship between educational level and the prevalence of oral-genital stimulation?
   a. Positive correlation between educational level and prevalence
   b. Negative correlation between educational level and prevalence
   c. There is no correlation.
   d. Relationships don't correlate for receiving vs. performing oral sex.

   p. 269-7   LO 6

8. All of the following are advantages of the male-superior position, EXCEPT:
   a. It can be highly arousing for the man.
   b. Kissing can continue.
   c. The woman can control the amount of clitoral stimulation she receives.
   d. The male's buttocks and scrotum can be stimulated more easily.

   p. 269   LO 6

9. Which of the following, if any, does your text suggest as an effective way to relieve concerns about offensive odors or cleanliness of one's genitals?
   a. Abstinence from oral sex
   b. Thorough washing of genitals immediately before oral sex
   c. All of the above
   d. None of the above

   p. 269   LO 7

10. Which of the following is a TRUE statement about semen?
    a. Swallowing semen can result in pregnancy.
    b. Semen is high in calories.
    c. Swallowing semen can cause indigestion.
    d. Semen tends to taste salty.

    p. 268   LO 7

(LO = Learning Objective)

1. What features of intercourse VARY according to which of the four positions discussed in your text is being used?
   a. Depth and rate of thrusting
   b. Ease at which additional sexual stimulation can be applied
   c. How readily the penis may pop out of the vagina
   d. All of the above
   e. Both A and B
                  p. 269-271   LO 8

2. Which of the four sexual positions discussed in this chapter tends NOT to be favored by women who enjoy manual clitoral stimulation from their partners during coitus?
   a. Male-superior
   b. Female-superior
   c. Lateral-entry
   d. Rear-entry
                  p. 269   LO 8

3. Which of the four sexual positions discussed in this chapter is said to be excellent for prolonged coitus?
   a. Male-superior
   b. Female-superior
   c. Lateral-entry
   d. Rear-entry
                  p. 270   LO 8

4. Which of the four sexual positions discussed in this chapter is sometimes perceived to create a sense of emotional distance?
   a. Male-superior
   b. Female-superior
   c. Lateral-entry
   d. Rear-entry
                  p. 271   LO 8

5. Historically, fantasizing during coitus has been considered:
   a. Negatively, as a sinful activity stimulated by the devil
   b. Positively, as an impetus to reproduction
   c. Positively, if the couple was married
   d. Negatively, as extremely abnormal and rare
                  p. 273-274   LO 9

6. Researchers find that _____ married people have engaged in coital fantasies to enhance their sexual arousal.
    a. very few
    b. emotionally distant
    c. unfaithful
    d. the majority of
        p. 273   LO 9

7. What does current research say about the relationship between sexual fantasies and the level of satisfaction in one's sexual relationship?
    a. Use of fantasies does not seem to be related to quality of sex life.
    b. Use of fantasies is necessary to have a high-quality sex life.
    c. Fantasies are a way to compensate for a poor sex life.
    d. Fantasies can ruin a good sex life.
        p. 273   LO 9

8. The risk of HIV infection through anal intercourse is higher:
    a. For men than for women.
    b. For women than for men.
    c. Than for vaginal intercourse.
    d. Even when both partners are infection-free.
        p. 272   LO 10

9. What does the desire to be entered anally by one's partner indicate about one's sexual orientation?
    a. It indicates a sexual attraction to men, whether you are male or female.
    b. It indicates that men are homosexual, but does not indicate anything about women.
    c. It indicates that women have gender dysphoria, but does not indicate anything about men.
    d. It does not indicate anything about sexual orientation in men or women.
        p. 272   LO 10

10. Which of the following sociocultural factors are associated with a HIGHER likelihood of engaging in anal sex?
    a. Lower levels of education
    b. Higher levels of education
    c. Self-identification as a male Christian
    d. Self-identification as a female Christian
        p. 272   LO 10

Multiple Choice

1. Among women, research has shown that there is an association between:
   a. Early masturbation and later sexual promiscuity later in life.
   b. Negative attitudes toward masturbation and difficulty reaching orgasm.
   c. Positive attitudes towards masturbation and multiple sex partners.
   d. Masturbation after marriage and marital dissatisfaction.

2. Who engages in sexual fantasies?
   a. Men and women without regular sexual partners
   b. Those who find tactile and visual stimulation insufficient
   c. Individuals who are reluctant to masturbate
   d. A vast majority of both men and women, especially during masturbation

3. All of the following are true regarding breast stimulation, EXCEPT:
   a. Some women report achieving orgasm from breast stimulation alone.
   b. The nipples are erotically sensitive in both genders.
   c. Female breast size is proportional to level of arousal when stimulated.
   d. The type of breast stimulation desired varies among individuals.

4. Why has masturbation been condemned by Judeo-Christian tradition?
   a. It is more pleasurable than intercourse.
   b. It spreads disease more easily.
   c. It is not a form of procreative sex.
   d. It debilitated those who engaged in it frequently.

5. Foreplay:
   a. May be a prelude to coitus.
   b. May be engaged in without coitus in mind.
   c. In some form, is engaged in by virtually all species of mammals.
   d. All of the above
   e. None of the above

6. What features of intercourse VARY according to which of the four positions discussed in your text is being used?
   a. Depth and rate of thrusting
   b. Ease at which additional sexual stimulation can be applied
   c. How readily the penis may pop out of the vagina
   d. All of the above
   e. Both A and B

7. What would the authors of the text say about someone who fantasizes about other people during sex with his or her partner?
    a. They should seek couples counseling.
    b. They are perfectly normal.
    c. They should be sure to tell their partner so they can enjoy it together.
    d. They have unsatisfying sex lives.

8. Fellatio refers to:
    a. Oral stimulation of the clitoris.
    b. Anal stimulation with the tongue.
    c. Anal intercourse.
    d. Oral stimulation of the male genitals.

9. Which of the four sexual positions discussed in this chapter is said to be excellent for prolonged coitus?
    a. Male-superior
    b. Female-superior
    c. Lateral-entry
    d. Rear-entry

10. If you were a 19th century parent who was concerned that your teenager masturbated, you would be likely to do all of the following, EXCEPT:
    a. Prepare a daily bowl of corn flakes for him/her.
    b. Introduce the teenager to strong coffee and tea.
    c. Serve graham crackers and whole wheat bread frequently.
    d. Purchase a medically approved masturbation-prevention device.

11. Researchers find that _____ married people have engaged in coital fantasies to enhance their sexual arousal.
    a. very few
    b. emotionally distant
    c. unfaithful
    d. the majority of

12. Cunnilingus refers to:
    a. A type of venereal disease.
    b. Oral stimulation of the female genitals.
    c. Sexually deviant behavior with animals.
    d. Oral stimulation of the penis.

13. What does current research say about the relationship between sexual fantasies and the level of satisfaction in one's sexual relationship?
    a. Use of fantasies does not seem to be related to quality of sex life.
    b. Use of fantasies is necessary to have a high-quality sex life.
    c. Fantasies are a way to compensate for a poor sex life.
    d. Fantasies can ruin a good sex life.

14. What does the desire to be entered anally by one's partner indicate about one's sexual orientation?
    a. It indicates a sexual attraction to men, whether you are male or female.
    b. It indicates that men are homosexual, but does not indicate anything about women.
    c. It indicates that women have gender dysphoria, but does not indicate anything about men.
    d. It does not indicate anything about sexual orientation in men or women.

15. Which statement most accurately describes the statistical relationship between educational level and the prevalence of oral-genital stimulation?
    a. Positive correlation between educational level and prevalence.
    b. Negative correlation between educational level and prevalence.
    c. No correlation.
    d. Relationships don't correlate for receiving vs. performing oral sex.

True/False

_____ 1. Cultural expectations do not tend to influence our sexual behavior.

_____ 2. Graham crackers were originally developed to help people control their sexual impulses.

_____ 3. Soap suds are a good choice of lubricant for men during masturbation.

_____ 4. Like snowflakes, the masturbation styles of women are all unique.

_____ 5. Some forms of individual sexual experience, like sexual fantasy, may or may not be accompanied by genital stimulation.

_____ 6. It is clear that having violent and/or sadistic sexual fantasies is connected to committing aggressive sex crimes.

_____ 7. Higher education tends to have a liberalizing effect on sexual behavior.

_____ 8. In the Biblical story, Onan was struck down by God because he had "spilled upon the ground" while masturbating.

Essay Questions

1. Discuss the main techniques used in manual stimulation of the genitals, including both the mechanics of stimulation and preferences related to it in men and women.

_____

_____

_____

_____

_____

_____

_____

_____

2. Compare and contrast the four major positions and techniques for sexual intercourse examined in your text. Please be sure to include the non-physical implications of each method. (For example, what does the male-superior position tend to symbolize socially?)

_____

_____

_____

_____

_____

_____

_____

_____

When You Have Finished...

Rev up your search engines and see where the Web takes you as you explore the following activities related to Sexual Behaviors and Fantasies.

1. Many places in the U.S. do not have stores for sex toys along with a good source of instruction on use readily available. Find out what's out there for you, but before you do your own search, you might want to get an overview of what's available, how to select, store, use, and care for them properly The following educational guide from "My Pleasure" can get you started. It even gives tips on how to travel with them and not excite airport security too much!
http://www.mypleasure.com/education/

2. Now that you've become acquainted with the basics—hold the phone! Literally. Read this article and think about the future of sex toys. It's about a British company's new software called "Purring Kitty" that turns cellular phones into mobile vibrators. (And no, we didn't make this up!) Do you think this will sell? Why or why not? http://www.wired.com/news/business/0,1367,58442,00.html

3. It is time for you to explore sexual positions. Google "Kama Sutra -.com" (You will remove a lot of the pornography from the web using the "-.com" in Google.) Log into your local library and check out a copy of the Kama Sutra. It is difficult to read, but it has almost every conceivable sexual position available. You can also search images for posters of various sexual positions.

4. Sexual fantasies. We all have them, and we all wonder if ours are "normal"—whatever that means! As was mentioned in the *As You Read* section of this chapter, a well-respected author who collects and writes about such issues is Nancy Friday. Take a look around the Web and find out what you can on the subject. For example, here's a site that claims to know women's Top 10 fantasies: http://www.askmen.com/love/vanessa/27_love_secrets.html. We particularly liked the way this one reminded you that it's healthy to have fantasies—even when you have no desire to act on them.

5. Tantric anyone? Is there a way to have sex for hours achieving mind blowing orgasms? Check out Google results for "Tantric Sex." There are some clips on YouTube and many websites where sexual meditation becomes therapy and healing. Has yoga gone too far with this?

Chapter 10
Sexual Orientation

Before You Begin...

Chapter Summary

Commonly across American society and its media, one often may hear the terms "straight," "bi," "lesbian," or "gay" in reference to other people different from him or her own self. Particularly so, with the latter two terms, there are some other variants that are rather unkind—lending the idea that this surely is a topic of controversy and misunderstanding in U.S. society. So what is all the fuss about and can sexual orientation really be boiled down to something as simple as a choice? All this and more in this chapter—so please get comfortable in your chair and we'll get going!

Sexual orientation describes the gender directionality of one's sexual preferences; importantly though, one's sexual partner may not always be consistent with one's sexual orientation. Too, heterosexual, bisexual, or homosexual orientations include more than just an emphasis on the erotic or sexual aspect of a relationship. Your text authors explain that any of the given orientations include an interest in developing a romantic relationship. The romantic element is important in further clarifying the distinct difference between—for example, same-sex sexual behavior in a prison versus that of a person with a homosexual orientation. Those in the latter case often desire love, intimacy, and sexual expression in the context of a romantic relationship over a period of time. Among those lesser educated in sexuality (which will not be you), there is an assumption, too, that people with homosexual orientations would prefer to actually be members of the other sex. As noted in your book, research does not support this notion.

Interestingly, Kinsey and his colleagues found evidence of degrees of homosexual and heterosexual orientations, with bisexuality representing a midpoint between the two. Alternatives to the Kinsey continuum point to the possibility that Kinsey's framework may not be complex enough to capture the reality of sexual orientation—especially in females. Storms suggests the possibility that gay and heterosexual orientations may be independent dimensions, rather than mutually exclusive polar opposites, whereas Lippa and Arad's research suggests that Storms' two-dimensional model may not be complex enough to fully characterize the picture either, and that gender differences need to be taken into account when considering sexual orientation. Bisexuality, the orientation wherein people are attracted to both males and females, is discussed, including controversies and incidence rates associated with being bisexual.

Same-sex behaviors are not unusual in the animal kingdom. They have been observed in over 450 species. The study of this and the relationship to humans is referred to scientifically as the "cross-species" perspective. You will find that your text explains how elements of this perspective apply (or "generalize") to humans—wise people are careful, though, in their generalizations since some animal sexual behaviors do not match up with human behaviors.

Attitudes in contemporary society have varied greatly over time. Throughout history, there is evidence that people have engaged in same-sex sexual behaviors, but social and cultural acceptance along with tolerance of such behavior has fluctuated. In recent times, some of these practices, such as sodomy, have been restricted or prohibited by law. From a religious perspective, some denominations have condemned same-sex sexual activity as sinful since its purpose is pleasure, not procreation. During the past generation, gay people have organized effective political groups to fight discrimination, overturn sodomy laws (e.g., Lawrence v. Texas in 2003), combat the AIDS epidemic, and even change perspectives in some organized religions. Information from the cross-cultural perspective concludes that male-male sexual behavior is practiced today by at least some members of most societies. Little is known about female-female sexual behavior in non-Western cultures. Although there are continued efforts to fight institutional and interpersonal discrimination against same-sex relationships, contemporary attitudes in American society indicate a great deal of ambivalence towards equality still exists for many heterosexual people.

The NSFGS found that the attitude in the United States has shifted in the past 10 years by 21 percent. While negative attitudes toward same-sex relationships are still over 50%, there are more and more states allowing marriage between same sex couples and even more states have provisions for civil unions. The marriage debate has been on many ballots and will continue to be an emotional and highly contested issue.

Theorists and researchers have tried to find the "causes" of same-sex attraction. A discussion of the many forms of homophobia is included in this review of the scholarly theories about sexual orientation. Various controversies and trends dealing with same sex attraction as they are evidenced in laws, activism, and social issues are discussed. The biological perspective seeks evidence of genetic and brain structure contributions to gay sexual orientation. Concordance (or agreement) of sexual orientation between identical (or monozygotic) twins is explained. The text authors also examine Hamer's study of the X chromosome and its potential connection to sexual orientation. The significance of hormonal variations during pre-natal sexual differentiation of the fetus is illuminated. Within the psychological perspective, psychoanalytic theory connects gay orientation to unconscious castration anxiety and/or improper resolution of the Oedipal complex, while learning theory focuses on the role of reinforcement of early sexual behavior. Gay men and lesbians are more likely than heterosexuals to report childhood behavior stereotypical of the other gender. Each of these perspectives has significant strengths and weaknesses and is further explained in your text.

Your authors also explore gender non-conformity—which is not behaving in a way that is expected given one's anatomical sex. Childhood onset is outlined and how gender non-conformity distinctly applies to gay men and to lesbians. With lesbians, your authors highlight the butch-femme dimension. With gay men, they examine the masculine-feminine variation—and how childhood effeminacy relates to the adult gay male orientation. Further, the accuracy of the popular stereotypes about butch lesbians and of effeminate gay men is spotlighted. (Hint: There is some truth in them but it is far from absolute as you will learn from your text.)

In terms of psychology and adjustment, evidence has failed to show that gay men and lesbians are more emotionally unstable than heterosexuals. Though, there is support that shows that homosexuals do have, on average, more issues with anxiety, depression, and suicide. Too, gay males are more likely to have eating disorders such as bulimia nervosa and anorexia nervosa. Some researchers associate societal oppression as correlates—even amongst the enlightened Dutch people. Across the various socioeconomic lifestyles, few homosexuals wish to change their sexual orientation—if it were readily possible. Also, new details on how Mexican Americans view sexual orientation are shared in the text.

Along the lines of societal oppression, a subset of people demonstrate varying degrees of homophobia (and biphobia too). Homophobia is fear of homosexual people. Manifestations of homophobia range from using derogatory terms, denying housing, to gay bashing. Gay bashing is the use force to injure, or in some cases to permanent maim and kill, those who are perceived to be gay, lesbian, or bisexual by the basher(s). Homophobic attitudes strongly relate to certain genders, political preferences, and religious orientations as further described by your authors.

Because of the social stigma in many societies—and especially in the U.S.—many lesbian, gay, and bisexual people encounter difficulty, at least at first, with coming to terms about being different. The coming-to-terms process is actually called "coming out." Coming out usually refers to two separate processes leading to acknowledgements of one's sexual orientation: coming out to oneself and coming out to others.

Gay couples generally express themselves sexually through as wide a range of activities as heterosexuals. However, gay males and lesbians spend more time caressing their partners' bodies before approaching the genitals. Gay males living with partners are more likely to engage in sexual activity outside the primary relationship than are lesbians. However, many gay men have changed their sexual behaviors since the advent of AIDS. The varied lifestyles of gay men and lesbians have been studied and classified; this includes both across group and within group diversity.

Learning Objectives

---

1. Define sexual orientation and distinguish between sexual orientation and gender identity.

2. Compare and contrast the Kinsey continuum and Storm's two-dimensional model of sexual orientation, including the limitations of both as addressed by Lippa & Arad.

3. Discuss the various definitions and societal views of bisexuality.

4. Examine Western culture's historical and religious perspectives on gay male and lesbian sexual orientations.

5. Describe the incidence of and societal reaction to gay male and lesbian sexual orientations and behaviors across world cultures and U.S. ethnicities.

6. Summarize the information on same-gender sexual behavior in other species.

7. Define and categorize forms and cultural expressions of homophobia.

8. Describe legislative and gay activist initiatives to combat discrimination against lesbians, gays, and bisexuals—and also to disseminate information about HIV infection.

9. Evaluate contemporary research conclusions on the genetics, sex hormonal influences, prenatal hormonal effects and brain structure differences as they attempt to explain adult sexual orientation.

10. Evaluate and describe the perspectives of psychoanalytic and learning theories as they explain gay male and lesbian sexual orientations.

11. Examine the link between early gender nonconformity and other familial influences on later gay male and lesbian sexual orientations.

12. Summarize the research about the adjustment of gay men and lesbians, the prevalence of those who wish to change their orientation and the relative success of these attempts.

13. Explain the "coming out" process.

14. Compare the sexual techniques of gay male, lesbian, and heterosexual partners.

15. Examine and explain the variations in the lifestyles of gay men and lesbians—including the concept of "Brokeback" marriages.

Term Identification

You know the drill; these are the terms you need to learn, and making flashcards will help. This might be a good chapter to double-up some of the flash cards, since many of them are defined in contrast to one another (e.g., make a flashcard comparing and contrasting close and open couples).

Chapter 10 Table of Key Terms

Activating effects	Functionals
Asexuals	Gay bashing
Biphobia	Gay males
Bisexuality	Heteroerotic
Butch	Heterosexual orientation
Castration anxiety	Homoerotic
Close couples	Homophobia
Concordance	Homosexual orientation
Cruising	Lesbians
Dizygotic (DZ) twins	Monozygotic (MZ) twins
Dysfunctionals	Open couples
Femme	Sexual orientation

As You Read...

❖ ***Getting Oriented Toward Sexual Orientation***

➤ *Coming to Terms with Terms, Sexual Orientation, and Gender Identity*

The first part of this chapter discusses definitions and controversies about the words we use to describe people who are sexually attracted to people who are the same sex as they are. It raises some interesting issues about the ambiguity of the term we use most often to describe this category of human sexuality: "homosexual." Think back to the assumptions about sexual orientation with which you came into this class. Use the space below to make notes about how you defined the following words before you read this chapter. Then, use the text to support the confirmations or corrections you now wish to make to your definitions. If you do not agree with the book, please be sure to acknowledge the book's definitions as you argue your point of view instead.

❑ Heterosexual

    o My definition before….

_____

_____

_____

_____

    o My definition now….

_____

_____

_____

_____

❑ Homosexual

    o My definition before….

_____

_____

_____

_____

o My definition now....

_____

_____

_____

_____

❑ Bisexual

o My definition before....

_____

_____

_____

_____

o My definition now....

_____

_____

_____

_____

➢ *Classification of Sexual Orientation: Is Yes or No (or Bi) Enough?*

Using the information in your book to support your argument, answer the following question in the space below.

Do you think that sexual orientation is categorical (Straight or Gay with no "in between"), a continuum (like Kinsey's model), or something else altogether (like Storms or Lippa and Arad)? Please include in your answer consideration of the relationship between people's sexual orientation and their sexual behavior.

_____

_____

_____

_____

_____

_____

_____

_____

_____

_____

_____

_____

_____

_____

_____

_____

_____

TRY PRACTICE TEST #1 NOW!
GOOD LUCK!

❖ **_Perspectives on Gay Male and Lesbian Sexual Orientation_**

Directions: Complete the chart below by supplying a summary of the theories and the support for each of the following perspectives on homosexuality.

Perspective	Description and Supporting Evidence
Historical	
Cross-cultural	
Cross-species	

Biological
 	
    Genetics
 	
    Hormonal influences
 	
    Brain structure	

Psychological
 	
    Psychoanalytic
 	
    Learning theories	

TRY PRACTICE TEST #2 NOW!
GOOD LUCK!

❖ *Adjustment of Gay Males and Lesbians*

    ➢ *Treatment of Gay Male and Lesbian Sexual Orientations*

Directions: After carefully reading the section of this chapter on the treatment of gay and lesbian orientations, consider the following two questions and answer them in the space below. Use the information in the text to argue your opinion.

1   Do you believe it is possible to change one's sexual orientation?

_____

_____

_____

_____

_____

_____

_____

_____

_____

_____

2   Examining your answer to question one above and assuming that sexual orientation cannot be changed, is it okay to just change a homosexual's sexual behavior? Why or why not?

_____

_____

_____

_____

_____

_____

_____

_____

_____

_____

❖ *Coming Out: Coming to Terms with Being Gay*

➢ *Coming Out to Oneself & to Others—"Field Assignment"*

Your text describes several components of coming out to oneself and to others. Using the prompts below, find a story of someone's coming out, and make note of the details of the person's story that correspond to the text's description of the process. You may do any of the following to get the information to apply to this exercise:

→ Interview someone you know who is gay and "out."
→ Watch a YouTube video about coming out and use their story.
→ Think of a gay character from a television story.
→ Find a blog online, written by someone gay about his/her own coming out experience.

My chosen person is named:

_____

How did you learn of his/her story?

_____
_____
_____
_____

How did s/he experience these parts of the coming out process?

1. Attraction to members of the same sex:

_____
_____
_____
_____

2. Self-labeling as gay or lesbian:

_____
_____
_____
_____

3. Sexual contact with members of the same sex:

_____
_____
_____
_____

4. Disclosure of one's sexual orientation to other people:

_____
_____
_____
_____

❖ *Gay Lifestyles*

It is clear from the information in your text that there is no singular way to live a gay or lesbian lifestyle, just as there is no one way to live a "straight" lifestyle. For example, your book discusses Bell and Weinberg's development of five lifestyle classifications based on their research on gay couples. Although these five surely do not cover every possibility, they are useful as a means to begin understanding the diversity of relationship styles among gay men and lesbians. Using the chart below, describe the main characteristics of each of Bell and Weinberg's "types"

Type of Relationship	Characteristics
Close couples	
Open couples	
Functionals	
Dysfunctionals	
Asexuals	

TRY PRACTICE TEST #3 NOW!
GOOD LUCK!

After You Read...

(LO = Learning Objective)

1. Which statement is accurate?
    a. Heterosexuals do not have sexual fantasies about erotic encounters with people of the same sex.
    b. Gays and lesbians do not have sexual fantasies about erotic encounters with partners of the other sex.
    c. One's sexual orientation is not always expressed in sexual behavior.
    d. People who perceive themselves as gay or lesbian are heterosexual until they have had a same sex encounter.

    p. 282   LO 1

2. Which of the following, if any, are among the objections raised by some gay people to the use of the term "homosexual"?
    a. The word draws attention to sexual behavior.
    b. The word is often used to refer to gay men, and thus makes lesbians invisible.
    c. The word is unclear as to whether it refers to sexual behavior or orientation.
    d. All of the above are objections raised by some.
    e. Only A and C are objections raised by some.

    p. 281   LO 1

3. According to many recent surveys, greater public acceptance of people who are gay and lesbian has come from:
    a. More experimental sexual behavior among young adults.
    b. More people knowing someone who is gay or lesbian.
    c. More "gay rights" news coverage.
    d. More people "coming out of the closet."

    p. 298   LO 1

4. What percentage of the population is gay, according to Kinsey?
    a. He reported that 4% of men and 1–3% of women are gay (meaning that they are either a 4, 5, or 6 on his scale).
    b. The percentage depends on how "gay" is defined on his scale (i.e., just 6's or just 5's and 6's, etc.)
    c. He reported that it varied depending on a given country's culture
    d. Universally, 10% of men, 8% of women

    p. 283-284   LO 2

5. Kinsey's research showed that sexual behavior patterns:
   a. Are fairly consistent across one's lifespan.
   b. Tend to reveal at least one same-sex experience for about half of all women.
   c. Are likely to vary over time, sometimes dramatically so.
   d. Tend to reveal at least one same-sex experience for about half of all women.

   p. 289   LO 2

6. According to your text, all of the following are factors that tend to affect the results of surveys concerning human sexuality EXCEPT:
   a. The phrasing of the questions.
   b. Volunteer bias.
   c. The social desirability of the behavior being examined.
   d. The past sexual behavior of the interviewer.

   p. 283   LO 2

7. Storms' two-dimensional alternative to the Kinsey sexual continuum model allows for:
   a. Heteroerotic and homoerotic stimulation to be considered separate dimensions.
   b. One to be characterized as "high" in both dimensions at the same time.
   c. Heteroerotic and homoerotic stimulation to be considered along the same dimension.
   d. Both A and B are true.
   e. Both B and C are true.

   p. 284   LO 2

8. The term *bisexual* refers to:
   a. A person with sex organs of both genders.
   b. Someone who is not erotically attracted to either gender.
   c. A person who enjoys both coitus and anal intercourse.
   d. Someone who responds sexually to both genders.

   p. 281   LO 3

9. According to the NHSLS study, about _____ of those surveyed, reported having bisexual _____.
   a. 1%; attractions to both women and men
   b. 4%; experiences with both women and men
   c. 1%; identities
   d. 4%; identities

   p. 286   LO 3

10. A "bi-bi" is a person who:
    a. Is bisexual and appears to be unable to carry on a monogamous relationship with a person of either gender.
    b. Is bisexual and appears to be equally attracted to people of their own sex and the other sex.
    c. Is bisexual and appears to be ambivalent about his or her own sexual identity.
    d. Is bisexual and appears to be attracted primarily to other bisexual people.

    p. 286   LO 3

(LO = Learning Objective)

1. Anal intercourse has historically been legally prohibited by:
   a. Federal legislation in the U.S.
   b. Death in some European countries.
   c. Sodomy laws at the state level.
   d. Public censure.

   p. 301   LO 4

2. Cross-culturally, societies that highly value female virginity before marriage and segregate young men and women:
   a. Have more female-female sexual behaviors among adults.
   b. Have more male-male sexual behaviors among adults.
   c. Are more warlike and encouraging of all types of sexual expression.
   d. Are less tolerant of sexual activities among children and adolescents.

   p. 302   LO 5

3. According to your text, researchers who study monkeys and apes, specializing in cross-species perspectives on sexuality, have found that:
   a. Only humans appear to exhibit same-sex *activities* on a consistent and ongoing basis.
   b. Some, but not all, species appear to exhibit same-sex, long-term *partnering* behaviors.
   c. Sexual motivation appears to play a role in some, but not all same-sex *activities* among animals.
   d. Both A and C are true.
   e. Both B and C are true.

   p. 290   LO 6

4. In the study of homophobic males, _____ increased arousal while   negative attitudes remain persistent.
   a. homosexual erotica.
   b. heterosexual erotica.
   c. homophobic literature.
   d. transvestites.

   p. 305   LO 7

5. Research has linked homophobia to all of the following, EXCEPT:
   a. Being exclusively heterosexual.
   b. A belief in male dominance.
   c. Support of stereotypical gender roles.
   d. A belief in the naturalness of female subservience.

   p. 306   LO 7

6. Research indicates that heterosexual men are less tolerant overall than heterosexual women, and that they tend to hold more:
   a. Negative attitudes toward gay men than toward lesbians.
   b. Negative attitudes toward lesbians than toward gay men.
   c. Negative attitudes toward gay men than toward bisexual men.
   d. Negative attitudes toward bisexual women than toward lesbians.

   p. 301   LO 7

7. Political organizing of gays and lesbians in large cities has led to:
   a. Reduced government funding of HIV/AIDS education initiatives as gays have largely assumed the funding of these initiatives in those cities themselves.
   b. Creation of laws to provide gays and lesbians equal treatment in areas like housing and employment.
   c. Substantial increases in the variety and number of sexually-transmitted infections both in amongst gay males and lesbians.
   d. None of the above.

   p. 301   LO 8

8. According to LeVay, gay men have a _____ than is found in heterosexual men.
   a. larger, more complex cerebral cortex
   b. less developed sperm producing apparatus
   c. cluster of cells in the anterior hypothalamus that is smaller
   d. smaller fiber connecting hypothalamus and the pituitary gland

   p. 295   LO 9

9. Learning theories:
   a. Are similar to Freudian concepts of the Oedipus Complex.
   b. Emphasize the resolution of intrapsychic conflicts.
   c. Believe there is a genetic component to our sexual orientation.
   d. Focus on the role of reinforcement of early patterns of sexual behavior.

   p. 295-296   LO 10

10. Which is *not* accurate regarding gays and lesbians?
    a. They follow a variety of lifestyles.
    b. They are more highly educated than Americans in general.
    c. They report levels of satisfaction with their relationships similar to heterosexual couples.
    d. They are primarily from lower socioeconomic levels.

    p. 306-307   LO 11

(LO = Learning Objective)

1. Identify what factors about sexual orientation and sexual behavior are TRUE.
   a. A person's sexual orientation is able to be altered once sustained change in sexual behavior has occurred.
   b. If a person's sexual behavior is altered, underlying sexual orientation always, or most always, remains unaltered
   c. It is usually uncommon, or even rare, that people demonstrate sexual behavior that is in conflict with their declared sexual orientation.
   d. All of the above are true.
   e. None of the above are true.

        p. 281-282   LO 12

2. Which of the following statements, if any, are FALSE?
   a. Gay men are more likely than heterosexuals to experience feelings of anxiety and depression, and are more prone to suicide.
   b. Lesbians are less likely than heterosexuals to experience feelings of anxiety and depression, and are more prone to suicide.
   c. Gay males are more likely to have anorexia and/or bulimia than heterosexual males.
   d. Both A and C are FALSE.
   e. Both B and C are FALSE.

        p. 303   LO 12

3. To "come out" to others usually involves:
   a. Wearing the clothing of the opposite gender.
   b. Fears of rejection and loss of love from family and friends.
   c. Retaliation against those who have created the situation.
   d. Changing one's name and identity to gain anonymity.

        p. 307-308   LO 13

4. According to recent research, development of sexual identity in gay males and lesbians involves all of the following steps EXCEPT:
   a. Attraction to others of the same sex.
   b. Labeling as gay or lesbian by others.
   c. Sexual contact with members of the same sex.
   d. Disclosure of one's sexual orientation to other people.

        p. 308   LO 13

5. During the "coming out" process, lesbians tend to focus on the _____ aspects of their growing feelings, and gay males are more likely to focus on the _____ aspects.
    a. negative; positive
    b. sexual; emotional
    c. positive; negative
    d. emotional; sexual
                p. 307-308   LO 13

6. Which statement(s) about gay or bisexual men in opposite-sex marriages is/are TRUE?
    a. These are usually marriages of convenience or to provide cover.
    b. The males typically have no sexual interest in their wives.
    c. The reasons for these kinds of marriages are usually complex.
    d. All of the above are true
    e. None of the above are true
                p. 307   LO 14

7. According to your text, "cruising" is the word used by gay people to mean:
    a. Searching for sex partners, mainly for casual sex.
    b. Searching for relationship partners among their friends.
    c. Attending informal social gatherings among other gay people.
    d. Engaging in sex with multiple partners at once.
                p. 309   LO 14

8. In comparison to married heterosexual males who had been living with a partner for over two years, their gay partnered male counterparts:
    a. Were less likely to have engaged in "extracurricular" sexual activities than the heterosexual men.
    b. Were less likely to have reported major shifts in their identity related to being part of a couple than the heterosexual men.
    c. Were more likely to have engaged in "extracurricular" sexual activities than the heterosexual men.
    d. Were more likely to have reported major shifts in their identity related to being part of a couple than the heterosexual men.
                p. 299   LO 14

9. One asset that gays and lesbians enjoy and heterosexuals do not is:
    a. Fewer religious prohibitions on extramarital sex.
    b. Right to privacy about sexuality while in the military.
    c. Gathering places legally reserved for exclusive use.
    d. An organized local and national advocacy movement.
                p. 302   LO 15

10. Kayla and Monica have been a cohabiting, lesbian couple for the past five years. At one time or another, each of them has had sexual relationships outside their long-term relationship, but neither of them know about the other's infidelity. Using Bell and Weinberg's typology, Kayla and Monica appear to be which of the following type of gay couples?
    a. Close couples
    b. Open couples
    c. Functionals
    d. Dysfunctionals
          p. 303   LO 15

Multiple Choice

1. Which statement(s) about gay or bisexual men in opposite-sex marriages is/are TRUE?
    a. These are usually marriages of convenience or to provide cover.
    b. The males typically have no sexual interest in their wives.
    c. The reasons for these kinds of marriages are usually complex.
    d. All of the above are true
    e. None of the above are true

2. Kinsey's research showed that sexual behavior patterns:
    a. Are fairly consistent across one's lifespan.
    b. Tend to reveal at least one same-sex experience for about half of all women.
    c. Are likely to vary over time, sometimes dramatically so.
    d. Tend to reveal at least one same-sex experience for about half of all women.

3. Which statement is accurate?
    a. Heterosexuals do not have sexual fantasies about erotic encounters with people of the same sex.
    b. Gays and lesbians do not have sexual fantasies about erotic encounters with partners of the other sex.
    c. One's sexual orientation is not always expressed in sexual behavior.
    d. People who perceive themselves as gay or lesbian are heterosexual until they have had a same sex encounter.

4. Cross-culturally, societies that highly value female virginity before marriage and segregate young men and women:
    a. Have more female-female sexual behaviors among adults.
    b. Have more male-male sexual behaviors among adults.
    c. Are more warlike and encouraging of all types of sexual expression.
    d. Are less tolerant of sexual activities among children and adolescents.

5. Anal intercourse has historically been legally prohibited by:
    a. Federal legislation in the U.S.
    b. Death in some European countries.
    c. Sodomy laws at the state level.
    d. Public censure.

6. According to your text, researchers who study monkeys and apes, specializing in cross-species perspectives on sexuality have found that:
    a. Only humans appear to exhibit same-sex *activities* on a consistent and ongoing basis.
    b. Some, but not all, species appear to exhibit same-sex, long-term *partnering* behaviors.
    c. Sexual motivation appears to play a role in some, but not all same-sex *activities* among animals.
    d. Both A and C are true.
    e. Both B and C are true.

7. Research has linked homophobia to all of the following, EXCEPT:
    a. Being exclusively heterosexual.
    b. A belief in male dominance.
    c. Support of stereotypical gender roles.
    d. A belief in the naturalness of female subservience.

8. Political organizing of gays and lesbians in large cities has led to:
    a. Reduced government funding of HIV/AIDS education initiatives as gays have largely assumed the funding of these initiatives in those cities themselves.
    b. Creation of laws to provide gays and lesbians equal treatment in areas like housing and employment.
    c. Substantial increases in the variety and number of sexually-transmitted infections both in amongst gay males and lesbians.
    d. None of the above.

9. According to LeVay, gay men have a _____ compared to heterosexual men.
    a. larger more complex cerebral cortex
    b. less developed sperm producing apparatus
    c. cluster of cells in the anterior hypothalamus which is smaller
    d. smaller fiber connecting hypothalamus and the pituitary gland

10. Learning theories:
    a. Are similar to Freudian concepts of the Oedipus Complex.
    b. Emphasize the resolution of intrapsychic conflicts.
    c. Believe there is a genetic component to our sexual orientation.
    d. Focus on the role of reinforcement of early patterns of sexual behavior.

11. Which is *not* accurate regarding gays and lesbians?
    a. They follow a variety of lifestyles.
    b. They are more highly educated than Americans in general.
    c. They report levels of satisfaction with their relationships similar to heterosexual couples.
    d. They are primarily from lower socioeconomic levels.

12. Which of the following statements, if any, are FALSE?
    a. Gay men are more likely than heterosexuals to experience feelings of anxiety and depression, and are more prone to suicide.
    b. Lesbians are more likely than heterosexuals to experience feelings of anxiety and depression, and are more prone to suicide.
    c. Gay males are more likely to have anorexia and/or bulimia than heterosexual males.
    d. Both A and C are FALSE.
    e. Both B and C are FALSE.

13. During the "coming out" process, lesbians tend to focus on the _____ aspects of their growing feelings, and gay males are more likely to focus on the _____ aspects.
    a. negative; positive
    b. sexual; emotional
    c. positive; negative
    d. emotional; sexual

14. Kayla and Monica have been a cohabiting, lesbian couple for the past five years. At one time or another, each of them has had sexual relationships outside their long-term relationship, but neither of them know about the other's infidelity. Using Bell and Weinberg's typology, Kayla and Monica appear to be which of the following type of gay couples?
    a. Close couples
    b. Open couples
    c. Functionals
    d. Dysfunctionals

15. According to the NHSLS study, about _____ of those surveyed, reported having bisexual _____.
    a. 1%; attractions to both women and men
    b. 4%; experiences with both women and men
    c. 1%; identities
    d. 4%; identities

True/False

_____ 1. Sexual motivation does not appear to play a role in any male-male and female-female sexual interactions among animals.

_____ 2. Men and women tend to be equally homophobic.

_____ 3. Freud believed that unresolved castration anxiety played a role in lesbian sexual orientation.

_____ 4. By definition, gay people cannot be homophobic.

_____ 5. In the past, Masters and Johnson ran a program to "reverse" gay male and lesbian sexual orientations through activities such as massage and genital stimulation.

_____ 6. The great majority of homosexual people have a gender identity that is consistent with their anatomic sex.

_____ 7. Lesbians and gay men who are considered members of ethnic minorities tend to find a greater sense of belonging in the gay community than they do in their respective ethnic communities.

_____ 8. Researchers have found evidence linking a region on the X sex chromosome to a gay male sexual orientation.

Essay Questions

1. Compare and contrast the theoretical frameworks developed by Kinsey, Storms, and more recent models, such as Lippa and Arad, that address additional issues. Include the strengths and weaknesses of each framework in your discussion.

_____

_____

_____

_____

_____

_____

_____

_____

2. Describe Savin-Williams and Diamond's 4-stage model of sexual identity development in gay males and lesbians. Include attention to gender differences in this process.

_____

_____

_____

_____

_____

_____

_____

_____

_____

When You Have Finished...

Let's see where the Web takes you as you explore the following activities related to Sexual Techniques and Behavior Patterns.

1. Why mess around with "wannabes" when you can go to the source? Check out the site for the Kinsey Institute and see what you think of the research findings as they exist outside your text: http://www.indiana.edu/~kinsey/index.html. Be sure to try out the heterosexual-homosexual continuum rating scale for yourself while you are there: http://www.indiana.edu/~kinsey/research/ak-hhscale.html

2. As your text has said, there is significant controversy considering the issue of bisexuality. After reading this chapter, where do you stand? Why not see what you can find on the Web to help you make some tentative conclusions. For example, this site provides more information to support or form your opinion about bisexuality (and whether it exists). If you have any questions about your own orientation as bisexual, this might be a starting place as well. It also includes forums, political and sexual information about bi-orientation. Note that this site is a link attached to a larger site for gay males and lesbians: http://www.planetout.com/pno/people/bi/splash.html

3. Where do you stand on the issue of homophobia? Are you an "ally"? A silent bystander? Or are you grappling with some feelings of homophobia yourself? Explore these issues in the privacy of your own computer. This link will connect you to information from a previous special on homophobia from PBS's *Frontline*. It is connected to a homophobia scale developed by Wright, Adams, and Bernat as part of a research project designed to test the theory that homophobia is a manifestation of repressed homosexual desire. Despite the purpose of the research, please note that the scale is not a measure of homosexuality. It is, however, designed to measure your thoughts, feelings, and behaviors with regards to homosexuality. There are no right or wrong answers, but you can compare your scores to others who have answered the same questions, as well as being able to find links to interesting web pages putting homophobia in a socio-historical context. http://www.pbs.org/wgbh/pages/frontline/shows/assault/etc/quiz.html

4. What are your thoughts on the US Supreme Court's ruling in Lawrence v. Texas—the ruling that said that the Texas sodomy law (and others like it) are unconstitutional? As a bonus, the "Prior Case Law" part of this webpage illuminates historical court decisions allowing married couples to *legally* use contraception. A mention of the infamous Roe v. Wade decision affecting abortion choice is featured. Importantly, the Lawrence decision was NOT a unanimous decision by the court and the dissenting opinion was viewed as caustic by some. Glance over the logic of featured highlights in Justice Kennedy's majority opinion. Using your critical analysis skills (instead of any emotions), what element(s) do you agree or disagree? (What are the strengths, what are the faults you see?) On the opposing side, Justice Scalia wrote the dissenting opinion—again, what do you agree (or disagree) with in some of the extracts shown of his opinion. Again, in a critical manner, why? How do your personal views align with your critical analysis—does it fit well or do you have some reconciliation to make?

Overview—http://en.wikipedia.org/wiki/Lawrence_v._Texas
Full majority opinion— http://www4.law.cornell.edu/supct/html/02-102.ZS.html

5. Along the lines of law and homophobia, which in a way combines the previous two numbered items, how common is hate crime on the basis of perceived sexual orientation? How does it compare to other bias crimes (i.e., race, disability, national origin, or religion)? How does your state compare— is it higher or lower than many or most others? The U.S. government's Department of Justice, via the Federal Bureau of Investigation (FBI), tracks data for all these questions and the time of the writing of this Grade-Aid, Search the FBI website for hate crimes and see how the statistics have changed. As a nation are we actually changing? http://www.fbi.gov

6. What do you think about the issue of sexual re-orientation (also called "reparative therapy")? Does it appear to be a viable reality to you, or are its chances of success roughly that of a person finding a unicorn in the Bronx Zoo? Here are some sites that present overviews of the debate on re-orientation along with two sites from the point of view of those who believe in it. Google "sexual orientation therapy." What are you finding? Can you find a theme on reorientation websites?

Chapter 11
Conception, Pregnancy, and Childbirth

Before You Begin...

Chapter Summary

Conception, pregnancy, and childbirth all have effectively millions of details, if not more, that come together to produce a miracle. It is this miracle that dad and mom call their new baby! In this chapter, we will explore the key details at each one of these steps to producing a new person. We hope you will enjoy the journey through this chapter and that it better prepares you for producing your own new persons (when and if it is right for you)! Let's start.

Fertilization is the first step, and it is the union of a sperm cell and ovum. It normally occurs in a woman's fallopian tube. As your text authors note, there are optimal times for fertilization and sometimes it can be especially important to optimize the couple's chances. Optimizing conception involves engaging in coitus during ovulation, which can be detected in three separate ways and is explained further in your book.

Sometimes the desired fertilization never occurs—leading to a diagnosis of infertility. This can result from problems in one or even both of the potential parents. The causes of infertility in males and females are explained—along with methods to overcome it. Methods for overcoming infertility include such things as:

- Artificial insemination by the father's (or a donor's) sperm
- In-vitro fertilization
- GIFT

- ZIFT
- Donor IVF
- Embryonic transfer
- Surrogate motherhood

Note that today both sperm and egg donation is becoming a more routine procedure. Too, prospective egg or sperm customers can go to websites and browse through lists of donor characteristics.

Probably predictably to most people, pregnancy goes through a series of stages from fertilization to removal of the placenta after the child has been delivered. The early signs and effects of pregnancy may include increased breast tenderness, need for more sleep, and morning sickness. In the early stages of pregnancy, spontaneous abortions—also called miscarriages—are most likely to occur. A woman's psychological responses to pregnancy reflect whether she or the couple wanted her to become pregnant, her physical changes, and her attitudes toward them. Men's responses reflect similar considerations, with the emphasis tending to be on financial and emotional readiness since he does not carry the baby to term. Let us also note that despite some popular ideas to the contrary, coitus during a normal pregnancy is medically safe until the start of labor.

Prenatal development can be divided into three periods. The germinal stage is the period from conception to implantation. The embryonic stage begins with implantation and extends to about the eighth week of development; it is characterized by differentiation of major organ systems. The fetal stage (characterized by continued maturation of the organ systems and dramatic increases in size) begins by the ninth week and continues until birth.

Environmental factors affect prenatal development, as well as the success of a pregnancy. A list of these factors include:

- Maternal diet and/or malnutrition
- Maternal health problems
- Presence of STIs
- Rubella
- Toxemia
- Ectopic pregnancy
- RH incompatibility
- Parental drug use
- Exposure to teratogens during critical periods of vulnerability

- Smoking, in particular, is a risk factor for:
  o Low birth weight
  o Impairment of intellectual development
  o Fetal heart rate abnormalities
  o Sudden infant death syndrome
  o Impaired lung functions.
- Chromosomal/genetic abnormalities

Particular defects and syndromes can result from chromosomal and genetic abnormalities contributed by either parent's genetic material. Blood tests, amniocentesis, and ultrasound can detect many of these fetal disorders. Too, the authors discuss research on optimal time intervals between successive pregnancies.

In the first stage of childbirth, uterine contractions efface and dilate the cervix. The second stage begins when the baby first appears at the opening of the birth canal and ends with the birth of the baby. During the third stage, the placenta is expelled. Contemporary methods of childbirth are explained. Some parents may choose to deliver at a birth center or at home instead of at a hospital. Prenatal anoxia, preterm delivery, and low birth weight are significant problems that can arise during the birthing process. Delivery method options and variations are discussed and weighed against each other. The probable difficulties with and consequences of babies born preterm and with low birth weights are discussed.

Finally, we examine the postpartum period, as there can be mood changes or depression that occurs during it. Also, decisions about breast-feeding versus bottle-feeding are examined. We then review resumption of normal ovulation and menstruation during the postpartum period along with resumption of coitus. If both the man and woman desire coital sexual activity, it can usually be resumed six weeks after birth.

1. Describe the process of fertilization and conception.

2. Identify how to optimize the chances of conception. Know the various methods and their associated success rates.

3. Describe what physical factors influence the higher likelihood that the zygote is male. Describe factors that offset these factors such that it evens out for females.

4. Describe the causes of infertility in males and females.

5. List and describe contemporary methods for overcoming infertility.

6. Examine the biological and psychological effects of pregnancy on women.

7. Trace prenatal development through the germinal, embryonic, and fetal stages.

8. Describe how environmental factors, before and during pregnancy, affect the embryo and fetus.

9. Discuss possible chromosomal and genetic abnormalities in the fetus and the tests used to detect them.

10. Describe maternal physical changes associated with the three stages of childbirth.

11. Discuss historical and current methods of childbirth, including the use of anesthesia, preparation for childbirth, and the need for and frequency of Cesarean sections.

12. Complications: Explain the suspected causes, the effects at birth and the effects later in a child's life of anoxia, preterm delivery, and low birth weight.

13. Postpartum period: Explain the emotional and physical changes that women may experience during this period.

14. Breast-feeding versus bottle-feeding: Discuss the advantages and disadvantages of both.

Term Identification: This chapter has many more terms than most all of the other chapters—two tables of them one below and then the page following. This does add some difficulty in making flashcards to quiz yourself but it is not impossible. If it helps you to keep them straight, group them according to their topic area (e.g., anatomy, illness, during embryonic stage, etc.). Just be careful to know them well enough to recognize them out of context, too. Another strategy is to "work" the tables in say two sittings so as to not be overwhelmed—it does start flowing (we urge you to trust us on that).

Chapter 11 Table of Key Terms

Acquired immunodeficiency syndrome (AIDS)	Ectoderm
Age of viability	Ectopic pregnancy
Amniocentesis	Efface
Amniotic fluid	Embryonic disk
Amniotic sac	Embryonic stage
Anoxia	Embryonic transfer
Artificial insemination	Endoderm
Auto-immune response	Endometriosis
Blastocyst	Episiotomy
Braxton-Hicks contractions	Fetal alcohol syndrome
Breech presentation	Gamete intrafallopian transfer (GIFT)
Cephalic presentation	General anesthesia
Cephalocaudal	Germinal stage
Cesarean section	Human chorionic gonadotropin
Critical period of vulnerability	Hyaluronidase
DES	Hysterosalpingogram
Dilate	In vitro fertilization
Donor IVF	Infertility
Down syndrome	Intracytoplasmic sperm injection

Chapter 11 Table of Key Terms (Continued)

Laparoscopy

Local anesthesia

Lochia

Mesoderm

Miscarriage

Morning sickness

Motility

Neural tube

Oxytocin

Perineum

Period of the ovum

Placenta

Postpartum

Postpartum depression

Preterm

Prolactin

Prostaglandins

Proximodistal

Recessive trait

Respiratory distress syndrome

Rh incompatibility

Rubella

Rubin test

Spontaneous abortion

Stillbirth

Surfactant

Surrogate mother

Syphilis

Teratogens

Toxemia

Transition

Transverse position

Trophoblast

Umbilical cord

Zona pellucida

Zygote

Zygote intrafallopian transfer (ZIFT)

As You Read....

<table>
<tr><td>Activities</td></tr>
</table>

❖ *Conception: Against All Odds*

➢ *The Discovery Zone: The Next Generation*

Think back to your childhood for a moment. What did you believe about pregnancy and where babies came from? How does it compare with the truth? For example, instead of telling her how babies were made, my grandmother told my mother that you could get pregnant from sitting on a man's lap. Considering that this was long enough ago that there were "rumble seats" in many cars where you'd have to double up on laps to fit everyone in the car for a group date, this was a big deal. So when she was old enough to go on car dates, she took a phone book to put between herself and her date's lap in case they had to pile into the rumble seat!

OR

If you didn't get direct information from peers or family members about pregnancy, think back on how conception and pregnancy were handled in movies you saw and books you read.

Using your text to compare and contrast what you first learned with the "state of the art" knowledge on conception in the book, respond to the questions below:

How old were you when you first found out (at least in theory) how babies were made?

_____

_____

How did you think conception worked? _____

_____

How accurate was this information?_____

_____

Where were you and with whom (if anyone)? _____

How did you feel about what you found out? (e.g., Did you think it was exciting, gross, scary, beautiful, etc.?)

_____

_____

How did you feel about the *difference* between what you found out as a child and what you found to be true as an adult?

_____

_____

What messages were you internalizing, according to your emotions about what you found out? (e.g., Was it another way to let you know sex was shameful? Beautiful? Appropriate under the right circumstances?)

_____

_____

❖ *Infertility and Alternative Ways of Becoming Parents*

Directions: Your text details many ways to address infertility. Using that information, fill in the chart below.

	Definition	Advantages	Disadvantages	Would YOU Do It?	Why/Why Not?
IVF					
GIFT					
ZIFT					

Definition	Advantages	Disadvantages	Would YOU Do It?	Why/Why Not?
Donor IVF				
Embryonic Transfer				
ICSI				
Surrogate Motherhood				
Adoption				

TRY PRACTICE TEST #1 NOW!
GOOD LUCK!

Pregnancy

Directions: Match the following pregnancy-related terms to their definitions below.

a. amniotic sac

_____ A condition in which antibodies produced by a pregnant woman are transmitted to the fetus and may cause brain damage or death.

b. amniotic fluid

_____ A life-threatening condition characterized by high blood pressure.

c. placenta

_____ An estrogen formerly given to women at risk for miscarriage to help maintain pregnancy.

d. umbilical cord

_____ Environmental influences or agents that can damage an embryo or fetus.

e. age of viability

_____ Following birth.

f. cephalic presentation

_____ A pregnancy in which the fertilized ovum implants someplace other than the uterus.

g. breech presentation

_____ The sac containing the fetus.

h. teratogens

_____ A cluster of symptoms caused by maternal drinking in which the child shows develop-mental lags and characteristic facial features, such as an underdeveloped upper jaw, flattened nose and widely spaced eyes.

i. critical period of vulnerability

_____ A tube that connects the fetus to the placenta.

j. toxemia

_____ Emergence of the baby feet first from the womb.

k. ectopic pregnancy

_____ Fluid within the amniotic sac that suspends and protects the fetus.

l. Rh incompatibility

_____ A period of time during which an embryo or fetus is vulnerable to the effects of a teratogen.

m. DES (diethylstilbestrol)

_____ An organ connected from mother to fetus by the umbilical cord, which allows the exchange of nutrients and wastes.

n. fetal alcohol syndrome

_____ Emergence of the baby headfirst from the womb.

o. postpartum

_____ The age at which a fetus can sustain independent life.

❖ Prenatal Development

Directions: Fill in the blanks about prenatal development below.

The seven- or eight-day period from conception to implantation in the uterine wall is termed the _____ stage. The period from implantation to about the eighth week of development is called the _____ stage. Development of the embryo follows two general trends: _____ (from the head downward), and _____ (from the center of the body outward). The embryo (or fetus) is suspended within the _____ sac in the _____ fluid.

Nutrients and waste products are exchanged between mother and embryo (or fetus) through the _____. The fetus is connected to this organ by the _____ cord. The _____ passes from the woman's body after delivery and is also called the "afterbirth."

The _____ stage begins about the ninth week and continues until the birth. During the second trimester, the fetus increases its weight from _____ to _____. Usually the mother can feel movement by the middle of the _____ month. Near the end of the second trimester, the fetus approaches the _____ _____. However, only a _____ of babies born at the end of the second trimester who weigh under two pounds will survive.

Environmental influences or agents that can harm the embryo or fetus are called _____. These include drugs taken by the mother, substances produced by the mother's body, and disease-causing organisms. For example, nearly 40% of children whose mothers drank heavily during pregnancy develop _____ _____ _____. Babies whose mothers _____ during pregnancy weigh less on the average at birth. These babies are also more likely to experience asthma and a variety of other problems. _____ and CVS (_____ _____ _____) are two tests used to detect chromosomal and genetic abnormalities in the fetus.

TRY PRACTICE TEST #2 NOW!
GOOD LUCK!

❖ Childbirth

Directions: Complete the chart below by supplying information about the events that take place during the three stages of childbirth.

Stage	Events Taking Place and Average Length of Stage
FIRST STAGE **Transition**	
SECOND STAGE	
THIRD STAGE	

❖ *The Postpartum Period*

One of your authors has often joked with new parents about the need for an operator's manual for newborns. The miracles of prenatal development and childbirth are complicated enough—but that's the *easy* part compared to what happens when you get home! Your text discusses some of the key issues related to the first part of childrearing—the postpartum period. Being sure to address the postpartum phenomena listed below, take a few moments to think about what could be done to support new parents during this time. Use the information in your text to support your choices.

❑   Maternal Depression

_____

_____

_____

❑   Breast-feeding vs. Bottle-Feeding

_____

_____

_____

❑   Resumption of Ovulation and Menstruation

_____

_____

_____

❑   Resumption of Sexual Activity

_____

_____

_____

TRY PRACTICE TEST #3 NOW!
GOOD LUCK!

After You Read...

(LO = Learning Objective)

1. A fertilized ovum is called a/an:
   a. Embryo
   b. Fetus
   c. Follicle
   d. Zygote

   p. 315   LO 1

2. Which of the following is responsible for locking other sperm out once an ovum is fertilized?
   a. Hyaluronidase
   b. Luteinizing hormone
   c. Vaginal mucus
   d. Zona pellucida

   p. 317   LO 1

3. Basal body temperature charting allows for:
   a. Identification of the optimal time for conception.
   b. Predicting the time of ovulation.
   c. Both of the above.
   d. None of the above.

   p. 317-318   LO 2

4. Sperm are the most active within _____ after ejaculation.
   a. 12 hours
   b. 24 hours
   c. 48 hours
   d. 72 hours

   p. 317   LO 2

5. Y-bearing sperm are _____, while X-bearing sperm are _____.
   a. bigger; faster
   b. smaller and faster; more durable
   c. bigger and faster; more abundant
   d. smaller and faster; more aggressive

   p. 316   LO 3

6. Despite the higher rates of spontaneous abortion of male fetuses, more males are born than females. What is the equalizing factor that brings it more into balance between the sexes?
    a. Male adolescents assume more risks that result in their deaths
    b. Male fetuses suffer a higher rate of infant mortality.
    c. Both A and B
    d. Neither B and C
        p. 316-317   LO 3

7. Causes of infertility in females include all of the following EXCEPT:
    a. Inability to achieve orgasm during coitus, which lowers acidity levels in the vagina.
    b. Failure to ovulate.
    c. Obstructions of the reproductive tract.
    d. Endometriosis.
        p. 321   LO 4

8. Which of the following are commonly associated with male fertility problems?
    a. Diabetes
    b. Thyroid disease
    c. High sperm motility
    d. Both A and B
    e. Both A and C
        p. 320   LO 4

9. Which of the following refers to the test in which carbon dioxide gas is blown through the cervix and reproductive tract in order to determine whether the fallopian tubes are blocked?
    a. Hysterosalpingogram
    b. Colposcopy
    c. Laparoscopy
    d. Rubin test
        p. 322   LO 5

10. According to follow-up studies of couples who give birth using IVF, the greatest success rates appear to be achieved when ____ embryos are implanted.
    a. 5
    b. 4
    c. 3
    d. 2
        p. 322   LO 5

(LO = Learning Objective)

1. Rosalia missed her period about three weeks ago and asks her physician for a pregnancy test. She is confirmed as pregnant if there is _____ in her urine.
   a. follicle stimulating hormone
   b. hyaluronidase
   c. luteinizing hormone
   d. human chorionic gonadotropin
   　　　　　p. 324　　　　　LO 6

2. Women carrying more than one child usually experience _____ during morning sickness.
   a. less nausea
   b. more nausea
   c. about the same amount of nausea
   d. None of the above; there is no relationship between multiple births and nausea
   　　　　　p. 325　　　　　LO 6

3. In the developing fetus, arm buds appear before hands and fingers. This is in keeping with:
   a. The cephalocaudal principle.
   b. The proximodistal principle.
   c. Nagele's Rule.
   d. The concept of critical period.
   　　　　　p. 330　　　　　LO 7

4. The correct order of the stages of prenatal development is:
   a. Trophoblast stage, embryonic stage, fetal stage.
   b. Germinal stage, embryonic stage, fetal stage.
   c. Blastocyst stage, embryonic stage, fetal stage.
   d. Embryonic stage, germinal stage, fetal stage.
   　　　　　p. 329-332　　　　　LO 7

5. During the germinal stage, it takes the zygote about _____ to reach the uterus.
   a. 1–2 hours
   b. 3–4 hours
   c. 1–2 days
   d. 3–4 days
   　　　　　p. 329　　　　　LO 7

6. At which stage of development are the major organ systems considered most vulnerable to the effects of teratogens?
   a. Germinal stage
   b. Embryonic stage
   c. Fetal stage
   d. Teratogenic stage
                     p. 334   LO 8

7. Toxemia, a life-threatening condition related to high blood pressure of the mother during pregnancy, begins with:
   a. Eclampsia.
   b. Erythroblastosis.
   c. Preeclampsia.
   d. Preerythroblastosis.
                     p. 334   LO 8

8. Debra is concerned about the possibility that her fetus has inherited a familial disease. To check for this genetic problem, she will undergo:
   a. Basal body temperature testing.
   b. Shettles' procedure.
   c. Amniocentesis.
   d. Urine analysis.
                     p. 342   LO 9

9. In most cases, Down Syndrome is transmitted:
   a. Through the mother.
   b. Through the father.
   c. Through a side effect of Rubella during the first trimester.
   d. Through maternal drug use.
                     p. 339   LO 9

10. Phenylketonuria, a disorder that causes mental retardation, can be diagnosed at birth and controlled by:
    a. Administering a one-time vaccine.
    b. Diet and nutrition.
    c. Periodic intravenous treatments during childhood.
    d. Allergy medicine.
                     p. 334   LO 9

(LO = Learning Objective)

1. The second stage of childbirth ends with:
    a. The transition period.
    b. Birth of the baby.
    c. Crowning.
    d. Episiotomy.
           p. 344   LO 10

2. An episiotomy during the second stage of pregnancy may prevent:
    a. Hymen perforation.
    b. Prostaglandin secretion.
    c. Injuring the perineum.
    d. Premature delivery.
           p. 344   LO 11

3. Which of the following are the result of using anesthetic drugs, including tranquilizers and narcotics, to eliminate pain during childbirth?
    a. Increased strength of uterine contractions
    b. Weakened ability to *stop* pushing the baby through the birth canal before it's time
    c. Lowered overall responsiveness of the newborn
    d. Both A and B
    e. Both B and C
           p. 346   LO 11

4. All of the methods below can be used to facilitate childbirth:
    a. Lamaze method.
    b. General anesthesia.
    c. Local anesthesia.
    d. Only A and B are methods to facilitate childbirth.
    e. A, B, and C are all methods to facilitate childbirth.
           p. 346   LO 11

5. The third stage of childbirth has one (or more) of the following characteristics?
    a. It is also where the placenta is evacuated or expelled.
    b. The breasts tend to enlarge, sometimes substantially.
    c. It is also called the post-partum.
    d. None of the above
    e. All of the above
           p. 344   LO 10

6. Gestation lasts for approximately _____ weeks.
    a. 37
    b. 48
    c. 57
    d. 40
                p. 349   LO 12

7. Preterm babies often experience respiratory distress syndrome because of:
    a. Too much anoxia.
    b. Too little anoxia.
    c. Too much surfactant.
    d. Too little surfactant.
                p. 348   LO 12

8. The term *postpartum* refers to the time:
    a. Following the midpoint of pregnancy.
    b. Following birth.
    c. Following conception.
    d. When a mother first feels her fetus move.
                p. 350   LO 13

9. Although recent news coverage of infanticide due to postpartum depression (PPD) make it seem as if it may be an epidemic, cases of PPD severe enough to include "psychotic features" tend to occur in about:
    a. 1 woman in 250–500.
    b. 1 woman in 500–1000.
    c. 1 woman in 1000–1500.
    d. 1 woman in 1500–2000.
                p. 351   LO 13

10. Breast-feeding tends to reduce the general risk of infections to the baby by transmitting:
    a. The mother's prolactin to the baby.
    b. The mother's oxytocin to the baby.
    c. The mother's circadian rhythms to the baby.
    d. The mother's antibodies to the baby.
                p. 352   LO 14

Multiple Choice

1. The term postpartum refers to the time:
    a. Following the midpoint of pregnancy.
    b. Following birth.
    c. Following conception.
    d. When a mother first feels her fetus move.

2. All of the methods below can be used to facilitate childbirth:
    a. Lamaze method.
    b. General anesthesia.
    c. Local anesthesia.
    d. Only A and B are methods to facilitate childbirth.
    e. A, B, and C are all methods to facilitate childbirth.

3. Breast-feeding tends to reduce the general risk of infections to the baby by transmitting:
    a. The mother's prolactin to the baby.
    b. The mother's oxytocin to the baby.
    c. The mother's circadian rhythms to the baby.
    d. The mother's antibodies to the baby.

4. The correct order of the stages of prenatal development is:
    a. Trophoblast stage, embryonic stage, fetal stage.
    b. Germinal stage, embryonic stage, fetal stage.
    c. Blastocyst stage, embryonic stage, fetal stage.
    d. Embryonic stage, germinal stage, fetal stage.

5. Debra is concerned about the possibility that her fetus has inherited a familial disease. To check for this genetic problem, she will undergo:
    a. Basal body temperature testing.
    b. Shettles' procedure.
    c. Amniocentesis.
    d. Urine analysis.

6. The second stage of childbirth ends with:
    a. The transition period.
    b. Birth of the baby.
    c. Crowning.
    d. Episiotomy.

7. Which of the following refers to the test in which carbon dioxide gas is blown through the cervix and reproductive tract in order to determine whether the fallopian tubes are blocked?
   a. Hysterosalpingogram
   b. Colposcopy
   c. Laparoscopy
   d. Rubin test

8. Basal body temperature charting allows for:
   a. Identification of the optimal time for conception.
   b. Predicting the time of ovulation.
   c. Both of the above
   d. Neither of the above

9. Rosalia missed her period about three weeks ago and asks her physician for a pregnancy test. She is confirmed as pregnant if there is _____ in her urine.
   a. follicle stimulating hormone
   b. hyaluronidase
   c. luteinizing hormone
   d. human chorionic gonadotropin

10. Y-bearing sperm are _____, while X-bearing sperm are _____.
   a. bigger; faster
   b. smaller and faster; more durable
   c. bigger and faster; more abundant
   d. smaller and faster; more aggressive

11. Gestation lasts for approximately _____ weeks.
   a. 37
   b. 48
   c. 57
   d. 40

12. Which of the following is responsible for locking other sperm out once an ovum is fertilized?
   a. Hyaluronidase
   b. Luteinizing hormone
   c. Vaginal mucus
   d. Zona pellucida

13. Which of the following are commonly associated with male fertility problems?
   a. Diabetes
   b. Thyroid disease
   c. High sperm motility
   d. Both A and B
   e. Both A and C

14. At which stage of development are the major organ systems considered most vulnerable to the effects of teratogens?
    a. Germinal stage
    b. Embryonic stage
    c. Fetal stage
    d. Teratogenic stage

15. An episiotomy during the second stage of pregnancy may prevent:
    a. Hymen perforation.
    b. Prostaglandin secretion.
    c. Injuring the perineum.
    d. Premature delivery.

True/False

_____ 1. In some states, surrogate mothering contracts have been invalidated so the surrogate does not have to keep their promise to give up the baby.

_____ 2. Men with lower sperm counts may be advised to increase their frequency of ejaculation per week to build up the count.

_____ 3. The placenta is developed from material supplied by both mother and embryo.

_____ 4. In about 40% of infertility cases, problems are found in *both* partners.

_____ 5. Postpartum depression with occasional psychotic features have only been reported inside the United States so far.

_____ 6. The majority of babies born to mothers with HIV become infected themselves.

_____ 7. Only 1 in 1000 sperm tends to arrive in the vicinity of an ovum.

_____ 8. Some women experience normal menstrual periods throughout pregnancy.

Essay Questions

1. What are the major sources of infertility among men and women? Include in your answer a brief mention of the suggestions for dealing with these problems.

_____

_____

_____

_____

_____

_____

_____

_____

2. Describe the pros and cons of breast-feeding, including the influence of social and historical trends.

_____

_____

_____

_____

_____

_____

_____

_____

When You Have Finished....

Let's see where the Web takes you as you explore the following activities related to Conception, Pregnancy, and Childbirth.

1. Think back to what you were told about how babies are made. Possibly it was from health class or your parents. Did that information really sink in? Go to YouTube and find the following video: "How Does a Woman get Pregnant." The video is rather crude but how does it do telling the story of conception? Is it accurate?

2. This chapter mentions a lot of thought provoking information about ways to manage the birth of your child. See what you can find out about the method that captured your attention the most. In the meantime, here's a fairly comprehensive site about childbirth options asserting that "birth is a natural process, not a medical procedure": http://www.childbirth.org/

3. What did you think about all of the ways people have tried to influence the gender of their children? Luckily for those of us who currently live in the U.S., the gender of our children is NOT a life or death issue. Nonetheless, a baby's gender influences the family system on all sorts of levels, no matter how many members there are in the family. For a collection of methods to choose your child's gender, Google the following statement "Choose the gender of my child." How much of the information is real? Look up the Chinese birth calendars and see if you are the correct gender for when your parents conceived you.

4. Infertility is such a difficult and personal issue, it seems well-suited to a Web search due to the relative anonymity the searcher can have. Go to YouTube and follow the fertility treatment of an individual. (There are many Blogs on IVF.) How much does it cost the individual in emotional stress and physical pain?

5. Teratogens? Search the Web for known teratogens that can harm the developing fetus. How is it possible any of us have turned out healthy?

Chapter 12
Contraception and Abortion

Before You Begin…

Chapter Summary

Even today, contraception and abortion can often lead to contentious debate—especially in some religious circles. Generally the latter (abortion) is a little more socially and politically charged than the former (contraception). Relative to contraception though, there are some who think of intercourse as *only* for procreation and therefore look disapprovingly toward contraceptives and their use. Indeed, contraception—when used correctly—does effectively separate reproduction from the pleasure and intimacy-building aspects of intercourse. On the other topic, abortion is used to terminate pregnancy for a variety of reasons (as your text will outline) and is viewed positively and negatively depending on where one sits on the continuum. Let's now explore this exciting and engaging topic further.

New contraceptive methods are being researched, including mechanical and chemical barrier methods, hormone-delivery systems, intrauterine devices (IUDs), and methods for men to use. The ideal contraceptive would suspend fertility, have no side effects, and be reversible on demand. Historically, contraceptive methods have been mechanical and chemical in nature: plugging the cervix, sheathing the penis, douching with substances thought to make the vaginal environment inhospitable to sperm, absorbing the sperm after ejaculation in the vagina, and, perennially the least popular, practicing abstinence.

Margaret Sanger, a nurse practitioner in the early 1900s, was an early advocate for disseminating information about birth control in the United States. Her work was responsible for overturning the Comstock Law of 1873, which prohibited sending contraceptive information or devices through the mail due to its "obscenity." In 1918, the courts ruled that physicians could disseminate such information to aid in the cure and prevention of disease. In 1965, the Supreme Court struck down the last legal impediment to informing about, selling, or using contraception, although the use of artificial contraception continues to be opposed by some groups (as alluded to in the opening paragraph).

Talking about contraception with your partner is not always easy to do. With this in mind, your authors provide helpful strategies for not only selecting a contraceptive method but raising the topic of contraception for discussion with your potential sex partner. Some contraceptives (but by no means all) offer an additional benefit in reducing risk in getting an STI. Contemporary methods of contraception are explained and evaluated for effectiveness and ease of use. These include oral contraceptives, Norplant, intrauterine devices (IUD), diaphragms, cervical caps, spermicides, condoms, douching, withdrawal, timing of ovulation (rhythm), and sterilization—voluntary and forced. Emergent contraceptives now under development are also discussed.

Hormonal methods of pregnancy prevention, such as oral contraceptives, include combination pills, minipills, the morning-after pill, and rather new contraceptive patches. Some methods require implantation or injection into the body. Norplant is progestin packaged in six small tubes that are implanted in a woman's upper arm. Depo-Provera and Lunelle are injected hormonal methods. All the hormonal methods are highly effective but have side effects, ranging from unpleasant to potentially quite dangerous. Your text authors fully inventory these for you and it might be wise to know some of these for your course's exam.

Barrier devices work on the principle of blocking the sperm from reaching an egg or killing it, or even a combination of both. Barrier devices include the IUD, which is highly effective but has potentially serious side effects. Other barrier devices require the use of spermicide to increase effectiveness. The diaphragm covers the cervix and has few health risks but some disadvantages. The cervical cap is similar to the diaphragm but smaller. Both have high failure rates in reality. Latex condoms have a high failure rate when used alone, but when used with spermicides, their effectiveness rivals that of birth-control pills. They also afford protection against STIs. A female condom that covers the vagina is also available. Both male and female condoms are available in polyurethane, which people who are sensitive or allergic to latex can use.

Let's look at sterilization and some common non-methods in contrast. One of your writer's professors asked the class, "What do you call a man who uses the withdrawal method? … Daddy." The converse of this also applies to women who attempt douching (or even jumping up and down afterward)—except that she is called mommy instead. Even before visiting your text, it should be clear that douching and withdrawal are unreliable and, therefore, considered contraceptive non-methods. At the other end of the spectrum, sterilization (through male vasectomy or female tubal ligation) has a very low failure rate (thus, are considered highly effective). Though, sterilization is *not* advised for individuals who believe that they might later decide that they want to biologically participate in conception. In fact, many physicians may refuse to sterilize young adults for fear that five or ten years down the road, the sterilized person can have a change of heart (and the doctor could be viewed as having some costly legal liability).

Let's now talk fertilization… There are women (and couples) in the world who wish to have a baby but can't because of some kind of a fertility issue. Especially in these cases, fertility is an important topic to understand. Fertility awareness methods rely on detecting when a woman ovulates using a calendar, basal body temperature readings, inspecting the viscosity of cervical mucus, and daily urine luteinizing hormone (LH) test kits.

Now the politically loaded topic, abortion—or more correctly "induced abortion." An induced abortion is the purposeful termination of a pregnancy. It is commonly and widely practiced in Canada, Japan, Russia, Europe, and the United States. Moral concerns about abortion turn on the question of when human life begins and whether a woman should have the right to terminate her own pregnancy. Historically, from 1607–1828, abortions in the U.S. were legal until "quickening" occurred. During the last half of the 1800s, all states passed laws outlawing abortion. In the late 1960s, some states began to liberalize their abortion laws. In the United States, the legal right to an abortion was established by the United States Supreme Court in *Roe v. Wade* (1973). A heated national debate continues between the self-named pro-choice and right-to-life movements. Since congressional passage of the Hyde amendment in 1977, Supreme Court decisions have allowed states to adopt greater restrictions than those set forth in *Roe v. Wade.* Research and public polls indicate that the majority of United States citizens favor legalized abortion but not under all circumstances.

Abortion methods in use today in the United States include vacuum aspiration, dilation and curettage (D & C), dilation and evacuation (D & E), induction of labor by intra-amniotic infusion, hysterotomy, and a drug-induced abortion method, RU-486 or Plan B. Importantly, choosing to have an abortion is typically an emotionally painful decision and there are widely varying reports of the psychological effects women experience as a result of choosing to have an abortion.

Learning Objectives

1. Define contraception and trace the history of methods of contraception.

2. Discuss the history of contraception law in the United States.

3. List eight issues to consider when choosing a contraceptive.

4. Describe how oral contraceptives work and discuss their effectiveness, reversibility, advantages, and disadvantages.

5. Describe how Norplant and Lunelle work and discuss their effectiveness, reversibility, advantages, and disadvantages.

6. Describe how IUDs work and discuss their effectiveness, reversibility, advantages, and disadvantages.

7. Describe the diaphragm, and discuss how it works, its effectiveness, reversibility, advantages, and disadvantages.

8. Identify the types of spermicides and discuss their use alone or with other methods, their effectiveness, reversibility, advantages, and disadvantages.

9. Describe the cervical cap and discuss how it works, its effectiveness, reversibility, advantages, and disadvantages.

10. Describe how condoms are used, and discuss their effectiveness, reversibility, advantages, and disadvantages.

11. Describe douching and withdrawal and explain why both are considered non-methods of contraception.

12. Name and explain the four fertility awareness techniques and discuss their effectiveness, advantages, and disadvantages.

13. Explain the procedures used in male and female sterilization and discuss the effectiveness, advantages, and disadvantages of the procedures.

14. Describe the advantages and disadvantages of the female condom, Depo-Provera, Lunelle, and discuss possible future developments in contraception.

15. Summarize the history of abortion, the changing abortion laws in the United States and attitudes toward abortion.

16. Describe the four methods most commonly used for first and second trimester abortions, including RU-486 and Plan B, the possible complications associated with each, and the time period during pregnancy in which each can be performed.

17. Explain how Americans' support for legalized abortion varies as a function of the stages of pregnancy.

18. Contrast the pro-life and pro-choice interpretations of known psychological consequences of abortion in the United States.

Term Identification

You know what we suggest you do here by now! The repetition from flashcards (or some new electronic equivalent) will help you!

Chapter 12's Table of Key Terms

Artificial contraception	Intrauterine device
Basal body temperature (BBT) method	Laparoscopy
Calendar method	Microbicide
Coitus interruptus	Minilaparotomy
Combination pill	Minipill
Condom	Oral contraceptive
Culpotomy	Ovulation method
D&C	Peak days
D&E	Prophylactic
Diaphragm	Sterilization
Douche	Tubal sterilization
Hysterectomy	Vacuum aspiration
Hysterotomy	Vasectomy
Induced abortion	Vasovasotomy
Intra-amniotic infusion	Viscosity

As You Read...

Activities

❖ **Contraception**

Reading the text's account of the history of contraception in the United States really makes one of your writers appreciate being born when she was, and being able to make choices about what kind of contraception she wanted and where to obtain it. However, there is another barrier to making contraception choices—communication. Why is it so hard to talk to one another about protection when we are being as physically intimate as two people can be? With that in mind, read the following scenarios. Using the five communication guidelines presented in your text to support your response, describe the advice you would give to each of the people who came to you for help with their dilemmas.

Scenario 1:
Tori is a high-school senior, and has dated Michael for two years. This year he is away at college, so they've had to endure a long-distance relationship for the first time. They each agreed that they would see other people, but only casually so that their social activity wouldn't end while they were apart; theirs would be the primary romantic relationship. Because they've been together and in love for so long, they have agreed long ago that Tori will take "the pill" as a contraceptive. Although Tori hasn't slept with anyone in Michael's absence, she has heard about how cute and sexually "open-minded" the girls are at college and is worried that Michael's world is full of temptations for casual sex. She thinks they should start using condoms along with the pill, so that no STI's are "shared." Michael takes great offense at this suggestion and Tori ends up having sex with him without a condom to "prove" that she still trusts him. How can she re-open this discussion without it ending in an argument?

Response: _____

_____

_____

_____

Scenario 2:

Damon and Monique have just left his fraternity semi-formal. Even though it is their first "official" date, they have been friends for a while and have even hooked-up a little after a couple of parties recently. It being a special occasion, with alcohol, Damon played it safe and booked a room at the hotel where the event was held. This is no surprise to Monique, because Damon was nice enough to both ask her if she'd like to share the room, and to guarantee her that he'd book a room with two beds, so that there wouldn't be any expectations. Nevertheless, they both know there is a possibility that their relationship will progress to the next level that evening at the hotel. Damon is so busy preparing for the event with his frat brothers, birth control is the last thing on his mind. How can Monique handle this issue responsibly while minimizing the chances that she will offend Damon?

Response: _____

_____

_____

_____

Scenario 3:

Rob and Alexa have been together for a few weeks. Though they have not defined their relationship to any great extent, they are having sex and are both comfortable with the pace of their relationship. However, Rob is worried because he's not really satisfied with the choice of birth control Alexa has made. She already had a diaphragm when they met, and assured him that she had things taken care of. But he has read about them. Not only is he uncomfortable with their failure rate, but he's also not crazy about the way the spermicide tastes when they have oral sex. How can he bring up this discussion without upsetting Alexa, and without making their relationship seem like it's "farther along" than it is?

Response: _____

_____

_____

_____

Scenario 4:

Jorge is starting college and is still a virgin. He has been through an abstinence-only education program in his private school. After about four weeks Jorge met someone in his dorm with whom he really hit it off. On their first date, things progressed rapidly and his partner told him to go and buy condoms and get back as soon as he could.

Response: _____

_____

_____

_____

Scenario 5:

Mike (33) and Kelly (42) have been together for a few months. They like spending time together, but Kelly is feeling the need to get married and have children. Mike is not so sure about the commitment. They plan a romantic getaway to Mexico for Mike's birthday. Mike is unsure about contraceptive methods for the week, as Kelly is sensitive to latex so condom usage would be ill-advised for the week. A few days before the trip, Kelly gets a prescription for birth control pills. She starts taking them the day they go. Six weeks later, she calls Mike and says that she is pregnant and would like to get married.

Response: _____

_____

_____

_____

TRY PRACTICE TEST #1 NOW!
GOOD LUCK!

Methods of Contraception

Directions: Complete the chart below by listing the variations within each method, its effectiveness, and the advantages and disadvantages of using each method.

Methods	Effectiveness	Advantages	Disadvantages
Oral contraceptives *(daily dose)*			
Emergency Oral Contraception			
Norplant			
Intrauterine devices			
Diaphragm			
Spermicides			
Contraceptive Sponge			
Cervical cap			
Condoms			
Douching			
Coitus interruptus			

Methods	Effectiveness	Advantages	Disadvantages
Fertility awareness methods			
Sterilization			

TRY PRACTICE TEST #2 NOW!
GOOD LUCK!

❖ *Abortion*

Directions: Your book raises many important issues about abortion. Rather than confine your work here to the pro-life/pro-choice debate, let's focus on the whole context as well. To that end, please answer the short questions below.

1. Briefly describe the history of abortion in the United States.

2. Summarize the *Roe v. Wade* decision.

3. Explain the impact Americans' views on abortion and the *Roe v. Wade* decision have had on legal access to late second trimester and third trimester abortions.

4. During what part of pregnancy are most abortions in the United States done? How safe are abortions?

5. Briefly describe the psychological consequences of induced abortion.

TRY PRACTICE TEST #3 NOW!
GOOD LUCK!

After You Read...

(LO = Learning Objective)

1. Which of the following, if any, were referred to as contraceptives in the Bible?
    a. Vaginal sponges
    b. Coitus interruptus
    c. Oral concoctions
    d. None of the above
    e. All of the above
        p. 359   LO 1

2. The term "condom" was not used to describe penile sheaths until:
    a. The sixteenth century.
    b. The seventeenth century.
    c. The eighteenth century.
    d. The nineteenth century.
        p. 359   LO 1

3. How did the Ancient Egyptian contraceptive made of sour milk and crocodile dung function?
    a. It changed the acidity of the vagina so that sperm could not travel to the ovum.
    b. It eliminated ovulation temporarily.
    c. It caused the uterus to expel any fertilized eggs that might reach it.
    d. It absorbed semen before it could enter the cervix
        p. 359   LO 1

4. The 1960s were important in the history of contraception because:
    a. Sending contraceptive information through the mail became legal.
    b. The last law preventing the free sale of contraceptives was defeated and and oral contraceptives became available.
    c. Women won the right to terminate a pregnancy.
    d. Condoms were developed and mass marketed.
        p. 360   LO 2

5. The landmark *Roe v. Wade* decision legalizing abortion was made by the Supreme Court in:
   a. 1973.
   b. 1978.
   c. 1983.
   d. 1988.

   p. 360   LO 2

6. Why was the Comstock Law a barrier to the availability of contraception?
   a. It outlawed research about contraception.
   b. It made contraception too expensive to be readily available.
   c. It outlawed family planning.
   d. It ruled information about contraceptives to be obscene and therefore un-mailable.

   p. 360   LO 2

7. The issue of _____ refers to the effect a contraceptive method will have upon the ability to conceive in the future.
   a. shared responsibility
   b. moral acceptability
   c. reversibility
   d. safety

   p. 363,364   LO 3

8. The convenience of a birth control method depends on which of the following factors?
   a. How quickly it takes effect
   b. How much attention it requires during lovemaking
   c. How much protection it provides from STIs
   d. Both A and B
   e. Both A and C

   p. 382   LO 3

9. Why do the effectiveness rates of contraceptives go down when the usage is referred to as typical?
   a. Repeated use reduces effectiveness.
   b. Real-world usage is not as carefully controlled as research usage.
   c. Factory standards are not as high as laboratory standards for production.
   d. Psychological factors can influence the effectiveness levels.

   p. 382   LO 3

10. Although many still consider it to be reversible, your text encourages the assumption that sterilization is irreversible because:
    a. Reversing the procedures is cost-prohibitive.
    b. Sometimes the reverse procedures are not effective.
    c. Sterilization can adversely affect sex drive
    d. Both A and C
    e. Both A and B

    p. 379-380   LO 3

(LO = Learning Objective)

1. Oral contraceptives work most directly by:
   a. Interfering with penetration of the ova by the sperm.
   b. Thickening the uterine mucosa, thus preventing passage of sperm.
   c. Suppressing follicle maturation and ovulation.
   d. Preventing attachment of the fertilized egg to the wall of the uterus.
       p. 362   LO 4

2. Lunelle and Depo-Provera are:
   a. Contraceptive implants.
   b. Injectable contraceptives.
   c. Most effective when taken orally.
   d. Need removal after about two years.
       p. 366,367   LO 5

3. The IUD's effectiveness appears to be due to its ability to:
   a. Suppress ovulation.
   b. Kill sperm or reduce their motility.
   c. Prevent uterine implantation.
   d. Decrease the sperm's ability to penetrate the zona pellucida.
       p. 367   LO 6

4. A diaphragm and condom are similar in each respect, EXCEPT:
   a. Both act to prevent implantation of the fertilized ovum.
   b. Both are put on/in directly prior to intercourse.
   c. Both act as barriers between sperm and ova.
   d. Both are made of a latex rubber material.
       p. 370   LO 7

5. What have recent clinical trials revealed about nonoxynol-9, a widely used spermicide thought to prevent STIs like HIV?
   a. At least not to HIV, it is not a good microbicide.
   b. It causes irritation that makes the genital membranes susceptible to HIV.
   c. Neither of the above are true.
   d. Both A & B are true.
       p. 372   LO 8

6. All of the following are safety guidelines regarding condom usage, EXCEPT:
    a. Use only water-based lubricants with condoms.
    b. Unroll the condom all the way to the bottom of the penis.
    c. Use only oil-based lubricants with condoms.
    d. Check condoms for tears and cracks.
                    p. 373-374   LO 10

7. Why is the rhythm method considered an acceptable method of birth control by the Catholic Church?
    a. It is endorsed specifically in the Bible.
    b. It was made law in the 1700s by the Vatican.
    c. It does not involve the use of artificial devices.
    d. It facilitates conception.
                    p. 376   LO 11

8. According to the ovulation method, the ovulatory mucus discharge becomes thin, clear, slippery, and stringy:
    a. During the week before ovulation.
    b. During the peak days for conception.
    c. During the week before menstruation.
    d. During the first days following menstruation.
                    p. 378   LO 12

9. A vasectomy is performed by:
    a. Severing the epididymis.
    b. Removal of the prostate gland.
    c. Cauterizing a small section of the urethra.
    d. Severing the two vas deferens.
                    p. 379   LO 13

10. The most common technique of female sterilization is:
    a. Culpotomy.
    b. Tubal ligation.
    c. Laparoscopy.
    d. Minilaparotomy.
                    p. 380   LO 13

(LO = Learning Objective)

1. According to national public opinion polls taken since *Roe v. Wade*, the attitude toward legalized abortion is:
   a. Shifting from year to year.
   b. Antagonistic, except when the mother's life is in danger.
   c. Supportive under all circumstances.
   d. Supportive under some circumstances.

   p. 387   LO 15

2. What is the key issue that the pro-life movement hinges upon?
   a. Human life begins at conception.
   b. Abortion is taken too lightly.
   c. Abortions are too dangerous for women.
   d. All contraception is wrong and abortion is just an extreme form of it.

   p. 389   LO 15

3. When abortion was legal in the U.S. from 1607 to 1828, it was permitted until the "quickening." What is the event to which this term refers?
   a. Braxton-Hicks contractions that the mother could feel
   b. The beginning of the 3rd trimester
   c. Fetal movement that the mother could feel
   e. The end of morning sickness

   p. 387   LO 15

4. Which of the following is the most common and safest abortion method?
   a. Vacuum aspiration
   b. Induction
   c. Dilation and evacuation
   d. Intra-amniotic infusion

   p. 391   LO 16

5. When is the most common time to use the Dilation and Evacuation (D&E) method of abortion?
   a. During the first six weeks of pregnancy
   b. During the 1st trimester of pregnancy
   c. During the 2nd trimester of pregnancy
   d. During the 3rd trimester of pregnancy

   p. 391   LO 16

6. The hysterotomy method of abortion is, in effect:
    a. A sterilization procedure.
    b. A cesarean section.
    c. A dilation and curettage.
    d. A dilation and evacuation.
        p. 393   LO 16

7. Since *Roe v. Wade*, the principle state restrictions on access to legal abortion have concerned:
    a. Minors' rights and religious freedom.
    b. Religious freedom and fetal viability.
    c. Minors' rights and stage of pregnancy.
    d. Teen pregnancy and parental consent.
        p. 360, 388   LO 17

8. According to your text, about _____ of Americans believe parental consent should be required before teenage girls can have abortions.
    a. half
    b. three-quarters
    c. one-third
    d. two-thirds
        p. 387   LO 17

9. Which of the following, if any, are factors associated with more resilient reactions to abortion among women who have them?
    a. Support they receive from others
    b. Higher socioeconomic status
    c. Strong relationships with their partners
    d. Both A and B
    e. Both A and C
        p. 393   LO 18

10. The conclusion best drawn from research on the psychological effect of abortion on women is:
    a. That it is always a long-term source of emotional pain.
    b. That it is seldom a long-term source of emotional pain.
    c. That it is always a short-term source of emotional pain.
    d. That it is impossible to predict the level of emotional pain.
        p. 493-394   LO 18

Multiple Choice

1. Oral contraceptives work most directly by:
   a. Interfering with penetration of the ova by the sperm.
   b. Thickening the uterine mucosa, thus preventing passage of sperm.
   c. Suppressing follicle maturation and ovulation.
   d. Preventing attachment of the fertilized egg to the wall of the uterus.

2. How did the Ancient Egyptian contraceptive made of sour milk and crocodile dung function?
   a. It changed the acidity of the vagina so that sperm could not travel to the ovum.
   b. It eliminated ovulation temporarily.
   c. It caused the uterus to expel any fertilized eggs that might reach it.
   d. It absorbed semen before it could enter the cervix

3. All of the following are safety guidelines regarding condom usage, EXCEPT:
   a. Use only water-based lubricants with condoms.
   b. Unroll the condom all the way to the bottom of the penis.
   c. Use only oil-based lubricants with condoms.
   d. Check condoms for tears and cracks.

4. The IUD's effectiveness appears to be due to its ability to:
   a. Suppress ovulation.
   b. Kill sperm or reduce their motility.
   c. Prevent uterine implantation.
   d. Decrease the sperm's ability to penetrate the zona pellucida.

5. A vasectomy is performed by:
   a. Severing the epididymis.
   b. Removing the prostate gland.
   c. Cauterizing a small section of the urethra.
   d. Severing the two vas deferens.

6. What is the key issue that the pro-life movement hinges upon?
   a. Human life begins at conception.
   b. Abortion is taken too lightly.
   c. Abortions are too dangerous for women.
   d. All contraception is wrong and abortion is just an extreme form of it.

7. Since *Roe v. Wade*, the principle state restrictions on access to legal abortion have concerned:
   a. Minors' rights and religious freedom.
   b. Religious freedom and fetal viability.
   c. Minors' rights and stage of pregnancy.
   d. Teen pregnancy and parental consent.

8. A diaphragm and condom are similar in each respect, EXCEPT:
    a. Both act to prevent implantation of the fertilized ovum.
    b. Both are put on/in directly prior to intercourse.
    c. Both act as barriers between sperm and ova.
    d. Both are made of a latex rubber material.

9. Which of the following, if any, are factors associated with more resilient reactions to abortion among women who have them?
    a. Support they receive from others
    b. Higher socioeconomic status
    c. Strong relationships with their partners
    d. Both A and B
    e. Both A and C

10. Why was the Comstock Law a barrier to the availability of contraception?
    a. It outlawed research about contraception.
    b. It made contraception too expensive to be readily available.
    c. It outlawed family planning.
    d. It ruled information about contraceptives to be obscene and therefore un-mailable.

11. The most common technique of female sterilization is:
    a. Culpotomy.
    b. Tubal ligation.
    c. Laparoscopy.
    d. Minilaparotomy.

12. Which of the following is the most common and safest abortion method?
    a. Vacuum aspiration
    b. Induction
    c. Dilation and evacuation
    d. Intra-amniotic infusion

13. Lunelle and Depo-Provera are:
    a. Contraceptive implants.
    b. Injectable contraceptives.
    c. Most effective when taken orally.
    d. Need removal after about two years.

14. What have recent clinical trials revealed about nonoxynol-9, a widely used spermicide thought to prevent STIs like HIV?
    a. At least not to HIV, it is not a good microbicide.
    b. It causes irritation that makes the genital membranes susceptible to HIV.
    c. Neither of the above are true.
    d. Both A & B are true.

15. The issue of _____ refers to the effect a contraceptive method will have upon the ability to conceive in the future.
    a. shared responsibility
    b. moral acceptability
    c. reversibility
    d. safety

True/False

_____ 1. The pill was not marketed as a contraceptive until 1960.

_____ 2. Spermicides have a very high level of reversibility.

_____ 3. In typical use, the failure rate of the condom is estimated at 3%.

_____ 4. The Bible specifically prohibits abortion.

_____ 5. About 43% of women in the U.S. have a voluntary abortion at some time.

_____ 6. The minipill contains estrogen only.

_____ 7. Douching after sex may actually propel sperm toward the uterus.

_____ 8. IUDs have been used since Greek times.

Essay Questions

1. Choose five of the categories of contraceptives described in your text. Define them and discuss their advantages and drawbacks, including their level of effectiveness.

_____

_____

_____

_____

_____

_____

_____

_____

_____

_____

_____

2. Discuss the six major kinds of abortions described in your text, including what they entail, when they are best utilized, and which one is the most widely used and safest method.

_____

_____

_____

_____

_____

_____

_____

_____

_____

_____

_____

When You Have Finished....

Let's see where the Web takes you as you explore the following activities related to Contraception and Abortion.

1. It is clear that there are many forms of contraception in use AND many new ones on the horizon. How does the information on the Web stack up against that in your book? What's coming down the line? Start at good old Wikipedia where most young people go for answers. Is the information accurate? If it is not, edit it and correct it based on your textbook.

2. Abortion is quite politically volatile and can be a sharply divisive topic in many circles. Be informed and check out what the Web has to offer on the subject of abortion related laws. What exactly is allowed in your region?

3. Now that you have the laws, look up any additional information you need to be able to argue your own opinion. Where does the support for abortion come from? Where does the opposition take its roots? Are there any moderate sites or are they all radical? Please be warned that some of the sites may contain graphic images and could be disturbing to some.

4. Time to talk to your teen about safe sex. Google the following "talk to teen about sex." Now filter out the teen sex chat sites and see how many of the sites talk about birth control and abortion. What is the emphasis on parent/teen talks? What do you wish your parents told you?

5. Finally, it would be remiss of me to not mention this chapter's source of one-stop Web surfing— Planned Parenthood has it all. Check it out. Get information about contraceptives, find out what's going on with abortion rights, and get involved one way or another. (The video links are really good.) http://www.plannedparenthood.org/

Chapter 13
Sexuality in Childhood and Adolescence

Before You Begin...

Chapter Summary

Childhood and adolescent sexuality, this is often a politically-charged social topic—if people are even willing to talk about it openly at all in the first place. As you might expect, sexuality talk in this area contrasts dramatically to eager gossip about latest popular reality television program! Parental ability to sort between the abundance of myths and what is known scientifically prepares the parent to do his/her job better (and with less stress we'll note). Your knowledge here will help you lead your current or future daughter, son, niece, or nephew to become a well-adjusted adult—clearly a gift that can keep on giving and be appreciated for a lifetime! As with some other chapters, get comfortable and we'll get going.

Humans show a capacity for sexual responsiveness in utero; for example, male fetuses develop erections. Pelvic thrusting has been observed in infants as young as eight months old, and stimulation of the genitals in infancy may produce pleasurable sensations. Masturbation is typical behavior for young children, and some infants display sexual responses that resemble orgasm. In the United States, children typically begin showing curiosity about sexual anatomy and may engage in genital play with others around the age of 2. Studying childhood sexuality is difficult because parents may not allow others to interview their children about sexual matters, and parents may not fully or accurately answer such questions about their children's behavior.

Your text further explains research in emotional stability, sexual orientation, gender identity, or intellectual functioning for children raised by homosexual parents (compared to those reared by heterosexual parents). Despite what some politicians may like, the findings reveal no differences. We also examine same-sex sexual play among peers in childhood and preadolescence. Here findings say it is primarily exploration and that engaging in these activities does *not* predict adult sexual orientation (which is a common myth). Masturbation is examined, as it is the primary means of achieving orgasm during ages 9 to 13; boys are more likely than girls to masturbate, and social norms suggest masturbation is more acceptable for males.

Nearly all states mandate or recommend school-based sex education, but the content varies considerably, and most programs emphasize the biological aspects of puberty. Adolescents have reported receiving more information about sex from friends and the media than from school or their parents. There is no evidence that sex education increases sexual activity in adolescence.

In the U.S., adolescence is viewed as a conflicted period in which adults need to restrict impulsive adolescents "for their own good." Adolescence begins with the advent of puberty and development of secondary sex characteristics such as the growth of pubic hair. Sex hormones such as estrogen direct pubertal changes in primary sex characteristics. The principal markers of reproductive potential are menarche in girls and first ejaculation in boys.

Today, adolescents date and engage in sexual intercourse earlier than in the past, and most adolescents engage in petting to achieve sexual gratification. Research indicates that teens who have higher educational goals and good communication with their parents are less likely to engage in coitus. Teens who initiate intercourse earlier are least likely to use contraception and more likely to incur an unwanted pregnancy. Unplanned teenage pregnancy is correlated with higher school dropout rates and greater reliance on public assistance for adolescent mothers. More details are within your text.

Note that this chapter has a much larger number of learning objectives than other chapters—please take a deep breath and try not to be overwhelmed. Focus on a little at a time and you will do well. After all, children are a very important asset to you as parents (either now or someday) and to society, and we want to maximize the benefits you will receive in studying this chapter (and it won't hurt to help you boost your test grades either). Enjoy!

Learning Objectives

1. List three indicators of the capacity for sexual response in infancy, and state at what age these responses generally appear.

2. Indicate the age at which humans typically begin to masturbate and describe what techniques young children generally use for masturbation.

3. Recognize why some parents react negatively to their children's masturbation, discuss the implications of such reactions, and recommend an alternative response parents could utilize.

4. Identify two reasons why it is difficult to conduct research into childhood sexuality.

5. Using Friedrich's study of children's sexuality, list two common sexual behaviors for children ages 2 to 5 and children ages 6 to 9 years old.

6. Assess the relationship between same-sex sexual play in childhood and preadolescence on the development of sexual orientation in adulthood.

7. Cite at least one reason why masturbation is more common for male than female adolescents.

8. Discuss two limitations of school-based sex education programs in the contemporary U.S.

9. Outline the five suggestions Calderone and Johnson offer parents for improving parent-child communication about sexuality.

10. Cite one reason why the age at menarche has declined among girls in Western nations.

11. Describe the four general stages of pubertal development in females by specifying several changes that occur at each stage and indicating the average age at which each change occurs.

12. Describe the four general stages of pubertal development in males by specifying several changes that occur at each stage and indicating the average age at which each change occurs.

13. List three ways that parents attempt to limit their children's computer use and three ways that youths attempt to gain greater control over their use of the Internet.

14. Indicate the prevalence of petting, oral sex, and sexual intercourse among adolescents today, noting any variations in sexual activity by gender and ethnicity.

15. Recognize the primary biological, social, and psychological reasons why adolescents report initiating sexual intercourse, and evaluate how gender influences feelings about sexual activity.

16. List three factors that decrease the likelihood that female adolescents will be sexually active.

17. Identify the prevalence of same-sex sexual activity among adolescents, and evaluate the consequences of stigmatization for gay and lesbian teenagers.

18. Discuss the implications of becoming sexually active since the emergence of HIV/AIDS in the 1980s, noting how the disease has differently impacted youth of various ethnic heritages.

19. Provide an overview of the consequences of teenage childbearing for adolescent mothers, their children, and society at large.

20. Identify at least three factors that contribute to the incidence of teenage pregnancy in the U.S.

21. Cite three factors correlated with adolescents' use of contraceptives and list three reasons why sexually active adolescents report not using contraceptives.

22. Evaluate the influences of good parental communication and school-based prevention programs on curtailing unplanned pregnancy and the spread of STIs among adolescents.

23. Relate cross-cultural findings on the relationship of sex-education to teen pregnancy.

24. Understand the effects of child-parent co-sleeping versus some of the common myths historically associated with it.

Term Identification

You know the drill; these are the terms you will need to learn, and making flashcards will help.

Chapter 13 Table of Key Terms	
Anovulatory	Nocturnal emission
Critical fat hypothesis	Primary sex characteristics
Gynecomastia	Puberty
Larynx	Secondary sex characteristics
Menarche	

As You Read...

Sexuality in Childhood and Adolescence

> ➤ *Infancy (0 to 2 Years): The Search for the Origins of Human Sexuality*

What is your reaction to...?
Most people cannot remember anything before the age of 2 or 3 due to development of the brain. Therefore, you may not be aware, unless you have spent much time with infants, that sexuality begins very early in life. However, it typically is different from what adults consider sexual behavior. While reading the text's coverage of sexuality in infancy (0 to 2 years), write down your first responses to what you are reading.

_____

_____

_____

_____

What did you read that was surprising to you?

_____

_____

_____

_____

> ➤ *Early Childhood (3 to 8 Years)*

What should be someone's response if...?

Based on what you have learned, what might you do if one day you discover your child masturbating? If you have experienced this already, what did you do? This is a potentially difficult situation. Do you feel you handled it appropriately? Why or why not? Fill in the boxes below with your responses. If you never plan to be a parent, complete the table and share the information with someone who has children.

Reactions to Your Child Masturbating	
Inappropriate Reaction	Appropriate Reaction

➢ *Preadolescence (9 to 13 Years)*

Talking to Kids about Sex: How much should you tell them and when?
What do you remember being told about sex when you were a child?

I was told:

What do you wish you were told?

I wish I were told:

What were you told but wish you were not told?

I wish I were not told:

Of what you were told, will you tell (have you told) your child any of it?

Why or why not?

Of what you were told, which things will you tell (have you told) your child about sex?

If I become a parent, I plan to talk (have talked) to my child about the following topics in human sexuality:

Why is it important for parents not to rely on sources of information, like a child's peers, for information about sexuality?

TRY PRACTICE TEST #1 NOW!
GOOD LUCK!

What is your perspective? Clarify your perspective on sex education in schools.
Take this opportunity to think about two controversial issues in human sexuality: sex education and the distribution of contraceptives in schools. To do this, summarize the current state of sex education and of contraceptive distribution in schools. Then, list the arguments for and against sex education and contraceptive distribution—use research shared by your authors beyond the borders of the U.S. (e.g., cross-cultural findings) too. Finally, draw your own conclusions about what should be done regarding these topics.

Sex education in schools:

    Current situation:

    Pros:

    Cons:

    My position:

Contraceptive distribution:

    Current situation:

    Pros:

    Cons:

    My position:

❖ **If it were your decision...? How would you design a Sex Education Program?**

In this activity, imagine you are charged with designing a sex education program for preadolescent children (9 to 13 years) to be implemented in the public school system in your district. To help plan your approach, respond to the following statements.

My Plan for a Sex Education Program
The program will be implemented when children are the age of:
The program will focus on:
Sex education teachers will have a background in:
The program (will/will not) be coeducational:
The program will focus on biological issues such as:
The program will focus on psychological issues such as:
The following human sexuality topics will be discussed:

➢ *Adolescence*

What happens during Puberty? in Females? in Males?

Complete the two charts below indicating the main changes that happen to females and males as they experience the different aspects of development during puberty. Refer to the text if you have trouble filling out the charts.

Puberty for Females	
Between the ages of about 8 and 15	These changes occur:
Between the ages of about 10 and 16	These changes occur:
Between the ages of about 12 and 19	These changes occur:

Puberty for Males	
Between the ages of about 9 and 16	These changes occur:
Between the ages of 11 and 17	These changes occur:
Between the ages of 14 and 18	These changes occur:

TRY PRACTICE TEST #2 NOW!
GOOD LUCK!

Do you know the definitions of the terms in this chapter?

Find out how well you are learning the definitions of the vocabulary words in the chapter by completing the following matching exercise. Match each key vocabulary term listed in the left-hand column with the correct definition in the right-hand column. Good luck!

a. puberty

_____ Physical characteristics that differentiate males and females and are directly involved in reproduction, such as the sex organs.

b. secondary sex characteristics

_____ A structure of muscle and cartilage at the upper end of the trachea that contains the vocal cords; the voice box.

c. primary sex characteristics

_____ Without ovulation.

d. menarche

_____ The stage of development during which reproduction first becomes possible. It begins with the appearance of *secondary sex characteristics* and ends when the long bones make no further gains in length.

e. anovulatory

_____ Involuntary ejaculation of seminal fluid while asleep. Also referred to as a "wet dream," although the individual need not be dreaming about sex, or dreaming at all, at the time.

f. nocturnal emission

_____ Physical characteristics that differentiate males and females and that usually appear at puberty but are not directly involved in reproduction, such as the bodily distribution of hair and fat, development of the muscle mass, and deepening of the voice.

g. larynx

_____ The view that girls must reach a certain body weight to trigger puberty.

h. gynecomastia

_____ The onset of menstruation; first menstruation.

i. critical fat hypothesis

_____ Overdevelopment of a male's breasts.

How can we reduce teenage pregnancy?

Indicate strategies to reduce teenage pregnancy by completing the table. For each factor that contributes to teen pregnancy, list a strategy to combat it. Also, consider what research has shown regarding the effects of sex education programs that distribute condoms to their teenage students on adolescent pregnancy rates.

Factors that Contribute to Teenage Pregnancy	Strategy to Combat

TRY PRACTICE TEST #3 NOW!
GOOD LUCK!

After You Read...

1. Erections in males first occur:
    a. While they are in utero.
    b. Minutes after they are born.
    c. At about age 2.
    d. When puberty begins around age 9.
        p. 400   LO 1

2. According to Friedrich's research, the most common sexual behavior for both boys and girls to engage in during early childhood is:
    a. Attempting to look at adults while they are nude or undressing.
    b. Fondling the genitals of their same-sex peers.
    c. Touching their private parts when at home.
    d. Touching their mothers' breasts.
        p. 404-405   LO 5

3. Despite surveys showing that over 87 percent of parents want their children's sex education classes to teach them about sexual orientation, abortion, birth control, STIs, and HIV/AIDS transmission, which nation's elected representatives have strongly endorsed "abstinence only" education programs?
    a. Iran
    b. the Netherlands
    c. the United States of America
    d. This situation currently exists in all of the above nations.
        p. 422   LO 8

4. In the U.S., children typically begin to engage in genital play with others at what age?
    a. 12
    b. 8
    c. 4
    d. 2
        p. 402   LO 5

5. Which of the following statements accurately describes the influence of parental response on children's masturbation according to sex educators?
    a. Children whose parents respond to masturbation with disgust or ridicule usually stop masturbating completely.
    b. Children whose parents punish them for masturbating usually continue to masturbate, but become secretive and guilty about it.
    c. Children whose parents teach them that masturbation causes mental and physical maladies will never be able to receive erotic pleasure as adults.
    d. The way in which parents respond to children's masturbation is not correlated with positive *or* negative consequences for children's self-esteem or body image.
        p. 402   LO 3

6. The Kaiser Family Foundation survey on sexual health and knowledge indicates that most adolescents and young adults receive information about sex from:
    a. Their doctors.
    b. Their parents.
    c. Their friends.
    d. Classes at school.
        p. 409   LO 8

7. Best friends Sam and Michael are both nine years old. They display their genitals to each other and sometimes engage in mutual masturbation. This probably indicates that:
    a. The boys are typical preadolescents.
    b. Both of the boys have homosexual sexual orientations.
    c. One of the boys has been sexually molested by an adult.
    d. The boys will exhibit attachment problems in their intimate adult relationships.
        p. 409   LO 6

8. The text authors report that information about masturbation and other sexual activities during childhood is highly speculative because:
    a. Some parents do not define genital touching as masturbation.
    b. Many parents won't allow their children to be interviewed about sex.
    c. Parents often underreport their children's sexual activity as a social nicety.
    d. All of the above factors make information about children's sexuality speculative.
        p. 400, 403   LO 4

9. Your textbook's authors suggest that parents can most effectively respond to their older children's questions about sex by:
   a. Telling their children exactly what their punishment will be if they engage in sexual behavior that violates their parents' values.
   b. Providing children with objective statistics about the prevalence of STIs while showing them pictures of people who are ill due to HIV infection.
   c. Describing sexual anatomy using proper terminology, rather than silly words, to convey that sexual organs are neither embarrassing nor mysterious.
   d. Non-verbally communicating their discomfort with the topic and redirecting the conversation to less emotionally demanding topics.
      p. 410   LO 9

10. According to psychiatrist Anke Ehrhardt:
    a. The U.S. has an exemplary sex education curriculum in place at most of the schools in the nation; the incidence of STI and HIV infection among U.S. adolescents is lower than in every other industrialized nation.
    b. Sex is such a highly controversial and value-laden topic in Iran; most sex education materials distributed there are vague about puberty and reproduction and avoid mentioning contraception completely.
    c. In the Netherlands, where sex education materials are explicit and free condoms are provided to adolescents at school-based clinics, rates of HIV infection and STI transmission are higher than in almost every other industrialized nation.
    d. None of the above statements are true according to psychiatrist Anke Ehrhardt report.
       p. 409   LO 8

1. What characteristic is often the first visible sign of puberty in both sexes?
   a. Onset of fertility
   b. Appearance of pubic hair
   c. Growth of fatty tissue in the breast and hip areas
   d. Development of ability to achieve orgasm from self-stimulation
      p. 412   LO 11

2. The principal marker of reproductive potential in males is:
   a. First ejaculation.
   b. Deepening of the voice.
   c. Development of muscle mass.
   d. Growth of facial and chest hair.
      p. 413   LO 12

3. Which of the following statements about nocturnal emissions is accurate?
   a. These emissions involve the involuntary ejaculation of seminal fluid.
   b. These emissions may occur while a person is either asleep or awake.
   c. Both males and females experience these emissions during adolescence.
   d. All of the above statements about nocturnal emissions are accurate.
      p. 414   LO 12

4. Physical characteristics that differentiate males and females and usually appear at puberty, but are not directly involved in reproduction, are referred to as:
   a. Gynecomastia.
   b. Anovulatory traits.
   c. Primary sex characteristics.
   d. Secondary sex characteristics.
      p. 412   LO 11

5. At puberty, the breasts and uterus begin to grow, the pelvis widens, and the vaginal lining thickens. These changes in the female body are due mainly to the secretion of:
   a. Testosterone.
   b. Androgen.
   c. Estrogen.
   d. Insulin.
      p. 413   LO 11

6. All of the following statements about adolescent sexual behavior in the United States today are true EXCEPT:
    a. Teenagers' participation in oral sex increases with age.
    b. Nearly all teenagers have engaged in some form of petting by age 15.
    c. Significantly fewer girls than boys engage in coitus during adolescence.
    d. Masturbation is a major source of sexual gratification for both boys and girls.
        p. 417   LO 14

7. Which of the following statements concerning changes in menarche are true?
    a. Girls living in wealthy nations (such as Sweden) typically reach menarche at younger ages than do girls living in poor nations (such as Bangladesh).
    b. In Western nations, the age at menarche has been declining since the mid-1800s.
    c. Variations in menarche seem to be a result of improved nutrition and healthcare.
    d. All of the above statements concerning changes in menarche are true.
        p. 413   LO 10

8. Which of the following strategies do parents report using to exert greater control over their child's understanding of sexuality?
    a. Being honest with the child
    b. Letting the child ask questions
    c. Talk with their kids about it early in childhood
    d. Parents report using all of the above strategies
        p. 410   LO 13

9. According to Gates and Sonenstein's research on adolescent male sexual activities,
    a. African American males are more likely than both European and Latino American males to have engaged in vaginal intercourse during adolescence.
    b. European American males are more likely than both African and Latino American males to have engaged in anal intercourse during adolescence.
    c. Latino American males are more likely than both African and European American males to have received oral sex from a female.
    d. Their research revealed all of the above ethnic differences in sexual activities.
        p. 419   LO 14

10. Parent-child co-sleeping has recently been associated with the following outcomes when the child reaches adulthood?
    a. It can delay social development.
    b. It reduces the general level of intellectual development.
    c. It has not been linked to any negative outcome.
    d. Both A and C are outcomes associated with co-sleeping.
        p. 402   LO 24

1. Males are more likely than females to report _____ as a primary motivating factor for initiating sexual intercourse during adolescence.
   a. curiosity about sex
   b. love or affection for partner
   c. pressure from their partners
   d. Males are more likely than females to report all of the above reasons for initiating sexual intercourse during adolescence.
      p. 419   LO 15

2. Research by Sprecher indicates that a majority of girls report feeling _____ after their first intercourse.
   a. disappointed
   b. ambivalent
   c. guilty
   d. glad
   e. Both A and C.
      p. 418   LO 15

3. Which of the following factors decreases the likelihood that an adolescent female will become sexually active?
   a. Living in a two-parent household
   b. Beginning to date at an older age
   c. Having high educational goals
   d. All of the above factors decrease the likelihood that an adolescent female will become sexually active.
      p. 420   LO 16

4. What percentage of adolescent respondents in Mosher's study of sexual behavior reported having same-sex sexual experiences?
   a. 20
   b. 10
   c. 5
   d. 1
      p. 418   LO 17

5. The use of cell phones and texting is doing what to adolescent sexuality?
   a. Letting them express themselves.
   b. Opening them to embarrassment and/or harassment.
   c. Making them start menarche sooner.
   d. Normal adolescent behavior.
      p. 416   LO 18

6. Which of the following statements about adolescent pregnancy in the U.S. is true?
    a. Approximately 10 percent of girls ages 15 to 19 become pregnant each year.
    b. Only one-fourth of the nearly 800,000 teen pregnancies that occur each year result in live births, whereas the remainder of the pregnancies end in abortion.
    c. The rate of births for teenagers has been gradually increasing since 1990.
    d. All of the above statements about adolescent pregnancy in the U.S. are true.
       p. 420   LO 20

7. The text authors assert that the main cause of the largest number of unplanned teen pregnancies in the U.S. is:
    a. Impaired family relationships.
    b. Increased sexual explicitness in the mainstream culture.
    c. Girls' desire to elicit a commitment from their boyfriends.
    d. Misunderstandings about how reproduction and contraception work.
       p. 421   LO 20

8. Which of the following factors decreases the likelihood that sexually active teenage girls will use contraceptives?
    a. Having peers who use contraceptives
    b. Being in a monogamous relationship
    c. Engaging in intercourse infrequently
    d. All of the above factors lower the likelihood of using contraceptives.
       p. 421-422   LO 21

9. According to a National Campaign to Prevent Teenage Pregnancy poll, approximately what proportion of teenagers reported that they had never discussed sex, contraception, or pregnancy with their parents?
    a. One-fourth
    b. One-third
    c. One-half
    d. Two-thirds
       p. 422   LO 22

10. According to research by Blake and colleagues, what consequence(s) did schools making condoms available to high school students have on their behavior?
    a. Distributing condoms increased the percentage of students who became sexually active during high school.
    b. Among students who were already sexually active in high school, condom use became more consistent.
    c. Distributing condoms increased the number of partners with whom sexually active students had intercourse.
    d. All of the above occurred as a result of schools distributing condoms to students.
       p. 423   LO 22

Multiple Choice

1. All of the following statements about adolescent sexual behavior in the United States today are true EXCEPT:
   a. Teenagers' participation in oral sex increases with age.
   b. Nearly all teenagers have engaged in some form of petting by age 15.
   c. Significantly fewer girls than boys engage in coitus during adolescence.
   d. Masturbation is a major source of sexual gratification for both boys and girls.

2. According to Friedrich's research, the most common sexual behavior for both boys and girls to engage in during early childhood is:
   a. Attempting to look at adults while they are nude or undressing.
   b. Fondling the genitals of their same-sex peers.
   c. Touching their private parts when at home.
   d. Touching their mothers' breasts.

3. Your textbook's authors suggest that parents can most effectively respond to their older children's questions about sex by:
   a. Telling their children exactly what their punishment will be if they engage in sexual behavior that violates their parents' values.
   b. Providing children with objective statistics about the prevalence of STIs while showing them pictures of people who are ill due to HIV infection.
   c. Describing sexual anatomy using proper terminology, rather than silly words, to convey that sexual organs are neither embarrassing nor mysterious.
   d. Non-verbally communicating their discomfort with the topic and redirecting the conversation to less emotionally demanding topics.

4. Best friends Joe and Michael are both nine years old. They display their genitals to each other and sometimes engage in mutual masturbation. This probably indicates that:
   a. The boys are typical preadolescents.
   b. Both of the boys have homosexual sexual orientations.
   c. One of the boys has been sexually molested by an adult.
   d. The boys will exhibit attachment problems in their intimate adult relationships.

5. Which of the following statements about adolescent pregnancy in the U.S. is true?
   a. Approximately 10 percent of girls ages 15 to 19 become pregnant each year.
   b. Only one-fourth of the nearly 800,000 teen pregnancies that occur each year result in live births, whereas the remainder of the pregnancies end in abortion.
   c. The rate of births for teenagers has been gradually increasing since 1990.
   d. All of the above statements about adolescent pregnancy in the U.S. are true.

6. The principle marker of reproductive potential in males is:
    a. First ejaculation.
    b. Deepening of the voice.
    c. Development of muscle mass.
    d. Growth of facial and chest hair.

7. Erections in males first occur:
    a. While they are in utero.
    b. Minutes after they are born.
    c. At about age 2.
    d. When puberty begins around age 9.

8. The text authors assert that the main cause of the largest number of unplanned teen pregnancies in the U.S. is:
    a. Impaired family relationships.
    b. Increased sexual explicitness in the mainstream culture.
    c. Girls' desire to elicit a commitment from their boyfriends.
    d. Misunderstandings about how reproduction and contraception work.

9. Which of the following statements concerning changes in menarche are true?
    a. Girls living in wealthy nations (such as Sweden) typically reach menarche at younger ages than do girls living in poor nations (such as Bangladesh).
    b. In Western nations, the age at menarche has been declining since the mid-1800s.
    c. Variations in menarche seem to be a result of improved nutrition and healthcare.
    d. All of the above statements concerning changes in menarche are true.

10. At puberty, the breasts and uterus begin to grow, the pelvis widens, and the vaginal lining thickens. These changes in the female body are due mainly to the secretion of:
    a. Testosterone.
    b. Androgen.
    c. Estrogen.
    d. Insulin.

11. According to sex educators Calderone and Johnson, which of the following statements accurately describes the influence of parental response on children's masturbation?
    a. Children whose parents respond to masturbation with disgust or ridicule usually stop masturbating completely.
    b. Children whose parents punish them for masturbating usually continue to masturbate, but become secretive and guilty about it.
    c. Children whose parents teach them that masturbation causes mental and physical maladies will never be able to receive erotic pleasure as adults.
    d. The way in which parents respond to children's masturbation is not correlated with positive *or* negative consequences for children's self-esteem or body image.

12. What percentage of adolescent respondents in Mosher's study of sexual behavior reported having same-sex sexual experiences?
    a. 20
    b. 10
    c. 5
    d. 1

13. Males are more likely than females to report _____ as a primary motivating factor for initiating sexual intercourse during adolescence.
    a. curiosity about sex
    b. love or affection for partner
    c. pressure from their partners
    d. Males are more likely than females to report all of the above reasons for initiating sexual intercourse during adolescence.

14. Despite surveys showing that over 75 percent of parents want their children's sex education classes to teach them about sexual orientation, abortion, birth control, STIs, and HIV/AIDS transmission, which nation's elected representatives have strongly endorsed "abstinence only" education programs?
    a. Iran
    b. the Netherlands
    c. the United States of America
    d. This situation currently exists in all of the above nations.

15. Physical characteristics that differentiate males and females and usually appear at puberty, but are not directly involved in reproduction, are referred to as:
    a. Gynecomastia.
    b. Anovulatory traits.
    c. Primary sex characteristics.
    d. Secondary sex characteristics.

True/False

_____ 1. According to Pinkerton, preadolescent boys are more likely than girls to masturbate because females are not able to achieve orgasm until after pubertal changes are complete.

_____ 2. Blake's research clearly indicates that school distribution of condoms increases the percentage of adolescents who become sexually active during high school.

_____ 3. The earlier teens initiate sexual intercourse, the less likely they are to use contraception.

_____ 4. Although sex games such as "show" and "playing doctor" may begin earlier, they are most common among children ages 6 to 10.

_____ 5. Based on an extensive review of research, Anderssen and colleagues concluded that children reared by gay and lesbian parents are less emotionally stable and have more adjustment problems than do children reared by heterosexual parents.

_____ 6. Cross-cultural findings reveal that the presence of comprehensive sexuality education (over that of abstinence-only) reduces teen pregnancy rates.

_____ 7. Following the onset of menstruation, most girls' first few cycles are anovulatory.

_____ 8. Among adolescent males, European American men are less likely than both African American and Latino American men to have engaged in vaginal intercourse.

Essay Questions

1. Explain how gender influences the decision to engage in first sexual intercourse, and discuss the implications of these differences in motivation for how young women and men tend to feel about their first intercourse experience.

_____

_____

_____

_____

_____

_____

_____

_____

_____

2. Discuss why African American youth have become "the new face of HIV" in the U.S., and suggest at least two specific strategies for reducing HIV transmission among youth.

_____

_____

_____

_____

_____

_____

_____

_____

_____

When You Have Finished....

Let's see where the Web takes you as you explore the following activities related to childhood and adolescent sexuality.

1. The Planned Parenthood Federation of America site focuses on the challenge of how and when to talk with children about sex and sexual expression—and provides more helpful tips than what is already in your textbook and has guides for teens and families.
   http://www.plannedparenthood.org/

   As a companion site for teens, Planned Parenthood runs TeenWire.com at:
   http://www.teenwire.com

2. This site offers very interesting material on the truth about sex education from the Sexuality Information and Education Council of the United States (SIECUS): http://www.siecus.org/ Visitors can link to more information on community advocacy. First, click on "site navigation" and scroll down the page, you will find links for public policy, sexuality education and religion, and school health.

3. This site offers easy-to-understand information about the tough topic of puberty and how to talk to your child about it. The site is sponsored by the medical experts of the Nemours Foundation.
   http://www.kidshealth.org/parent/positive/talk/talk_about_puberty.html

4. How prevalent is teen pregnancy? Google "teen pregnancy rate" and check out some of the results. Is the rate increasing or decreasing? What do you think is causing the changes?

5. It is amazing the things that high school kids think about sex. Search for common teen myths about sex, contraception, and puberty. Where do these myths come from and how are they perpetuated?

6. Puberty Information for Boys and Girls: http://www.aap.org/family/puberty.htm
   This offers a public education brochure on the changes to expect during puberty for both males and females from the American Academy of Pediatrics. Compare the results to that of other sites about the age of onset of menarche. What is causing the decline in age of onset of puberty?

7. While YouTube changes all the time, search for the "Puberty Fairy." There are a few student made animations which are entertaining, and for the most part accurate. If you are into animation, this is your time to create something for teens that they will watch and remember.

Chapter 14
Sexuality in Adulthood

Before You Begin…

Chapter Summary

Adulthood in the contemporary United States offers people more lifestyle options than in the past. Remaining single by choice, cohabiting with a partner, getting divorced, and having a child outside of marriage have all become more socially acceptable options since the advent of the sexual revolution. Despite the high incidence of cohabitation in Western nations, marriage is still the most common lifestyle in the U.S. Throughout history, marriage has legitimized sexual relations, sanctioned the permanence of relationships, provided for the orderly transmission of wealth, and provided a context for raising children. The patriarchal marriage supported by the Hebrew, Greek, Roman, and Christian traditions has generally been replaced by the modern marriage, in which women are viewed as loving companions who have the same rights as their husbands. Marriages can be classified by how many spouses and/or sexual partners an individual has, as well as by the degree of social similarity the members of a couple exhibit. Although people in the U.S. are presumably free to choose their partners on the basis of love, most people marry others of their same race, ethnicity, educational level, and religion as outlined by your text.

Changes in marital sexuality since the 1930s include greater frequency of coitus, longer duration of intercourse, more variety in sexual activities, higher levels of sexual and emotional satisfaction, and increased attention to women's sexual pleasure. Although most Americans believe extramarital sex is wrong, infidelity does occur, and affairs seriously damage marriages in most instances. Women and men report different motives for engaging in extramarital sex. Half of all marriages in the U.S. end in divorce. People cite communication problems and lack of understanding as the most common reasons for divorcing. Divorce is usually connected with financial and emotional problems, especially for women, and it puts people at greater risk for illness; however, it can also be an opportunity for personal growth and renewal. Both chronic marital conflict and divorce are connected with psychological distress for children and youth.

The growth in the elderly population of the U.S. may help challenge the cultural myth that older people are either uninterested in or incapable of having sex. Physical changes influence older people's feelings about themselves, and their capacity to be sexual may be influenced by normal hormonal changes or illness; however, most older people report liking sex. For both the elderly and people with sensory, physical, and psychological disabilities, the availability of an interested and supportive partner is perhaps the most important determinant of sexual activity. Among the disabled population, sexual wellness involves positive self-concept, knowledge about sexuality, positive relationships, resources to cope with barriers to sexual activity, and maintenance of general health.

1. Compare the frequency of singlehood, cohabitation, marriage, and divorce in the United States today and note how the prevalence of these adult lifestyles have changed since the 1970s.

2. Discuss the reasons why more people in the U.S. are remaining single for longer periods of their lives and sometimes choosing singlehood as a permanent lifestyle.

3. State what the acronym POSSLQ stands for and recognize why the U.S. Bureau of the Census introduced it.

4. Identify at least three reasons why some couples choose to cohabit prior to, or instead of, marriage; and provide a profile of the people who are most likely to cohabit in the United States.

5. Discuss the selection factors that influence the likelihood of divorce among couples that cohabit prior to marriage.

6. Considering marriage of today, note how the weakening of Christian patriarchal foundation in Western culture has altered men and women's roles and expectations of marriage.

7. List at least three functions of marriage for society and consider whether other types of domestic arrangements can fulfill these societal needs.

8. Identify two functions of marriage for individuals in the contemporary United States and indicate the primary reason most adults report wanting to get married today.

9. Define *monogamy*, *polygyny*, and *polyandry*; note which type of marriage is most common and which type is illegal in the United States.

10. Discuss the legal status of same-sex couples in the U.S. and other Western nations.

11. Define *homogamy* and *mating gradient* and discuss to what extent these patterns of mate selection are found in the U.S. population.

12. Compare the patterns of marital sexuality typical of couples today to those of the married couples in Kinsey's research from the 1930s and 1940s.

13. Identify three societal changes of the 1960s and 1970s that had a "liberalizing influence" on sexual attitudes and behavior in the United States.

14. Using data from Laumann and colleagues' surveys, compare the levels of physical and emotional satisfaction with their partners that individuals reported, noting any patterns that emerged according to gender, age, marital status, and/or race-ethnicity.

15. Estimate the frequency of extramarital sex for women and for men, and describe the consequences an affair typically has on a marriage.

16. Discuss why women and men tend to report different motivations for participating in extramarital affairs.

17. Assess the influence of *no-fault* divorce laws on the prevalence of divorce in the U.S.

18. Indicate which three spousal behaviors are key predictors of divorce and list the two most common reasons given for a divorce today.

19. Compare how divorce typically affects children in the United States, China, and Africa.

20. Recognize which parental behaviors exacerbate children's psychological distress, and which parental behaviors promote children's successful adjustment, when divorce occurs.

21. Identify the problems that adults who are parents tend to experience as a result of divorce, and explain why divorce tends to affect women and men differently.

22. Consider how changes in the composition of the U.S. population may affect cultural views about sexuality among older people.

23. Cite evidence to support the finding that older people are interested in, and capable of, having satisfying sex lives.

24. List the most common changes in sexual arousal associated with the biological process of aging.

25. Recognize which factor the text authors suggest is probably the most important determinant of sexual fulfillment for both older people and people with disabilities.

26. Discuss the five factors Nosek identifies as central to sexual wellness among the disabled.

27. Identify three physical disabilities and the limitations those conditions may impose on sexual activities, and discuss the strategies people with disabilities can use to maintain sexual activity.

28. Explain why people with physical, sensory, and psychological disabilities often lack the knowledge and skills necessary to participate in sexual relationships.

Term Identification

You know the drill; these are the terms you need to learn in your mastery of this broad chapter, and making flashcards will help.

Chapter 14's Table of Key Terms

Arthritis	Homogamy
Celibacy	Mating gradient
Cerebral Palsy	Monogamy
Cohabitation	Open marriage
Consensual adultery	Polyandry
Conventional adultery	Polygamy
Extramarital sex	Polygyny
Friends with benefits	Serial monogamy
Gay marriage	Swinging
Group marriage	

As You Read...

Sexuality in Adulthood

> *Singlehood*

Being Single

What are the benefits of being single? What are the costs of being single?

Provide your answers to these questions by responding to the following statements.

The benefits of singlehood include:

The disadvantages of singlehood include:

> *Cohabitation: Darling, Would You Be My POSSLQ?*

Living Together versus Getting Married

What are the motives behind cohabitation? Would you ever or have you ever cohabited with your partner? Why or why not? Do you think that cohabitation will replace marriage in the future? Why or why not? Consider your responses to these questions as you complete the chart below.

People Cohabit Because:	People Get Married Because:

TRY PRACTICE TEST #1 NOW!
GOOD LUCK!

➢ *Marriage: Tying the Knot*

Characteristics of Marriage

What are the characteristics of traditional marriages? Have marriages changed over the last fifty years? If so, how?

Characteristics of traditional marriages include:

Characteristics of nontraditional or modern marriages include:

Have the changes you mention benefited men, women, or both genders?

Why?

How have people's needs and wants regarding marriage changed over the last half-century?

Today, people are looking for:

Possible consequences of changes in what people want from marriage include:

Speaking of nontraditional marriage... What about the gay marriage debate?
Take both sides of this issue and argue for each position: *homosexuals should be allowed to marry* and *homosexuals should not be allowed to marry*. I know this exercise may be difficult if you hold a strong opinion about whether the marriages of gay men and lesbians should be recognized by government entities. However, it is a wonderful opportunity to empathize with the "other side."

Arguments in favor of gay marriage include:

Arguments in opposition to gay marriage include:

What has research found regarding marital sexuality?
Using what you have learned from your text and the data provided by the Kinsey survey and the NHLS study, write a paragraph that summarizes the findings on marital sexuality. In your paragraph, indicate which results surprised you and why.

The costs of divorce: What are they?
Consider both the economic and emotional costs of divorce.

The financial costs of a divorce are:

The psychological costs of a divorce are:

TRY PRACTICE TEST #2 NOW!
GOOD LUCK!

> *Sex in the Later Years*

Sexuality and Aging
What effects, if any, on sexuality can people expect as they age? Complete the table with what you learn from the text about sex in the later years.

Effects of Aging on Sexuality			
Physical Changes		Patterns of Activity	
Changes in Males	Changes in Females	Changes in Males	Changes in Females

> *Sex and Disability*

The Effects of Disability on Sexuality
What are the effects of disability on sexuality? After reading the text's coverage of this material, complete the chart with this information.

Disability	Effects on Sexuality
Physical Disabilities Cerebral Palsy Spinal Cord Injuries Sensory Disabilities Other	
Psychological Disabilities	

TRY PRACTICE TEST #3 NOW!
GOOD LUCK!

Do you know the definitions of the terms in this chapter?

Find out how well you are learning the definitions of the vocabulary words in the chapter by completing the following matching exercise. Match each key vocabulary term listed in the left-hand column with the correct definition in the right-hand column. Good luck!

a.   serial monogamy

_____ Living together as though married but without legal sanction.

b.   celibacy

_____ Complete sexual abstinence. (Sometimes used to describe the state of being unmarried, especially in the case of people who take vows to remain single.)

c.   cohabitation

_____ A pattern of involvement in one exclusive relationship after another, as opposed to engaging in multiple sexual relationships at the same time.

d.   gay marriage

_____ Simultaneous marriage to more than one person.

e.   monogamy

_____ Marriage to a person of the same sex.

f.   polygamy

_____ Marriage to one person.

g.   polygyny

_____ A form of consensual adultery in which both spouses share extramarital sexual experiences.

h.   polyandry

_____ A progressive disease that is characterized by inflammation and pain in the joints.

i.   homogamy

_____ The tendency for women to "marry up" (in social or economic status) and for men to "marry down."

j.   mating gradient

_____ A muscular disorder that is caused by damage to the central nervous system (usually prior to or during birth) and characterized by spastic paralysis.

k.   extramarital sex

_____ Extramarital sex that is engaged in openly with the knowledge and consent of one's spouse.

l.   conventional adultery

_____ The practice of marrying people who are similar in social background and standing.

m.   consensual adultery

_____ Sexual relations between a married person and someone other than his or her spouse.

n. swinging   _____ A marriage that is characterized by the personal privacy of the spouses and the agreed-upon liberty of each spouse to form intimate relationships, which may include sexual relationships, with people other than the spouse.

o. open marriage   _____ A form of marriage in which a woman is married to more than one man at the same time.

p. group marriage   _____ A form of marriage in which a man is married to more than one woman at the same time.

q. cerebral palsy   _____ Swinging; mate-swapping.
r. arthritis   _____ Extramarital sex that is kept hidden from one's spouse.

s. comarital sex   _____ A social arrangement in which three or more people share an intimate relationship.

Time to Test Yourself by Filling in the Blanks

Test your knowledge of the content of this chapter by reading the following paragraphs and completing them. If you need to, use your text as a guide. Good luck!

_____ is the most common lifestyle among people in their early twenties. By the end of the last century, _____ woman in _____ and _____ men in _____ in the U.S. age 15 and older have never married. Most singles are _____ and _____. Most singles are sexually active, and many practice _____ _____, or one exclusive relationship after another. Some practice _____ or complete sexual abstinence.

_____ is the U.S. Bureau of Census' abbreviation for cohabitation. The number of cohabiting couples (doubled/remained about the same) _____ between 1980 and the early 1990s. People who cohabit are generally (more/less) _____ educated and (more/less) _____ affluent compared to their peers who are not cohabiting. Some studies suggest that the likelihood of divorce within ten years of marriage is nearly _____ as great among those who cohabited before marriage.

The institution of _____ is found in all human societies and is the most common lifestyle. Until the nineteenth century, _____ was not considered to be a basis for marriage.

There are two major types of marriage: _____ and _____. Among the world's societies, _____ is by far the most prevalent form of polygamy; _____ is practiced only rarely.

The concept of "like marrying like" is termed _____. We tend to marry others who are "like" us in _____ _____, _____ _____, and _____.

The _____ _____ of the 60s and 70s led to increases in the _____ of marital sex and the _____ of coital positions. The frequency of coitus tends to decrease with _____ and with _____ _____ _____. The duration of both _____ and _____ has increased since Kinsey's time.

One measure of marital sexual satisfaction is _____ _____; nearly all men report this but lower numbers of women do. Another measure of marital sexual satisfaction is how _____ satisfying the sexual relations are.

Extramarital sex can be divided into two types: _____ _____ (clandestine affairs) and _____ _____ (relationships conducted openly with the knowledge and consent of the partner). In the NHSLS study, _____ percent of married women and _____ percent of married men reported remaining loyal to their spouses. Most people in the United States (disapprove of/accept) _____ extra-marital affairs. _____, or "mate swapping," is a form of consensual adultery.

Nearly _____ of all marriages in the United States end in divorce. About _____ of children under eighteen live in single-parent households. Fewer (men/women) _____ than (men/women) _____ remarry. The divorce rate in remarriages is (higher/lower) _____ than that of first marriages.

Most older people (retain/lose) _____ their capacity to respond sexually. Age-related changes tend to occur more gradually in _____ than in _____. The most important determinant of continued sexual activity may be the _____ of a _____ _____ and _____ _____.

_____ _____, a muscular disorder caused by central nervous system damage, does not generally impair sexual interest, capacity for orgasm, or fertility. Some _____-_____ _____ cause a loss of sensation in the parts of the body that lie beneath the site of injury. Most women with this type of disability can become _____.

_____ _____ do not directly affect genital responsiveness but people with these disabilities may require special sex-education curricula and help in developing self-confidence and social skills. Despite the negative stereotypes about people with _____ _____, most are capable of learning the basics of reproduction and the social rules for responsible expression of their sexuality.

After You Read...

PRACTICE TEST #1

1. The U.S. Census Bureau uses the term POSSLQ to refer to:
   a. A divorced or widowed woman who shares a household with minor children.
   b. A single adult who lives in the same household as his or her elderly parents.
   c. Two adults who are married but living in separate households.
   d. Two adults who live together without marrying.

   p. 431   LO 3

2. Research indicates that compared to couples who do not cohabit prior to marriage, couples who first cohabit and later marry are more likely to:
   a. Have a successful marriage that only ends when one spouse dies.
   b. Separate due to both partners having an affair.
   c. Get divorced.
   d. None of the above is true, because researchers have found no differences between couples who do and do not cohabit prior to marriage.

   p. 433   LO 5

3. Among which of the following groups in the U.S. is cohabitation most prevalent?
   a. European American couples
   b. African American couples
   c. Middle-to-upper class couples
   d. College-educated couples

   p. 432   LO 4

4. Approximately what proportion of adults living in the U.S. has cohabited at some time?
   a. One-tenth
   b. One-fourth
   c. One-half
   d. Three-fourths

   p. 432   LO 1

5. Which of the following is true about the average age at marriage in the United States?
   a. The age at marriage for the typical woman has increased from 20 to 25 years old in the last 50 years.
   b. The age at marriage for the typical man has remained constant at about 26 years old for the last 50 years.
   c. Although the age at marriage for the typical woman was historically younger than the age at marriage for men, the average age at marriage is now 28 for both.
   d. The average age at marriage for both men and women has steadily increased during every decade since 1890.

   p. 429   LO 1

6. Single-mother family groups, which comprised 12 percent of all families in the 1970s, now represent _____ percent of all families in the United States.
   a. 15
   b. 26
   c. 35
   d. 46

   p. 429   LO 1

7. Social scientists refer to the practice of having a succession of exclusive sexual relationships as:
   a. Homogamy.
   b. Ritual partnering.
   c. Marital infidelity.
   d. Serial monogamy.

   p. 430   LO 2

8. Which of the following attitudinal factors is correlated with the willingness to cohabit?
   a. Liberal attitudes about sexual behavior
   b. Traditional attitudes toward gender roles
   c. Conservative attitudes about childbearing
   d. All of the above attitudes are related to a greater willingness to cohabit.

   p. 433   LO 5

9. Approximately what proportion of U.S. households with never-married cohabiting couples has children living with them?
   a. One-fifth
   b. One-third
   c. One-half
   d. One-tenth

   p. 432   LO 1

1. The sexual revolution of the 1960s and 1970s contributed to which of the following developments in the U.S.?
   a. Women became more informed about orgasm and felt more entitled to sexual pleasure.
   b. Married couples began engaging in coitus more frequently and for longer periods of time.
   c. The increased availability of effective contraception made it possible for more people to separate sexual activity from reproduction.
   d. The sexual revolution contributed to all of the above developments.
   p. 441   LO 13

2. The term *mating gradient* refers to the:
   a. Fact that college-educated people are more likely than people with lower education levels to support gay marriage.
   b. Situation in which both parties in a marriage agree to support their spouse's involvement in sexual relationships with other people.
   c. Tendency for women to marry men who are somewhat older, better educated, and of higher economic status than themselves.
   d. Trend toward delaying marriage and childbearing that has emerged since 1970.
   p. 441   LO 11

3. Which of the following characteristics distinguishes marriages of today from those based on the Christian patriarchal tradition in Western cultures?
   a. In traditional marriages, husbands initiate sexual activity and wives comply; but in today's marriages, either spouse may initiate or refuse sex.
   b. The emphasis in traditional marriages is on companionship, whereas the emphasis in today's marriages is on having and rearing children.
   c. The husband is dominant in traditional marriages, but the wife is dominant in today's marriages.
   d. All of the above accurately describe the distinctions between traditional marriages and those of today.
   p. 435   LO 6

4. Which of the following statements concerning *homogamy* in the U.S. is accurate?
   a. On average, women marry men who are 2 to 5 years older than them.
   b. In recent years, more African Americans have entered mixed-race marriages than any other racial-ethnic group.
   c. Because people in the U.S. are free to marry whomever they love, there is no systematic pattern of mate selection according to education level or occupation.
   d. All of the above statements concerning homogamy are accurate.
   p. 440   LO 11

5. Which of the following findings emerged from the NHSLS study of sexual behavior?
   a. Married couples engage in sexual relations an average of 14 times per month, which represents a notable increase in frequency since Kinsey's studies.
   b. Consistent with Kinsey's findings, there were no notable differences in the frequency of coitus for couples who are younger than 50 years old compared to couples who are aged 50 and older.
   c. The average duration of the last sexual event for couples surveyed was between 15 minutes and one hour, which represents a notable increase in duration since Kinsey's studies.
   d. Consistent with Kinsey's findings, only half of the women surveyed reported usually reaching orgasm, and orgasmic consistency for women declined with age.
      p. 442   LO 12

6. According to the NHSLS study, women with which marital status are most likely to report orgasmic consistency?
   a. Noncohabiting
   b. Cohabiting
   c. Engaged
   d. Married
      p. 442   LO 14

7. The majority of women who have had extramarital affairs cite _____ as their motivation.
   a.   revenge
   b.   curiosity
   c.   need for sexual excitement
   d.   desire for emotional closeness
      p. 445   LO 16

8. The practice of mate-swapping, also known as *swinging*, is a form of _____ adultery.
   a. accidental
   b. consensual
   c. conventional
   d. psychological
      p. 445   LO 16

9. Alterman suggests that the main reason men may not be able to forgive their wives when they have affairs is because men:
   a. Experience the affair as a massive blow to their pride or ego.
   b. Have difficulty conceiving of sex without emotional intimacy.
   c. Perceive the affair as a threat to the basic structure of their lives.
   d. Resent that they were denied the same opportunity to seek sexual fulfillment.
      p. 445   LO 15

1. Paula, a disabled adult who lives in her parents' household, is more likely than her peers without physical disabilities to experience:
    a. Confusion about her sexual orientation.
    b. A general lack of sexual feelings and disinterest in sex.
    c. Interference in her sexual life from overprotective parents.
    d. All of the above.
       p. 454   LO 28

2. Most of the physical changes that women experience as they age are due mainly to:
    a. Insomnia brought on by the emotional stress of the transition to old age.
    b. The inevitable weight gain that comes with menopause.
    c. A decline in the production of estrogen.
    d. Poor nutrition and loss of bone density.
       p. 451   LO 24

3. Which of the following factors tends to exacerbate the psychological distress many children experience after their parents divorce?
    a.   Continued involvement of both parents in the child's educational activities
    b.   Persistence of high level of conflict between the parents
    c.   Provision of financial support from the nonresident parent
    d.   All of the above factors exacerbate children's distress after divorce.
       p. 448   LO 20

4. Which of the following is true concerning divorce and remarriage in the United States?
    a. Second marriages are more likely than first marriages to end in divorce.
    b. Divorced men are more likely than divorced women to remarry, particularly among older people.
    c. One of the most common reasons that stepfamilies disband is parental conflict over children from the previous marriage(s).
    d. All of the above statements are true.
       p. 449-450   LO 21

5. All of the following characteristics of husbands are key predictors of divorce EXCEPT:
    a. Criticism.
    b. Contempt.
    c. Defensiveness.
    d. Financial neglect.
       p. 447   LO 18

6. According to the authors of the text, one of the most important factors contributing to the rising U.S. divorce rate after the 1960s was the:
    a. Relaxation of legal restrictions on divorce.
    b. Failure of couples to take marriage seriously.
    c. Media portrayal of divorce as a great opportunity to experience personal growth.
    d. Publication of scientific evidence revealing that most children do not exhibit psychological distress after their parents divorce.
    p. 447   LO 17

7. Which of the following changes in sexual arousal are associated with the aging process in healthy males?
    a. Nocturnal emissions disappear.
    b. More semen is emitted during ejaculation.
    c. More time is required to develop an erection.
    d. All of the above changes are associated with aging in males.
    p. 452   LO 24

8. One of the most common issues concerning sexuality among people with *sensory* disabilities is:
    a. Having difficulty physically positioning themselves in ways conducive to intercourse.
    b. Experiencing stronger-than-normal sex drives and lacking control over sexual urges.
    c. Lack of knowledge about sexual anatomy and positions used for sexual activities.
    d. Losing the physical capacity to become aroused through genital stimulation.
    p. 456   LO 28

9. In what way does cerebral palsy generally affect sexuality?
    a. People with cerebral palsy do not usually exhibit any sexual interest.
    b. People with cerebral palsy are usually unable to achieve orgasm.
    c. People with cerebral palsy are unable to become pregnant.
    d. None of the above statements are true because cerebral palsy does not generally impair sexual interest, capacity for orgasm, or fertility.
    p. 455   LO 27

10. Which of the following factors inhibits the development of satisfying sexual relationships among people with physical, psychological, *and* sensory disabilities?
    a. Lowered intellectual capacity that limits the ability to consent to sexual activity
    b. Neurological damage that impairs the ability to feel erotic sensations
    c. Chronic pain that limits flexibility and movement
    d. Lack of self-confidence due to social rejection
    p. 454   LO 26

COMPREHENSIVE PRACTICE TEST

Multiple Choice Questions

1. Which of the following is true about the average age at marriage in the United States?
   a. The age at marriage for the typical woman has increased from 20 to 25 years old in the last 50 years.
   b. The age at marriage for the typical man has remained constant at about 26 years old for the last 50 years.
   c. Although the age at marriage for the typical woman was historically younger than the age at marriage for men, the average age at marriage is now 28 for both.
   d. The average age at marriage for both men and women has steadily increased during every decade since 1890.

2. Which of the following characteristics distinguishes marriages of today from those based on the Christian patriarchal tradition in Western cultures?
   a. In traditional marriages, husbands initiate sexual activity and wives comply; but in today's marriages, either spouse may initiate or refuse sex.
   b. The emphasis in traditional marriages is on companionship, whereas the emphasis in today's marriages is on having and rearing children.
   c. The husband is dominant in traditional marriages, but the wife is dominant in today's marriages.
   d. All of the above accurately describe the distinctions between traditional marriages and those of today.

3. Research indicates that compared to couples that do not cohabit prior to marriage, couples that first cohabit and later marry are more likely to:
   a. Have a successful marriage that only ends when one spouse dies.
   b. Separate due to both partners having an affair.
   c. Get divorced.
   d. None of the above is true, because researchers have found no differences between couples that do and do not cohabit prior to marriage.

4. Approximately what proportion of adults living in the U.S. has cohabited at some time?
   a. One-tenth
   b. One-fourth
   c. One-half
   d. Three-fourths

5. The majority of women who have had extramarital affairs cite _____ as their motivation.
   a. revenge
   b. curiosity
   c. need for sexual excitement
   d. desire for emotional closeness

6. The term *mating gradient* refers to the:
   a. Fact that college-educated people are more likely than people with lower education levels to support gay marriage.
   b. Situation in which both parties in a marriage agree to support their spouse's involvement in sexual relationships with other people.
   c. Tendency for women to marry men who are somewhat older, better educated, and of higher economic status than themselves.
   d. Trend toward delaying marriage and childbearing that has emerged since 1970.

7. Which of the following statements concerning *homogamy* in the U.S. is accurate?
   a. On average, women marry men who are 2 to 5 years older than them.
   b. In recent years, more African Americans have entered mixed-race marriages than any other racial-ethnic group.
   c. Because people in the U.S. are free to marry whomever they love, there is no systematic pattern of mate selection according to education level or occupation.
   d. All of the above statements concerning homogamy are accurate.

8. According to the authors of the text, one of the most important factors contributing to the rising U.S. divorce rate after the 1960s was the:
   a. Relaxation of legal restrictions on divorce.
   b. Failure of couples to take marriage seriously.
   c. Media portrayal of divorce as a great opportunity to experience personal growth.
   d. Publication of scientific evidence revealing that most children do not exhibit psychological distress after their parents divorce.

9. One of the most common issues concerning sexuality among people with *sensory* disabilities is:
   a. Having difficulty physically positioning themselves in ways conducive to intercourse.
   b. Experiencing stronger-than-normal sex drives and lacking control over sexual urges.
   c. The lack of knowledge about sexual anatomy and positions used for sexual activities.
   d. Losing the physical capacity to become aroused through genital stimulation.

10. All of the following characteristics of husbands are key predictors of divorce EXCEPT:
    a. Criticism.
    b. Contempt.
    c. Defensiveness.
    d. Financial neglect.

11. Social scientists refer to the practice of having a succession of exclusive sexual relationships as:
    a. Homogamy
    b. Ritual partnering.
    c. Marital infidelity.
    d. Serial monogamy.

12. Most of the physical changes that women experience as they age are due mainly to:
    a. Insomnia brought on by the emotional stress of the transition to old age.
    b. The inevitable weight gain that comes with menopause.
    c. A decline in the production of estrogen.
    d. Poor nutrition and loss of bone density.

13. Among which of the following groups in the U.S. is cohabitation most prevalent?
    a. European American couples
    b. African American couples
    c. Middle-to-upper class couples
    d. College-educated couples

True/False

_____ 1. Social scientists refer to the practice of completely abstaining from sexual relations with other people as *celibacy*.

_____ 2. The ancient Greeks, Hebrews, and Romans considered wives *chattel*, or part of the husband's property.

_____ 3. As of 2007, the United States and Canada were the only nations in the world to extend marriage rights to same-sex couples.

_____ 4. One significant attitudinal change that has emerged since the sexual revolution is that less than half of all Americans now view extramarital affairs as "always wrong."

_____ 5. About three-fourths of men who admit to having an extramarital affair cite "being in love" as the primary justification for the affair.

_____ 6. Research by Laumann and colleagues indicates that between the ages of 25 and 39 years old, a higher percentage of men than women report being both "extremely physically satisfied" and "extremely emotionally satisfied" with their partners.

_____ 7. Among couples that divorce today, the most common reason cited for divorce is physical abuse.

1. Identify several factors contributing to divorce—noting the factor that is strongest. Explain the impacts of divorce (or even staying together in an unrewarding marriage) and children. Identify what parental behaviors in staying together are most damaging to the children. Note the typical behavioral impacts on children post-divorce and what parents can do to offset them.

_____

_____

_____

_____

_____

_____

_____

_____

2. Outline the five factors Margaret Nosek asserts are necessary for sexual wellness among the disabled population. Suggest one specific mechanism through which a person with a disability could secure the resources they need to achieve each component.

_____

_____

_____

_____

_____

_____

_____

When You Have Finished...

Let's see where the Web takes you as you explore the following activities related to adult sexuality.

1. Cohabitation: A Snapshot. Go to the National Institute of Child and Health and Human Development (http://www.nichd.nih.gov/) and see what they have to say about living together without marriage.

2. Single and Older: What do you do when you are 35 and still single? Search for online singles and see what resources are out there for you if you have not settled down yet. Check Craigslist.org in your area. What are you finding? What are people looking for?

3. Equal Marriage for Same-Sex Couples: http://www.samesexmarriage.ca/. Read articles regarding gay marriage at this site. Review the sites from the previous chapters... has your opinion changed?

4. Extramarital affairs: Why do good men and women have affairs? Google "causes of affairs" and see what comes up. Check the news link to see what is in the popular culture at the time. From the President of the United States to famous golfers, is there anyone who is immune?

5. How do you know if you are cheating? Search Google for "is it cheating if" and check out some of the results. What does infidelity actually mean? Is there a boundary or line that needs to be crossed?

   Divorce and its child impacts: An article by Robert Hughes, Jr., Ph.D. of the Department of Family Relations and Human Development at The Ohio State University deals with aspects of divorce and how it may affect children: http://hec.osu.edu/famlife/family/divorce.htm

6. Aging and sexuality: This website, http://www.siecus.org/pubs/biblio/bibs0012.html, lists resources on aging and sexuality from the Sexuality Information and Education Council of the United States (SIECUS).

7. Go to Ted.com and search for Helen Fisher. Watch the video on why we love and cheat. If you watched it in a previous chapter and watch it again. It is totally worth it.

Chapter 15
Sexual Dysfunctions

Before You Begin...

Chapter Summary

This chapter explores the wide variety of sexual dysfunctions and what can be done to effectively accommodate them. Clinicians categorize the sexual dysfunctions presented in this chapter as disorders of desire, arousal, orgasm, or pain. Women more often report experiencing painful sex, lack of desire or pleasure, and inability to reach orgasm, whereas men more often report having anxiety about their performance and reaching orgasm too soon. Dysfunctions may also be classified as lifelong or acquired, and general or situational. Sexual dysfunction is related to biological factors, such as a reduction in testosterone levels as men age; interpersonal factors, such as conflict in the couple's relationship; psychosocial factors, such as stress, depression, guilt, or fear; and cultural factors, such as norms governing communication about sexual matters or the social stigma attached to a gay or lesbian sexual orientation.

Sex therapies designed to treat sexual dysfunctions have five main goals—to change self-defeating beliefs and attitudes, teach sexual skills, enhance sexual knowledge, improve sexual communication, and reduce performance anxiety. Masters and Johnson, who pioneered the use of direct behavioral approaches, focus on the couple as the unit of treatment. Other professionals treat the individual who manifests the dysfunction. In addition to therapy, some people with sexual dysfunctions undergo biological treatments, such as hormone therapy and vascular surgery. All of these have specific scenarios where they demonstrate strengths and your text authors have done a fine job explaining.

Learning Objectives

1. Name and describe the four categories of sexual dysfunctions identified in the *DSM*.

2. Give examples of at least two disorders from each category of sexual dysfunctions and identify the primary factors that contribute to the development of each disorder.

3. Using data from Laumann and colleagues' research, compare the self-reported incidence of various sexual problems for European American men and women with that of African American men and women, noting what patterns the data reveal by race and gender.

4. Provide an overview of the biological factors most often implicated in sexual dysfunction and give examples of hormonal, vascular, neurological, and chemical causes of sexual dysfunction.

5. Demonstrate familiarity with the nine psychosocial factors associated with sexual disorders, and consider how these factors may interact with biological causes to foster sexual dysfunction.

6. State which models of treatment are collectively referred to as sex therapy and list the five main goals of sex therapies.

7. Recognize why Masters and Johnson are considered "pioneers" in the field of sex therapy, provide an overview of their approach to treating sexual dysfunction, and consider how Helen Singer Kaplan's approach to sex therapy differs from the Masters and Johnson model.

8. Describe the process the text authors suggest you use to find a qualified sex therapist.

9. Identify the most common methods of treating sexual desire disorders and classify the methods according to the type of treatment they represent, e.g., biological or psychological.

10. Identify the most common methods of treating sexual arousal disorders and classify the methods according to the type of treatment they represent, e.g., biological or psychological.

11. Identify the most common methods of treating orgasmic disorders and classify the methods according to the type of treatment they represent, e.g., biological or psychological.

12. List the seven elements commonly found in direct-masturbation programs designed to treat women who experience orgasmic disorders.

13. Identify the most common methods of treating sexual pain disorders and classify the methods according to the type of treatment they represent, e.g., biological or psychological.

14. Explain why the development of treatments for sexual dysfunction in women has lagged behind the development of treatments for men, and identify at least two treatments originally designed for men that are currently being investigated as treatments for women.

Term Identification

You know the drill; these are the terms will help you learn what you need, and making flashcards will help.

Chapter 15's Table of Key Terms

Anorgasmic	Sex therapy
Biopsychosocial model	Sexual arousal disorders
Dyspareunia	Sexual desire disorders
Hypogonadism	Sexual dysfunctions
Male erectile disorder	Sexual pain disorders
Neurotransmitter	Spectator role
Orgasmic disorders	Squeeze technique
Performance anxiety	Tumescence
Premature ejaculation	Vaginismus
Sensate focus exercises	Vasocongestion

As You Read...

Sexual Dysfunctions

> ➤ *Types of Sexual Dysfunctions*

Cultural Influences: When is sexual behavior dysfunctional? How is it decided?

What are the common expectations about females in U.S. culture relative, say, to assertiveness and overall knowledge of sex? What other expectations can you think of from your text (if any)?

_____

_____

_____

_____

_____

What are the common expectations about males in U.S. culture relative to their readiness and overall knowledge of sex? What other expectations can you think of from your text (if any)?

_____

_____

_____

_____

_____

What happens if a man is unable to meet cultural expectations at the moment expected? Does it (or can it) lead to a dysfunction? If so, how and what type(s)? Please explain.

_____

_____

_____

_____

_____

For the females, what happens (or can happen) when one or two of the cultural expectations you've outlined above for females isn't met? What kind(s) of dysfunctions can manifest and how? Please explain.

_____

_____

_____

_____

_____

Take a moment to reflect on whether the media (news, films, books, etc.) have influenced how you feel about your sexuality in terms of whether it is functional or dysfunctional. Has a movie or novel ever made you question your sexual abilities? In what ways did what you viewed or read affect you? Can a film bring doubts to oneself regarding one's sexual prowess or that of one's partner? If so, what are some examples of this? Since culture can have an impact on whether sexual behavior is considered dysfunctional, note your thoughts about the media below.

_____

_____

_____

_____

_____

_____

_____

What are effective coping strategies that both females and males can use to offset an individual's thoughts that can set the stage for sexual dysfunction? What about how one would offset some of the popular media ideas you've just noted above?

_____

_____

_____

_____

_____

_____

_____

TRY PRACTICE TEST #1 NOW!
GOOD LUCK!

➤ *Origins of Sexual Dysfunctions*

What are the causes of sexual dysfunctions?

Sexual dysfunctions may have many origins. What are some biological causes of sexual dysfunctions? What are the psychosocial causes of sexual dysfunctions? Can some sexual dysfunctions be due to both types of causes? Fill out the chart below with your responses to these questions by checking the appropriate box for each type of sexual dysfunction.

Categories of Sexual Dysfunction	*Cause(s)*		
	Biological	*Psychosocial*	*Possibly Both*
Sexual desire disorders			
Sexual arousal disorders			
Orgasmic disorders			
Sexual pain disorders			

➤ *Treatment of Sexual Dysfunctions*

If you were a sex therapist...

Choose three biological causes and three psychosocial causes of sexual dysfunctions that you thought of as you completed the chart above and suggest a strategy to treat each of them. Use the information in the text to back up your treatment methods.

Biological Cause:

Strategy:

Biological Cause:

Strategy:

Biological Cause:

Strategy:

Psychosocial Cause:

Strategy:

Psychosocial Cause:

Strategy:

Psychosocial Cause:

Strategy:

TRY PRACTICE TEST #2 NOW!
GOOD LUCK!

Masters and Johnson versus Helen Singer Kaplan
Two approaches to the treatment of sexual dysfunctions are mentioned in the text: the Masters and Johnson Approach and the Helen Singer Kaplan Approach. What are the techniques associated with each approach?

      <u>Masters and Johnson Approach</u>

          Main Techniques:

      <u>Helen Singer Kaplan Approach</u>

          Main Techniques:

Which treatment for which disorder?
Fill out the following table indicating the types of treatment methods used by professionals to treat each main type of sexual dysfunction: sexual desire disorders, sexual arousal disorders, orgasmic disorders, and sexual pain disorders. Check your answers by referencing the textbook.

Categories of Sexual Dysfunction	Treatment Methods
Sexual desire disorders	
Sexual arousal disorders	

Orgasmic disorders	
Sexual pain disorders	

Does sex therapy work?
Summarize the effectiveness of sex therapy by answering the questions below.

Which dysfunctions have a better success rate?

What factors are associated with success in sex therapy?

How do you find a good sex therapist?
What advice would you give a friend who asks you (since you are taking a course in human sexuality) how to go about finding a qualified sex therapist?

What questions should your friend ask a sex therapist before deciding who to see?

About what should you warn your friend?

TRY PRACTICE TEST #3 NOW!
GOOD LUCK!

Time to Test Yourself by Filling in the Blanks
Test your knowledge of the content of this chapter by reading the following paragraphs and completing them. If you need to, use your text as a guide. Good luck!

Most sexual dysfunctions can be grouped into four categories: 1) _____ _____ disorders, 2) _____ _____ disorders, 3) _____ disorders and 4) _____ _____ disorders.

_____ _____ _____ is one of the most commonly diagnosed sexual dysfunctions. Abrupt changes in sexual desire can often be explained by psychological and interpersonal factors such as _____, _____ and problems in the _____. People with _____ _____ disorder find sex disgusting or aversive and they avoid genital contact.

Sexual arousal disorders have in the past been labeled with the pejorative terms of _____ in the male and _____ in the female. As many as 30 million men in the United States experience some degree of _____ _____ or persistent difficulty in achieving or maintaining an erection.

In _____ _____, a person experiences a delay in reaching or a failure to reach orgasm. This disorder is more common in _____ than in _____. Women who have never achieved orgasm are sometimes labeled _____ or _____. The most common male sexual dysfunction is _____ _____.

_____ or painful coitus can affect men or women. The causes can be (for example, vaginal infections, STIs, PID, smegma under the foreskin, endometriosis) _____ or (for example, guilt, anxiety, effects of sexual trauma) _____. In women the most common cause is _____ _____. Another sexual dysfunction, _____, occurs reflexively during attempts at vaginal penetration. It is caused by a _____ ____ _____ and these women often have histories of sexual traumas, which resulted in _____ _____.

People with sexual dysfunctions are generally advised to have a physical exam to determine whether their problems are _____ based. Medical conditions that can cause sexual dysfunctions include heart disease, _____ mellitus, _____ _____, _____ _____ _____, complications from _____, _____ problems, or the use of some _____ and other _____. Many cases of sexual dysfunction involve the interaction of _____ and _____ factors.

Children reared in cultures or home environments that are _____ _____ may experience anxiety and guilt about sex. In the United States the double standard has a greater impact on

_____. Experiences such as rape, incest or child molestation may cause _____ _____, which can stifle arousal or cause anxiety.

_____ _____ _____ such as little foreplay, lack of variety or lack of clitoral stimulation can contribute to sexual dysfunctions. High levels of _____ are associated with lessened sexual interest and response. Troubled relationships are often characterized by _____ _____ about sex and other matters.

People who are overly concerned about how they will perform are experiencing _____ _____; a sexual failure can then lead to increased anxiety and begin a vicious cycle.

_____ and _____ pioneered the use of a male and female therapy team with a focus on direct behavior changes. Couples perform daily homework including _____ _____ exercises in which partners take turns giving and receiving stimulation in nongenital areas of the body. Kaplan's approach, termed _____ _____, combines _____ and _____ methods.

For men with abnormally low levels of testosterone _____ _____ may help restore sexual drive and erectile ability. A _____ _____ is a prosthetic device that is surgically implanted as a treatment for erectile dysfunction. _____ surgery may be used for specific blockages of blood vessels that supply the penis. _____ of phentolamine into the penis can produce long-lasting erections. A recently introduced treatment is the _____ _____ _____, which forces an increased flow of blood into the penis. _____ _____ is one of the major treatments for anorgasmic women. Two methods of treating premature ejaculation are the _____ techniques and the _____ method.

After You Read...

PRACTICE TEST #1
---

1. A woman who is *anorgasmic*:
   a. Is able to achieve orgasm through self-stimulation but not from intercourse.
   b. Has never reached orgasm.
   c. Takes so long to reach orgasm that she usually becomes discouraged and frustrated during sex.
   d. Experiences multiple, intense orgasms during a single sexual encounter.
      p. 468   LO 2

2. The most common male sexual dysfunction reported in the NHSLS study was :
   a. Impotence.
   b. Dyspareunia.
   c. Delayed ejaculation.
   d. Premature ejaculation.
      p. 462-463   LO 3

3. The physiological process involving the engorgement of blood vessels with blood, an important component of sexual arousal for both men and women, is called:
   a. Vaginismus.
   b. Hypogonadism.
   c. Vasocongestion.
   d. Masturbation.
      p. 465   LO 2

4. Hypoactive sexual desire is often accompanied by:
   a. Infertility.
   b. Severe PMS.
   c. Excessive lubrication.
   d. Absence of sexual fantasies.
      p. 464   LO 2

5. Women who experience complete aversion to sexual contact are classified as having a(n):
   a. Pain disorder.
   b. Desire disorder.
   c. Arousal disorder.
   d. Orgasmic disorder.
      p. 464   LO 1

6. The *most* common cause of coital pain in women is:
    a. Inadequate lubrication.
    b. Penile contact with the cervix.
    c. An allergic reaction to latex condoms or spermicide.
    d. Involuntary contractions of the vaginal musculature.
         p. 464   LO 2

7. U.S. culture places certain expectations on men and women. Many times these expectations contribute to sexual dysfunctions. Which statement(s) is (are) true?
    a. Our culture expects sexual competence of both men and women. Outcomes of not meeting the expectation include diminished self-esteem, guilt, anxiety, and shame for both sexes.
    b. Men are expected to always be eager and ready for sex in the U.S. When one fails to have or sustain an erection, even occasionally when expected, it can lead to dysfunction.
    c. Repressive social attitudes interfere with women's ability to learn of the sexual potentials.
    d. All the above are true
    e. Only A and B are true.
         p. 462,467   LO 3

8. Which of these groups reported the highest incidence of the sexual problem, "lack of interest in sex," in the NHSLS study?
    a. African American women
    b. African American men
    c. European American women
    d. European American men
         p. 471   LO 3

9. The root cause of the sexual pain disorder, *vaginismus*, is:
    a. Psychological fear of penetration due to emotional trauma.
    b. Injury to the vagina sustained during strenuous physical activities.
    c. Development of scar tissue from a problematic childbirth experience.
    d. A structural disorder of the reproductive organs due to genetic factors.
         p. 471   LO 2

10. One of the least frequently diagnosed sexual disorders, male _____ disorder, tends to appear in men when there are feelings of performance anxiety, sexual guilt, and hostility toward one's partner.
    a. pain
    b. desire
    c. arousal
    d. orgasmic
         p. 469   LO 1

1. The common *biological* condition underlying erectile dysfunction in men with large waists, low levels of physical activity, and high consumption of alcohol is probably:
   a. A high degree of performance anxiety due to poor body image.
   b. Insufficient production of testosterone due to an endocrine disorder.
   c. Insufficient flow of blood to the penis due to high cholesterol levels.
   d. Impaired sensation due to depression of the central nervous system.
   p. 472   LO 4

2. Laumann and colleagues found that whereas poor physical health can contribute to a wide variety of sexual dysfunctions in men, it contributes *mostly* to _____ in women.
   a. performance anxiety
   b. poor body image
   c. delayed orgasm
   d. sexual pain
   p. 475   LO 4

3. Consumption of which of the following substances tends to impair genital blood flow, thus impairing erectile function in men and reducing lubrication in women?
   a. Cocaine
   b. Diuretics
   c. Prescription tranquilizers
   d. All of the above substances may impair genital blood flow for men and women.
   p. 474   LO 4

4. The following way(s) are good at locating qualified sex therapists EXCEPT:
   a. The telephone yellow pages.
   b. Local university counseling department.
   c. American Association of Sex Educators, Counselors, and Therapists.
   d. All of the above are good ways.
   p. 481   LO 5

5. All the below are true about Viagra, Levitra, and Cialis EXCEPT:
   a. They increase arterial blood flow in the penis.
   b. They are called PDE5 inhibitors.
   c. They can directly contribute to HIV infection by immune system suppression.
   d. They can cause migraine headaches.
   p. 484   LO 10

6. According to Leiblum and Rosen, which of the following couples is unlikely to derive much benefit from consulting a sex therapist about their sexual problems that manifest in the bedroom?
    a. Sam and his wife Pam, who believes that "losing control" is unfeminine
    b. Lynn and her boyfriend Dan, whose limited knowledge about female anatomy prevents him from experimenting with different sexual techniques
    c. Mark and Lori, who quietly but deeply resents her husband Mark for having an affair last year
    d. Donna and her fiancé, Bill, who limits foreplay to a few minutes before coitus
        p. 480.490   LO 5

7. Sex therapists note that individuals who experience sexual dysfunction due to performance anxiety often adopt a _____ role in sexual relationships.
    a. performer
    b. spectator
    c. dominant
    d. victim
        p. 468   LO 5

8. Learning theorists suggest that women who have experienced sexual trauma such as rape or incest are conditioned to experience _____ when exposed to sexual stimuli.
    a. anger
    b. social stigma
    c. heightened anxiety
    d. excessive lubrication
        p. 476   LO 5

9. Laumann and his colleagues identified what notable relationship between alcohol consumption and sexual dysfunction?
    a. The consumption of alcohol consistently increases sexual arousal in women by promoting vasocongestion.
    b. The consumption of alcohol significantly depresses testosterone production and frequently leads to erectile failure in men.
    c. Although the consumption of alcohol increases sexual desire and fosters arousal in men, alcohol consumption dampens both desire and arousal in women.
    d. None of the above is accurate, because Laumann found no general relationship between alcohol consumption and sexual dysfunction.
        p. 475   LO 4

10. Some drugs used to treat depression (called SSRIs) have the following attribute:
    a. They can cause priapism (sustained erections causing physical harm) in some people.
    b. Used by people needing blood pressure control too.
    c. Often used for diabetes in regulating the metabolizing of glucose.
    d. Unlike some medications, once they are stopped, the negative effect on sexual functioning may not disappear.
        p. 473   LO 4

1. Which perspective on sexual dysfunction assumed that the only way to treat sexual problems was for an individual to resolve unconscious psychological conflicts through long-term therapy?
   a. Direct behavioral intervention model
   b. Cognitive modification model
   c. Psychoanalysis model
   d. Skill-building model

         p. 478   LO 7

2. Masters and Johnson introduced all of the following components to the field of sex therapy EXCEPT:
   a. Using direct behavioral approaches to treat sexual dysfunction.
   b. Having patients reside at a clinic for the duration of their treatment.
   c. Focusing treatment on the couple instead of the individual reporting the problem.
   d. Assigning female therapists to men, and male therapists to women, to give patients insight into their partner's perspective on sexuality.

         p. 479   LO 7

3. When Rob and Leslie meet with their sex therapist, she instructs them to go home, take off their clothes, create a relaxing atmosphere, and take turns giving and receiving non-genital stimulation. Therapists refer to this treatment technique as:
   a. Intimacy orientation.
   b. Sensate focus exercise.
   c. Squeeze technique.
   d. Cognitive reevaluation.

         p. 480   LO 9

4. Administering the drug *alprostadil* treats erectile disorders by:
   a. Reducing men's anxiety about performing sexually.
   b. Artificially increasing the level of testosterone produced.
   c. Increasing sexual interest by first addressing clinical depression.
   d. Relaxing the muscles around the arteries in the penis to increase blood flow.

         p. 483-484   LO 10

5. In what way does getting penile implants affect a man's sexuality?
   a. Implants direct fluid into the penis to create an erection in cases where normal blood flow into the penis is physically blocked.
   b. Implants enhance a man's sex drive by increasing the production of testosterone.
   c. Implants promote sexual arousal by increasing sensitivity to touch in men who have genital nerve damage.
   d. Penile implants affect men's sexuality in all of the above ways.

         p. 485   LO 10

6. All of the following are tools used in effective biological treatments for erectile dysfunction EXCEPT:
    a. Vacuum pump(s)
    b. Psychotherapy
    c. Medication(s)
    d. Surgery
       p. 485   LO 13

7. Which of the following medical treatments currently used to address men's problems with sexual arousal are now being adapted and tested for use in women?
    a. Medications such as Viagra and alprostadil
    b. Testosterone skin patches
    c. Vacuum pumps
    d. All of the above medical treatments are under investigation for use in women.
       p. 488   LO 14

8. Which of the following positions did Masters and Johnson recommend heterosexual couples use for intercourse in cases where the woman experiences an orgasmic disorder?
    a. Male-superior (man on top)
    b. Female-superior (woman on top)
    c. Parallel (laying face-to-face on their sides)
    d. Rear-entry (laying stomach-to-back on their sides)
       p. 488   LO 12

9. Urologist James Semans introduced what popular method of helping men tolerate longer periods of sexual stimulation, thereby reducing the likelihood of premature ejaculation?
    a. Intimacy orientation
    b. Squeeze technique
    c. Sensate focus exercise
    d. Cognitive reevaluation
       p. 492   LO 11

10. Healthcare providers generally treat female _____ disorders by instructing a woman to insert dilators into the vagina as a way to help relax the vaginal musculature.
    a. desire
    b. arousal
    c. orgasmic
    d. pain
       p. 493   LO 13

Multiple Choice Questions

1. The *most* common cause of coital pain in women is:
   a. Inadequate lubrication.
   b. Penile contact with the cervix.
   c. An allergic reaction to latex condoms or spermicide.
   d. Involuntary contractions of the vaginal musculature.

2. Some drugs used to treat depression (called SSRIs) have the following attribute:
   a. They can cause priapism (sustained erections causing physical harm) in some people.
   b. Used by people needing blood pressure control too.
   c. Often used for diabetes in regulating the metabolizing of glucose.
   d. Unlike some medications, once they are stopped, the negative effect on sexual functioning may not disappear.

3. The most common male sexual dysfunction reported in the NHSLS study was:
   a. Impotence.
   b. Dyspareunia.
   c. Delayed ejaculation.
   d. Premature ejaculation.

4. Learning theorists suggest that women who have experienced sexual trauma such as rape or incest are conditioned to experience _____ when exposed to sexual stimuli.
   a. anger
   b. social stigma
   c. heightened anxiety
   d. excessive lubrication

5. The common *biological* condition underlying erectile dysfunction in men with large waists, low levels of physical activity, and high consumption of alcohol is probably:
   a. A high degree of performance anxiety due to poor body image.
   b. Insufficient production of testosterone due to an endocrine disorder.
   c. Insufficient flow of blood to the penis due to high cholesterol levels.
   d. Impaired sensation due to depression of the central nervous system.

6. The root cause of the sexual pain disorder, *vaginismus*, is:
   a. Psychological fear of penetration due to emotional trauma.
   b. Injury to the vagina sustained during strenuous physical activities.
   c. Development of scar tissue from a problematic childbirth experience.
   d. A structural disorder of the reproductive organs due to genetic factors.

7. Which perspective on sexual dysfunction assumed that the only way to treat sexual problems was for an individual to resolve unconscious psychological conflicts through long-term therapy?
    a. Direct behavioral intervention model
    b. Cognitive modification model
    c. Psychoanalysis model
    d. Skill-building model

8. All of the following are tools used in effective biological treatments for erectile dysfunction EXCEPT:
    a. Vacuum pump(s).
    b. Psychotherapy.
    c. Medication(s).
    d. Surgery.

9. Masters and Johnson introduced all of the following components to the field of sex therapy EXCEPT:
    a. Using direct behavioral approaches to treat sexual dysfunction.
    b. Having patients reside at a clinic for the duration of their treatment.
    c. Focusing treatment on the couple instead of the individual reporting the problem.
    d. Assigning female therapists to men, and male therapists to women, to give patients insight into their partner's perspective on sexuality.

10. A woman who is *anorgasmic*:
    a. Is able to achieve orgasm through self-stimulation but not from intercourse.
    b. Has never reached orgasm.
    c. Takes so long to reach orgasm that she usually becomes discouraged and frustrated during sex.
    d. Experiences multiple, intense orgasms during a single sexual encounter.

11. When Rob and Leslie meet with their sex therapist, she instructs them to go home, take off their clothes, create a relaxing atmosphere, and take turns giving and receiving non-genital stimulation. Therapists refer to this treatment technique as:
    a. Intimacy orientation.
    b. Sensate focus exercise.
    c. Squeeze technique.
    d. Cognitive reevaluation.

12. Which of these groups reported the highest incidence of the sexual problem, "lack of interest in sex," in the NHSLS study?
    a. African American women
    b. African American men
    c. European American women
    d. European American men

13. Consumption of which of the following substances tends to impair genital blood flow, thus impairing erectile function in men and reducing lubrication in women?
    a. Cocaine
    b. Diuretics
    c. Prescription tranquilizers
    d. All of the above substances may impair genital blood flow for men and women.

14. Which of the following positions did Masters and Johnson recommend heterosexual couples use for intercourse in cases where the woman experiences an orgasmic disorder?
    a. Male-superior (man on top)
    b. Female-superior (woman on top)
    c. Parallel (laying face-to-face on their sides)
    d. Rear-entry (laying stomach-to-back on their sides)

15. Women who experience complete aversion to sexual contact are classified as having a(n):
    a. Pain disorder.
    b. Desire disorder.
    c. Arousal disorder.
    d. Orgasmic disorder.

True/False

_____ 1. Masters and Johnson are considered pioneers in the treatment of sexual dysfunction because they taught, and had couples practice, sexual techniques in large group settings.

_____ 2. The reason why drugs used to treat psychological problems such as depression often help with premature ejaculation is that both problems are connected with insufficient levels of testosterone.

_____ 3. Recent research indicates that Viagra is an effective biological treatment for both men and women who experience sexual desire and arousal disorders.

_____ 4. The results of the NHSLS study indicate that men are more likely than women to report lack of sexual desire and pleasure.

_____ 5. Sexual arousal disorder in women is more likely to be caused by psychological factors such as anger, guilt, and anxiety than by biological causes such as hormonal imbalances.

_____ 6. The most common cause of sexual pain disorders in men is genital infection.

_____ 7. Based on findings from both Rimm's study and the Massachusetts Male Aging Study, the best thing men can do to prevent erectile dysfunction is exercise regularly.

Essay Questions

1. Explain how cultural ideology and social norms contribute to the definition and experience of sexual dysfunction. Illustrate your points about the importance of culture using the example of premature ejaculation.

    _____
    _____
    _____
    _____
    _____
    _____
    _____
    _____

2. Discuss why orgasmic disorders are relatively rare among men but quite common among women in the United States. Considering both the physiological and social factors that contribute to the development of female orgasmic disorders, assess the relevance of the main elements included in most directed-masturbation programs, and identify any other components you think could enhance the effectiveness of these programs.

    _____
    _____
    _____
    _____
    _____
    _____
    _____
    _____

When You Have Finished...

What Does the World Think?

Let's see where the Web takes you as you explore what happens when there are problems or concerns about your sex life?.

1. Dyspareunia: http://www.dyspareunia.org/
   Interesting information and links regarding dyspareunia are provided in this site.

2. Sensate Focus Therapy: You can search Google with and without the "-.com" and see what shows up. Are there good resources for learning how to pleasure you partner?

3. A Sex-Positive Primer: http://sexuality.org/aspp.html
   This is an interesting introduction to having a positive attitude about sex. Provides some basic information about enjoying sex from the Sexuality Organization sponsored by the Society for Human Sexuality.

4. Vaginismus: On YouTube, there are a series of videos about overcoming this disorder.
   Search for "VAGINISMUS Diary" and experience this from a different perspective.

5. Anorgasmia: http://adam.about.com/encyclopedia/Orgasmic-dysfunction.htm. From the ADAM Health Center on About.com (from the New York Times).

6. For help with Female Sexual Dysfunction: http://www.aafp.org. Search for female sexual disorders. This site contains information on female sexual dysfunction including a comprehensive list of factors associated with female sexual dysfunction. From the American Academy of Physicians.

Chapter 16
Sexually Transmitted Infections

Before You Begin...

Chapter Summary

As with all things in our world, one cannot have the good without some consequences. Some of the consequences can be irritating and, at worst, can lead to an untimely and painful death. Here we want you to be able to make deliberate and intelligent choices to avoid sexually-transmitted infections (STIs) or recognize them quickly to get the right kind of care without delay. Though, if you are reading this and do already have one of the STIs in the more painful category, we hope to inspire you with solid coping strategies to optimize your life.

Your text authors provide a comprehensive overview of the many sexually transmitted infections (STIs) that are prevalent in the human population. They note that there has been a surge in the incidence of STIs, and STIs such as chlamydia and genital warts are epidemics in the U.S. and around the world. Factors such as increases in the number of young persons who engage in coitus and their average number of sexual partners, as well as a failure to use condoms consistently, contribute to STI epidemics. Because some STIs have no symptoms, many people do not realize they are infected, so they do not seek treatment. Untreated STIs may foster the development of other medical problems, such as cervical cancer, pelvic inflammatory disease (PID), and infertility.

Sexually transmitted infections are classified as bacterial, viral, or ectoparasitic. Bacterial STIs, such as gonorrhea and syphilis, are diagnosed by clinical inspection and fluid cultures. They are cured with antibiotics. Viral infections, such as Acquired Immunodeficiency Syndrome (HIV) and genital herpes (HSV-2), are diagnosed by clinical inspection and fluid cultures too, but they cannot be cured. People with these STIs often take medications to relieve their symptoms though. Ectoparasitic infestations such as pediculosis ("crabs") are diagnosed by clinical inspection and can be cured by using medicated shampoo. Although some STIs can be contracted after kissing an infected person or having contact with contaminated objects (like linens), other STIs are transmitted only through vaginal, oral, or anal sexual activity with an infected person. Mothers can also transmit gonorrhea, chlamydia, and AIDS to their infants during childbirth.

The only ways to completely prevent the sexual transmission of STIs are abstinence and the maintenance of a monogamous sexual relationship with an uninfected partner. To lower the risk of contracting STIs, you need to be fully informed of the risks of sexual activity, know how to communicate well with sexual partners, and always practice safer-sex by consistently using latex condoms correctly. Alcohol and drug use increase the likelihood of engaging in risky sexual behavior so you can lower your risk of contracting STIs by remaining sober.

Women and men who notice symptoms such as burning urination, lower abdominal pain, genital itching, thick or odorous vaginal or penile discharge, or bumps or sores around the genital, anal, or mouth areas should avoid sexual activity until after they consult a healthcare provider. This is important not only for you, those you might care about, and for overall public health. (Yes, there is good reason that county health departments often treat many STIs for little or no cost to you.)

Learning Objectives

1. Cite evidence to support the assertion that STIs are epidemic in the United States.

2. Identify the cause of each major STI presented in this chapter using the bacterial-viral- ectoparasitic classification scheme, and note which category includes the STIs that are incurable.

3. List the STIs that mothers can transmit to their infants during pregnancy, childbirth, and/or breast-feeding, and indicate whether medical intervention can stop mother-to-child transmission.

4. Distinguish between those STIs that are almost exclusively transmitted by sexual contact and those that can be transmitted by *both* sexual contact and contact with contaminated objects.

5. Keeping in mind that some infected people are symptom-free, describe the most common symptom associated with each of these sexually transmitted infections: gonorrhea, syphilis, chlamydia, bacterial vaginosis, candidiasis, trichomoniasis, oral herpes, genital herpes, viral hepatitis, AIDS, genital warts, pediculosis, and scabies.

6. Recognize the techniques that are currently used to diagnose each of the major STIs.

7. Distinguish between those STIs that are currently incurable and those that can be cured with appropriate treatment. Identify the primary treatment method used for each major STI.

8. List two serious reproductive health problems that may develop in men and women who have an STI (such as gonorrhea) if the STI goes untreated.

9. Identify at least three reasons there has been a surge in the incidence of STIs in the U.S.

10. Provide an overview of the four stages involved in the development of syphilis.

11. Describe how the incidence of HIV/AIDS in the United States varies by gender, race-ethnicity, age, and sexual orientation, and explain why subpopulation differences exist.

12. Compare and contrast how HIV/AIDS has affected the populations of the U.S. and Africa.

13. Summarize the process through which the human immunodeficiency virus (HIV) disables the immune system and promotes the development of AIDS.

14. List at least three factors that scientists think increase the risk of communicating HIV.

15. Indicate at least three ways that people commonly, *but incorrectly*, believe HIV is transmitted.

16. Discuss three psychosocial factors underlying risky sexual behavior among young people.

17. Recognize how the safer-sex recommendations outlined in your text decrease your risk of communicating or contracting a sexually transmitting infection.

Term Identification

You know the drill; these are the terms you need to learn, and making flashcards will help you on your destination toward mastery.

Chapter 16 Table of Key Terms

Acquired immunodeficiency syndrome (AIDS)	Inflammation
Antibodies	Jaundice
Antigen	Leukocytes
Asymptomatic	Lymphogranuloma venereum
Bacteria	Molluscum contagiosum
Bacterial vaginosis	Neurosyphilis
Candidiasis	Ocular herpes
Cervicitis	Ophthalmia neonatorum
Chancre	Opportunistic diseases
Chancroid	Outercourse
Congenital syphilis	Pathogen
Ectoparasites	Pediculosis
Elephantiasis	Pelvic inflammatory disease
Epididymitis	Pharyngeal gonorrhea
General paresis	Prodromal symptoms
Genital herpes	Scabies
Genital warts	Seronegative
Gonorrhea	Seropositive
Granuloma inguinale	Sexually transmitted infections (STIs)
HAART	Shigellosis
Hepatitis	Syphilis
Herpes simplex virus type 1	Trichomoniasis
Herpes simplex virus type 2	Vaginitis
Human immunodeficiency virus	VDRL
Immune system	

As You Read...

Sexually Transmitted Infections

> *Types of Sexually Transmitted Infections*

Sexually Transmitted Infections: How do you get them? What are their symptoms? What should you do about it? It is important to know how each sexually transmitted infection (STI) is transmitted and which symptoms are associated with them. Complete the following chart by supplying this information for each STI.

Sexually Transmitted Infections	Transmission	Symptoms	Treatment
Bacterial Infections			
Gonorrhea			
Syphilis			
Chlamydia			
Other Bacterial			
Vaginal Infections			
Bacterial Vaginosis			
Candidiasis			
Trichomoniasis			

Sexually Transmitted Infections	Transmission	Symptoms	Treatment
Viral Infections			
HIV/AIDS			
Genital Herpes			
Viral Hepatitis			
Genital Warts			
Molluscum Contagiosum			
Ectoparasitic Infestations			
Pediculosis			
Scabies			

What are your attitudes toward sexually transmitted infections?
Take the STI Attitude Scale on page 502 in your text and check the key to interpret your score.
Did you learn anything about yourself that you did not realize? Why or why not? If so, what did you learn?

_____
_____
_____
_____

Can people's fears about contracting an STI lead them to engage in risky sexual behaviors? Why or why not? Please explain.

_____
_____
_____
_____

You are in a long-term committed relationship. You have not been unfaithful or thought about someone else. Your partner just announces that he or she has an STI and that you have some explaining to do. Are they cheating on you? What should you do?

_____
_____
_____
_____

TRY PRACTICE TEST #1 NOW!
GOOD LUCK!

What have you learned about...? What would you do if...?
Further clarify your knowledge and practice your empathy skills with this exercise. Choose a sexually transmitted infection and write a short essay detailing ways that it is transmitted, its symptoms, how it is diagnosed, and how it is treated. Also, consider what you would do if you or someone you know had contracted the STI. In your essay address the following questions:

What would you do or advise a friend or family member?

Which sexually transmitted infections, besides HIV and AIDS, may be the hardest to deal with psychologically? Why?

What would it be like to be told that you had a bacterial STI or a viral STI?

How would these diagnoses change your sexual behavior?

Why is it difficult for some people to talk about STIs?

Is it hard for you to talk about STIs with your peers or your family? Why or why not?

What associations do people have with STIs that interfere with open and honest discussions about them?

Do only dirty people get STIs?

TRY PRACTICE TEST #2 NOW!
GOOD LUCK!

Do you know the definitions of the terms in this chapter?
Find out how well you are learning the definitions of the vocabulary words in the chapter by completing the following four matching exercises. For each exercise, match each key vocabulary term listed in the left-hand column with the correct definition in the right-hand column. Good luck!

I. Vocabulary Exercise 1

a. sexually transmitted infections

_____ Inflammation of the cervix.

b. bacteria

_____ Inflammation of the pelvic region—possibly including the cervix, uterus, fallopian tubes, abdominal cavity and ovaries—that can be caused by organisms such as *Neisseria gonorrhoeae*. It may lead to infertility. Abbreviated *PID*.

c. gonorrhea

_____ Syphilitic infection of the central nervous system, which can cause brain damage and death.

d. pharyngeal gonorrhea

_____ Infections that are communicated through sexual contact. Abbreviated STIs.

e. ophthalmia neonatorum

_____ An STI caused by a bacterium and that may progress through several stages of development—often from a chancre to a skin rash to damage to the cardiovascular or central nervous system.

f. cervicitis

_____ A gonorrheal infection of the pharynx that is characterized by a sore throat.

g. asymptomatic

_____ Inflammation of the epididymis.

h. epididymitis

_____ A sore or ulcer.

i. pelvic inflammatory disease

_____ A class of one-celled microorganisms that have no chlorophyll and can give rise to many illnesses.

j. syphilis

_____ Without symptoms.

k. chancre

_____ A syphilis infection that is present at birth.

l. congenital syphilis

_____ An STI caused by bacteria and characterized by a discharge and burning urination. Left untreated, it can give rise to PID and infertility.

m. neurosyphilis   _____ A gonorrheal infection of the eyes of newborn children who contract the disease by passing through an infected birth canal.

II. Vocabulary Exercise 2

a. general paresis   _____ An STI caused by the *Hemophilus ducreyi* bacterium. Also called *soft chancre*.

b. VDRL   _____ A tropical STI caused by the *Chlamydia trachomatis* bacterium.

c. antibodies   _____ A progressive form of mental illness caused by neurosyphilis and characterized by gross confusion.

d. chancroid   _____ Specialized proteins produced by the white blood cells of the immune system in response to disease organisms and other toxic substances. They recognize and attack the invading organisms or substances.

e. shigellosis   _____ A tropical STI caused by the *Calymmatobacterium granulomatous* bacterium.

f. granuloma inguinale   _____ A form of vaginitis usually caused by the *Gardnerella vaginalis* bacterium.

g. lymphogranuloma venereum _____ A form of vaginitis caused by the protozoan *Trichomonas vaginalis*.

h. vaginitis   _____ A form of vaginitis caused by a yeastlike fungus, *Candida albicans*.

i. bacterial vaginosis   _____ Any type of vaginal infection or inflammation.

j. candidiasis   _____ The test named after the Venereal Disease Research Laboratory of the U.S. Public Health Service that tests for the presence of antibodies to *Treponema pallidum* in the blood.

k. trichomoniasis   _____ An STI caused by the *Shigella* bacterium.

III. Vocabulary Exercise 3

a. acquired immunodeficiency
    syndrome (AIDS)

_____ Redness and warmth that develop at the site of an injury, reflecting dilation of blood vessels that permit the expanded flow of leukocytes to the region.

b. human immunodeficiency
    virus (HIV)

_____ A protein, toxin or other substance to which the body reacts by producing antibodies.

c. immune system

_____ Diseases that take hold only when the immune system is weakened and unable to fend them off. Kaposi's sarcoma and *pneumocystis carinii* pneumonia (PCP) are examples found in AIDS patients.

d. pathogen

_____ White blood cells that are essential to the body's defenses against infection.

e. leukocytes

_____ A term for the body's complex of mechanisms for protecting itself from disease-causing agents, such as pathogens.

f. antigen

_____ A sexually transmitted virus that destroys white blood cells in the immune system, leaving the body vulnerable to life-threatening diseases.

g. inflammation

_____ An agent, especially a microorganism, which can cause a disease.

h. opportunistic diseases

_____ A condition caused by the human immunodeficiency virus (HIV) and characterized by destruction of the immune system so that the body is stripped of its ability to fend off life-threatening diseases.

IV. Vocabulary Exercise 4

a. *Herpes simplex* virus type I

_____ Parasites that live on the outside of the host's body—as opposed to endoparasites, which live within the body.

b. genital herpes

_____ An inflammation of the liver.

c. *Herpes simplex* virus type 2   _____ An STI that is caused by the *human papilloma virus* and takes the form of warts that appear around the genitals and anus.

d. ocular herpes   _____ A parasitic infestation caused by a tiny mite (*Sarcoptes scabiei*) that causes itching.

e. prodromal symptoms   _____ A herpes infection of the eye, usually caused by touching an infected area of the body and then touching the eye.

f. hepatitis   _____ A parasitic infestation by public lice (*Pthirus pubis*) that causes itching.

g. genital warts   _____ Warning symptoms that signal the onset or flare-up of a disease.

h. molluscum contagiosum   _____ An STI caused by the *Herpes simplex* virus type 2 and characterized by painful shallow sores and blisters on the genitals.

i. ectoparasites   _____ The virus that causes oral herpes, which is characterized by cold sores or fever blisters on the lips or mouth. Abbreviated *HSV-1*.

j. pediculosis   _____ The virus that causes genital herpes. Abbreviated *HSV-2*.

k. scabies   _____ Caused by a pox virus that causes painless raised lesions to appear.

What does HIV/AIDS do to the immune system? How does it progress?
In order to understand the effects of HIV/AIDS on the immune system, first define what the human immunodeficiency virus (HIV) and acquired immunodeficiency syndrome (AIDS) are. Then, define the relevant components of the immune system. Finally, describe the progression of HIV/AIDS. Be sure to reference your text as needed.

The *human immunodeficiency virus (HIV)* is a virus that _____
_____.
It attacks the immune system by destroying _____.

The condition know as the *acquired immunodeficiency syndrome (AIDS)* is caused by
_____ and is characterized by _____
_____.

The *immune system* is _____
_____.

A *pathogen* is a _____
_____ .

Leukocytes are _____
_____ .

An *antigen* is _____
_____ .

Now consider the progression of HIV/AIDS.
What is the progression of HIV/AIDS? Below, please indicate the symptoms and events associated with each stage of the disease.

Just after infection:

The symptoms may include:

These symptoms usually last:

For years following infection:

The symptoms may include:

If no symptoms are present, the person is said to be:

In about 50 percent of people with HIV, about a decade after infection the virus overtakes their bodies:

The symptoms of the beginning of full-blown AIDS include:

AIDS is associated with the appearance of diseases such as:

These diseases are called:

People are most vulnerable to these diseases when:

About 10 percent of people with AIDS have the:

If untreated, AIDS, within a few years, typically results in:

What increases a person's risk of HIV infection?
The factors that make someone more likely to be infected with HIV and develop AIDS are:

What are ways that a person CANNOT get HIV?
HIV is not transmitted by:

> ➤ *Prevention of Sexually Transmitted Infections*

Preventing Sexually Transmitted Infections
Now that you know much about the sexually transmitted infections in this chapter, focus on what can be done to prevent their transmission. What prevention strategies does the book offer to keep someone free from contracting or transmitting an STI? Do you think that all of the strategies are realistic? Why or why not? Which ones may be difficult to implement? Why? Do you have any suggestions as to how to make these strategies more feasible and more likely to be followed, for example, how to increase positive attitudes toward condom use? Indicate your responses to these questions below.

Prevention Strategy Mentioned in the Text	Realistic	Not Realistic (Provide Explanation)	An Alternative or How to Implement
Be Knowledgeable about the Risks			
Remain Sober			
Inspect Yourself and Your Partner			
Use Latex Condoms			

Use Barrier Devices when Practicing Oral Sex			
Avoid High-Risk Sexual Behaviors			
Wash the Genitals before and after Sex			
Have Regular Medical Checkups			
Discuss Whether You and Your Partner Should be Tested before Having Sex			
Engage in Noncoital Sexual Activities			
Consult Your Physician if You Suspect You Have an STI			
Get to Know Your Partner before Having Sex			
Avoid Other High-Risk Behaviors			

TRY PRACTICE TEST #3 NOW!
GOOD LUCK!

After You Read...

PRACTICE TEST #1

1. Which industrialized country is believed to have the highest rate of infection by STIs?
   a. England
   b. Sweden
   c. Canada
   d. United States

   p. 499   LO 1

2. Dubbed the "silent disease" because so many infected people have no noticeable symptoms, _____ is now the most common STI found in the U.S. population.
   a. syphilis
   b. chlamydia
   c. pediculosis
   d. trichomoniasis

   p. 511   LO 1

3. The VDRL is a(n):
   a. Oral medication that women can take immediately after having intercourse to prevent pregnancy.
   b. Cervical smear test used to detect the presence of chlamydia bacterium.
   c. Powerful "cocktail" of antiviral drugs used to treat HIV/AIDS.
   d. Blood test used to definitively diagnose second-stage syphilis.

   p. 503   LO 6

4. If a hard, round, painless chancre appears in the genital area within 2 to 4 weeks of sexual contact with an infected person, you have probably contracted:
   a. Scabies.
   b. Syphilis.
   c. Gonorrhea.
   d. Candidiasis.

   p. 503   LO 5

5. Miscarriage, stillbirth, and bone and teeth deformities in newborns are all possible outcomes of pregnancy when a pregnant woman is infected with _____, which may be transmitted through the placental membrane.
   a.   syphilis
   b.   chlamydia
   c.   herpes simplex virus – type 1
   d.   human papilloma virus (HPV)

   p. 503   LO 3

6. The most effective way to treat gonorrhea and chlamydia in both men and women is to:
    a. Administer antiviral drugs such as acyclovir to provide relief from the symptoms.
    b. Administer oral or injectable antibiotics such as ofloxacin.
    c. Apply antibiotic cream to the affected areas.
    d. Insert anal suppositories of miconazole.
        p. 503   LO 7

7. During the _____ stage of syphilis, which generally develops within a few months of becoming infected, the affected person develops a sore throat, headaches, fever, and a painless, reddish skin rash.
    a. latent
    b. primary
    c. secondary
    d. tertiary
        p. 507   LO 10

8. Researchers estimate that at least 20 percent of Americans over the age of 12, and about one-third of all college women in the U.S. are infected with _____, an organism that is linked to the development of genital warts and cervical cancer.
    a. viral hepatitis—type C
    b. human papilloma virus (HPV)
    c. human immunodeficiency virus (HIV)
    d. gardnerella vaginalis bacterium (GVB)
        p. 527   LO 1

9. Often referred to using the slang term, "the clap," _____ is a highly contagious bacterial infection that produces a burning sensation and thick yellow penile discharge in men.
    a. genital herpes
    b. viral hepatitis
    c. gonorrhea
    d. syphilis
        p. 525   LO 5

10. When gonorrhea is not treated early in women, the bacterium can spread through the cervix to the uterus and fallopian tubes, sometimes resulting in a painful condition called:
    a. Epididymitis.
    b. Pharyngeal gonorrhea.
    c. Opthalmia neonatorum.
    d. Pelvic inflammatory disease.
        p. 525   LO 8

1. Although _____ is considered an STI because it can be passed back and forth between sex partners through vaginal intercourse, this common fungal infection can also develop in women who are not sexually active due to changes in the vaginal environment.
    a. syphilis
    b. candidiasis
    c. trichomoniasis
    d. bacterial vaginosis
        p. 514   LO 2

2. The primary route of HIV infection in Africa, Latin America, and Asia today is:
    a. Male-to-female transmission via vaginal intercourse.
    b. Mother-to-infant transmission through breastfeeding.
    c. Transfusion of infected blood during medical procedures.
    d. Male-to-male transmission via anal or oral intercourse.
        p. 515   LO 12

3. Although researchers cannot prove definitively that HIV is not transmitted through _____, they consider it highly unlikely that a person will contract HIV from having contact with this bodily fluid.
    a.   blood
    b.   urine
    c.   semen
    d.   vaginal secretions
        p. 515   LO 15

4. The most effective treatment available for bacterial vaginosis (BV), which can infect both women and men, is:
    a. The topical application of Lindane, a medicated shampoo.
    b. Surgical removal of the painless bumps that appear as a result of infection.
    c. Administration of the oral medication produced under the brand name, Flagyl.
    d. None of the above is effective for treating BV because it is an incurable STI.
        p. 514   LO 7

5. Which of the following is a drawback of using the ELISA to test for HIV infection?
    a. It only reveals HIV antibodies, rather than directly detecting HIV.
    b. It is more expensive than the other commonly used test called OraQuick.
    c. Unlike other tests that can detect HIV in blood, saliva, and urine, the ELISA only detects HIV in blood, and many people are wary about getting blood tests.
    d. All of the above are drawbacks of the ELISA test.
        p. 516   LO 6

6. The drug combination known as HAART is the best treatment currently available to people infected with:
    a. Human immunodeficiency virus (HIV)
    b. Gardnerella vaginalis bacterium (GVB)
    c. Human papilloma virus (HPV)
    d. Viral hepatitis – type B
        p. 522   LO 7

7. Which of the following strategies has proven effective for considerably reducing the transmission of HIV from seropositive women to their newborns?
    a. Oral administration of Zidovudine during at least part of the pregnancy
    b. Having an elective C-section to avoid vaginal delivery
    c. Substituting formula for breast milk
    d. All of the above are effective strategies for reducing HIV transmission.
        p. 522, 523   LO 3

8. The most common parasitic STI, _____, is nearly always sexually transmitted, but it can also be communicated through direct contact with infected semen or vaginal discharges found on towels and bedclothes.
    a. syphilis
    b. chancroid
    c. shigellosis
    d. trichomoniasis
        p. 514   LO 4

9. As of 2005, which of the following statements about AIDS cases in the United States is accurate?
    a. Both European American and African American ethnicities are each at about 40% with the remaining groups composing the 20% balance.
    b. About 25 percent of people with AIDS are of African American ethnicity.
    c. Men who engage in sex with other men represent 95 percent of AIDS cases.
    d. AIDS is the top cause of death among Americans aged 25 to 44.
        p. 515   LO 11

10. The World Health Organization 2006 model reveals what about people "living with HIV:"
    a. There are nearly 20 million people in the world (inclusive of the US/North America) living with HIV.
    b. Outside of Africa (the unfortunate leader), the US/North America ranks second in number of cases of people living with HIV.
    c. The African continent has about 5.2 million people living with HIV or about equal to that of North America.
    d. The African continent has about 25.2 million people living with HIV, more than seventeen times that of North America.
        p. 499   LO 12

1. Although there is no cure for this viral infection, people who contract _____ can take drugs such as acyclovir to provide relief from the symptoms they experience.
    a. genital herpes
    b. trichomoniasis
    c. venereal warts
    d. vaginosis
        p. 525   LO 7

2. Which of the following STIs is caused by an ectoparasitic infestation, leads to intense itching in the pubic area, and can be treated using a medicated shampoo?
    a. Vaginosis
    b. Pediculosis
    c. Candidiasis
    d. Trichomoniasis
        p. 528   LO 7

3. What is the most common symptom of infection by the human papilloma virus in men?
    a. Painless warts on the penis, scrotum, or anus
    b. Intense itching in the pubic area
    c. Mild, flu-like symptoms
    d. Reddening of the penis
        p. 527   LO 5

4. One of the few pathogens that can be easily contracted by kissing or drinking from the same cup as an infected person, as well as through oral-genital contact, is:
    a. Herpes simplex virus – type 1 (HSV-1).
    b. Human papilloma virus (HPV).
    c. Viral hepatitis – type D.
    d. Pthirus pubis.
        p. 523   LO 4

5. Although most people with viral hepatitis have no symptoms, when symptoms do appear, they are likely to include:
    a. Burning on urination.
    b. Vomiting and abdominal pain.
    c. Odorous penile or vaginal discharge.
    d. Sores or blisters on the lips, mouth, or genitals.
        p. 526   LO 5

6. Although using latex condoms reduces the risk of contracting human papilloma virus (HPV), the risk is not completely eliminated because the virus:
    a. May be transmitted from contact with genital warts located on areas other than the genitals of the infected person's body.
    b. Is still present in the infected person's body even after the warts caused by HPV have been removed.
    c. Can be transmitted through physical contact with the towels and clothing used by the infected person.
    d. All of the above factors contribute to the possibility of contracting HPV even when latex condoms are used during sexual intercourse with an infected person.
        p. 532   LO 17

7. Ectoparasitic infestations are transmitted by direct sexual contact, as well as by:
    a. Eating raw infected shellfish.
    b. Receiving a transfusion with contaminated blood products.
    c. Physical contact with towels and sheets used by an affected person.
    d. Oral contact with contaminated saliva, nasal mucus, menstrual blood, or semen.
        p. 528   LO 4

8. One of the less common STIs, _____ is characterized by painless, pinkish, raised lesions that appear on the genitals, buttocks, thighs, or lower abdomen that often disappear on their own within 6 months, or can be treated with applications of silver nitrate.
    a. shigellosis
    b. pediculosis
    c. molluscum contagiosum
    d. lymphogranuloma venereum
        p. 506   LO 5

9. To reduce the likelihood of contracting an STI, sexually active people should avoid engaging in which of the following high-risk sexual behaviors with their partners?
    a. Kissing
    b. Rimming
    c. Taking a bubble bath
    d. Mutual masturbation
        p. 533   LO 17

10. Which of the following factors is associated with high-risk sexual behavior among adolescents?
    a. An adventurous spirit and feeling of invulnerability typical of youth
    b. Persistence of negative attitudes toward condom use, especially among males
    c. Lack of specific communication and social skills necessary for assuring their interests are respected
    d. All of the above contribute to adolescent involvement in high-risk sexual behavior even when they are knowledgeable about STIs.
        p. 534   LO 17

Multiple Choice Questions

1. Dubbed the "silent disease" because so many infected people have no noticeable symptoms, _____ is now the most common STI found in the U.S. population.
   a. syphilis
   b. chlamydia
   c. pediculosis
   d. trichomoniasis

2. Although there is no cure for this viral infection, people who contract _____ can take drugs such as acyclovir to provide relief from the symptoms they experience.
   a. genital herpes
   b. trichomoniasis
   c. venereal warts
   d. vaginosis

3. One of the few pathogens that can be easily contracted by kissing or drinking from the same cup as an infected person, as well as through oral-genital contact, is:
   a. Herpes simplex virus—type 1 (HSV-1).
   b. Human papilloma virus (HPV).
   c. Viral hepatitis—type D.
   d. Pthirus pubis.

4. Which of the following strategies has proven effective for considerably reducing the transmission of HIV from seropositive women to their newborns?
   a. Oral administration of Zidovudine during at least part of the pregnancy
   b. Having an elective C-section to avoid vaginal delivery
   c. Substituting formula for breast milk
   d. All of the above are effective strategies for reducing HIV transmission.

5. Which of the following STIs is caused by an ectoparasitic infestation, leads to intense itching in the pubic area, and can be treated using a medicated shampoo?
   a. Vaginosis
   b. Pediculosis
   c. Candidiasis
   d. Trichomoniasis

6. The main reason why drug therapy has not been nearly as successful at reducing the death rate from HIV/AIDS in Africa as it has been in the United States is that:
    a. The African governments will not allow pharmaceutical companies to distribute the medications within the country's borders.
    b. African people refuse to take the prescribed drugs because Western scientific medical practices are in conflict with their traditional cultural beliefs.
    c. The medications are too expensive for people in this impoverished nation to purchase.
    d. Doctors do not get the opportunity to treat most of the people who become infected because they are too ashamed to seek treatment after diagnosis.

7. When gonorrhea is not treated early in women, the bacterium can spread through the cervix to the uterus and fallopian tubes, sometimes resulting in a painful condition called:
    a. Epididymitis.
    b. Pharyngeal gonorrhea.
    c. Opthalmia neonatorum.
    d. Pelvic inflammatory disease.

8. Although using latex condoms reduces the risk of contracting human papilloma virus (HPV), the risk is not completely eliminated because the virus:
    a. May be transmitted from contact with genital warts located on areas other than the genitals of the infected person's body.
    b. Is still present in the infected person's body even after the warts caused by HPV have been removed.
    c. Can be transmitted through physical contact with the towels and clothing used by the infected person.
    d. All of the above factors contribute to the possibility of contracting HPV even when latex condoms are used during sexual intercourse with an infected person.

9. If a hard, round, painless chancre appears in the genital area within 2 to 4 weeks of sexual contact with an infected person, you have probably contracted:
    a. Scabies.
    b. Syphilis.
    c. Gonorrhea.
    d. Candidiasis.

10. The most effective way to treat gonorrhea and chlamydia in both men and women is to:
    a. Administer antiviral drugs such as acyclovir to provide relief from the symptoms.
    b. Administer oral or injectable antibiotics such as ofloxacin.
    c. Apply antibiotic cream to the affected areas.
    d. Insert anal suppositories of miconazole.

11. Ectoparasitic infestations are transmitted by direct sexual contact with the affected person as well as by:
    a. Eating raw infected shellfish.
    b. Receiving a transfusion with contaminated blood products.
    c. Physical contact with towels and sheets used by an affected person.
    d. Oral contact with contaminated saliva, nasal mucus, menstrual blood, or semen.

12. Researchers estimate that at least 20 percent of Americans over the age of 12, and about one-third of all college women in the U.S. are infected with _____, an organism that is linked to the development of genital warts and cervical cancer.
    a. viral hepatitis – type C
    b. human papilloma virus (HPV)
    c. human immunodeficiency virus (HIV)
    d. gardnerella vaginalis bacterium (GVB)

13. The most common parasitic STI, _____, is nearly always sexually transmitted, but it can also be communicated through direct contact with infected semen or vaginal discharges found on towels and bedclothes.
    a. syphilis
    b. chancroid
    c. shigellosis
    d. trichomoniasis

14. Which of the following statements about AIDS cases in the United States is accurate?
    a. Nearly half of the women with AIDS are of European American ethnicity.
    b. About 25 percent of people with AIDS are of African American ethnicity.
    c. Men who engage in sex with other men represent 75 percent of AIDS cases.
    d. AIDS is the fifth leading cause of death among Americans aged 25 to 44.

15. Miscarriage, stillbirth, and bone and teeth deformities in newborns are all possible outcomes of pregnancy when a pregnant woman is infected with _____, which may be transmitted through the placental membrane.
    a. syphilis
    b. chlamydia
    c. herpes simplex virus – type 1
    d. human papilloma virus (HPV)

True/False

_____ 1. Trichomoniasis is one of the few disease agents that can be picked up from a contaminated toilet seat if direct contact with the penis or vulva occurs.

_____ 2. Research indicates that pregnant women infected with HIV reduce the likelihood of transmitting the virus to their newborns when they deliver by C-section.

_____ 3. Although HAART cures HIV, most people with AIDS cannot take the drug "cocktail" long enough to eliminate the virus from their bodies because the side effects of the medications in HAART are so debilitating.

_____ 4. Syphilis is the only STI that once the symptoms go away it means the immune system was effective in eliminating it.

_____ 5. Among men who are infected with HIV, circumcised men are more likely than men who are not circumcised to transmit the virus to their sexual partners.

_____ 6. Hepatitis is a viral STI characterized by painless red lesions that appear on the genitals, buttocks, thighs, or lower abdomen.

_____ 7. The most common way of contracting the hepatitis A virus is through oral contact with infected fecal matter found in contaminated food or water.

_____ 8. The fastest growing exposure category for cases of AIDS in the United States is male-to-female sexual contact.

Essay Questions

1. Assume you are a peer educator on your college campus and prepare a fun, engaging talk about safer sex practices to be presented at a coed dorm meeting. Consider how you could challenge the negative attitudes toward condom use and the myth of personal invulnerability that may be prevalent among your peers. In addition to offering your peers general knowledge about STI transmission, teach them some specific skills they could use to protect themselves in sexually-charged situations.

    _____
    _____
    _____
    _____
    _____
    _____
    _____
    _____
    _____

2. Describe how the incidence of HIV/AIDS in the United States varies by gender, race-ethnicity, age, and sexual orientation, and discuss why these subpopulation differences exist. Explain what implications this disparity has for preventing the further transmission of HIV and other STIs.

    _____
    _____
    _____
    _____
    _____
    _____
    _____
    _____
    _____

When You Have Finished...

What Does the World Think?

Let's see where the Web takes you as you explore the following activities related to STIs.

1. Sexually Transmitted Infections: http://plannedparenthood.org/sti/
   This site contains an index with links to STIs and ways to prevent them. The Planned Parenthood website has a wealth of easily accessible information. It also includes a link to stories about children and AIDS.

2. Ted.com rears its head again. What is the impact of AIDS? Watch the videos from the following speakers to change your thought process about AIDS: "Emily Oster," "Nathan Wolfe," and, the best, "Hans Rosling" with his solidified laser pointer.

3. When you think of STIs, think of education. Check out the graphs from the CDC (www.cdc.gov/std/stats/). If you are feeling statistical, also check out the graphs of the demographics from the last election. Can you see similarities in the United States? (http://www-personal.umich.edu/~mejn/election/2008/ or Google "2008 Election results by state.")

4. The Lost Children of Rockdale County: http://www.pbs.org/wgbh/pages/frontline/shows/georgia/
   This is the companion website to PBS's Frontline film, which covered a syphilis outbreak among teens in an affluent Georgia suburb.

Chapter 17
Atypical Sexual Variations

Before You Begin...

Chapter Summary

Here is when communication is really important in a relationship.

Social judgments about what constitute "normalcy" and "deviance" vary across cultures and over time. Prior to 1973, for example, the American Psychiatric Association (APA) defined homosexual sexual orientation as a mental disorder. The authors of this text, who define "normality" based on the frequency of a given behavior in a population, have chosen to label unusual patterns of sexual activity as "atypical variations" rather than "sexual deviations."

Paraphilia is a diagnostic category used by the APA to describe atypical patterns of sexual behavior that are viewed as problematic for society or distressing to the individual who experiences the recurrent urge to become sexually aroused in response to unusual stimuli. These stimuli include non-consenting persons, nonhuman objects and animals, and pain or humiliation. In *fetishism*, for example, an inanimate object such as shoes elicits sexual arousal, whereas in *transvestism*, the object of clothing is only alluring when it is worn. For some people, paraphilias represent a type of sexual compulsion or addiction, whereas others function sexually in the absence of the stimuli all or most of the time. It is difficult to determine the prevalence of paraphilias because people are usually unwilling to discuss them, but experts believe that all paraphilias except sexual masochism occur almost exclusively among men.

Some paraphilias, such as fetishism, are mostly harmless and victimless; however, others may cause injury and/or violate the law. In *pedophilia*, for example, children are the objects of sexual arousal. The sexual coercion or molestation of children in the U.S. is always illegal, and being victimized has serious consequences for children's physical and mental health. Unwilling adult participants in atypical sexual activities such as *exhibitionism* may also experience negative consequences such as feelings of violation, recurrent nightmares, misplaced guilt, and anxiety.

There are several theories that attempt to explain paraphilic behavior. Biological perspectives examine how the endocrine and nervous systems may be involved in producing paraphilias. Psychoanalytic theory suggests that paraphilias develop in response to unconscious psychological dilemmas. Learning-theory perspectives, which emphasize the influence of direct experience and environment on the development of paraphilias, suggest that conditioning and modeling are important factors to examine. A sociological perspective, which emphasizes the effects of the group on individual behavior, is useful for understanding the patterns of dominance and submission characteristic of *sadomasochism*.

Although the courts often refer sexual offenders for mental health treatment, many are not motivated to change their behavior because the paraphilia is a source of pleasure. Offenders who view society's intolerance, rather than their own behavior, as the real problem are likely to resist therapeutic treatment. The most common treatments for paraphilias are psychoanalysis, cognitive-behavioral therapy, and the administration of medications such as antidepressants and antiandrogen drugs.

Learning Objectives

1. Consider why the authors of this text chose to refer to paraphilias as "atypical variations" instead of "sexual deviations."

2. Recognize the difference between statistical and cultural definitions of "normality."

3. Provide a technical definition of *paraphilia*, list the paraphilias that are known to occur in the population, and identify the central object of sexual arousal for each of these paraphilias.

4. Explain the different reasons why heterosexual men, gay men, and transsexuals may engage in *transvestism*.

5. Assess how the personal characteristics of the average exhibitionist, voyeur, and obscene phone caller are related to the victim population they typically select to act out their paraphilias.

6. Summarize the most common consequences of exhibitionism, voyeurism, and obscene phone calling for the victims of these sexual offenses, and suggest at least two things women should do if confronted with these behaviors.

7. Evaluate why *masochism* is the only paraphilia found among women, and use a sociological perspective to explain why women tend to assume submissive roles within the S&M subculture.

8. Use a biological perspective to explain why experiencing certain levels of pain may result in heightened sexual arousal and pleasure.

9. Summarize the classic psychoanalytic perspective on the origin of paraphilic behavior.

10. Apply the principles of learning theory to the development of *fetishism*.

11. Recognize the utility of a *lovemap* for investigating the origins of paraphilia in childhood.

12. Outline the four problems with why sex offenders resist treatment for their paraphilias.

13. Describe how experts use these techniques to treat paraphilic behavior: covert sensitization, aversion therapy systematic desensitization, orgasmic reconditioning, and social-skills training.

14. Assess the effectiveness of psychoanalysis, cognitive-behavioral therapy, and drug therapy for treating paraphilic behavior—both individually and in combination with one another.

Key Terms

Term Identification

You know the drill; these are the terms you need to learn, and making flashcards will help.

Chapter 17 Table of Key Terms

Antiandrogen drug	Paraphilia
Autogynephilia	Partialism
Aversion therapy	Pedophiles
Bondage	Sadomasochism
Chat scatophilia	Sexual masochism
Cognitive-behavioral therapy	Sexual sadism
Coprophilia	Sexual sadists
Covert sensitization	Social-skills training
Exhibitionism	Systematic desensitization
Fetishism	Telephone scatologia
Frotteurism	Toucherism
Hypoxyphilia	Transvestism
Klismaphilia	Urophilia
Lovemap	Voyeurism
Necrophilia	Zoophilia
Orgasmic reconditioning	

As You Read...

Activities

Atypical Sexual Variations

> ### *Normal versus Deviant Sexual Behavior*

How do you define normal sexual behavior?

Consider the above question for a moment. What criteria would you use to evaluate whether a sexual behavior is deviant or normal? Would you use yourself or a protagonist in a movie or novel as a standard? When one considers what is normal versus atypical versus deviant sexual activity, what factors should be considered? Answering these questions reminds us of the difficulties involved with figuring out what is normal and functional versus abnormal and dysfunctional. In this chapter you will learn about what professionals call "atypical variations" in sexual behavior. It may be difficult for some of you to keep an open mind as you read about people who engage in behaviors in which you do not. However, attempting to do so will help you learn the material better and perhaps gain a semblance of understanding of differences regarding human sexuality.

Time to play "What would you do if...?"

Read the three case stories in this chapter—Archie, the transvestite; Michael, the exhibitionist; and Ron the masochist—and respond to the following questions.

First, take a look at Archie.

What was your initial reaction to the story of Archie, a transvestite?

Do you think that Archie was harming anyone? Why or why not?

Was he harming himself? Why or why not?

What would you have done in Myrna's situation?

Do you respect her decision? Why or why not?

Now consider Michael.

What was your initial reaction to the story of Michael, an exhibitionist?

Do you think that Michael was harming anyone? Why or why not?

Was he harming himself? Why or why not?

What would you have advised someone if she was approached by Michael?

Do you think that Michael can be treated for his "problem"? Why or why not?

Now consider Ron.

What was your initial reaction to the story of Ron, a masochist?

Do you think that Ron was harming anyone? Why or why not?

Was he harming himself? Why or why not?

What would you have advised someone who wanted to be spanked for pleasure?

Do you think that Ron can be treated for his "problem"? Why or why not?

> *The Paraphilias*

Do you know the definitions of the terms in this chapter?

Find out how well you are learning the definitions of the paraphilias in the chapter by completing the following two matching exercises. For each exercise, match each key vocabulary term listed in the left-hand column with the correct definition in the right-hand column. Good luck!

I. Vocabulary Exercise 1

a.	paraphilia	____	Ritual restraint, as by shackles, as practiced by many sexual masochists
b.	fetishism	____	When a person has persistent urges to cross-dress or repeatedly cross-dresses to achieve sexual arousal
c.	partialism	____	Achieving sexual arousal by observing unsuspecting strangers who are naked, disrobing or engaged in sexual relations
d.	transvestism	____	Related to fetishism, in which sexual arousal is associated with a particular body part, such as feet, breasts or buttocks
e.	exhibitionism	____	Making obscene telephone calls
f.	telephone scatologia	____	People who become sexually aroused by inflicting pain or humiliation on others
g.	voyeurism	____	When an inanimate object, such as an article of clothing or items made of rubber or leather, elicits sexual arousal
h.	sexual masochism	____	The desire or need to receive pain or humiliation to enhance sexual arousal
i.	sexual sadists	____	A diagnostic category used by the American Psychiatric Association to describe atypical patterns of sexual arousal or behavior that may or may not become problematic in the eyes of the individual or society
j.	bondage	____	Having persistent, powerful urges and sexual fantasies involving exposing one's genitals to unsuspecting strangers to achieve sexual arousal

II. Vocabulary Exercise 2

a. sexual sadism

_____ A mutually gratifying sexual interaction between consenting sex partners in which sexual arousal is associated with the infliction and receipt of pain or humiliation. Commonly known as S&M.

b. sadomasochism

_____ A paraphilia in which sexual arousal is associated with urine.

c. frotteurism

_____ A practice related to frotteurism and characterized by the persistent urge to fondle non-consenting strangers.

d. toucherism

_____ A paraphilia in which sexual arousal is attained in connection with feces.

e. zoophilia

_____ A paraphilia characterized by the desire or need to inflict pain or humiliation on others to enhance sexual arousal so that gratification is attained.

f. necrophilia

_____ A paraphilia in which sexual arousal is derived from use of enemas.

g. klismaphilia

_____ A paraphilia characterized by recurrent, powerful sexual urges and related fantasies involving rubbing against or touching a non-consenting person.

h. coprophilia

_____ A paraphilia characterized by desire for sexual activity with corpses.

i. urophilia

_____ A paraphilia involving persistent or repeated sexual urges and related fantasies involving sexual contact with animals.

j. hypoxyphilia

_____ A practice in which a person seeks to enhance sexual arousal, usually during masturbation, by becoming deprived of oxygen.

TRY PRACTICE TEST #1 NOW!
GOOD LUCK!

> *Theoretical Perspectives*

Who Said What? Understanding the Theories.

Your text discusses five theoretical perspectives relevant to the study of paraphilias. Read each statement about paraphilias and indicate who is most likely to have said it. Your choices are someone from a biological perspective, a psychoanalytic perspective, a learning-theory perspective, a sociological perspective, and an integrated perspective.

1. In order to understand and treat paraphilias, one must consider how gender roles and societal expectations may play a role in their development. _____

2. The best indicator of the causes of people's paraphilia is their reinforcement history. Most of the time it is the associations that people make to objects or situations when they are sexually aroused that explain the origin of paraphilias. _____

3. Important factors in the development of paraphilias are hormone levels and the brain's neural circuitry. _____

4. Most cases of paraphilias involve unresolved conflicts that arose during the phallic stage when boys feared that they would be castrated due to their feelings toward their mothers.

_____

5. Many factors underlie the formation of one's lovemap. One cannot consider biological factors or societal factors in isolation but instead must look at the entire sphere of influences on an individual to fully understand why someone has a paraphilia. _____

Theoretical Perspectives on the Paraphilias

Summarize the explanations for paraphilias from each of the following theoretical perspectives by filling out this chart. After completing this table, what can you conclude about the origins of paraphilias?

Biological Perspectives:
Psychoanalytic Perspectives:
Learning Perspectives:
Sociological Perspectives:
Integrated Perspective   **The "Lovemap":**

TRY PRACTICE TEST #2 NOW!
GOOD LUCK!

➢ *Treatment of the Paraphilias*

How are Paraphilias Treated?

Summarize the methods used to treat paraphilias within each type of therapy by filling out this chart. As you complete this table, suggest which treatment might be the most effective at treating a particular paraphilia.

Type of Therapy	Methods Used
Psychoanalytic Psychotherapy	
Cognitive-Behavioral Therapy	
Medical Approaches	

Do you know the definitions of the terms in this chapter?

Find out how well you are learning the definitions of the therapies and treatment methods in the chapter by completing the following matching exercise. Match each key vocabulary term listed in the left-hand column with the correct definition in the right-hand column. Good luck!

I. Vocabulary Exercise

a. lovemap

_____ Persons with pedophilia, a paraphilia involving sexual interest in children.

b. behavior therapy

_____ Strengthening the association of sexual arousal with sexual stimuli by repeatedly pairing the desired stimuli with orgasm.

c. systematic desensitization

_____ Behavior therapy for building social skills using coaching and practice.

d. aversion therapy

_____ A form of aversion therapy in which thoughts of engaging in undesirable behavior are paired repeatedly with imagined aversive stimuli.

e. covert sensitization

_____ The systematic application of the principles of learning to help people modify problem behavior.

f. pedophiles

_____ A chemical substance that reduces the sex drive by lowering the level of testosterone in the bloodstream.

g. social skills training

_____ An integrated perspective on paraphilia, which claims that childhood experience establishes brain patterns of sexual arousal.

h. orgasmic reconditioning

_____ A method for terminating undesirable sexual behavior in which the behavior is repeatedly paired with an aversive stimulus, such as electric shock, so that a conditioned aversion develops.

i. antiandrogen drug

_____ Progressive muscle relaxation is practiced in connection with an arousing stimulus, such as a fetishistic object, so that the person learns to remain unaroused in their presence.

Time to Test Yourself by Filling in the Blanks

Test your knowledge of the content of this chapter by reading the following paragraphs and completing them. If you need to, use your text as a guide. Good luck!

The authors of the text prefer the term "_____ _____ in sexual behavior" to the term "sexual deviations." The American Psychiatric Association term for these behaviors is _____.

_____ involves sexual arousal to unusual stimuli, nonhuman objects or pain or humiliation. Paraphilic urges have a _____ quality; that is, people describe themselves as being overcome by seemingly irresistible urges. Except for sexual masochism, paraphilias are believed to occur almost exclusively in (men/women)_____.

In _____, an inanimate object comes to elicit sexual arousal. In a related paraphilia, _____, people are excessively aroused by a particular body part. Most fetishes and partialisms are _____. In _____, people become excited by wearing articles of clothing of the other gender.

_____ involves powerful urges to expose one's genitals to unsuspecting strangers for the purpose of sexual arousal or gratification. Although many people with this paraphilia are single males, the typical exhibitionist is _____, _____ _____ and _____ _____. Exhibitionism usually begins before age _____.

_____ _____ or obscene telephone calling, involves achieving sexual arousal by shocking the victims. Most exhibitionists and obscene telephone callers (are/are not) _____ dangerous. The typical obscene phone caller is a _____ _____ _____ male who has difficulty forming intimate relationships with women. Very few obscene phone callers are _____.

_____, found almost exclusively among males, involves urges to observe unsuspecting strangers who are undressing or engaging in sexual behaviors. The voyeur may _____ while "peeping" or afterward while "replaying" the incident in his mind. Compared to other types of sex offenders, voyeurs tend to be (more/less) _____ sexually experienced and they are (more/less) _____ likely to be married.

_____ _____ are people who associate pain or humiliation with sexual arousal. This paraphilia is the only one found with some frequency among women. Still, males may outnumber females by _____ to one. The association of sexual arousal with mildly painful stimuli is (rare/common) _____. In _____, people may place plastic bags over their heads or nooses around their necks to become sexually aroused by being temporarily deprived of oxygen.

_____ _____ is characterized by urges and fantasies involving infliction of pain on others for sexual arousal and gratification. Sadomasochism involves _____ _____ sexual interactions between _____ partners. Participants often engage in elaborate rituals involving _____ and _____. If pain is employed, it is often mild or moderate. One survey showed that about ____ of four participants are male. Most were (married/single) _____.

_____ involves urges to rub against or touch a non-consenting person. It has been reported exclusively among (men/ women) _____. These acts usually take place in _____ _____. _____ is the persistent urge to fondle non-consenting strangers.

_____ involves persistent urges to have, and fantasies about, sexual contact with animals. In most cases, it is associated with _____-_____ _____ _____ and difficulty relating to members of the other gender. In _____, a very rare paraphilia, a person desires sex with corpses. Many of the people with this paraphilia are clearly _____ _____. In _____, sexual arousal is derived from the use of enemas. In _____, sexual arousal is connected to feces. And, in _____, sexual arousal is associated with urine.

Regarding the role of biology in paraphilic behavior, one study found elevated levels of a specific measure of testosterone among _____. Psychoanalytic theory views paraphilias as psychological defenses, usually against unresolved _____ _____. There is (sufficient/a lack of) _____ evidence to support this theory. Learning theorists believe that paraphilias are _____ _____ that are acquired through experience.

One proposal for a _____ explanation of sadomasochism focuses on the social and gender roles that exist in the larger society. Money and his colleagues propose a theory that incorporates multiple perspectives. _____ _____ etch a pattern in the brain, called a _____, that determines the stimuli and activities that will be sexually arousing to the individual.

Paraphiles do not usually seek treatment _____. Traditional _____ tends to be a lengthy process of exploration of the childhood origins of problem behaviors. _____ _____ is briefer and focuses directly on changing the problem behaviors. _____ _____ attempts to break the link between the sexual stimulus and the inappropriate response of sexual arousal by pairing relaxation (not arousal) with the stimulus. In _____ _____, the undesirable sexual behavior is paired with an aversive stimulus, such as an electric shock. _____ _____

_____ focuses on helping the paraphile improve his ability to relate to the other gender.

_____ _____ focuses on pairing culturally appropriate imagery with orgasmic pleasure.

_____ drugs reduce the level of testosterone circulating in the bloodstream.

_____-_____ is the drug most often used in the treatment of sex offenders. It reduces the intensity of sexual drives, fantasies, and urges, so that the man may feel less compelled to act upon them.

TRY PRACTICE TEST #3 NOW!
GOOD LUCK!

After You Read...

1. The text authors recommend that women respond to obscene phone and Chat-Scatophilia calls by:
   a. Crying, because it invokes sympathy in the caller.
   b. Saying nothing at all and immediately hanging up the phone.
   c. Having a brief, polite conversation about paraphilias with the caller.
   d. Yelling obscenities, because it shows the caller you are not afraid of him.
   p. 548   LO 6

2. Atypical sexual variation is typically used in place of which term(s)?
   a. Sadomasochism
   b. Sexual deviance
   c. Sexual abnormity
   d. Fetishism
   p. 549   LO 1

3. The text authors define "normality" based on the:
   a. Proscriptions for behavior offered by the Christian Bible.
   b. Legal status of particular sexual activities in the contemporary U.S.
   c. Social acceptability of particular sexual practices around the world.
   d. Estimated frequency of certain sexual practices in the total population.
   p. 551   LO 2

4. *Most* people with paraphilias describe their sexual urges as:
   a. Severe, constant, and disabling.
   b. Insistent, repeated, and distressing.
   c. Mild and occasional.
   d. Harmless and rare.
   p. 542   LO 3

5. Some _____ appear to be motivated by *autogynephilia*, a condition in which the individual is sexually stimulated by fantasies that their own bodies are female.
   a. sadists
   b. pedophiles
   c. transvestites
   d. exhibitionists
   p. 543, 544   LO 4

6. Among men with the following paraphilias, which group is most likely to keep their activities to themselves and refrain from engaging in antisocial or illegal behavior?
   a. Telephone scatologia
   b. Exhibitionism
   c. Transvestism
   d. Voyeurism
   p. 542   LO 4

7. Paraphilias may involve sexual arousal in response to which of the following stimuli?
   a. Bodily fluids
   b. Inanimate objects
   c. Non-consenting persons
   d. All of the above may serve as sexual stimuli for people with paraphilias.
   p. 542, 543   LO 3

8. Which of the following paraphilias is characterized by strong, repetitive urges and related sexual fantasies of observing unsuspecting strangers who are naked or engaged in sex?
   a. Sadism
   b. Voyeurism
   c. Masochism
   d. Exhibitionism
   p. 550   LO 3

9. Compared to other types of sex offenders, voyeurs are more likely to be:
   a. Married.
   b. Socially inept.
   c. Sexually experienced.
   d. Voyeurs typically have all of the above characteristics.
   p. 550   LO 5

10. Among the few women who are caught and charged with making obscene telephone calls, the motivation for the offense is generally:
    a. Rage.
    b. Boredom.
    c. Curiosity.
    d. Sexual arousal.
    p. 549   LO 4

1. Which paraphilia involves consenting adults engaging in mutually gratifying sexual interaction in which sexual arousal is promoted by the infliction and receipt of pain and/or humiliation?
   a. Voyeurism
   b. Frotteurism
   c. Hypoxyphilia
   d. Sadomasochism
   p. 552   LO 3

2. Which of the following paraphilias involves rubbing against or touching a non-consenting person, usually in a crowded place such as a bus or elevator?
   a. Sadism
   b. Zoophilia
   c. Frotteurism
   d. Klismaphilia
   p. 554   LO 3

3. Which paraphilia is the only one found among women with some frequency?
   a. Masochism
   b. Necrophilia
   c. Pedophilia
   d. Fetishism
   p. 552   LO 7

4. Although the prevalence of _____ in the general population is unknown, Kinsey and his colleagues reported that about eight percent of the men and three percent of the women interviewed admitted to having sexual contact with animals.
   a. klismaphilia
   b. coprophilia
   c. necrophilia
   d. zoophilia
   p. 555   LO 2

5. Kinsey and his colleagues estimated that about _____ of adults have experienced erotic sensations in response to mildly painful stimuli such as being bitten during lovemaking.
   a. three-fourths
   b. one-half
   c. one-fourth
   d. one-tenth
   p. 552   LO 2

6.   Social scientists have noted that in addition to inflicting or receiving pain, _____ is/are a central component in deriving sexual pleasure from sadomasochistic behavior.
    a.   ritualistic games of dominance and submission
    b.   being under the influence of alcohol or drugs
    c.   causing or receiving a visible injury
    d.   psychological torture
        p. 553   LO 7

7.   Which of the following potentially lethal paraphilias involves depriving oneself of   oxygen during masturbation?
    a.   Urophilia
    b.   Necrophilia
    c.   Coprophilia
    d.   Hypoxyphilia
        p. 552   LO 3

8.   Psychiatrists consider individuals who have a persistent, powerful urge to inflict pain and suffering on others to achieve sexual excitement or gratification to be:
    a.   Sadists.
    b.   Masochists.
    c.   Pedophiles.
    d.   Nymphomaniacs.
        p. 552   LO 3

9.   Which of the following paraphilias always involves engaging in behavior that is   considered illegal in the contemporary United States?
    a.   Klismaphilia
    b.   Frotteurism
    c.   Masochism
    d.   Sadism
        p. 554,555   LO 2

10.   The primary motivation for _____ appears to be the desire to possess a completely unresisting sexual partner who will not reject the person who initiates sexual activity.
    a.   Klismaphilia
    b.   Coprophilia
    c.   Necrophilia
    d.   Urophilia
        p. 556   LO 3

1. Which biological factor (from research by Haake et al.) is associated with the development of paraphilia in men?
    a.   Below-average levels of testosterone
    b.   Genetic predisposition to alcoholism
    c.   Heightened sex drive
    d.   Serotonin deficiency
         p. 557   LO 8

2. Classic psychoanalytic theorists view paraphilias in men as:
    a.   Normal expressions of excessive libidinal energy.
    b.   Exaggerated expressions of affection for their intimate partners.
    c.   Unfortunate outcomes of brain damage incurred during the birth process.
    d.   Psychological defenses against unresolved castration anxiety from childhood.
         p. 558   LO 9

3. Which model would a healthcare provider use to eliminate paraphilic behaviors while also strengthening the patient's sexual response to socially appropriate stimuli?
    a.   Cognitive-behavioral therapy
    b.   Long-term psychotherapy
    c.   Social skills training
    d.   Drug therapy
         p. 558, 559   LO 13

4. According to John Money, paraphilic behavior develops because:
    a.   Every society includes a certain number of rebellious individuals who will violate cultural norms just to gain attention.
    b.   Some people are traumatized by exposure to distorted ideas about sexuality or to abusive sexual behavior during childhood.
    c.   People who live in highly industrialized, consumption-oriented societies are motivated to continually search for novel ways to entertain themselves.
    d.   Adults are exposed to so much violent, sexually-explicit material in the mass media that they fail to distinguish between moral and immoral behavior.
         p. 560   LO 11

5. Which of the following factors interferes with providing effective treatment for people   with paraphilias?
    a.   Most people with paraphilias do not want treatment because the behavior is a source of pleasure for them.
    b.   Most people with paraphilias do not accept personal responsibility for their behavior because they claim they are unable to control the urges they feel.
    c.   Many people with paraphilias perceive their problem as stemming from society's intolerance for sexual variety rather than from their own actions.
    d.   All of the above factors interfere with effective treatment of paraphilias.
         p. 560-2   LO 12

6. According to the _____ model, a boy who masturbates in the bathroom where his mother's stockings are hanging on the towel rack may develop a fetish for stockings because orgasm in the presence of the object reinforces an erotic connection.
   a. psychoanalytic
   b. conditioning
   c. subcultural
   d. medical
   p. 561   LO 10

7. Which technique attempts to terminate paraphilic behavior by repeatedly pairing the undesirable sexual behavior with an undesirable stimulus such as a nauseating smell?
   a. Psychoanalysis
   b. Aversion therapy
   c. Chemical castration
   d. Orgasmic reconditioning
   p. 561, 562   LO 13

8. Taking antiandrogen drugs sometimes helps curb paraphilic urges because the drugs:
   a. Induce vomiting every time a man ejaculates.
   b. Reduce testosterone levels, thus lowering sexual desire.
   c. Block the flow of blood to the penis, thus preventing erection.
   d. Reduce performance anxiety, thus allowing men to fulfill their sexual needs with appropriate sexual partners.
   p. 562, 563   LO 14

9. Which technique attempts to increase sexual arousal to socially appropriate stimuli by allowing the patient to begin masturbating to paraphilic images or fantasies, but having the patient switch his focus to culturally approved imagery before he ejaculates?
   a. Aversion therapy
   b. Covert sensitization
   c. Orgasmic reconditioning
   d. Systematic desensitization
   p. 562   LO 13

10. Which technique attempts to break the link between the sexual stimulus and sexual arousal by pairing muscle relaxation with paraphilic images or fantasies?
   a. Psychoanalysis
   b. Aversion therapy
   c. Orgasmic reconditioning
   d. Systematic desensitization
   p. 561   LO 13

Multiple Choice Questions

1. Taking antiandrogen drugs sometimes helps curb paraphilic urges because the drugs:
   a. Induce vomiting every time a man ejaculates.
   b. Reduce testosterone levels, thus lowering sexual desire.
   c. Block the flow of blood to the penis, thus preventing erection.
   d. Reduce performance anxiety, thus allowing men to fulfill their sexual needs with appropriate sexual partners.

2. Which paraphilia is the only one found among women with some frequency?
   a. Masochism
   b. Necrophilia
   c. Pedophilia
   d. Fetishism

3. Which technique attempts to terminate paraphilic behavior by repeatedly pairing the undesirable sexual behavior with an undesirable stimulus such as a nauseating smell?
   a. Psychoanalysis
   b. Aversion therapy
   c. Chemical castration
   d. Orgasmic reconditioning

4. The text authors define "normality" based on the:
   a. Proscriptions for behavior offered by the Christian Bible.
   b. Legal status of particular sexual activities in the contemporary U.S.
   c. Social acceptability of particular sexual practices around the world.
   d. Estimated frequency of certain sexual practices in the total population.

5. Social scientists have noted that in addition to inflicting or receiving pain, _____ is/are a central component in deriving sexual pleasure from sadomasochistic behavior.
   a. ritualistic games of dominance and submission
   b. being under the influence of alcohol or drugs
   c. causing or receiving a visible injury
   d. psychological torture

6.   Which of the following factors interferes with providing effective treatment for people   with paraphilias?
    a. Most people with paraphilias do not want treatment because the behavior is a source of pleasure for them.
    b. Most people with paraphilias do not accept personal responsibility for their behavior because they claim they are unable to control the urges they feel.
    c. Many people with paraphilias perceive their problem as stemming from society's intolerance for sexual variety rather than from their own actions.
    d. All of the above factors interfere with providing effective treatment for people with paraphilias.

7.   Paraphilias may involve sexual arousal in response to which of the following stimuli?
    a. Bodily fluids
    b. Inanimate objects
    c. Nonconsenting persons
    d. All of the above may serve as sexual stimuli for people with paraphilias.

8.   Kinsey and his colleagues estimated that about _____ of adults have experienced erotic sensations in response to mildly painful stimuli such as being bitten during lovemaking.
    a. three-fourths
    b. one-half
    c. one-fourth
    d. one-tenth

9.   According to John Money, paraphilic behavior develops because:
    a. Every society includes a certain number of rebellious individuals who will violate cultural norms just to gain attention.
    b. Some people are traumatized by exposure to distorted ideas about sexuality or to abusive sexual behavior during childhood.
    c. People who live in highly industrialized, consumption-oriented societies are motivated to continually search for novel ways to entertain themselves.
    d. Adults are exposed to so much violent, sexually-explicit material in the mass media that they fail to distinguish between moral and immoral behavior.

10.   According to the _____ model, a boy who masturbates in the bathroom where his mother's stockings are hanging on the towel rack may develop a fetish for stockings   because orgasm in the presence of the object reinforces an erotic connection.
    a. psychoanalytic
    b. conditioning
    c. subcultural
    d. medical

11. Which of the following paraphilias involves rubbing against or touching a nonconsenting person, usually in a crowded place such as a bus or elevator?
    a. Sadism
    b. Zoophilia
    c. Frotteurism
    d. Klismaphilia

12. Classic psychoanalytic theorists view paraphilias in men as:
    a. Normal expressions of excessive libidinal energy.
    b. Exaggerated expressions of affection for their intimate partners.
    c. Unfortunate outcomes of brain damage incurred during the birth process.
    d. Psychological defenses against unresolved castration anxiety from childhood.

13. Among the few women who are caught and charged with making obscene telephone calls, the motivation for the offense is generally:
    a. Rage.
    b. Boredom.
    c. Curiosity.
    d. Sexual arousal.

14. Which technique attempts to break the link between the sexual stimulus and sexual arousal by pairing muscle relaxation with paraphilic images or fantasies?
    a. Psychoanalysis
    b. Aversion therapy
    c. Orgasmic reconditioning
    d. Systematic desensitization

15. Which of the following potentially lethal paraphilias involves depriving oneself of oxygen during masturbation?
    a. Urophilia
    b. Necrophilia
    c. Coprophilia
    d. Hypoxyphilia

_____ 1. Men who practice *transvestism* are almost always homosexuals who truly wish to be members of the other sex.

_____ 2. The phenomenon of cross-dressing appears to exist only in highly industrialized nations such as England and the United States.

_____ 3. Most experts consider *frotteurism* a harmless, victimless paraphilia.

_____ 4. There is strong clinical evidence that medical treatments such as drug therapy are more effective than psychoanalysis for eliminating paraphilic urges in men.

_____ 5. In 1973, the American Psychiatric Association deleted homosexuality from the Diagnostic and Statistical Manual because it was no longer considered a mental disorder.

6. *Pedophilia* is a paraphilia in which sexual arousal is exaggeratedly associated with a
_____ particular body part such as the feet.

7. Chat scatophilia differs from telephone scatologia in that it is done, for example, via email
_____ and instant messages.

8. In nearly all cases, *fetishism* is practiced in private during masturbation or is incorporated into coitus with a willing partner.

Essay Questions

1. Compare and contrast the psychological and sociological perspectives on participation in sadomasochistic behavior. Pay particular attention to how each theory accounts for gender differences in this particular form of paraphilic behavior.

_____

_____

_____

_____

_____

_____

_____

_____

2. At one time, homosexuality was considered a mental disorder that warranted psychiatric treatment. Some people with paraphilias have suggested that their behaviors should also be declassified as psychiatric disorders. Drawing on what you have learned in this chapter, discuss whether you think any of these paraphilias should be defined as abnormal and/or illegal behaviors that warrant treatment.

_____

_____

_____

_____

_____

_____

_____

_____

When You Have Finished....

Let's see where the Web takes you as you explore the following activities related to atypical sexual variation.

1. Right off the start, Google "Fetish." Make sure you have your Internet filter in place unless you are in a situation where you can see graphic material. What do you find? Do you think the Internet helps paraphilic individuals or does the fantasy create more deviance? http://www.sexuality.org/l/fetish/ is a nice place to start if you are feeling timid.

2. Sexual Addiction: http://www.sexaddictionhelp.com/
   Contains general information, a self-test, information for partners, and treatment information.

3. Inhibiting Sexual Tendencies: http://pslgroup.com/dg/5aede.htm
   Provides an article on drug therapy to inhibit deviant sexual activity by PSL Doctor's guide.

4. Search for "autoerotic asphyxiation" in Google. How common is this behavior? Check out David Carradine, and Michael Hutchence. Did they die this way or not?

5. Paraphilias: http://allpsych.com/disorders/paraphilias/
   Provides links to many paraphilias including sexual sadism, sexual masochism, voyeurism, and pedophilia from AllPsych Online—The Virtual Psychology Classroom.

Chapter 18
Sexual Coercion

Before You Begin...

Chapter Summary

This chapter provides not only information about the types of coercion but also ways to protect yourself (or at least minimize the damage). Let's get into the details for your personal benefit and for those whom you love (and will love in the future).

Your text authors examine the causes and consequences of three forms of sexual coercion—rape, sexual harassment, and the sexual abuse of children. The actual incidence of sexual crimes is much higher than reflected in official reports because many victims do not report the assault. Although the legal definition of rape varies state to state, it generally refers to nonconsensual sexual activity that takes place as a result of threats and/or force. Rape is sometimes classified by the relationship of the perpetrator to the victim, resulting in subcategories such as:

- Stranger rape
- Acquaintance rape
- Date rape

- Gang rape
- Male rape
- Partner rape

- Marital rape
- Rape by women

Other times it can be defined by law, such as statutory rape. This is a legal term referring to even consensual sexual activity between an adult and a person below the age of consent in that state—even if the minor fully and eagerly cooperates in the activity. Rapes can also be classified according to perpetrators' motives, which may be anger, power, or sadism.

Rape, somewhat predictably, creates a crisis for many of its victims. Your authors examine the adjustments required to be a rape survivor and how to be supportive to those in your life that may have been raped—either of recent or earlier moments in time.

Rape occurs in a social climate that reinforces male dominance by linking male sexuality with competition and aggression. Self-identified sexually aggressive men tend to share traits, such as traditional gender-role attitudes, hostility toward women, irresponsibility, and lack of social conscience. In addition to physical injury, rape survivors often experience psychological trauma and develop difficulties relating to their partners—this is explained further by your text authors. At-the-moment-afterward information is presented on how to preserve evidence and seek immediate help. There is much period-afterward information presented both in terms of protecting oneself from further bodily harm (from STIs) and contacting a rape crisis center for information, referrals, and emotional support. Also, where posttraumatic stress disorder fits in all of this is further explained.

Your authors also address broader treatment-of-rape-survivors issues. These include items like group and individual therapies not just for the survivor but for his/her family members. (Often family members, in trying to be helpful, are not.) Mediation, where a counselor trains family members is also covered.

With the old proverb in mind that says "an ounce of prevention is worth a pound of cure," your text writers thoroughly cover techniques to help prevent rape. Respectfully, we do recognize that there are times where no amount of prevention can prevent some attacks—but knowing and using the correct prevention techniques provides a peace of mind and sense of confidence. Aspects of whether to fight, flee, or plead are outlined—along with the odds associated with each one.

In your text, we spend a significant amount of time reviewing sexual abuse of children in greater detail—though, *any* sexual contact between an adult and a child is considered abuse because children are legally incapable of consenting to sexual activity. Children who are sexually assaulted suffer numerous emotional and behavioral problems that impair their development. Although victims of child sexual abuse are predominantly female, an estimated 18 percent of boys and 25 percent of girls are sexually abused in the U.S. Genital fondling is the most common form of molestation of children and the perpetrators are likely to be male relatives and family friends, not strangers.

In terms of intra-family sex, all known cultures have some form of incest taboo, or prohibition against sexual relations between people who are related by blood. In the U.S., incest occurs more frequently in families with high levels of disruption, especially those headed by alcoholic and/or physically abusive parents. Individual and group therapy in adulthood are covered as tools that can help survivors improve self-esteem and better manage stress.

Pedophilia, the sexual attraction to children, is explained along with personality characteristics of pedophiles. Criminal punishments of these offending pedophiles (and rapists) are reviewed along with therapeutic techniques that could help reduce recidivism rates. As with rape prevention, your authors note techniques that are effective in preventing child sexual abuse.

Back in the 1990s, sexual harassment became more visible when a nominee to the U.S. Supreme Court (later confirmed anyhow) was accused of it. Sexual harassment is another form of victimization. It includes a range of actions from verbal abuse, leering, to unwanted physical contact. Men may engage in this behavior as a way of expressing power and exerting control over women. (Note that certain minorities are more likely to be victims too.) Because sexual harassment in schools and workplaces is a form of sex discrimination, employers and academic institutions can be held legally accountable if they fail to prevent or stop such behavior.

Finally, it is important to remember that although the perpetrators of sexual harassment and other assaults are always responsible for their actions, there are many things that adults can do to reduce their risk of being victimized and to cope with the consequences of being victimized if it has already occurred. This chapter provides an extensive list of strategies one can adopt to protect herself/himself at work and on campus.

Learning Objectives

1. Discuss *how* and *why* the definition of rape has varied across cultures and over time.

2. Cite the incidence of rape in the United States. State three reasons why official rape statistics are flawed.

3. Using data from the NHSLS, compare the frequency of being raped by a stranger, spouse, acquaintance, person the respondent knew well, and person the respondent loved.

4. Consider why rape is classified and discussed in terms of subcategories reflecting the victim's relationship to the perpetrator, and assess the implications of making such distinctions.

5. Recognize why the issue of *consent* is central to the legal definitions of "rape" for adults and "sexual abuse" for children.

6. Indicate how rapes committed by individual men tend to differ from gang rapes.

7. Discuss why rape by women is rare and indicate what role women tend to play when they do participate in rape.

8. List the most common motives for male-to-male rape, describe the conditions under which most male rapes occur, and state why male rape victims are unlikely to report the assault.

9. Provide evidence to support the assertion that the social climate of the United States fosters and legitimizes rape, particularly among young people.

10. Using information derived primarily from studies of incarcerated rapists, identify some of the common psychological and behavioral traits found within this group.

11. Develop a profile of the self-identified sexually aggressive man.

12. Summarize the evolutionary view of rape offered by Archer and Vaughan and recognize why this perspective is highly controversial.

13. Using Groth's and Birnbaum's classification scheme, distinguish among the three types of rape —anger, power, and sadistic—in terms of motive for, and nature of, the attack.

14. Provide an overview of the emotional, psychological, and interpersonal consequences of sexual victimization for children and adults.

15. Repeat the five suggestions provided for individuals who have been raped.

16. Recognize the benefits of contacting a rape crisis center or mental health hotline if you or someone you care about has been sexually assaulted.

17. Demonstrate familiarity with the list of precautions a woman can take to help protect herself from rape and share them with others you know.

18. Review the list of suggestions for avoiding date rape, examine how you currently communicate with your dating partners, and identify any positive changes you could make in your dating behavior. Explain how the drug Rohypnol fits into date rape, what it does and techniques to avoid becoming a sexual assault victim because of it.

19. Assess the potential costs and benefits of responding to an attack by fighting back, trying to escape, and pleading with an assailant.

20. Estimate the prevalence of the sexual abuse of children in the United States and note how this form of victimization varies by the gender of both the perpetrator and the victim.

21. Identify the people most likely to molest children, and indicate which factor is most important in determining whether an adult who becomes aware of the abuse will report it to authorities.

22. Note which types of sexual behavior adult perpetrators are most likely to engage in with child victims, and discuss why physical force is rarely needed to gain abused children's compliance.

23. Summarize the factors that seem to motivate the women who sexually abuse children.

24. Distinguish between child molesters and pedophiles, and use a sociocultural framework to explain why both child molesters and pedophiles are almost always male.

25. Assess the importance of the *incest taboo* in promoting the survival of the human species and the stability of families and kinship groups.

26. Compare the prevalence of, motivations for, and consequences of father-child incest to those of brother-sister incest.

27. Describe the family context in which incest typically occurs, and indicate how social factors such as poverty may further support the development of the sexual abuse of children.

28. Recommend at least three ways society could empower children in an attempt to both prevent child sexual abuse and effectively respond to cases of suspected abuse.

29. Evaluate the effectiveness of the U.S. legal system's current response to convicted rapists and child molesters and identify some of the techniques that may be helpful in treating offenders.

30. Provide a legal definition of sexual harassment and explain why this behavior is considered a form of sex discrimination when it occurs in schools and workplaces.

31. Cite the incidence of sexual harassment at workplaces and colleges in the United States. Identify how (and what) minority status impacts the likelihood of becoming a victim.

32. Outline the strategies individuals can use to respond more effectively to sexual harassment, and consider why it might be difficult for a victim of harassment to adopt these suggestions.

Term Identification

You know the drill; these are the terms you need to learn, and making flashcards will help. Most of the terms (all but four) are in the margins of your text book. Date rape, male rape, and partner rape are *not* in those boxes and can instead be found in their respectively-named sections in the main body of the textbook. Crisis is defined within the main body near the beginning.

Chapter 18 Table of Key Terms

Acquaintance rape	Partner rape
Crisis	Post-traumatic stress disorder
Date rape	Rape
Forcible rape	Sexual assault
Gang rape	Sexual harassment
Incest	Statutory rape
Male rape	Stranger rape
Pedophilia	

As You Read...

Activities

Sexual Coercion

➢ *Rape: The Most Intimate Crime of Violence*

Something to think about...

One person out of five has had unwanted sexual advances placed on them. While much of this chapter is difficult to talk about and read, education is your best defense for dealing with this material. Starting the conversation is often the best way to help prevent offenses and help people overcome the emotional trauma involved.

Time to Offer and Back Up Your Opinion.

What is your reaction to the material in the "A Closer Look" box on page 573?

Is this a case of date rape? Why or why not?

What could Jim and Ann have done differently to avoid this incidence of date rape?

Who has the primary responsibility for avoiding this type of situation?

Do you think gender affects how one would answer these questions? If so, what does that tell us about how well we understand and can prevent date rape?

Please make sure to explain your responses.

What's in a Myth?

This exercise asks you to explore the myths regarding rape. *List the rape myths that you have heard. When listing them, try to include (if you remember) where and when and by whom you were told them. Finally, take the self-assessment the text offers on page 577 of your textbook.*

The rape myths that I have heard include:

The following rape myths are accurate, because...

Myths regarding rape serve the following purposes and people:

I think that rape myths affect society by:

Cultural factors that may help foster sexual coercion include:

Who Rapes?

Read the section in the text regarding the psychological characteristics of rapists and their motives. Consider each of the theoretical perspectives to which you have been exposed in the text (for example, see chapters 1 and 17): biological, psychoanalytic, learning, sociological, and an integrated perspective. Write a statement from each of these perspectives explaining how men who rape came to have these characteristics and motives that the text mentions.

Biological Perspective:

Psychoanalytic Perspective:

Learning-Theory Perspective:

Sociological Perspective:

Integrated Perspective:

Other:

What Can You Do If Someone...?

List four strategies you can take if someone you know comes to you and tells you that he or she has been raped.

Strategy: Strategy:

Strategy: Strategy:

What Have You Learned about Rape Prevention?

Construct two lists of preventive measures, one to avoid being raped by a stranger and another to avoid being raped by a date.

Precautions to Protect Oneself	Suggestions for Avoiding Date Rape

Despite these measures, if someone is raped, it is important to remember:

TRY PRACTICE TEST #2 NOW!
GOOD LUCK!

➤ *Sexual Abuse of Children*

What Have You Learned about the Sexual Abuse of Children?

Write down the page number and the example in the book addressing each of the following questions:

What are the known statistics regarding the sexual abuse of children?
Page:_____   Example: _____

What is known about the patterns of abuse and the types of abusers?
Page:_____   Example: _____

What is pedophilia and what is known about pedophiles?
Page:_____   Example: _____

What is known about incest and the families within which it occurs?
Page:_____   Example: _____

What is known about the effects of sexual abuse on children?
Page:_____   Example: _____

What can be done to prevent the sexual abuse of children?
Page:_____   Example: _____

What treatments are available to the survivors of sexual abuse?
Page:_____   Example: _____

➤ *Sexual Harassment*

On the Topic of Sexual Harassment...

Have you ever been at work where inappropriate words or gestures were exchanged? What are the realities of sexual harassment? How should one go about resisting sexual harassment according to your text?

The realities of sexual harassment in the workplace include:

The realities of sexual harassment on campus include:

Guidelines for resisting harassment include:

TRY PRACTICE TEST #3 NOW!
GOOD LUCK!

Time to Test Yourself by Filling in the Blanks

Test your knowledge of the content of this chapter by reading the following paragraphs and completing them. If you need to, use your text as a guide. Good luck!

_____ _____ is usually defined as sexual intercourse with a non-consenting person by the use of force or the threat of force. _____ _____ refers to sexual intercourse with a person below the age of consent, even if the victim cooperates. The vast majority of rapes go _____ in the U.S. The best available evidence suggests that between _____ in _____ and _____ in _____ women in the U.S. will be raped during their lifetimes.

_____ rape refers to a rape committed by an assailant not previously known to the victim. _____ rape refers to a rape committed by an assailant known to the victim. Of these two types, _____ rape is much less likely to be reported to the police. _____ rape is a form of acquaintance rape. About _____ to _____ percent of women report being forced into sexual intercourse by dates. Because date rape occurs within a context in which sex may occur voluntarily, the issue of _____ is usually the central question.

_____ rapes are those perpetrated by a group of assailants. Most _____ rapes occur in prison settings, but some occur elsewhere. Male victims are more likely to be attacked by (a single/multiple) _____ assailant(s). Most men who rape other men are (homosexual/heterosexual)_____.

Marital rape often occurs within a marriage where there is _____, _____, and _____ intimidation. Rape by _____ is rare, but when it does occur, it often involves aiding or abetting _____ who are attacking another _____.

College men who more closely identify with the _____ _____ gender role express a greater likelihood of committing rape and are more accepting of violence against women compared to their peers.

Studies of incarcerated rapists show that they are (more/no more) _____ likely to be mentally ill than comparison groups. The great majority of rapists (are/are not) _____ in control of their behavior and they (know/do not realize) _____ that it is illegal.

Rape victims often show signs of _____ _____ _____, a stress reaction that is brought on by a traumatic event. Treatment of rape survivors includes _____, which can help the survivor cope with the _____ consequences of rape and avoid _____.

Researchers estimate that about ____ percent of boys and about ____ percent of girls become victims of sexual abuse. Most _____ are relatives, family friends, and _____. Physical force is (often/seldom) _____ needed to gain compliance. Victimized children (often/rarely) _____ report the abuse. The overwhelming majority of child sexual abusers are _____.

_____ involves persistent or recurrent sexual attraction to children. _____ are almost exclusively (male/female) _____. Most (do/do not) _____ fit our image of the "dirty old man" hanging around the schoolyard. _____ involves sexual relations between people who are closely related. _____ incest is the most common type.

Many fathers who commit incest are _____ , _____, _____, and _____. Incestuous abuse is (often/rarely) _____ repeated from generation to generation. Child sexual abuse often results in (moderate/great) _____ psychological harm to the child. Although reactions by boys and girls are similar in many ways, boys are more likely to become more _____ _____ and girls are more likely to become _____. The effects of childhood sexual abuse are often (short-term/long-lasting) _____.

The results of rehabilitative treatment programs for incarcerated sex offenders (have been/remain to be)_____ demonstrated. Drugs such as _____-_____ may be used to reduce testosterone levels.

_____ _____ is defined as deliberate or repeated unsolicited comments, gestures or physical contact of a sexual nature that is unwelcome by the recipient. The great majority of the cases are perpetrated by _____ against _____. Sexual harassment may have more to do with abuse of _____ than with sexual desire. As many as ____ in ____ women encounters some form of sexual harassment in the workplace or on campus. Overall, ____ to ____ percent of college students report at least one incident of sexual harassment. Most forms of sexual harassment on college campuses involve _____ _____ relationships.

After You Read...

1. For most of recorded history, rape was considered:
    a. A violent crime that curtailed the rights of women.
    b. A crime against the property rights of fathers or husbands.
    c. The act of mentally deranged men.
    d. An act of adultery by the victim.
        p. 570   LO 1

2. Your text mentions that the incidence of reported rape translated to one woman being raped about every seven minutes. This is an extremely conservative estimate because:
    a. It is calculated based on crime statistics.
    b. Many rapes were discounted from the total based on state laws.
    c. Federal laws are new and would have resulted in higher numbers.
    d. Only stranger rape is prosecutable in the U.S.
        p. 570   LO 1

3. Acquaintance rapists:
    a. Tend to believe in sexual equality.
    b. Are less sexually aggressive.
    c. Tend to believe myths that serve to legitimize their behavior.
    d. Are more likely than stranger rapists to be reported to the police.
        p. 572   LO 2

4. All of the following statements about marital (or partner) rape are accurate, EXCEPT:
    a. Marital rape generally leads the couple to become involved in marital counseling.
    b. Marital rape is motivated by the need to dominate, intimidate, and subjugate.
    c. Many survivors of marital rape fear physical injury and/or death.
    d. Marital rapes are probably more common than date rapes.
        p. 575   LO 2

5. The lessons learned by males in competitive sports may:
    a. Increase their willingness to accept limits in sexual encounters.
    b. Teach them that rules of proper conduct are to be obeyed.
    c. Predispose them to sexual violence.
    d. Bear no relationship to how they behave in sexual interactions.
        p. 576   LO 3

6. Which of the following are socio-cultural factors that foster a social climate in which more rapes tend to occur?
   a. Gender role equality
   b. Acceptance of violence in relationships
   c. Perception of sex as non-adversarial
   d. Both A and B
   e. Both B and C
   p. 579   LO 3

7. All of the following "profile" characteristics of rapists are accurate EXCEPT:
   a. They are no less intelligent than non-rapists.
   b. They tend to feel socially inadequate.
   c. They do not fit into any one type of family background description.
   d. They tend to be more mentally ill than non-rapists.
   p. 579   LO 4

8. Power plays a principal role in the following type of rape (or rapes):
   a. Gang rape.
   b. Rape by women.
   c. Partner (marital) rape.
   d. All of the above.
   p. 574   LO 4

9. All of the following are features of posttraumatic stress disorder, EXCEPT:
   a. Intrusive flashbacks about the rape.
   b. Heightened arousal.
   c. Numbing or blunting of feelings.
   d. Unpredictable rage.
   p. 580   LO 5

10. After a rape, it is suggested that the survivor do all of the following, EXCEPT
    a. Seek medical help.
    b. Consider reporting the rape to the police.
    c. Ask questions regarding medical rights.
    d. Wash herself and obtain clean clothes as soon as possible.
    p. 581   LO 5

1. Resisting rape decreases the chances of the rape being completed and it:
   a. Increases pregnancies among survivors.
   b. Decreases the chances of being hurt.
   c. Increases the chances of being physically injured.
   d. None of the above
        p. 584   LO 6

2. Which of the following is accurate regarding verbal sexual coercion?
   a. It is common in dating relationships and is thus not recognized as sexual coercion.
   b. It employs devious means to exploit the person's emotional needs.
   c. It includes persistent verbal pressure or use of seduction "lines" to manipulate the person into sexual activity.
   d. All of the above
        p. 585   LO 6

3. Which of the following does your text suggest shouting as loudly as possible when a person is attempting to rape you?
   a. "Rape!"
   b. "Fire!"
   c. "Help!"
   d. "Police!"
        p. 583   LO 6

4. Parents are *least* likely to report the sexual abuse of their child if the perpetrator is:
   a. A stranger to the child.
   b. A family acquaintance.
   c. An older teenager.
   d. A relative of the child.
        p. 585   LO 7

5. Which of the following statements is accurate regarding childhood sexual abuse?
   a. The child is usually abused by a stranger.
   b. The abuser usually uses physical force to obtain compliance by the child.
   c. Submission to adult authority aids the abuser to gain compliance.
   d. Most children enjoy the sexual behaviors.
        p. 685   LO 7

6. The most common type of child abuse is:
   a. Genital fondling.
   b. Intercourse.
   c. Exhibitionism.
   d. Oral sex.
      p. 685   LO 7

7. Which statement regarding pedophilia is NOT true?
   a. It involves a persistent or recurrent sexual attraction to children.
   b. All child molesters are pedophiles.
   c. The prevalence in the general population in unknown.
   d. Pedophiles are almost exclusively male.'
      p. 687   LO 8

8. Incarcerated pedophiles usually:
   a. Receive longer sentences than incarcerated child molesters.
   b. Stop acting on their urges after completing their sentences.
   c. Are very aggressive, "masculine" men.
   d. Have committed many more offenses than those for which they were convicted
      p. 689   LO 8

9. Some theorists suggest that the incest taboo was established long ago to:
   a. Increase the amount of genetic variation in the societal gene pool.
   b. Reduce sexual competition within the family.
   c. Help ensure people would create cohesive communities by marrying outside their own families.
   d. All of the above
   e. None of the above
      p. 590   LO 9

10. Which of the following, if any, are descriptive of a family context that might foster incest?
   a. Uneven power relationship between the spouses
   b. Physically abusive parents
   c. Father experiencing stressful life events
   d. All of the above
   e. None of the above
      p. 90   LO 9

1. Although the effects of sexual abuse on children are variable, there are some trends your text details. All of the following are listed among those probable outcomes EXCEPT:
    a. Eating disorders.
    b. Inappropriate sexual behavior.
    c. Posttraumatic stress disorder.
    d. High trust of others.
        p. 592   LO 10

2. Researchers find that adolescent girls who are sexually abused tend to:
    a. Engage in consensual sex at earlier ages than non-abused peers.
    b. Engage in consensual sex at more advanced ages than non-abused peers.
    c. Engage in consensual sex at similar ages to non-abused peers.
    d. Engage in consensual sex with fewer partners than non-abused peers.
        p. 592   LO 10

3. Children who have received training in the prevention of sexual abuse are more likely to use which of the following strategies?
    a. Running away
    b. Fighting back physically
    c. Disabling the abuser with a weapon, such as pepper spray
    d. None of the above
    e. All of the above

        p. 593   LO 11

4. All of the following messages are likely to be used in school-based child abuse prevention programs EXCEPT:
    a. "It's not your fault."
    b. "Never keep a bad or scary secret."
    c. "Always tell your parents about this."
    d. "Just pretend to go along until you can escape."
        p. 593   LO 11

5. Why is group therapy the most common form of treatment of rapists and child molesters?
    a. It costs the judicial system less money than individual therapy; funding is tight.
    b. It is better than no treatment at all.
    c. They do not fool each other as easily as they fool non-peers.
    d. It is the only way to teach them empathy for others.
        p. 594   LO 12

6. All of the following are plausible reasons for using chemical castration as a treatment for rapists and child molesters EXCEPT:
    a. Research reports lower recidivism rates among castrated offenders.
    b. It costs less per offender than traditional surgical castration.
    c. It is a non-invasive process.
    d. It is a reversible process.
        p. 595   LO 12

7. According to the U.S. Supreme Court, sexual harassment is held to involve behavior of a sexual nature that:
    a. Causes harm to the victim that require psychological treatment.
    b. Must be flagrant and demeaning to the victim.
    c. Creates a hostile work environment or interferes with an employee's work performance.
    d. Must involve outright sexual advances.
        p. 598   LO 13

8. Research on sexual harassment in the workplace asserts that it sometimes has more to do with _____ than with _____.
    a. sexual desire; abuse of power.
    b. abuse of power; sexual desire.
    c. anxiety of the accuser; abuse of power.
    d. Both A and C
    e. Both B and C
        p. 597   LO 13

9. About _____% of students report at least one incident of sexual harassment in college.
    a. 5–10
    b. 15–20
    c. 25–30
    d. 35–40
        p. 598   LO 14

10. What is the best technique(s) for resisting sexual harassment either on campus or at work?
    a. Convey a professional attitude
    b. Politely ignore the behavior (it will decrease or go away on its own)
    c. Consider spending only a small amount of alone time with the harasser
    d. All of the above
        p. 599   LO 32

Multiple Choice Questions

1. Power plays a principal role in the following type of rape (or rapes):
    a. Gang rape.
    b. Rape by women.
    c. Partner (marital) rape.
    d. All of the above.

2. Which of the following, if any, are descriptive of a family context that might foster incest?
    a. Uneven power relationship between the spouses
    b. Physically abusive parents
    c. Father experiencing stressful life events
    d. None of the above
    e. All of the above

3. Which of the following statements is accurate regarding childhood sexual abuse?
    a. The child is usually abused by a stranger.
    b. The abuser usually uses physical force to obtain compliance by the child.
    c. Submission to adult authority helps the abuser to gain compliance.
    d. Most children enjoy the sexual behaviors.

4. Which of the following are socio-cultural factors that foster a social climate in which more rapes tend to occur?
    a. Gender role equality
    b. Acceptance of violence in relationships
    c. Perception of sex as non-adversarial
    d. Both A and B
    e. Both B and C

5. Researchers find that adolescent girls who are sexually abused tend to:
    a. Engage in consensual sex at earlier ages than non-abused peers.
    b. Engage in consensual sex at more advanced ages than non-abused peers.
    c. Engage in consensual sex at similar ages to non-abused peers.
    d. Engage in consensual sex with fewer partners than non-abused peers.

6. Your text mentions that the incidence of reported rape translated to one woman being raped about every seven minutes. This is an extremely conservative estimate because:
    a. It is calculated based on crime statistics.
    b. Many rapes were discounted from the total based on state laws.
    c. Federal laws are new and would have resulted in higher numbers.
    d. Only stranger rape is prosecutable in the U.S.

7. Why is group therapy the most common form of treatment of rapists and child molesters?
    a. It costs the judicial system less money than individual therapy; funding is tight.
    b. It is better than no treatment at all.
    c. They do not fool each other as easily as they fool non-peers.
    d. It is the only way to teach them empathy for others.

8. All of the following statements about partner/marital rape are accurate, EXCEPT:
    a. Marital rape generally leads the couple to become involved in marital counseling.
    b. Marital rape is motivated by the need to dominate, intimidate, and subjugate.
    c. Many survivors of marital rape fear physical injury and/or death.
    d. Marital rapes are probably more common than date rapes.

9. About _____% of students report at least one incident of sexual harassment in college.
    a. 5–10
    b. 15–20
    c. 25–30
    d. 35–40

10. After a rape, it is suggested that the survivor do all of the following, EXCEPT:
    a. Seek medical help.
    b. Consider reporting the rape to the police.
    c. Ask questions regarding medical rights.
    d. Wash herself and obtain clean clothes as soon as possible.

11. According to the U.S. Supreme Court, sexual harassment is held to involve behavior of a sexual nature that:
    a. Causes harm to the victim that requires psychological treatment.
    b. Must be flagrant and demeaning to the victim.
    c. Creates a hostile work environment or interferes with an employee's work performance.
    d. Must involve outright sexual advances.

12. Resisting rape decreases the chances of the rape being completed and it:
    a. Increases pregnancies among survivors.
    b. Decreases the chances of being hurt.
    c. Increases the chances of being physically injured.
    d. None of the above

13. For most of recorded history, rape was considered:
    a. A violent crime that curtailed the rights of women.
    b. A crime against the property rights of fathers or husbands.
    c. The act of mentally deranged men.
    d. An act of adultery by the victim.

14. Children who have received training in the prevention of sexual abuse are more likely to use which of the following strategies?
    a. Running away
    b. Fighting back physically
    c. Disabling the abuser with a weapon, such as pepper spray
    d. None of the above
    e. All of the above

15. Which statement regarding pedophilia is NOT true?
    a. It involves a persistent or recurrent sexual attraction to children.
    b. All child molesters are pedophiles.
    c. The prevalence in the general population in unknown.
    d. Pedophiles are almost exclusively male.

True/False

_____ 1. Much of our knowledge about psychological characteristics of rapists is based on studies of incarcerated rapists.

_____ 2. Only about one-quarter of the women in a national college survey who had been sexually assaulted saw themselves as rape victims.

_____ 3. Women who blame themselves for having been raped tend to suffer fewer depression problems than those who are able to see themselves as victims.

_____ 4. Children who are sexually abused by family members are more likely to suffer repeated abuse.

_____ 5. Survivors of gang rape are more likely to report the attack to police or seek support from a crisis center than are survivors of individual assaults.

_____ 6. Following sexual assault, the emotional distress tends to peak in severity about three weeks after the assault and remains high for about a month before beginning to subside.

_____ 7. The current definition of rape varies from state to state.

_____ 8. Male rape survivors suffer traumatic effects quite dissimilar from those suffered by female survivors.

Essay Questions

1. Compare and contrast the definitions and incidences of stranger rape, acquaintance rape, and date rape. Include a comparison of the likely emotional fallout for survivors of each type of assault.

_____

_____

_____

_____

_____

_____

_____

_____

2. Discuss two major issues that set the stage for rape: the social attitudes, myths, and cultural factors that encourage rape, and the psychological characteristics and motives of rapists.

_____

_____

_____

_____

_____

_____

_____

_____

When You Have Finished...

What Does the World Think?

Let's see where the Web takes you as you explore the following activities related to sexual coercion.

1. What does your campus have for you? Go to your campus website. Find information about sex crimes. What does it show you? For an example, here is the link for San Diego State University link: http://www.sa.sdsu.edu/cps/sexual_assault.html

2. This abstract of an article in *Health Psychology* describes a study that examined how the circumstances of a rape affect later sexual behavior: http://www.apa.org/monitor/feb04/rapehtml

3. Sexual harassment is not just a workplace phenomenon. It is, unfortunately, to be found in some educational settings. In this pamphlet, entitled "It's Not Academic," the Office for Civil Rights gives information about what constitutes sexual harassment and ways to handle harassment at school: http://www.ed.gov/ and search for sexual harassment. What are the guidelines and what should you do if you feel uncomfortable?

4. The Rape, Abuse, and Incest National Network provides statistics on the incidence of rape and other relevant information: http://www.rainn.org/

5. Is it rape? On NPR there was a story about a girl who thought she was having sex with her husband, but it turns out she was tricked into having sex with his brother. Go to NPR.org and search for "rape by fraud" listen to/read the story. Where is line between rape and bad judgment?

6. Get information on Rohypnol or "Roofies," a drug linked to the incidence of date rape, from http://www.drugs.com/rohypnol.html

7. This list of links will lead you to resources on these topics from the Feminist Majority Foundation: http://www.feminist.org/911/resources.html

8. National Center for PTSD provides a wide variety of information on this topic, including assessments for both children and adults: http://www.ncptsd.va.gov/

Chapter 19
The World of Commercial Sex:
A Disneyland for Adults?

Before You Begin...

Chapter Summary

Sex remains a powerful motivator of human behavior—and some people do not do well without it! Given the natural demand for it along with a lack of a "free" or easy way to get it, some males and females will eagerly exchange money or other valuable (and sometimes illicit) goods for it. Despite laws seeking to change behaviors, sex remains a timeless commodity that is widely available, and it is provided in the form of sexually-explicit movies and publications, sex shops and erotic clubs, and telephone, Internet, and escort services.

With the exception of a few Nevada counties, exchanging sex for money is illegal in the United States. Police officers generally consider prostitution a "nuisance" crime and impose penalties such as small fines or short jail terms. Prostitutes can be classified into four types based on the settings in which they work. At the bottom of the hierarchy are *streetwalkers*, who are at greatest risk for arrest because they operate out in the open. These prostitutes, many of whom are runaways, are usually raised in poor, conflict-ridden households. *House prostitutes* work in brothels or massage parlors. *Escorts* and *call girls*, many of whom are well-educated and come from the middle class, often attend social functions with their clients in addition to providing sexual services. The incidence of psychological disturbances, STIs, and other medical problems is unusually high among prostitutes in the U.S. and around the world.

Men who use prostitutes, called *johns* or *tricks*, may lack other sexual outlets, desire sexual variety or sex without commitment to a relationship, or enjoy the social aspects of engaging in recreational sexual adventures with their male peers. Men also work as prostitutes. *Gigolos* typically provide escort and sexual services to older, wealthy, single women. *Hustlers*, who may be of any sexual orientation, provide sexual services to gay men. Like streetwalkers, hustlers usually come from poor backgrounds, have low education levels and few job skills, and often enter prostitution after running away from troubled family situations. One of the most pressing concerns about prostitution is its role in transmitting HIV/AIDS.

The production and distribution of *pornography*—materials containing explicit words and images intended to arouse sexual desire—is a thriving industry. There is considerable social controversy over pornography; for example, many feminists argue it dehumanizes women and may encourage men to sexually assault them. The legal definition of obscenity depends on what offends "the average person" and violates community standards; thus, determining what is obscene or pornographic is highly subjective. Although both women and men physiologically respond to pornography, women report being more sexually aroused by romantic scenes than by explicit scenes, and men report greater interest than women in using pornographic materials.

Although one congressional commission concluded there was no evidence that using pornography leads to crimes of violence or sexual offenses, another commission convened 20 years later claimed exposure to violent pornography in which women are degraded increases viewers' tolerance for rape. There is evidence that pornography stimulates deviant urges in subgroups of men who are predisposed to commit crimes of sexual violence. Although there is no reliable link between pornography and aggression, extended exposure to pornography tends to make users more callous in their attitudes toward women, particularly victims of rape.

Learning Objectives

1. Recognize why prostitution is commonly referred to as "the world's oldest profession."

2. Indicate how prevalent prostitution is in the United States and around the world, noting why it is difficult to accurately determine the incidence of prostitution.

3. Identify the four types of female prostitutes and two types of male prostitutes, and note what criteria are used to classify them.

4. Compare the background characteristics, motivations, and work conditions of the various types of prostitutes.

5. Summarize the most common physical and psychological problems found among prostitutes.

6. Recognize how police in most areas of the U.S. perceive and respond to prostitution.

7. Recognize the terms assigned to men who purchase services from prostitutes, and list the six common motives men have for using prostitutes.

8. Assess the contribution of prostitution to HIV transmission in the U.S. and other nations.

9. Indicate how prevalent the use of pornography is in the U.S., note how usage varies by gender, and suggest at least one reason why men and women respond differently to pornography.

10. Outline the criteria used by the U.S. legal system to determine *obscenity*; state why it is difficult to determine what is considered obscene or pornographic using this definition.

11. Know of modern day regulation of pornography and of sex workers.

12. Evaluate the results of research investigating the relationship between consumption of pornography (both violent and nonviolent), attitudes toward women, and the commission of sexual crimes (sexual coercion).

13. Recognize what defines cybersex and cybersex addiction.

Key Terms

Term Identification

You know the drill; these are the terms you need to learn and they are in alphabetical order as with prior chapters. Again, making flashcards will help. Do note that there a few terms below in this chapter that are *not* in the margins of your text. These should nonetheless still be rather evident as you read (or perhaps even as you initially scan) the chapter. Familiarity with all the terms will help provide you a well-rounded understanding of this oftentimes socially controversial topic.

Chapter 19 Table of Key Terms	
Brothel	Pornography
Call boys	Posttraumatic stress disorder (PTSD)
Call girls	Prostitution
Cybersex	Prurient
Drag prostitutes	Punks
Erotica	Scores
Gigolo	Sex worker
Hustlers	Snuff film
Kept boys	Streetwalkers
Obscenity	Strippers
Pimps	Whore-Madonna complex

As You Read...

The World of Commercial Sex

> ➢ *Prostitution*

Types of Female Prostitutes

In the chart below, compare and contrast the different types of female prostitutes.

Types of Prostitutes	Characteristics of Prostitutes
Streetwalkers	
Brothel Prostitutes	
Massage Parlor Prostitutes	
Escort Service Prostitutes	
Call Girls	

TRY PRACTICE TEST #1 NOW!
GOOD LUCK!

What Can Be Discovered from Examining People's Backgrounds and Motives?
Find out by responding to the following questions about prostitutes and their customers.
First, think about your attitudes toward prostitutes, their customers, and prostitution.

Would you describe them as positive or negative?

Why do you think you have these attitudes?

Now, answer the questions below:

What are the characteristics of female prostitutes?

What psychological disturbance may affect prostitutes? Describe this disorder.

Prostitutes are likely to come from which type of family backgrounds?

What are the motives for using prostitutes? Describe the whore-Madonna complex.

What are characteristics of male prostitutes?

What are the motives for why people become prostitutes?

What are your attitudes toward prostitutes, their customers, and prostitution? Have they changed since completing this activity?

If so, how have they changed? If not, why not? Please explain.

TRY PRACTICE TEST #2 NOW!
GOOD LUCK!

> *Pornography and Obscenity*

What is Pornographic? What is Obscene?

How would you go about answering the above questions? What have the courts ruled in terms of defining what is pornographic or obscene? Briefly summarize each of the following laws/cases presented in the text.

Comstock Act (1873):

Roth v. United States, **1957:**

Miller v. California, **1973:**

Pope v. Illinois, **1987:**

Stanley v. Georgia, **1969:**

What Do We Know About...?

Summarize the findings of each of the following:

The Commission on Obscenity and Pornography and the Meese Commission Report

The Effects of Violent Pornography

The Effects of Nonviolent Pornography

TRY PRACTICE TEST #3 NOW!
GOOD LUCK!

Do you know the definitions of the terms in this chapter?
Find out how well you are learning the definitions of the terms in the chapter by completing the following matching exercise. Match each key vocabulary term listed in the left-hand column with the correct definition in the right-hand column. Good luck!

a. prostitution

_____ Written, visual or audiotaped material that is sexually explicit and produced for purposes of eliciting or enhancing sexual arousal.

b. streetwalkers

_____ Prostitutes who arrange for their sexual contacts by telephone (or even Internet e-mail).

c. pimps

_____ Characterized by flashbacks, emotional numbing, and heightened body arousal.

d. call girls

_____ Customers of hustlers.

e. whore-Madonna complex

_____ The sale of sexual activity for money or goods of value, such as drugs.

f. hustlers

_____ Tending to excite lust; lewd.

g. scores

_____ A rigid stereotyping of women as either sinners or saints.

h. pornography

_____ That which offends people's feelings or goes beyond prevailing standards of decency or modesty.

i. prurient

_____ Prostitutes who solicit customers on the streets.

j. obscenity

_____ Men who engage in prostitution with male customers.

k. posttraumatic stress disorder

_____ Men who serve as agents for prostitutes and live off their earnings.

➤ **Who uses Pornography?**

What kind of person looks at pornography? Are they social deviants , child molesters and social outcasts? Check out Figure 19.2 on page 624. and answer these questions:

Who is aroused by pornographic material?

When are most people first exposed to pornography?

What percentage of college students are using online pornography?

Does online pornography have as much stigma as in the past?

How much Internet usage is focused on sex websites?

Time to Test Yourself by Filling in the Blanks

Test your knowledge of the content of this chapter by reading the following paragraphs and completing them. If you need to, use your text as a guide. Good luck!

In the United States, _____ is illegal everywhere except in some counties in Nevada. In this activity, a person exchanges _____ _____ for money or items of value. Although _____ is also illegal in many states, police rarely arrest customers. Most prostitutes are (male/female) _____ and virtually all customers are (male/female) _____. The major motive for prostitution throughout history and currently is _____.

Kinsey's data indicated a decrease in sexual experience with prostitutes that seems to be linked to the decay of the _____ _____ _____. Of the different types of prostitutes, most are _____, who hold the lowest status and earn the lowest income. They are also most likely to be abused by _____ and _____. Many were _____ _____ who initially became prostitutes in order to survive on their own.

_____ prostitutes have a higher status than streetwalkers. Except in Nevada, these prostitutes are most likely to work in _____ _____ or for _____ _____. _____ _____ provide "outcall" services and are listed in the yellow pages of telephone directories. They are typically, but not always, fronts for prostitution. Prostitutes who work for these businesses are often from _____ - class backgrounds and are _____ educated.

_____ _____ occupy the highest status in female prostitution. They are usually the most attractive and most well educated. They are expected to provide not only sex but also _____ _____. They usually work (on their own/with a pimp)_____.

Two factors, which figure prominently in the backgrounds of many prostitutes, are _____ and _____ and/or _____ _____. One study found that nearly _____ of prostitutes could be diagnosed with post-traumatic stress disorder.

Motives for using prostitutes include _____ without negotiation, sex without _____, sex for eroticism and _____, prostitution as _____, _____ away from home, and _____ sex.

Male prostitutes who service female clients — _____ — are rare. They may or may not offer sexual services. The overwhelming majority of male prostitutes, usually called _____, service other men. The average age of male prostitutes is (14–15, 17–18, 20–22) _____. The majority comes from _____-class or _____-class backgrounds. Many are survivors of _____ _____. About half are (heterosexual/homosexual) _____ in orientation. Their major motive is _____.

_____ is writing, pictures, etc. intended to arouse sexual desire. Legislative bodies usually write laws about _____, but they have great difficulty defining it. The 1873 _____ Act banned information about _____ _____ and made it a felony to _____ obscene material.

The report of the 1960s Commission on Obscenity and Pornography found (persuasive/no) _____ evidence that pornography led to crimes of violence or sexual offenses. A recent review of the research literature found (significant/little or no) _____ differences in the level of exposure to pornography between incarcerated sex offenders and felons who had committed nonsexual crimes.

The 1986 Meese Commission (the United States Attorney General's Commission on Pornography) claimed they (found/were unable to find) _____ a causal link between sexual violence and exposure to violent pornography. Research suggests that it is (sex/violence) _____ with or without (sex/violence) _____ that has damaging effects on those who are exposed to it. Some studies on the effects of nonviolent pornography show that for some (men/women) _____, exposure to pornography can result in _____ _____toward women.

After You Read...

1. Of the four types of female prostitutes discussed in the text, which type occupies the lowest status in the hierarchy of prostitution?
   a. Escorts
   b. Call girls
   c. Streetwalkers
   d. House prostitutes
   p. 608   LO 3

2. In most areas of the U.S., the penalty for engaging in prostitution is usually a(n):
   a. Involuntary commitment to a psychiatric facility.
   b. Lengthy prison sentence.
   c. Monetary fine.
   d. Prostitution is not a crime in the United States, so none of the penalties above is applied.
   p. 609   LO 6

3. The primary motivation for most young women who enter prostitution is the:
   a. Desire to exert control over men.
   b. Need to earn money to support themselves.
   c. Opportunity to receive sexual gratification without commitment.
   d. Inability to control their psychological compulsion to be victimized.
   p. 607   LO 4

4. Kinsey's research on men's use of prostitutes in the 1940s indicates that:
   a. About two-thirds of European American males in the research sample had used a prostitute at least once.
   b. College-educated men were more likely than those without college educations to have visited a prostitute.
   c. Young men were more likely to become sexually initiated by their girlfriends than by a prostitute during that period in history.
   d. Kinsey's research indicates all of the above are true.
   p. 607   LO 2

5. Today's "massage parlor" prostitutes are most likely to perform their services at:
   a. Abandoned inner-city buildings.
   b. Suburban shopping malls.
   c. Their own homes.
   d. Expensive hotels.
   p. 610   LO 4

6. Which of the following statements about brothel prostitutes is accurate?
   a. They occupy the lowest status, and encounter the most risk, of all prostitutes.
   b. Although they perform manual stimulation and oral sex for their clients, they rarely engage in sexual intercourse with them.
   c. Although this category of prostitution was very common in the past, it is rarely found in the United States today.
   d. All of the above statements about brothel prostitutes are accurate.
      p. 610   LO 3

7. Which of the following statements about *call girls* is accurate?
   a. In the social hierarchy of prostitution, they are lower in status than house prostitutes but higher in status than streetwalkers.
   b. They have the highest rates of psychological disorders and medical problems of all prostitutes.
   c. They are usually the most attractive, best-educated, and highest paid prostitutes.
   d. They typically enter prostitution during adolescence as a way to escape poverty.
      p. 613   LO 3

8. Men who serve as agents for prostitutes in exchange for a percent of their earnings are:
   a. Hustlers.
   b. Scores.
   c. Johns.
   d. Pimps.
      p. 608   LO 4

9. Historical records indicate that prostitution:
   a. Is a relatively recent phenomenon that was brought on by industrialization.
   b. First emerged during the Victorian period in the nineteenth century.
   c. Can be traced back as far as ancient Mesopotamia.
   d. Developed in Europe during the medieval period.
      p. 607   LO 1

10. The Internet has marshaled in a new way for some to find sexual expression—cybersex. Some people are becoming cybersex addicts. Given this, all the behaviors listed below are congruent with addiction EXCEPT:
   a. Cybersex addicts will usually deny that there is a problem with the amount of time spent.
   b. Cybersex is typically sought out by men with little or no alternative outlets for sexual expression.
   c. The time spent by addicts sexually-engaged at the computer impairs any existing intimate love relationship—sometimes to the breaking point. It can also contribute to job loss.
   d. Intense orgasms can tend to reinforce the addictive behavior.
      p. 625   LO 13

1. What percent of the prostitutes in Farley's multinational study of prostitutes reported that they wanted to leave "the life"?
    a. 10
    b. 25
    c. 50
    d. 90
        p. 610   LO 5

2. Streetwalkers in the contemporary U.S. commonly, or even most commonly, accommodate men who:
    a. Have special sexual needs due to physical disabilities.
    b. Are suffering from a compulsive psychological disorder.
    c. Are away from home while attending business conventions or sporting events.
    d. Have such strong sex drives that their usual partners cannot fulfill all their needs.
        p. 608   LO 7

3. Which of the following statements about *hustlers* is FALSE?
    a. They are paid to provide sexual services primarily to gay male clients.
    b. They are typically poor young men who come from troubled families.
    c. They are equally as likely to describe their sexual orientation as homosexual as they are to describe it as heterosexual.
    d. They are just as likely as female prostitutes to have economic need as their major motive for entering prostitution.
        p. 615   LO 3

4. Which of the following best describes a *gigolo*'s typical client?
    a. 66-year-old divorced heterosexual female who needs an escort for a charity ball
    b. 16-year-old homosexual male who wants to have intercourse for the first time
    c. 36-year-old single heterosexual male who desires sex without commitment
    d. 26-year-old married heterosexual female who enjoys sexual variety
        p. 615   LO 3

5. Which of the following is an example of the "habitual john"?
    a. Chuck, a young man who is engaged to his childhood sweetheart and wants to gain some sexual experience before he gets married
    b. Dave, a wealthy, emotionally distant, middle-aged bachelor who values his freedom
    c. John, a traveling salesmen who regularly has sex with his wife but sometimes visits prostitutes when he is out of town and feeling lonely
    d. Todd, a middle-aged man who suffers from a psychological disorder that interferes with his ability to perform sexually with women he knows
        p. 614   LO 7

6. Which of the following is the *most* important factor in the male-to-female transmission of HIV/AIDS in Africa today?
   a. Sexually-active members of the population cannot buy and use condoms because the government has banned their distribution.
   b. A significant number of married men have sex with prostitutes, contract the virus, and transmit it to their wives.
   c. A significant number of married women have affairs, contract the virus, and transmit it to their husbands.
   d. A large percentage of young women are raped by foreign military personnel, thus spreading the virus among the local population.
      p. 617   LO 8

7. While U.S. court interpretations of the First Amendment protects people's right to produce, act in, and possess pornography, it has not prevented various governing bodies from imposing some regulations on the industry. Given this, what kind(s) of regulation is (are) currently in place in some places of the U.S.?
   a. Actors in pornographic films must be certified as free of STIs as frequently as once a month.

   b. Male actors in most U.S. states are now required to wear a condom to reduce the unanticipated spread of HIV to the other actor(s).
   c. Studios are required to keep accurate records of the actors' proof of age, health testing status, and all sexual contacts for inspection by state regulators or public health authorities.
   d. All of the above are examples of regulations imposed somewhere in the U.S.
   e. None of the above items are currently imposed regulations.
      p. 621   LO 11

8. Pedersen and Hegna's survey of Norwegian adolescents revealed that youth participation in prostitution was connected with all of the following factors EXCEPT:
   a. Identifying as homosexual.
   b. Abusing alcohol and other drugs.
   c. Being the victim of physical abuse.
   d. Initiating sexual intercourse at an early age.
      p. 616   LO 5

9. Male prostitutes typically refer to their male customers as:
   a. Pimps.
   b. Scores.
   c. Gigolos.
   d. Hustlers.
      p. 615   LO 7

10. Research suggests that men and women differ in which of the following ways?
    a. Men are more willing than women to engage in sexual activity in the absence of a commitment to a relationship.
    b. Men are more interested than women in greater sexual variety.
    c. Men have a stronger sex drive than women do.
    d. There is evidence that all of the above sex differences exist.
        p. 614   LO 7

1. In the U.S., the legal prohibition of pornography as a form of obscenity *began* with the:
   a. Adoption of the Bill of Rights in 1791.
   b. Passage of the Comstock Act in 1873.
   c. Supreme Court ruling, *Stanley v. Georgia*, in 1969.
   d. Meese Commission's recommendations in 1985.
      p. 620   LO 10

2. Based on their interpretation of research investigating the correlation between exposure to pornography and sexually aggressive behavior, the Meese Commission:
   a. Concluded that because there is no evidence that pornography leads to crimes of violence or to sexual offenses the government should not restrict access to it.
   b. Suggested that exposure to violent materials of any kind are more likely to have adverse effects on young people than is exposure to non-violent pornography.
   c. Recommended that the government better enforce existing obscenity laws and impose greater restrictions on the dissemination of all forms of pornography.
   d. Dismissed the results of current research after determining that data collected from small, unrepresentative samples is not reliable.
      p. 626-7   LO 10

3. Which of the following factors MUST be present to designate a product as *pornographic*?
   a. The product must use writing and/or pictures that refer to or depict sexual acts.
   b. The product must include words and/or images intended to arouse sexual desire.
   c. The product must present women or children in degrading or dehumanizing roles.
   d. All of these factors must be present to designate a product as pornographic.
      p. 619   LO 10

4. The text authors state that our ability to generalize the results of existing research concerning the effects of pornography on sexually aggressive behavior is limited by:
   a. An over-reliance on college students as research subjects.
   b. Conducting the research in artificially-created laboratory settings.
   c. Measuring the subjects' perceptions and attitudes about hypothetical situations, rather than measuring actual behavior.
   d. Existing research on pornography is limited by all of the above factors.
      p. 628   LO 12

5. One notable difference between men and women concerning pornography is:
   a. Most men are physiologically aroused by pornographic images, but very few women respond to pornographic stimuli with vasocongestion of the genitals.
   b. Women's subjective feelings of arousal increase with the degree of romance depicted, whereas men's arousal increases with the degree of sexual explicitness.
   c. Males are typically exposed to pornography by their male peers, whereas females are usually introduced to pornography by their older siblings.
   d. Research provides evidence for all of the above gender differences.
      p. 624   LO 9

6. In which of the following landmark cases did the Supreme Court rule that the portrayal of sexual activity was protected under the First Amendment to the Constitution *unless* its dominant theme dealt with "sex in a manner appealing to prurient interest"?
    a. Roth v. United States, 1957
    b. Miller v. California, 1973
    c. Stanley v. Georgia, 1969
    d. Pope v. Illinois, 1987
        p. 620   LO 10

7. Some observers note that _____ are the latest form of sexually explicit materials to threaten committed relationships in the contemporary United States.
    a. mass-produced romance novels
    b. interactive web sites on the Internet
    c. men's magazines such as *Penthouse*
    d. X rated videos available for home use
        p. 625   LO 12

8. Although the U.S. Supreme Court has ruled that the possession of obscene material in one's home is not a criminal act, states still have the right to criminalize the downloading and possession of pornography that depicts _____ in a sexual manner or context.
    a. animals
    b. children
    c. women
    d. weapons
        p. 621   LO 10

9. In the case of _____, the U.S. Supreme Court clarified the definition of *obscenity* by indicating that public perceptions of "prurient interest" depend on "contemporary community standards."
    a. Pope v. Illinois
    b. Stanley v. Georgia
    c. Miller v. California
    d. Roth v. United States
        p. 620   LO 10

10. One of the most interesting findings from Zillman and Bryant's classic study of exposure to non-violent pornography was that:
    a. The punishments subjects assigned to a rapist did not vary at all according to which "dose" of pornography they had received.
    b. Female subjects exposed to a "massive dose" of pornography assigned more lenient punishments to a rapist than did male subjects in the "massive dose" group.
    c. Both male and female subjects exposed to "massive doses" of pornography assigned more lenient punishments to a rapist than did men and women in the "no-dose" control group.
    d. Male subjects who were exposed to either "massive" or "intermediate" doses reported less acceptance of premarital and extramarital sex than did male subjects in the "no-dose" control group.
        p. 629   LO 12

Multiple Choice Questions

1. The most frequent use of prostitutes in the contemporary U.S. occurs among men who:
   a. Have special sexual needs due to physical disabilities.
   b. Are suffering from a compulsive psychological disorder.
   c. Are away from home while attending business conventions or sporting events.
   d. Have such strong sex drives that their usual partners cannot fulfill all their needs.

2. In which of the following landmark cases did the Supreme Court rule that the portrayal of sexual activity was protected under the First Amendment to the Constitution *unless* its dominant theme dealt with "sex in a manner appealing to prurient interest"?
   a. Roth v. United States, 1957
   b. Miller v. California, 1973
   c. Stanley v. Georgia, 1969
   d. Pope v. Illinois, 1987

3. Today's "massage parlor" prostitutes are most likely to perform their services at:
   a. Abandoned inner-city buildings.
   b. Suburban shopping malls.
   c. Their own homes.
   d. Expensive hotels.

4. Which of the following factors MUST be present to designate a product as *pornographic*?
   a. The product must use writing and/or pictures that refer to or depict sexual acts.
   b. The product must include words and/or images intended to arouse sexual desire.
   c. The product must present women or children in degrading or dehumanizing roles.
   d. All of these factors must be present to designate a product as *pornographic*.

5. The primary motivation for most young women who enter prostitution is the:
   a. Desire to exert control over men.
   b. Need to earn money to support themselves.
   c. Opportunity to receive sexual gratification without commitment.
   d. Inability to control their psychological compulsion to be victimized.

6. Which of the following is the *most* important factor in the male-to-female transmission of HIV/AIDS in Africa today?
    a. Sexually-active members of the population cannot buy and use condoms because the government has banned their distribution.
    b. A significant number of married men have sex with prostitutes, contract the virus, and transmit it to their wives.
    c. A significant number of married women have affairs, contract the virus, and transmit it to their husbands.
    d. A large percentage of female adolescents and young adults are raped by foreign military personnel, thus spreading the virus among the local population.

7. Historical records indicate that prostitution:
    a. Is a relatively recent phenomenon that was brought on by industrialization.
    b. First emerged during the Victorian period in the nineteenth century.
    c. Can be traced back as far as ancient Mesopotamia.
    d. Developed in Europe during the medieval period.

8. While U.S. court interpretations of the First Amendment protects people's right to produce, act in, and possess pornography, it has not prevented various governing bodies from imposing some regulations on the industry. Given this, what kind(s) of regulation is/are currently in place in some places of the U.S.?
    a. Actors in pornographic films must be certified as free of STIs as frequently as once a month.

    b. Male actors in most US states are now required to wear a condom to reduce the unanticipated spread of HIV to the other actor(s).
    c. Studios are required to keep accurate records of the actors' proof of age, health testing status, and all sexual contacts for inspection by state regulators or public health authorities.
    d. All of the above are examples of regulations imposed somewhere in the U.S.
    e. None of the above items are currently imposed regulations.

9. In the U.S., the legal prohibition of pornography as a form of obscenity *began* with the:
    a. Adoption of the Bill of Rights in 1791.
    b. Passage of the Comstock Act in 1873.
    c. Supreme Court ruling, *Stanley v. Georgia*, in 1969.
    d. Meese Commission's recommendations in 1985.

10. Which of the following statements about brothel prostitutes is accurate?
    a. They occupy the lowest status, and encounter the most risk, of all prostitutes.
    b. Although they perform manual stimulation and oral sex for their clients, they rarely engage in sexual intercourse with them.
    c. Although this category of prostitution was very common in the past, it is rarely found in the United States today.
    d. All of the above statements about brothel prostitutes are accurate.

11. Which of the following statements about *hustlers* is **false**?
    a. They are paid to provide sexual services primarily to gay male clients.
    b. They are typically poor young men who come from troubled families.
    c. They are equally as likely to describe their sexual orientation as homosexual as they are to describe it as heterosexual.
    d. They are just as likely as female prostitutes to have economic need as their major motive for entering prostitution.

12. In most areas of the U.S., the penalty for engaging in prostitution is usually a(n):
    a. Involuntary commitment to a psychiatric facility.
    b. Lengthy prison sentence.
    c. Monetary fine.
    d. None of the above penalties are usually imposed on prostitutes because prostitution is not a crime in the United States.

13. Although the U.S. Supreme Court has ruled that the possession of obscene material in one's home is not a criminal act, states still have the right to criminalize the downloading and possession of pornography that depicts _____ in a sexual manner or context.
    a. animals
    b. children
    c. women
    d. weapons

14. The text authors state that our ability to generalize the results of existing research concerning the effects of pornography on sexually aggressive behavior is limited by:
    a. An over-reliance on college students as research subjects.
    b. Conducting the research in artificially-created laboratory settings.
    c. Measuring the subjects' perceptions and attitudes about hypothetical situations, rather than measuring actual behavior.
    d. Existing research on pornography is limited by all of the above factors.

15. One notable difference between men and women concerning pornography is:
    a. Most men are physiologically aroused by pornographic images, but very few women respond to pornographic stimuli with vasocongestion of the genitals.
    b. Women's subjective feelings of arousal increase with the degree of romance depicted, whereas men's arousal increases with the degree of sexual explicitness.
    c. Males are typically exposed to pornography by their male peers, whereas females are usually introduced to pornography by their older siblings.
    d. Research provides evidence for all of the above gender differences.

True/False

1. ____Malamuth's research on pornography provided definitive evidence that men who regularly view pornographic movies are twice as likely to commit sexual crimes.

2. ____Sex with prostitutes is the most important factor in the transmission of HIV in Africa.

3. ____The major motive for occasional johns to use prostitutes is the desire for sexual variety and novelty.

4. ____The 1960s Commission on Obscenity and Pornography strongly recommended that obscenity laws be more strictly enforced and the dissemination of pornography curtailed.

5. ____Kinsey's survey results indicate that young men in the 1940s were more likely to be sexually initiated by a prostitute than by a girlfriend.

6. ____A majority of adult women show no physiological response while viewing sexually explicit images because most women perceive pornography as humiliating.

7. ____Zillman's research indicates that prolonged exposure to pornography fosters dissatisfaction with the physical appearance and sexual performance of both male and female viewers' partners.

8. ____In *Stanley v. Georgia* (1969), the U.S. Supreme Court ruled that it is constitutional to prohibit the distribution of sexually explicit materials depicting violence toward women because pornography prevents women from securing equal rights.

Essay Question

1. Citing evidence from the research presented in your text, outline the personal and societal problems fostered by prostitution. Recommend at least three specific measures you think should be implemented in the U.S. to effectively manage the problems you identified.

_____
_____
_____
_____
_____
_____
_____
_____

When You Have Finished...

Let's see where the Web takes you as you explore the following activities related to sex for sale in your community and around the world.

1. This article by Laurie Hall is based on her book, <u>An Affair of the Mind</u> (1996) (published by a Christian organization, Focus on the Family), which argues that pornography destroys families. As a critical thinker, read it so as to recognize Ms. Hall's key points and then factor in her religious beliefs. What do you conclude? http://bauercom.net/pornography_whats_the_big_deal.htm

2. This site, http://www.ifc.com/indiesex/, is a documentary series about pornographic material in cinema. If you can catch it on your local cable provider, it is not very graphic but it is very interesting.

3. At the following site, you can find the text of the 1986 Supreme Court decision that upheld the Georgia sodomy law: http://www.qrd.org/QRD/usa/legal/bowers-v-hardwick.txt. Near the very beginning, you will notice "Held: The Georgia statute is constitutional." Consider examining the Justices' rationale.

4. Although this site might be a bit dated (these pictures were taken by photojournalist Piet den Blanken in 1951), it is still an interesting cross-cultural look at the phenomenon of prostitution: http://www.denblanken.com/index-bordello.html (click on the photo to see the rest of the images).

5. What is the modern prostitute? Go to Craigslist.org. See how long it takes you to find someone willing to have sex for money. Look in the Adult Services section. See what is in your area and what is in the larger cities. Are you shocked?

6. <u>Be aware that the follow site contains nudity and adult language and sometimes a graphic video on the home page</u>: http://worldsexguide.org/ It lists prostitution information by country/continent. This site is intended for people looking for sexual experiences around the globe. Again, what are your thoughts and why?

7. This site presents a research article by Catharine A. MacKinnon that discusses the effects prostitution has on prostitutes and on society. It is titled "Prostitution and Civil Rights." http://prostitutionresearch.com/mackinnon1.htm

ANSWER KEY

CHAPTER 1

Practice Test 1

1. B
2. B
3. C
4. D
5. C
6. B
7. C
8. E
9. E

Practice Test 2

1. C
2. B
3. B
4. E
5. C
6. B
7. D
8. A
9. D
10. D

Practice Test 3

1. C
2. D
3. C
4. C
5. D
6. B
7. D
8. E
9. B
10. D

Comprehensive Test – Multiple Choice

1. B
2. B
3. B
4. C
5. C
6. B
7. B
8. D
9. D
10 D
11. C
12. C
13. D
14. D
15. E

True/False

1. F
2. F
3. T
4. T
5. F
6. T
7. T
8. T

CHAPTER 2

Practice Test 1

1. B
2. A
3. D
4. D
5. B
6. B
7. B
8. C
9. C
10. B

Practice Test 2

1. B
2. A
3. B
4. B
5. A
6. B
7. D
8. B
9. D
10. C

Practice Test 3

1. D
2. C
3. A
4. C
5. A
6. D
7. A
8. C
9. D
10. C

Comprehensive Test – Multiple Choice

1. A
2. B
3. C
4. C
5. D
6. D
7. D
8. B
9. C
10 A
11. A
12. C
13. A
14. B
15. A

True/False

1. F
2. T
3. F
4. T
5. T
6. T
7. F
8. T

CHAPTER 3

Practice Test 1

1. C
2. C
3. C
4. B
5. C
6. B
7. C
8. A
9. C
10. D

Practice Test 2

1. C
2. D
3. B
4. C
5. D
6. B
7. D
8. B
9. B
10. D

Practice Test 3

1. B
2. D
3. B
4. C
5. B
6. E
7. A
8. A
9. D
10. E

Comprehensive Test –
Multiple Choice

1. B
2. D
3. E
4. B
5. A
6. C
7. E
8. B
9. D
10 C
11. D
12. C
13. C
14. B
15. D

True/False

1. T
2. F
3. T
4. T
5. F
6. T
7. F
8. T

CHAPTER 4

Practice Test 1

1. C
2. A
3. C
4. E
5. E
6. B
7. D
8. B
9. C
10. B

Practice Test 2

1. A
2. B
3. D
4. C
5. C
6. B
7. A
8. B
9. C
10. D

Practice Test 3

1. D
2. B
3. D
4. D
5. C
6. B
7. D
8. C
9. D
10. C

Comprehensive Test –
Multiple Choice

1. E
2. C
3. C
4. C
5. C
6. B
7. C
8. B
9. C
10 B
11. D
12. C
13. A
14. D
15. B

True/False

1. T
2. T
3. F
4. F
5. T
6. F
7. T
8. F

CHAPTER 5

Practice Test 1

1. C
2. D
3. D
4. C
5. C
6. A
7. E
8. C
9. E
10. B

Practice Test 2

1. A
2. B
3. C
4. A
5. C
6. B
7. A
8. A
9. A
10. B

Practice Test 3

1. A
2. B
3. D
4. B
5. C
6. B
7. B
8. C
9. D
10. D

Comprehensive Test – Multiple Choice

1. C
2. D
3. C
4. C
5. A
6. A
7. B
8. B
9. B
10 C
11. B
12. C
13. D
14. D
15. D

True/False

1. F
2. T
3. T
4. F
5. T
6. F
7. T
8. T

CHAPTER 6

Practice Test 1

1. C
2. C
3. B
4. D
5. C
6. C
7. D
8. D
9. C
10. D

Practice Test 2

1. C
2. B
3. D
4. B
5. C
6. B
7. B
8. B
9. D
10. C

Practice Test 3

1. E
2. E
3. C
4. A
5. A
6. B
7. B
8. C
9. B
10. C

Comprehensive Test – Multiple Choice

1. B
2. C
3. C
4. C
5. D
6. C
7. B
8. B
9. C
10 B
11. A
12. C
13. D
14. C
15. B

True/False

1. F
2. T
3. T
4. T
5. F
6. F
7. F
8. F

CHAPTER 7

Practice Test 1

1. C
2. A
3. A
4. D
5. B
6. D
7. C
8. B
9. C
10. B

Practice Test 2

1. D
2. C
3. B
4. C
5. D
6. A
7. C
8. B
9. C
10. C

Practice Test 3

1. D
2. D
3. B
4. A
5. D
6. D
7. B
8. D
9. C
10. D

Comprehensive Test – Multiple Choice

1. D
2. C
3. D
4. B
5. C
6. C
7. B
8. D
9. B
10 C
11. B
12. D
13. A
14. B
15. D

True/False

1. F
2. F
3. T
4. T
5. F
6. F
7. T
8. F

CHAPTER 8

Practice Test 1

1. C
2. C
3. E
4. E
5. C
6. B
7. D
8. A
9. C
10. B

Practice Test 2

1. B
2. A
3. E
4. C
5. B
6. B
7. D
8. C
9. D
10. A

Practice Test 3

1. A
2. C
3. C
4. D
5. C
6. E
7. C
8. B
9. D
10. A

Comprehensive Test – Multiple Choice

1. C
2. C
3. D
4. C
5. D
6. C
7. B
8. A
9. B
10 C
11. E
12. D
13. A
14. C
15. C

True/False

1. T
2. T
3. T
4. T
5. T
6. T
7. F
8. T

CHAPTER 9

Practice Test 1

1. C
2. B
3. E
4. A
5. B
6. B
7. D
8. D
9. B
10. A

Practice Test 2

1. D
2. C
3. B
4. D
5. B
6. D
7. A
8. C
9. B
10. D

Practice Test 3

1. D
2. A
3. C
4. D
5. A
6. D
7. A
8. C
9. D
10. B

Comprehensive Test – Multiple Choice

1. B
2. D
3. C
4. C
5. D
6. D
7. B
8. D
9. C
10 B
11. D
12. B
13. A
14. D
15. A

True/False

1. F
2. T
3. F
4. T
5. T
6. F
7. T
8. F

CHAPTER 10

Practice Test 1

1. C
2. D
3. B
4. B
5. C
6. D
7. D
8. D
9. C
10. B

Practice Test 2

1. C
2. B
3. C
4. D
5. A
6. A
7. D
8. C
9. D
10. D

Practice Test 3

1. B
2. B
3. B
4. B
5. D
6. C
7. A
8. C
9. D
10. B

Comprehensive Test – Multiple Choice

1. B
2. C
3. C
4. B
5. C
6. C
7. A
8. B
9. C
10 D
11. D
12. B
13. D
14. B
15. C

True/False

1. F
2. F
3. F
4. F
5. T
6. T
7. T
8. T

CHAPTER 11

Practice Test 1

1. D
2. D
3. C
4. C
5. B
6. B
7. A
8. D
9. D
10. D

Practice Test 2

1. D
2. B
3. B
4. B
5. D
6. B
7. C
8. C
9. A
10. B

Practice Test 3

1. B
2. C
3. C
4. E
5. A
6. D
7. D
8. B
9. B
10. D

*Comprehensive Test –
Multiple Choice*

1. B
2. E
3. D
4. B
5. C
6. B
7. D
8. C
9. D
10 B
11. D
12. D
13. D
14. B
15. C

True/False

1. T
2. T
3. T
4. F
5. F
6. F
7. T
8. F

CHAPTER 12

Practice Test 1

1. E
2. C
3. D
4. B
5. A
6. D
7. C
8. D
9. B
10. E

Practice Test 2

1. C
2. B
3. C
4. A
5. D
6. C
7. C
8. B
9. D
10. B

Practice Test 3

1. D
2. A
3. C
4. A
5. C
6. B
7. C
8. D
9. E
10. D

*Comprehensive Test –
Multiple Choice*

1. C
2. D
3. C
4. C
5. D
6. A
7. C
8. A
9. E
10 D
11. B
12. A
13. B
14. D
15. C

True/False

1. T
2. T
3. F
4. F
5. T
6. F
7. T
8. T

CHAPTER 13

Practice Test 1

1. A
2. C
3. C
4. D
5. B
6. C
7. A
8. D
9. C
10. D

Practice Test 2

1. B
2. A
3. A
4. D
5. C
6. C
7. D
8. D
9. A
10. C

Practice Test 3

1. A
2. E
3. D
4. C
5. B
6. A
7. D
8. C
9. A
10. B

Comprehensive Test – Multiple Choice

1. C
2. C
3. C
4. A
5. A
6. A
7. A
8. D
9. D
10. C
11. B
12. C
13. A
14. C
15. D

True/False

1. F
2. F
3. T
4. T
5. F
6. T
7. T
8. T

CHAPTER 14

Practice Test 1

1. D
2. C
3. B
4. C
5. A
6. B
7. D
8. A
9. B

Practice Test 2

1. D
2. C
3. A
4. A
5. C
6. D
7. D
8. B
9. A

Practice Test 3

1. C
2. C
3. B
4. D
5. D
6. A
7. C
8. C
9. D
10. D

Comprehensive Test – Multiple Choice

1. A
2. A
3. C
4. C
5. D
6. C
7. A
8. A
9. C
10. D
11. D
12. C
13. B

True/False

1. T
2. T
3. F
4. F
5. F
6. T
7. F

CHAPTER 15

Practice Test 1

1. B
2. D
3. C
4. D
5. B
6. A
7. D
8. A
9. A
10. D

Practice Test 2

1. C
2. D
3. D
4. A
5. C
6. C
7. B
8. C
9. D
10. D

Practice Test 3

1. C
2. D
3. B
4. D
5. A
6. B
7. D
8. B
9. B
10. D

Comprehensive Test –
Multiple Choice

1. A
2. D
3. D
4. C
5. C
6. A
7. C
8. B
9. D
10 B
11. B
12. A
13. D
14. B
15. B

True/False

1. F
2. F
3. T
4. F
5. T
6. T
7. T

CHAPTER 16

Practice Test 1

1. D
2. B
3. D
4. B
5. A
6. B
7. C
8. B
9. C
10. D

Practice Test 2

1. B
2. A
3. B
4. C
5. A
6. A
7. D
8. D
9. A
10. D

Practice Test 3

1. A
2. B
3. A
4. A
5. B
6. D
7. C
8. C
9. B
10. D

Comprehensive Test –
Multiple Choice

1. B
2. A
3. A
4. D
5. B
6. C
7. D
8. D
9. B
10 B
11. C
12. B
13. D
14. D
15. A

True/False

1. T
2. T
3. F
4. F
5. F
6. F
7. T
8. T

CHAPTER 17

Practice Test 1

1. B
2. B
3. D
4. B
5. C
6. C
7. D
8. B
9. B
10. A

Practice Test 2

1. D
2. C
3. A
4. D
5. C
6. A
7. D
8. A
9. B
10. C

Practice Test 3

1. C
2. D
3. A
4. B
5. D
6. B
7. B
8. B
9. C
10. D

*Comprehensive Test –
Multiple Choice*

1. B
2. A
3. B
4. D
5. A
6. D
7. D
8. C
9. B
10 B
11. C
12. D
13. A
14. D
15. D

True/False

1. F
2. F
3. F
4. F
5. T
6. F
7. T
8. T

CHAPTER 18

Practice Test 1

1. B
2. A
3. C
4. A
5. C
6. B
7. D
8. A
9. D
10. D

Practice Test 2

1. C
2. D
3. B
4. D
5. C
6. A
7. B
8. D
9. D
10. D

Practice Test 3

1. D
2. A
3. A
4. D
5. C
6. B
7. C
8. B
9. C
10. A

*Comprehensive Test –
Multiple Choice*

1. A
2. E
3. C
4. B
5. A
6. A
7. C
8. A
9. C
10 D
11. C
12. C
13. B
14. A
15. B

True/False

1. T
2. T
3. F
4. T
5. F
6. T
7. T
8. F

CHAPTER 19

Practice Test 1

1. C
2. C
3. B
4. A
5. B
6. C
7. C
8. D
9. C
   B

Practice Test 2

1. D
2. C
3. C
4. A
5. B
6. B
7. A
8. A
9. B
10. D

Practice Test 3

1. B
2. C
3. B
4. D
5. B
6. A
7. B
8. B
9. C
10. C

Comprehensive Test –
Multiple Choice

1. C
2. A
3. B
4. B
5. B
6. B
7. C
8. A
9. B
10. C
11. C
12. C
13. B
14. D
15. B

True/False

1. F
2. T
3. T
4. F
5. T
6. F
7. T
8. F